SOUTHERN VOICES FROM THE PAST

Women's Letters, Diaries, and Writings

This series makes available to scholars, students,
and general readers collections of letters, diaries, and other
writings by women in the southern United States from
the colonial era into the twentieth century. Documenting
the experiences of women from across the region's economic,
cultural, and ethnic spectrums, the writings enrich our
understanding of such aspects of daily life as courtship
and marriage, domestic life and motherhood, social events
and travels, and religion and education.

Roots and Ever Green

Roots and Ever Green

THE SELECTED LETTERS OF
Ina Dillard Russell

EDITED BY SALLY RUSSELL

THE UNIVERSITY OF GEORGIA PRESS

ATHENS AND LONDON

© 1999 by the University of Georgia Press
Athens, Georgia 30602
All rights reserved
Designed by Erin Kirk New
Set in 10.5 on 14 Minion by G&S Typsetters
Printed and bound by Maple-Vail
The paper in this book meets the guidelines for
permanence and durability of the Committee on
Production Guidelines for Book Longevity of the
Council on Library Resources.

Printed in the United States of America

03 02 01 00 99 C 5 4 3 2 1

Library of Congress Cataloging in Publication Data

Russell, Ina Dillard, 1868–1953.
Roots and ever green : the selected letters of Ina Dillard Russell /
edited by Sally Russell.
p.   cm.
(Southern Voices from the past)
Includes index.
ISBN 0-8203-2138-9 (alk. paper)
1. Russell, Ina Dillard, 1868–1953—Correspondence.   2. Russell,
Richard B. (Richard Brevard), 1861–1938—Correspon-
dence.   3. Russell, Richard B. (Richard Brevard), 1897–1971—
Family.   4. Women—Southern States—Biography.   5. Russell
family.   6. Dillard family.   7. Georgia Biography.   I. Russell,
Sally, 1942– .   II. Title.
CT275.R88245A4   1999
975'.041'0922—dc21   99-25068
[B]

British Library Cataloging in Publication Data available

Beauty, strength, youth are flowers but fading seen;

Duty, faith, love are roots, and ever green.

—George Peele, "Blessed Be the Hearts That
Wish My Sovereign Well"

In memory of

Ina Dillard Russell Stacy,

who left me her mother's letters,

and

dedicated to my husband, Les Warrington,

whose love and faith inspired

the legacy of this book.

CONTENTS

PREFACE

This book contains some of the letters of Ina Dillard Russell, a woman who lived in rural North Georgia from 1868 to 1953. She entered time at a moment of despair and defeat for the state of Georgia, and grew to young womanhood in a poverty-stricken, insular country. When she married in 1891, the world was poised for a thrilling swing into a new age. A product of the old age, reared strictly in the revered code of the agrarian Old South, she rode the swoop into the new world with élan, yet retained her values from the old way with amazing grace. She valued a life of love, work, and family, ordered by the distilled tenets of Christian doctrine: love the Lord thy God with all thy heart, strength, and mind and thy neighbor as thyself.

Although she aspired to live simply, she was riding with an eccentric and brilliant husband whose political ambitions were tenacious—some might say obsessive—and ultimately thirteen children, active and original heirs to the multiple talents of their father and mother. The balancing act Ina maintained with this entourage reveals a remarkable story of the human capacity for equilibrium. And for love.

Through the letters in this book, written to her family over a period of nearly fifty years, she tells her own story. The narrative I give is simply to provide background to a complex life, to help focus its myriad events and characters. My help in accomplishing this end came in many forms. First, of course, I had Ina's letters. More than 1,200 survive, of the estimated 3,000 she wrote during her lifetime. All could not be used in this book, but I gleaned much information from the whole. In addition, I was fortunate to have other letters from the extended Dillard and Russell families—some letters dating back to the Civil War—as well as a number of other valuable documents such as family wills, ledgers, and Bibles. James Fielding Dillard, Ina's brother, kept a diary during the Civil War, which his granddaughter Lucy Virginia Dillard Bryant used in 1941 as the basis of a thesis written for part of the requirements in a master's degree program at the University of Georgia. This work, "James Fielding Dillard, Confederate Soldier," is a valuable source of material about the Dillards during their early period. The extensive Dillard genealogy compiled by Carlton Dillard, *Back to Old Virginia, With Dillard, Daniel, and Kin,* has been a reassuring resource, explaining how the Dillards migrated to Georgia from Virginia in about 1802 and showing clearly the relationships of the many families in Oglethorpe County. Carlton's scrupulous honesty in revealing errors in several family legends proves the work trustworthy. Several Dillards, thanks to Carlton's help in putting us in touch, have been kind enough to send me copies of family letters either from Ina or about her, as well as personal memories written through the years by a variety of Ina's relatives. Carlton's second book, *Fielding Dillard (1771–1818) and Descendants* records some of Ina's family stories and adds a lively facet to the genealogy.

On the Russell side, I have had the wealth of material at the Richard B. Russell Library for Political Research and Studies at the University of Georgia. The Russell Library has all the early family papers of Richard Sr. and Ina that related to their distinguished son's life, and they are neatly, clearly, *blessedly* catalogued. The family archives at the Russell homeplace—more than 130 years of material from a prolific family of packrats—have been a major source, though these can best be described on an optimistic day as slightly catalogued chaos. Nevertheless, serendipity and I have discovered many documents—letters, obituaries, inscriptions in books, notes on the backs of envelopes and pictures—that have helped me to put in missing pieces of the puzzle and to make reliable identifications of characters.

Fortunately I was working within a long and rich heritage of witness "from lips of those I love." My father and his twelve brothers and sisters were *all* great storytellers. Most of these loved ones are gone now, but we are a family who tells its stories over and over, keeping, as Eudora Welty has said of southern storytellers, "the past safe in the present." Many stories were tape-recorded at family reunions through the years (we also are record keepers, given a little leeway for chaos and packrattery). Thanks to the oral histories recorded following the death of Richard Russell Jr., a number of those stories are also available at the Russell Library. Ina's daughters Carolyn and Patience have been constant, reliable, and encouraging references. Ina's daughters-in-law Virginia Wilson Russell and Ala Jo Brewton

Russell have also been indefatigable sources of memories, help and encouragement, as was my mother, Sarah Eaton Russell, before her death in 1998.

For historical and political information I have used the two-volume *Dictionary of Georgia Biography,* edited by Kenneth Coleman and Steve Gurr,
a work that proved of inestimable value to me working in England most of
the time. I also used Gilbert Fite's biography, *Richard B. Russell, Jr., Senator
from Georgia,* and am indebted to him for his thorough work.

I was fortunate to have recommended to me along the way three classic
works on southern women that helped me understand the traditions that
shaped Ina's life: Anne Firor Scott's *The Southern Lady: From Pedestal
to Politics, 1830–1930* (1970), Catherine Clinton's *The Plantation Mistress:
Woman's World in the Old South* (1982) and Elizabeth Fox-Genovese's
Within the Plantation Household: Black and White Women of the Old South
(1988). Although Clinton's and Fox-Genovese's studies cover the antebellum period only, Ina's early letters prove how tenacious these traditions
were, while the progress of her life validates Scott's observations. I am con-
fident that Ina's letters will provide a useful record to further understanding
of the vast and fascinating subject of gender dynamics in the pre– and
post–Civil War South.

ACKNOWLEDGMENTS

This book has come into being because of the interest, patience, cooperation, and skill of many people. Steve Gurr, my friend and colleague at Gainesville College, was the first to suggest to me that Ina's letters would make a passionate book, and it was he who put me in touch with Karen Orchard at the University of Georgia Press. Karen's expert guidance and kind encouragement have been invaluable to the project from the beginning.

To my aunts and cousins who trusted me with their stashes of Ina's letters, I am indebted far beyond my ability to pay, but I wish to thank them now: Richard Russell Bowden; Nancy Green Carmichael and, after her death, her husband, Ben; Patience Elizabeth Russell Peterson; Virginia Wilson Russell; Ala Jo Brewton Russell; and Carolyn Russell Nelson. I thank, too, Richard Brevard Russell III for maintaining the Russell homeplace and Records House all these years so that I was able to uncover other stashes of letters in good condition. I explain further in the preface but mention here as well my debt to Cousin Carlton Dillard, a former FBI man, which may be what it takes to be the accurate genealogist Carlton is.

The staff at the Russell Library at the University of Georgia, particularly Sheryl Vogt and Jill Severn, were unfailingly helpful and patient through all of my work there.

My sisters Susan Russell Reynolds and Nancy Russell Parker and my friend Lynn Smith Roberts offered all kinds of practical aid and buoyed me up with humor and love. They are proof that in spite of changes in women's work, we are still capable of the sisterhood of Ina's day.

My daughter, Jessica Brevard Jackson-Keeley, and her husband, Howard John Keeley, were my ardent and capable staff across the Great Water. Their immediate, cheerful, and utterly competent responses to letters and phone calls begging them to search out various people and facts are tributes to their capabilities and, more important from a mother's viewpoint, their sterling characters.

A fellow American living in England, Nancy Allison, editor and friend, read the first manuscript as it was nearing completion and offered valuable feedback. Ann and Hugh Jones, my neighbors in Warwickshire, read the second, heavily edited manuscript and offered helpful comments.

For a quiet place and a friendly computer to work with in Georgia, I am indebted to my former colleagues at Gainesville College. I especially appreciated Brandon Haag's kindness and patience in getting me going on a "new" computer.

Although I have dedicated this book to my husband, Les Warrington, for his loving support, I could not let this page pass without noting his help in the technical category. His computer wizardry gave me, whose soul was cast long before the Industrial Revolution, courage to clack on, and when courage was lacking, Les dug me out of deep pits with the flick of a mouse and his sweet smile. What a teammate!

To all, I give my deepest gratitude and, in view of whose book this is, a heart of love.

EDITORIAL NOTE

Upon hearing that a woman with fifteen children wrote an estimated 3,000 letters during her childbearing and child-rearing years, if one can suspend disbelief enough to give the matter serious consideration, the first question inevitably is "How did she do it?" Probably this is the first question one asks regarding a woman who had fifteen children, never mind the letter writing.

Ina Dillard Russell's letters reveal how she accomplished her monumental task of rearing thirteen of those fifteen children to responsible adulthood. They also show how she managed to create such a body of superior written work. It's the lesson that artists in any medium must learn, that of self-discipline and dedication to the task at hand, using whatever tools and time are available. She learned quickly that it also helps to keep whining at a minimum. She sometimes states frankly the difficulties she is under in writing, but she doesn't belabor the point. Since she lived before the Paper Age and was in modest financial circumstances, she could not always find something suitable on which to write. She most often used her lawyer/judge husband's office paper, but she also used hotel stationery, which I surmise he brought home. Although she preferred to use pen and ink—the "proper" way to write a letter—she sometimes settled for pencil rather than be frustrated in losing time searching for tools. She welcomed boxes of stationery or tablets as gifts, for these were quickly and thoroughly used up as she wrote letter after letter. She improvised her stationery, too, saving scraps of odd-sized paper or the backs of pages left empty by wastrel letter writers. She rarely left any blank space on a page.

She wrote in the early morning hours, before her household was awake, or in the evenings when all had gone to bed, writing by kerosene lamplight, later by gaslight, and finally with the pleasure of electric lights. If she could not have peace and quiet to write, she wrote anyway, with a baby on her lap, small boys playing football in the hall behind her, or visitors talking business with her husband nearby. Sometimes these circumstances broke her concentration and intruded on her letters, yet each of the 1,200 extant letters is coherent, literate, interesting, and especially personal to the one to whom she was writing. While she had been taught to give descriptive detail, to write a full-bodied letter, time constraints sometimes forced her into a telegraphic style. Nevertheless, it is clear she enjoyed writing long, newsy letters and did so more often than not, working consciously to make her letters noteworthy. Consequently, they show remarkable powers of composition and composure.

Ina Dillard Russell saw her letters mainly as an extension of her work in homemaking and child rearing, and perhaps incidentally as a record of it, and it was her awareness of and belief in the importance of her task that motivated her to write after long days of labor that included hog killing and goober picking, in addition to the normal duties of housekeeping, cooking, and teaching in her numerous, boisterous household. Nevertheless, I believe she also found writing a satisfying and necessary creative act. In spite of her creativity in so many other spheres—child rearing, cooking, sewing, knitting, quilting, and gardening—she needed to create the written witness of her life. In 1942, writing to her daughter Carolyn, she says: "Here I come with a sorry letter. I have been so proud of my letters." It was this pride and joy in her creation, as well as her love for her children and her need to connect with them, that kept her writing.

Ina was not particularly introspective. She was not a diarist, pouring out thoughts and emotions. Rather, she was an observer, a lively, good-humored reporter, as well as one of the principal actors in the scenes she depicted. While an innate and sincere modesty prevented her commenting too much on her own part in anything, it is evident her power in and over her world was indisputable and complete. Her children, her husband, her siblings, her friends loved and admired her as a superior spirit. While they might be wandering barks, she was always the guiding star. Although she was practical and realistic about the difficulties of being stellar, her code did not allow her to shirk or even to admit growing weary in her role.

In her later years, as her eyesight grew steadily worse but her keen mind could not be still, Ina would ask for the help of an amanuensis. Her daughters-in-law sometimes took dictation from her, as well as granddaughters or practical nurses who were there to help when she had had a particularly difficult time with her health. It has been my great privilege to be her amanuensis in the work of editing her book. Like everyone who knew her in life, I have found her company delightful and uplifting. I believe you, her readers, will experience the same delight and inspiration. I would like to have included each letter in its entirety, but because her families were large and her range of friends and acquaintances widespread, it became important to simplify the cast of characters. Therefore, I have cut out some people, events, and places that were referred to only in passing, those who and which do not affect the whole story in any way.

Another subject that it was necessary to modify in the interest of space was that of sewing and fashion, most often found in the early letters to her daughters. I have left her accounts of sewing in general and the work involved but have omitted many passages regarding the specific details of making a dress, blouse, shirt, skirt, or suit.

Thanks to her telegraphic style and her attention to special items relating to her particular reader, Ina often tacked messages onto the top of a letter, where a little white space was left, or she inserted hurried one-line items between longer paragraphs within the letter. When these messages were not united to the rest of the letter or necessary to any understanding of it, I omitted them. When it seemed more appropriate, I moved the material added at the top of a letter to the end, which is surely where she would have put it if space had permitted.

Because she was writing to so many different children and giving at least some of the same news to each one, I omitted these repetitions. I have used ellipses to indicate all omissions.

I have left everything else as she gave it: the abbreviations, initials, ampersands, et ceteras, ignored apostrophes, and all, for they are witness to "how she did it." Although Ina's earlier letters, before her family grew so large and her life so complicated, were accurate in the use of apostrophes, to save time she later culled apostrophes, especially the possessive kind. Rarely did I have to correct a spelling or a diction error, but I have taken the liberty of doing that occasionally. I leave spellings that have changed with time. She was a careful speller, keeping her dictionary by her bed next to her Bible.

Brackets indicate my insertion of an omitted word or verb ending or of a name where she uses only an initial. All parentheses are Ina's. She used both dashes and periods, and it was sometimes difficult to tell the difference. In the interest of clarity, perhaps I leaned a little more toward the use of periods. I made other minor punctuation adjustments in the same interest. Capitalization or lack of is hers.

A final word about adjectives and adverbs: Although Ina was a staunch advocate of improving one's vocabulary, she often uses the two adjectives *nice* and *good* in formulaic description. I believe this combination was a family joke, a tongue-in-cheek reference to laziness about learning new words, perhaps. She plays with adverbs deliberately, especially *almost* and *really*. "He really ate dinner at Lucy Cobb." "After putting up hog meat all day I was almost tired." Again, I believe this is a family word play that would bring writer and reader together as it reminded of shared experience.

FAMILY TREES

The Fielding Dillard Family

America Frances Chaffin
(1826–1909)
and
Fielding Dillard
(1815–1896)
married March 1841,
Oglethorpe County, Georgia,
to whom were born:

- James Fielding (1842–1909)
- Joseph Lemuel (1844–1862)
- Harriet [Aunt Hattie] (1845–1919)
- Annie Elizabeth [Aunt Annie] (1846–1932)
- America Patience [Aunt Pipey or Pinkie] (1849–1931)
- Miles Hill (1851–1898)
- Samuel (1852–1863)
- Martha Tabitha [Aunt Mattie] (1853–1938)
- Thomas Benjamin [Uncle Ben] (?–1929)
- Mary Antionette [Aunt Mamie] (1860–1936)
- William Calvin (1862–1868)
- Walter Branham [Uncle Walter] (1866–1939)
- Blandina [Ina] (1868–1953)

The William John Russell Family

Rebecca Harriette Brumby
(1829–1902)
and
William John Russell
(1825–1897)
married December 30, 1859,
Cobb County, Georgia,
to whom were born:

- Richard Brumby/Brevard (1861–1938)
- William Edward (1863–1865)
- Robert Lee [Uncle Rob] (1864–1934)
- Mary Brevard [Auntney] (1866–1919)
- William John [Uncle John] (1868–1960)
- Edward Gaston [Uncle Ed] (1869–1962)
- Lewis Carolyn [Uncle Lewis] (1871–1950)

The Richard Brevard Russell Family

Ina Dillard
(1868–1953)
and
Richard Brevard Russell
(1861–1938)
married June 24, 1891,
Oglethorpe County, Georgia,
to whom were born: ———

— Mary Willie [Mary William, Bill, Billie]
(March 1, 1893–May 16, 1983)
m. Samuel Gordon Green, March 1, 1918

— Ina Dillard (June 22, 1894–May 13, 1991)
m. Jean Killough Stacy, June 4, 1938

— Frances Marguerite [Dicksie, Dixie, Marguerite,
Margo](April 11, 1896–August 30, 1967)
m. James Harris Bowden, June 24, 1920

— Richard Brevard Jr. [R. B., Dick]
(November 2, 1897–January 21, 1971)

— Harriette Brumby [Harriet]
(May 16, 1899–January 20, 1959)
m. Samuel Ralph Sharpton, October 5, 1927

— Robert Lee [Rob] (August 19, 1900–January 18, 1955)
m. Sybil Nannette Millsaps, June 27, 1923

— Patience Elizabeth [Pat] (b. January 4, 1902)
m. Hugh Peterson, June 24, 1930

— Walter Brown (June 18, 1903–December 17, 1986)
m. Dorothea Bealer [Dolly], January 1, 1927

— Susan Way (April 15, 1905–August 7, 1905)

— Lewis Carolyn (June 7, 1906–September 9, 1906)

— William John, twin (August 21, 1907–June 7, 1971)
m. Ethelene Huff Booth, March 10, 1948

— Fielding Dillard, twin
(August 21, 1907–February 15, 1993)
m. Virginia Boyce Wilson, August 3, 1931

— Henry Edward [Jeb, Jebs, Edward]
(September 26, 1909–March 26, 1979)
m. Ala Joanna Brewton, June 15, 1938

— Alexander Brevard [Dickson, Dick, Alec, Alex]
(October 19, 1910–February 10, 1995)
m. Sara [Sarah] Eaton, September 28, 1936,
    divorced 1957
m. Kate H. Roberts, April 15, 1958

— Carolyn Lewis (b. August 19, 1912)
m. Raymond Lee Nelson, February 18, 1942

Don't Marry One of Those Peculiar Russells

*J*une 24, 1891, dawned a day of celebration at the Fielding Dillard home near Lexington in Oglethorpe County, Georgia, for it was the day the Dillards were marrying their youngest daughter, Blandina. Their thirteenth and last child, Blandina was born February 18, 1868, and it is believed that her unusual name, that of a Christian martyr of the second century, was suggested by one of the circuit-riding Methodist parsons who frequently sought shelter with this pious family. Although the name was soon shortened to Ina, the child was deeply marked by Christian heritage as she grew in wisdom and favor within her large and affectionate family. When she was nine years old, she formally joined the church community at a tiny Methodist chapel called Cherokee Corner, built on a historic spot where an early treaty had been signed with the Cherokee and Creek nations.

That bright June day of Ina's wedding, her family and many friends in the rural community were early on their way to Farm Hill, for the hour of the nuptials was eight o'clock in the morning so that the couple could catch a train for Atlanta and there begin an "extended tour of the North," including Niagara Falls. Since Ina's engagement to Richard Brevard Russell of Athens had occurred only a scant three weeks earlier, everyone was curious to meet the bridegroom and hear details of the courtship. Although the Russells were a respected family in Athens, where Richard's father had managed a textile mill at Princeton for more than twenty years and Richard had begun practicing law in 1879, they were rumored to be a little strange, not the sociable, fun-loving people the Dillards were. Seven years older than the twenty-three-year-old Ina, Richard was a widower whose first wife had died in childbirth in 1886, and his grief had been long and deep. General opinion from the Dillard side, however, was that he was a good prospect, sober, industrious, and already successful in his law career. If anyone could bring him out of his melancholy, it was the petite, vivacious, and affectionate Ina Dillard. The Fielding Dillards were celebrated in their community as people to whom love in its finest manifestations was the highest ambition, and they were not afraid of challenges.

America Frances Chaffin and Fielding Dillard had come newly married to their farm early in 1841, when she was fifteen and he twenty-six. Orphaned in their youth, they hoped to raise a happy family and add to the two hundred acres Fielding had managed to buy at Farm Hill, named by the Hill couple to whom Fielding had been apprenticed in 1833 after his parents died. America's two younger sisters came with the newlyweds. Fielding and America's first child, a son, was born on January 24, 1842, one day after America's sixteenth birthday.

The farm and the family prospered. The couple acquired more land and a few slaves, perhaps ten or fifteen, by the April day in 1861 when their first son, James Fielding, left for service with the Confederate Army in Virginia. The family had grown to ten of their own children and had sheltered two others, in addition to America's sisters, by this date. Neither Fielding nor America could bear to shut their door on a homeless child, and because they were part of a close community, related by blood to many of the Dillards and Chaffins in the area, as well as related by brotherhood in the Christian community, they saw their obligations as numerous but apparently not overwhelming. They believed the Lord would provide.

As his family grew, Fielding brought an abandoned log house from another homestead and set it up in the yard at Farm Hill. This they called "the boys' house," while the girls had their rooms in the larger house, which the family began in 1851 and completed in 1858. The original house became the kitchen, safely separate to the east of the main house, a white, two-story wooden structure with six rooms, modest in size, adorned only with a columned portico at the front door. It sat on a knoll, sheltered by generous oaks, with outbuildings, barns, and slave cabins behind it. The yards were carefully swept and white picket fences guarded a number of flower beds bright with jonquils, roses, sweet peas, and hydrangeas in season. A long drive ran down to the main road. Beyond the grove, several hundred acres were under cultivation, fields of cotton and peanuts, pastures for horses and cows. Sugar cane brakes separated some of the fields. Even a cursory glance at the property was enough to say that the people who lived there were not lilies of the field. They were workers who did well what they set their hands to do, workers who did not need to be ashamed.

A picture of the Dillards at home is found in a poignant scene from a diary James Fielding Dillard kept during his four years' service in the Confederate Army. He returned home for one furlough during that time, arriving at Farm Hill on November 25, 1863. A neighbor brought him from the train station in Lexington.

I got out of the buggy and passed through the gate, unperceived by any of the family. Here I paused, and for several minutes stood in silent ecstacy [sic] of delight, gazing upon things around me, and thanking the Giver of all good, for a safe return to my "home sweet home." Then I proceeded up the walk to the house. And when about 75 yds. from the door, I was first discovered by my little Sister, Mattie, who was playing in the flower yard. Upon seeing me, she ran into the house, crying out, "Ma I do believe that Bud Jimmie is coming."

Then followed a scene of rejoicing that words cannot describe. Sister Hattie, who was the first to hear the news, came running to meet me. But fearing that she might be meeting some other soldier, instead of her brother, she suddenly stopped when within 20 yds. of me, and asked, "Bud Jimmie is that you." And when I assured her that it was I, she hastened to meet me. Then came Ma, the dearest of all. I never saw a person more completely overjoyed. I know that no one was gladder, or more thankful to see me than she. In half a minute Sisters Pink and Mattie came up. Then Pa came out, exclaiming, "Bless the boy, he's back at his old home again at last." After spending a few minutes there in the yard, we all walked into the house, where I saw sweet little Mamie, and Willie [born July 1862]. Buddie Milie and Ben were off feeding their pigs, and Cousin Matt[1] and Sister Annie had gone to walk. Messengers were immediately dispatched for them, and in a few minutes, they came in, almost breathless from running.

When they were seated, I had the pleasure of seeing the whole family together. But alas! Sadly different from what it was on the morning of the 23rd of Apr./61, when I last saw them all together. Since that morning, Death has robbed us of two dear brothers. And now, as I sat, and looked around upon the cheerful group, the absence of their sweet faces was the only cause of sadness, to mar my perfect happiness. One of them fills a soldiers grave,[2] in "Hollywood graveyard," at Richmond, Va., and the other, who was taken in the innocency of childhood, sleeps in the old family graveyard, in Oglethorpe Co. Georgia. We are a broken family on earth, But blessed thought: We may, by emulating the lives of those who have been taken from us, one day form an unbroken family around our Father's throne in Heaven, where there shall be no more sorrow, nor parting forever.[3]

James Fielding's diary and letters from the war, giving details of his experience and reflections on it, are strong illustrations of the importance the Dillards attached to education. This emphasis extended to daughters as well as sons, perhaps because of their sincere piety. Working out one's own salvation was a serious undertaking, and reading the Bible was a necessity in the endeavor. In addition, in the code of the Old South, women had many duties that required reading and writing, and Fielding Dillard intended for all his children to be able to carry out their duties in this world as well as achieve citizenship in the next. *Usefulness* was a Dillard ideal as important as loving one's neighbor.

According to Virginia Dillard's account of her grandfather's early life, the older children went to school first at the Barrow plantation, home of the family of David Crenshaw Barrow, later chancellor of the University of Georgia. Fielding Dillard served on the first board of trustees of this school. When their favorite teacher, Ripley P. Adams, left to start another school in Athens, Fielding Dillard helped to establish Rose Hill Academy, which was nearer to Farm Hill. It was at Rose Hill that Ina received her earliest formal education, but her sister, America Patience, better known as Sister Pinkie, unmarried and living at home, was her first teacher. A surviving report card, filled out by Principal A. P. Dillard on May 29, 1874, indicates that Ina made 100 in Spelling, Writing, and Neatness, but achieved only 98 in Punctuality and Deportment.

Ina continued to prove an apt and eager pupil, and the family united to send her to school. By the time she was twelve she was in school in Winterville, probably living with relatives there, and later she spent at least a year with her brother Miles Dillard, a Methodist minister, in Oxford, Georgia, in order to go to school at Palmer Institute. She formed deep attachments to his wife, Lella, and their first baby, Annie Zu. Finally, in 1888 Ina attended

Lucy Cobb Institute in Athens. Although Fielding could not afford to pay room and board at the girls' finishing school, he arranged for her to live with five women teachers in a place they called "Cottage Content," near the University of Georgia campus. Ina walked the considerable distance to Lucy Cobb each day, and wrote to Brother Miles in April that although the weather had been rainy, she had missed only one day of school, "and it was not on account of the weather then." She was especially happy to have the chance to study piano and reported frankly that her teacher said she was almost a year ahead of his other pupils in the exercises she was able to do. She was making plans to spend the summer helping another brother, Walter, in a sort of mission school he was offering at Cartecay [Church?]. Walter was training to become a minister.

In 1889 Ina began teaching third grade at the Washington Street School in Athens, where Richard Russell was a member of the school board. Richard's younger brothers Lewis and John were students at the University of Georgia, and after meeting Ina at a social gathering at Cottage Content, Lewis decided to introduce Richard to her. Although Richard called several times at Cottage Content, it appeared at first he was not ready to risk matrimony again, but Lewis persevered. Richard really ought not to let a woman like Ina get away, he said, and get away she surely would, for there were other suitors. Rather suddenly Richard saw the sense in Lewis's arguments, and on May 31, 1891, he proposed marriage to a surprised Ina. She could not consider the question, she said, because she was buying a piano. Richard assured her he could handle piano payments, declared he could not wait to make her his own true wife, and insisted on seeing her father and, with his approval, setting a June wedding date.

Richard Russell was a man of magnetic personality, extraordinary charm, and, although somewhat careless in his dress, handsome. It is easy to imagine that Ina was swept away by her ardent, take-charge suitor. However, it is equally probable that she considered the case and, seeing no reason for caution, agreed to the engagement and early wedding. She had been expecting God to reveal her partner to her for many years, and she was eager to get on with her life's calling, which she believed was to be a wife and mother.

Although it is important that Ina brought to her marriage a keen intellect reasonably trained by the standards of her day, it cannot be overemphasized that she was a product of her mother's age and her mother's example.

To the Dillards, there was no higher calling on earth than that of Christian wife and mother, and in America Dillard, Ina had seen stunning success in the role. In addition to raising eleven children of her own to adulthood, America had mothered at least eight other children, and because her family appreciated and recognized woman's work, she was revered, loved, and praised by husband, children, and friends. Coming at the end of her mother's career, seeing this well-deserved adulation, as well as being conditioned by everything else in society to revere homemaking, Ina longed to emulate her mother and was eager to prove herself. Teaching was only a temporary substitute for the more difficult and rewarding work of homemaking. Nevertheless, she had been content to wait for the right partner, watching, using her brain to help her heart.

In 1885, Ina's sister Mattie Dillard Morris, wife of a Methodist minister, gave her a book entitled *Advice to Young Ladies on Their Duties and Conduct in Life* by T. S. Arthur. The parts that Ina underlined indicate what she thought about woman's role in marriage and family and the kind of man she would choose to marry. Dates written in the book indicate she received it on July 14, 1885, and read it within three days, then reread the chapter "Conduct towards Parents" again in August 1887. In the latter she underlined several descriptive paragraphs on the nobility and difficulty of a mother's work, ending with the honor and aid due to her.

In a chapter entitled "Equality of the Sexes," there is a discussion of man's strength of intellect and woman's strength of will and affection. Ina underlined this: "By intellect, do not understand us to say mind: we are only speaking of a faculty of the mind by which man is peculiarly distinguished. Love, the sweeter, purer, stronger quality of mind is woman's. . . . As to which is highest or lowest, superior or inferior, that is another matter. Here we believe woman to be the equal of man; not born to obedience but to be his intelligent and loving companion."

Ina also underlined passages referring to duty and self-sacrifice, perhaps noting them as reasonable advice that would help her to fulfill her ambition to love and to serve. Nothing in her creed led her to believe that loving and serving were inferior to any other work. These lines from Longfellow's "The Building of the Ship"—likely learned at Lucy Cobb Institute—were part of her creed: "Ah, how skilful grows the hand / That obeyeth Love's command! / It is the heart and not the brain, / That to the highest doth attain,

/ And he who followeth Love's behest / Far exceedeth all the rest!" And had she not Christ's enigmatic directive from Matthew: "And whosoever will be chief among you, let him be your servant"? As Christ himself was servant.

Believing women divinely ordained to love, and this the highest calling, Ina also accepted as divinely directed the earthly hierarchy that placed men as masters "in the world" and women as subordinate, fulfilling myriad duties in the home. As Elizabeth Fox-Genovese shows throughout her distinguished study *Within the Plantation Household: Black and White Women of the Old South,* this was the attitude of most upper- and middle-class women of Ina's time and place. Their everyday lives conformed to prevailing notions of the appropriate division of labor by gender, following earlier British and other European conceptions of male and female spheres. For these white women, gender relations merged with their sense of their own social role and personal identity. Modern sensibilities may judge them victims of male dominance, but few of them would have agreed.[4]

Modern sensibilities also recoil before the absolute power invested in southern patriarchs, but Ina's family situation provided a paternal figure of a stern but benevolent character in Fielding Dillard. He was the kind of man who increased confidence in the system, making it more likely that she would accept her place without question. Although born in 1868, Ina's early experience validated the place of the plantation mistress, for it is certain that America Dillard's life was lived out in the most exacting script of that role.

Contrary to highly romanticized modern depictions, the life of a plantation mistress was not one of ease, nor were her days spent fluttering fans and eyelashes at suitors and other visitors, while nibbling a bit of barbecue, sipping cool drinks on the veranda, and chatting about the evening's ball to come. Women, black and white, were first of all servants in the Old South, and the white mistress worked alongside her black servants to provide food in large quantities, raising it, processing it for preservation or cooking, and serving it. "It" was anything from hogs, cows, chickens, and wild game such as rabbits and squirrels, to potatoes, cabbages, and other garden vegetables, as well as wild fruits common in the South: blackberries, plums, and muscadine grapes. Along with black servants, the mistress sewed to provide clothing for her household, and in addition, she had to teach both secular and religious subjects, keep the accounts of the plantation, do considerable personnel management, nurse the sick and elderly, and, of course, bear children (an enterprise of great physical peril) to give her husband heirs and her country white citizens. Her life was one of such unremitting labor that Catherine Clinton, in *The Plantation Mistress: Woman's World in the Old South,* calls her the slave of slaves.[5] Although the Dillards were not among the largest landholders in Oglethorpe County, they easily fall within the conventional divisions that Fox-Genovese accepts in defining the privileged classes of the Old South: planters, those holding twenty or more slaves; small planters, those holding ten to nineteen slaves; yeoman slaveholders, those holding nine or fewer slaves. It is likely that America lived on and helped to manage a farm on which there were an equal number of blacks and whites, given the size of her immediate family. That she worked hard in a physical as well as emotional sense cannot be doubted.

Although it is important to correct the erroneous picture of the southern lady's life as one of leisure, it must not be forgotten that her lot was far, far better than that of the enslaved black woman, a fact that white women certainly recognized at the time. As Fox-Genovese notes in more than one instance, it was several years after the end of slavery that white southern women emphasized the "oppression" such an abominable system brought to slaves and mistresses alike rather than stressing the mistresses' privileged status.

The circumstances of Ina's life following her marriage to Richard Russell in 1891 until the end of World War I show that black and white women continued to labor side by side as servants in post–Civil War Georgia, with the black women still subservient but obviously much more independent. On the other hand, white women of Ina's class often had to go out of the home to work, a circumstance rarely encountered in the antebellum period. Whereas before the war the southern woman was educated in order to make her a better servant at home, able to keep accounts and teach the young, she now received an education that might enable her to ease the poverty that dug deeply into all southern homes.

Teaching was the most frequent career choice of upper- and middle-class women, but women also became newspaper editors and journalists or authors. In addition, by the 1890s, not only were lower-class white women flocking to mills, laundries, and seamstress jobs, but women in classes above these were seeking employment, even against their families' wishes, at clerking, dressmaking, making patent medicines, in book binderies and in textile and cigarette factories.[6] Thus Ina not only learned the skills needed for homemaking from her mother and sisters, but she also eagerly prepared herself for independence should she not find her life's mate immediately.

Ina's advice book in fact recommends that a young woman remain single for two years or more after leaving school, choosing to wait until the age of at least twenty-one before marrying, and it does not neglect to emphasize the hard physical trials of a married woman's life. Nevertheless, Ina was not impressed enough with these passages to underline them. In the chapter on marriage, however, she underlined with double markings this sentence: "In marriage, there should always exist a harmonizing equality in intellect, education, taste and habit of thinking." In Richard Russell, Ina saw her best chance at this harmony. His charm and good looks notwithstanding, he had many other qualities to recommend him as a possible partner in a great marriage.

Two of these were his bright mind and thorough professional qualification indicated by two degrees from the University of Georgia and early success in his profession. The Russells were an intensely intellectual family. Richard's mother, Harriette Brumby, was daughter of Richard Trapier Brumby, professor of science at the University of Alabama and later the University of South Carolina. When Harriette had finished a girls' school education, she petitioned to attend her father's classes at the University of South Carolina. Although at first refused, she repeated the request until she finally was allowed to study chemistry with him, provided she sat behind a screen so she would not distract the all-male class. Being made to sit behind a screen did not improve Harriette's imperious nature.

Her brothers and uncles were in the textile business in Marietta, Georgia, and while she was there visiting them, she met William John Russell, a young man who was part owner and manager of a textile mill called Sweetwater Factory, in Cobb County. There was a working relationship between Harriette's brothers and William John, but the nature of it is not clear from family records. William John was from Walthourville, in Liberty County, Georgia, and although he was the eldest son of a family with large landholdings in South Georgia, after he attended the University of Georgia, he decided to remain in the north and go into textiles. He worked for a time with Governor Charles McDonald, who was impressed with the young man and asked him to help start the factory at Sweetwater. William John and

Harriette married in December 1859, and their first son, Richard Brumby,[7] was born on April 27, 1861.

The war fell heavy on the Russells. Because they manufactured material for tents and blankets for the Confederate army, their factory, warehouses, and all other outbuildings, including about one hundred laborers' cottages, were burned by Union troops in July 1864. Their home near the factory was reduced to ashes, and the workers and their families were taken prisoner and shipped north. A more total or humiliating devastation of life as they knew it is difficult to imagine.

William John joined the state militia assigned to the defense of Augusta, while Harriette refuged to an unknown location, perhaps in Hancock County. She had given birth to William Edward in 1863, and was expecting another child in November of 1864, so William John hoped she could go to Columbia and be with her parents. In a letter to her in late July 1864, he says that he has had word from her father that no provisions can be made for her in Columbia. Their third son, Robert Lee, was born in Edgefield County, South Carolina, and then Harriette came back to Hancock County, Georgia, where little Willie died on April 11, 1865, and was buried in a coffin made from the doors of a walnut cabinet. William John wrote a letter of sympathy and sorrow on April 19, 1865, and gave, too, the news of Lee's surrender at Appomattox. Although defeat is bitter, the thought of peace is sweet to him and his hopes are high that his family will soon be reunited.

Their bad luck continued. Although they had managed to escape with some gold and a few valuable goods for sale, after the war William John left Harriette in Marietta and took their funds to Pensacola, Florida, to establish a lumber mill with a business partner. According to an account written by Richard Russell Sr. in about 1937, his father had "embarked in the lumber business at a point on the gulf a few miles from Pensacola, Florida, called Escambra Bay. A partner collected more than $15,000.00 for lumber, and appropriated the proceeds to his own use and left this country for another which at that time had no extradition treaty with the United States, with another man's wife." William John came back to Harriette penniless and took the job as manager of the textile mill at Princeton, near Athens. Richard presented his father's new employment this way in the 1937 account: "Mr. Russell accepted the position of general agent for the directors with power of attorney giving him full powers of the directory, and this position he held for more than twenty years, until his retirement." It seems likely that young Richard was haunted by this story of his father's losses and felt keenly their lack of property and position. He resolved to make a name for himself and to own property, both land and buildings.

Harriette Brumby Russell, a sternly religious woman of the Presbyterian doctrine, had, however, consecrated her eldest son to the Lord, as Hannah had Samuel. She taught Richard the Scriptures as well as his other lessons, not trusting any of her children to the evil world of schools, public or private. Sometimes Professor Brumby came and lived with them to instruct Richard in Latin, Greek, and French as well as in math and science. The lad was exceptionally bright and eager to please and made rapid progress. By the time he was fourteen, he had read the Bible through aloud several times to his mother and could recite the Shorter and Larger Catechisms of his faith from memory. They attended the Athens First Presbyterian Church, and Richard sang in the choir.

There were five Russell sons, Richard, Robert, John, Edward, and Lewis, and one daughter, Mary Brevard. Harriette taught them all at home, and Richard gave her full credit to the end of his life and in glowing terms for his sound classical education.

In spite of his mother's iron-willed directive toward the ministry, young Richard looked to the male side of the house for guidance in his career choice. When he was not quite fifteen, he wrote in the friendship book of his cousin Mamie Glover, that the person he would most prefer to be if not himself was "Washington or my father." His preferred occupation was "a lawyer or a merchant." When he was seventeen, he entered the University of Georgia, where in a class of forty he resolved to stand always in the top four and did. Soon Richard told his mother that he did not feel he was called to the ministry and instead would prepare himself for a career in law and public service. For the rest of his life he recalled the day he told her his decision as one of the saddest in his life, but he could not be dissuaded.

That Richard was at least supposed to have become a minister no doubt endeared him to young Ina, to whom there was no higher calling for men than that of the ministry. In addition, she respected as noble his desire to serve his state in public office, and he had already proved he had the ability to do so. Having graduated from the University of Georgia Law School in

1879, he began to practice law in Athens and in 1881 was elected to the state legislature, becoming the youngest member of that body. He served three two-year terms, then ran for solicitor general of the Western Circuit and was elected to that office in 1888. In the 1886 General Assembly he introduced the first postwar bill in Georgia to provide state-supported higher education for women, attaching it to the bill that first funded Georgia Tech. Although the women's college bill failed to pass that year, it did pass in 1888, partly thanks to his continued lobbying for the bill among friends in the assembly. The school established at Milledgeville was first called Georgia Normal and Industrial College, and later Georgia State College for Women. His close association with this school and his pride in it would last until the end of his life.

Richard kept a diary intermittently from 1880 to early 1883, and his entries constantly refer to his ambitions and dreams of public recognition. It was not only his father's perceived failures following the war that sparked these dreams. The Russells of Liberty County were members of the Midway Presbyterian Church, where many famous men in the early history of Georgia worshipped, including Lyman Hall and Button Gwinnett. Richard's great-grandfather William Way was a founder of one of the first families of Georgia. His mother's grandfather was Alexander Brevard, "Captain Brevard," who served on General Washington's staff at Valley Forge. Professor Richard Brumby had achieved acclaim in academic circles for his mineral collections. Such personal stories of patriotism and public service awakened in young Richard an intense ambition to "make his mark" as well as a sincere desire to serve. On January 1, 1881, he wrote in his diary: "Ambition? Did I say, shall I admit I am ambitious? Ay[e], in this diary written for my eye alone I shall make any admission of any thought I feel so that in future days when I shall be known and honored by all, I shall look back with pleasure to this recaller of my past pleasures and simple joys when unknown to fame, or if it be my sad fate to fail, I shall rejoice oh, so greatly in my bitterness of spirit and misery that once I had at least a hope of doing great things."

Ina Dillard, too, had been reared on stories of public service and patriotism. The Dillards were reputed to be kin to George Washington. Other stories reported that Abner Dillard, cousin of the first Fielding Dillard who came to Georgia, was chosen by George Washington to design and manufacture guns during the Revolutionary War.[8] William H. Crawford, early

Georgia patriot and statesman, settled near Lexington in 1799, and stories of his near election to the presidency, as well as of his deeds as senator, ambassador to France, secretary of war, and secretary of the treasury, were told proudly in Oglethorpe County. No doubt Ina passed his home at Woodlawn many times. The thought of becoming the mother of a great son was an immediate possibility, not a far-off dream.

Ina and Richard were heirs to that peculiar patriotism that developed following the Civil War in the South. Postwar southerners looked to the founding of the United States as a glorious time, an era when they were as good as northerners, not second-class citizens of a conquered nation. Because of their separatist attitude, southern states were like countries unto themselves in many ways, and their view of life was colloquial. Well into the twentieth century, headlines in major state papers often were more about local people than about national or international events. Consequently, though Richard looked to his Revolutionary War ancestors with pride, his dreams of accomplishment were limited to Georgia. He wanted to become chief justice, then governor, then United States senator and thus serve in all branches of government.

Another facet of Richard's personality is revealed in his diaries and in the friendship book: He was romantic. In the friendship book entry, to the question "What is your idea of happiness?" he answered (at age fourteen), "A sweet and amiable wife." In his opinion, the sweetest words in the world were "I will be thine," and the saddest were "I cannot love you, no never." The sublimest passion of which human nature is capable? According to the young Richard, "Love & Fidelity."

By 1881 he was already thinking of taking a wife, writing in his diary that he believes even if his beloved, who doesn't yet know of his intentions, should refuse him, he has two others he will try! He is resolved to marry because "it is evident to me that I can never overcome my bad habits and evil propensities without a companion to cheer my loneliness and urge me on to greatness. . . . How great the pleasure to be derived from companionship with one whose every interest is identical with your own, to whom you can reveal if you like every thought and working of your inmost heart. . . . If I could get Miss B. she would make a most congenial companion, friend, counsellor, guide, and a guardian *angel* through life." He longs to "pop the question" but fears refusal. He finally concludes that he must ask her. "I am determined to know my fate, for despair is better than doubt." This unnamed young woman refused the gallant Mr. Russell, and he continued his search for the ideal companion.

In May 1883, Richard went to Barnesville, Georgia, to the wedding of a friend. While there, he met Marie Louise Tyler, called Minnie, a nineteen-year-old beauty, and the two fell wildly in love. Wedding celebrations of the time often went on for a week or more, and apparently the idea of marriage caught on with Richard and Minnie. Family legend has it that Richard took Minnie on a buggy ride and refused to bring her home until she consented to marry him. No one knows how long this buggy ride lasted, but the two were married after the briefest of courtships, and Richard brought his bride back to Athens to his mother's home. Harriette was so shocked she refused to greet the new Mrs. Russell for several hours.

Grief shadowed the union of Richard and Minnie. Their first child was stillborn, then the second. On January 6, 1886, a third child died, and Minnie, too, succumbed. Little is known of this marriage except that Richard grieved for many years and always honored the memory of his first wife. Her obituary as published in the *Barnesville Mail* rests in the Russell family Bible to this day. It speaks at length about a young woman who scattered sunbeams and dispelled shadows, one who possessed every virtue and attraction of pure and noble womanhood. From its style it is possible to suppose that Richard had a hand in composing it.

It is certain that this tragic loss would have aroused nothing but sympathy in Ina, and no doubt, because everyone knew of Richard's long grieving, she felt a certain pride in being the one to whom he finally turned for renewed happiness.

When Miss Dillard announced to her third-grade class that she was engaged to marry Richard Russell, there was great chagrin. The children did not want to lose their beloved teacher, and one little girl burst into tears, sobbing, "Oh, Miss Dillard, please don't marry one of those peculiar Russells!" Ina told this story to her own children with great amusement.

At the appointed hour on that morning of June 24, 1891, Dillard and Russell relatives and friends filled the parlor, hall, and dining room at Farm Hill, spilling over onto the small front porch. Sister Pipey, Ina's first teacher, was frying chicken in the kitchen several yards away from the main house, for the guests were to be served breakfast after the wedding. Coming to the house, Pipey found the front and back doors blocked by other relatives when the ceremony began. Determined to see her baby sister wed her handsome young widower, Pipey hitched up her skirts and climbed into the parlor through a front window in time to hear her brother Walter Dillard, recently ordained as a minister in the Methodist Church, perform his first wedding ceremony. Pipey, who never married, did well to insist that day on witnessing this marriage, for it turned out to be her life's work as well as Ina's.

Among the wedding guests were Russell family members who would influence Ina's life thereafter, for in southern tradition the wife must give priority to her husband's family. Richard's parents, his brothers William John, Edward Gaston, and Lewis Carolyn, and his sister, Mary Brevard, had come to celebrate, rising early to make the trip from Athens. Brother Robert Lee, the first Georgian to graduate from the U.S. Naval Academy following the Civil War, was at sea, but he too would now be a close part of Ina's family. The Russells honored family devotion as did the Dillards, though not with the Dillard all-embracing nature. The Russells were much more likely to be clannish. Blood was important, that of the Lamb notwithstanding. Harriette clearly saw her firstborn as heir-apparent, and admitted that she had sometimes neglected her other children in order to instruct Richard. Nevertheless, she instilled in him a sense of responsibility toward his younger brothers and his sister so that Richard was intensely loyal to them and ready to help them at all times. In turn, they supported his efforts in public and private life, rejoicing with him in his marriage to the vivacious young Ina following the long grieving after Minnie's death. Even Harriette, who had mourned Richard's first marriage, rejoiced to see her brooding son bright again, and welcomed Ina into the family with a warm note on the wedding day.

Having been nurtured within such families, it is not surprising that Richard and Ina believed parenthood an important and pleasant duty. Richard Russell wanted children, and, in southern tradition, sons were preferred, to carry on his name. Ina Dillard's greatest ambition was to fill with honor the role of wife and mother, supporting her husband from the home while rearing fine human beings—and sons were preferred if Richard preferred them—to carry on the work of the world. Richard was prepared to be a good provider; Ina was prepared to give herself wholly to the man she found worthy of calling husband. They both wanted a loving and close relationship in marriage, and in intellect and nature as well as in ideals, the couple were extraordinarily well matched.

"No bliss without alloy!" was a favorite Ina-phrase in her later life. June 24, 1891, was a blissful day, but there was a potential source of serious conflict in the union. Ina, whose parents lived and worked together, expected marriage to give her a companion with whom she would share the work and the play of daily life. A person of intense attachments, she gloried in the company of those she loved. Yet from their earliest days of marriage Richard's work and other activities took him away from home, a circumstance that meant a major adjustment in attitude for Ina. It would not come easy.

Intense bonding to friends and family, but especially to family, was Ina's bliss, enriching her emotional life, fulfilling her ambition to love. Its alloy was the pain of separation. In Ina's earliest letters to Richard, the whimperings of an immature spirit are evident. It would take time and experience to show that the seeds of love were in fertile ground in that young heart.

Notes

1. An orphaned cousin who lived with the family for several years.

2. Joseph Lemuel Dillard died of illness. Two years younger than James Fielding, he had not been well enough to go at the first call, and when he joined his brother, he was not strong enough to stand the rigors of a soldier's life.

3. Lucy Virginia Dillard, "James Fielding Dillard, Confederate Soldier" (master's thesis, University of Georgia, 1941).

4. Elizabeth Fox-Genovese, *Within the Plantation Household: Black and White Women of the Old South* (Chapel Hill and London: University of North Carolina Press, 1988), 192.

5. Catherine Clinton, *The Plantation Mistress: Woman's World in the Old South* (New York: Pantheon, 1982), 16–35.

6. Anne Firor Scott, *The Southern Lady: From Pedestal to Politics, 1830–1930* (Chicago and London: University of Chicago Press, 1970), 105–33.

7. Richard changed his name to Brevard about 1880.

8. Carlton Dillard's genealogy shows that Abner Dillard worked for a Fielding Lewis who was married to George Washington's sister Betty, which probably accounts for the kinship story.

1891–1897

How I Wish You Were
Here Tonight

*O*n August 5, 1891, under the heading "The Solicitor's Bride," the following appeared in a Monroe, Georgia, newspaper: "It is hoped by all that Solicitor General Russell will bring his bride with him court week. And no doubt he will, as the session here will be a lengthy one. Mrs. Russell, nee Miss Ina Dillard, is a sister of Rev. Walter Dillard, who is so much liked here. She is a very attractive young lady, loved and admired of all who know her."

Ina traveled occasionally with Richard on his solicitor's circuit during the two years before their first child was born, but often circumstances were not favorable to the solicitor's taking his bride along. Although the couple lived in Athens, a tradition of letter writing, which derived from the remote situations of plantation mistresses, remained prevalent, and early training in letter writing that Ina received from her mother and sisters was put to use right away.

In late 1893 Richard made the decision to move to Winder, a new town between Athens and Atlanta on the Seaboard Railroad, because he felt that his professional and political chances would be better in a new and growing area. Clarke County was set in its ways. Names well established there would always precede him. Winder, relatively unsettled but developing, was located where Jackson, Walton, and Gwinnett Counties met. Land was reasonably priced. Richard saw fertile fields, figurative and literal, opening around the new town.

Ina was bereft at this decision. Compared with the social and cultural life of Athens, living in Winder was akin to going into exile. Recently renamed for a railroad executive, the crossroads village had been called Jug Tavern until 1892, a name that did not inspire confidence. With feet dragging, the solicitor's wife packed up their ten-month-old baby and moved into a bungalow on a newly cut, muddy, treeless street behind the main thoroughfare, four blocks from the railroad station. She was three months pregnant.

To Hon. Richard B. Russell, Watkinsville, Ga.

Athens, Ga., July 27, 1891

O, my own precious darling,

I would give anything just to feel your dear strong arms around me right now! Here I sit, all alone. Father[1] has gone to bed and everything in the house is still, except my heart and that is beating just a little faster than usual. I love you my boy: I don't think I'm a sure enough coward, but I do love so much to be with you. It is so sweet. I envy anything that you may be touching now while you read this letter. I dread to go to bed. How can I ever go to sleep!

When I finished that page I stopped and read it over. Is it at all foolish? You don't think so, I feel sure.

Mr. Hughes came a second ago to know if you had come. He says he'll bring you home to-morrow night. Do come if you can, and if you wont have to neglect any business.

Poor father! I know he thinks I'm as stupid as a long summer day, but I can't talk or do anything but think of you.

Just then an old devils horse flew in at the window and made a terrible noise. Yonder he is on the wall. You know one side of the blinds is off.

I forgot to bring the pistol in here. If anything were to happen I could never wake father. But I'll try to "bear & grin it" until I see you once more.

I hired the boy you sent to draw water. He is real smart.

I did ever so many things to-day, and thought about you all the time. I really forgot to eat any dinner. Mrs. DuBose sent me a delicious dish of frozen peaches and cream. There was quite enough for two and I wished for you to have some.

That horrid thing (I mean the devils horse) has fallen on the floor and I'll never kill him.

It is five minutes to eleven o'clock. I have despaired of your coming. Just think! Mr. Hughes will see you before I will. But you won't kiss him, will you?

I imagine this is a very silly letter to send a man that is very busy. I hope you will get it at dinner time so you will have time to spare to read it.

I send—(Another big bug has come in the window.)

Yes, I send a cargo of my best love with this letter. My darling, your baby loves you with all the true love her heart and life is capable of giving. How my heart goes out to you! I feel so lonely without my boy. Good night sweetheart.

> Yours, now & forever,
> "Mina" [2]

1. Richard's father, William John Russell. Ina would not stay alone.
2. Richard's pet name for her, short for My Ina.

To Hon. Richard B. Russell [Monroe, Georgia]

Athens, Ga., February 27, 1893 [1]

My darling Richard,

I have been very well to-day, only everything I have eaten has made me sick. The *everything* means oatmeal, milk, biscuit and rice. I will have to stop eating entirely. I have tried to keep busy to-day and the time has passed more rapidly than I expected. I did not get up this morning until nearly ten o'clock, and I gave myself a good rubbing before I dressed. If I can only stay up until you get home again I will be so glad. Did you say you might come home Wednesday night? [March 1] I hope so if it won't interfere with your business.

I am going to take a good hot bath to-night and try to sleep just as well as if my Richard was here holding me in his precious arms. I think I will leave the light burning "just a little ways" and see if it helps me any. I have the headache and a pain in my side now, but I will trust to my bath to relieve both.

I have loved you devotedly to-day my precious husband, and have thought over all the sweet petting you have given me. It is no wonder that I miss you so terribly when you leave me.

It is nearly seven o'clock and I don't feel any different from what I did this morning. I will try so hard to keep well until my darling comes home, but I tell you baby, I can hardly get up sometimes when I am sitting down, & I don't see how I can possibly go much longer.

I wonder if you are going to write me one letter! I would be so glad.

My darling, I love you so much. Pray for your little wifer, and for your little baby. We love our little baby, don't we?

I'm so tired I can't write any more.

With kisses and tight hugs for you, my own loved one.

     Your devoted wife.

1. Ina's first child, a daughter, was born on March 1, 1893.

To Hon. Richard Russell, Carnesville, Ga.

Athens, Ga., Apr. 2, 1893

My darling,

How miserable it is not to have you with me on Sunday! such a lovely Easter Sabbath, and I had planned a walk with you out to see the calf! As it is, I took my little walk in the front yard alone. I was afraid to venture down the high back steps to-day without your dear strong arm to help me. I miss you *so* much to-day, and have looked for you every minute since last night when the North Eastern came in. What are you doing to-day? I wonder if you went to spend the day with Mr. Yow, or if you are resting. I wonder if you miss me, and if you want to see our baby. When you go to your room at night do you remember the lovely times we have had to-gether there?

O, baby, things will never be as they have been! I will be separated from you more than ever now. I love my baby, though, a great deal and will always try to take good care of her.[1] She has been sweeter to-day than usual. [Brother] Johnnie and [Sister] Mary came by to see her this morning on their way to church. Johnnie held the baby a long time and seemed to love her very much. He would talk to her and she would laugh the sweetest little

smiles you ever saw. I was so proud of her. She had just been bathed and dressed and looked lovely. She has grown a great deal since you saw her and has taken on several new accomplishments.

I put on my dress and white necktie this morning and tried to look like folks. Anne said I looked so "neat" in the waist that she hardly knew me. I wanted you to come and see me. While I was out in the yard, I knew you would be glad to see me there. I love you so dearly, my husband, that it is hard for me to be happy when we are apart.

I have had such terrible dreams about you every night since you left. I don't dream that you are hurt or in danger, but that you have ceased to care for me and that you treat me badly.

Your letter was *so* precious to me. I devoured every word of it and loved my boy and longed to put my arms around his neck and pet him. Were you blue, my baby? You have been too much rushed lately, and need rest and sleep. I imagine you felt as I do sometimes when I cry and you think I'm silly. I am ready to cry now because I want to see you so bad. My only hope is that Court will adjourn early in the week and that you will soon come home. I will look for you every day. If you don't write to me to-day I will be *so* disappointed. You don't know how the very sight of your hand writing thrills me when I get your letters. . . .

My darling, I want to see you so bad to-day. The sun is so bright, and every body seems so happy in their new Easter clothes. Nothing would make me happier than to be with you to-day. I will try to be happy any how, for I have the sweetest baby and the best husband in the world.

All my beer is gone.[2] Dr. Gerdine told me to get malt to make milk. I see no improvement in my milk, & it makes me very sad. I want you to get me some malt as soon as you get home. If that doesn't help, I will despair of ever giving enough.

Take care of yourself, my Richard. Baby sends kisses and love for her papa. God bless my husband.

Ina

1. The baby was first called Dixie, for her father. His first letter, written to her from court, when she is one week old, is addressed to Miss Dixie Russell, but her name was soon changed to Mary William, in honor of Richard's sister and his father. This later became Mary Willie. It appears at the time of this letter, however, that a name had not been decided.

2. Ina drank beer for the malt to help her make milk.

To Hon. Richard Russell, Carnesville, Ga.

Athens, Ga., Sep. 25, 1893

My darling Richard,

Here I am writing to you, and I have vowed that I would never write to you again unless you wrote to me. I love you Richard,—that is the reason why I am compelled to write and talk to you any how, if you are thirty-six miles from me, and if you do treat my poor little letters with silent contempt. I can not understand why you don't write to me when we are separated. But all this talk doesn't affect you in the least, and I may be my sweetest, but none of these things move you, you are so hard hearted.

The man came to-day and fixed the gutters and cleaned them out for $1.25. He got so much rotten trash out of the gutters and I had it all put on my rose bed. Its the very thing you know. I felt so proud that I did it and you were not here to tell me to do it.

The baby has seemed right well to-day, but has taken fresh cold some way, and the doctor gave her some more powders to-day.

Father stayed here all day and watched the man fix the gutters. He told he wanted the letter press that belonged to the Ledger.[1] He said charge him with it. Father is so lovely and good. I wish you could give him everything he wants. He is the father of the best man in the world and he has done so much for that man. Father thinks there is no one like Richard. Now isn't that so?

My baby, I have written enough. One long day has passed. I miss you so much and wish you never had to leave me. All this must be so stale to you. It is my old, old song, but Richard, I love you with my whole life and heart. My good husband, I have never tired of telling you and showing you my love.

Come to me as soon as Court is over. I wish it would adjourn this week if it would not affect your pocket.

Good-by my darling. Take good care of yourself and remember you promised not to go on the hotel porch.[2]

Pray for your wife and baby girl. May God bless my Richard.

Your devoted wife

Don't forget to show baby's picture and give my love to my friends.

1. Richard edited a paper called the *Athens Ledger* for a period in the 1880s.

2. This promise may have had to do with Ina's early and soon-abandoned attempts to get Richard to give up chewing tobacco.

To Hon. Richard Russell, Watkinsville, Georgia

Winder, Ga., January 25, 1894[1]

My dearest Richard,

I have been so happy to-day for I know that *no* sweetheart ever wrote a sweeter, dearer letter to his best girl, than the one I received last night, and if you had been my lover instead of my husband you couldn't have written me a more loving letter than the one dated Jan. 23, 1894. The short period of our courtship was full of bliss and genuine happiness for me, but our married life has been far sweeter. I love you more every day and I know my husband loves me.

I sent to the post office but no letter. I received an invitation to Lucy Aikens marriage. Just think of it! She marries a boy I went to school with in Winterville when you were speaking and going to the Legislature. She can make him a good living.

Darling, you must tell Dr. Gerdine about our baby being so badly constipated. She hasn't had a natural action since you left, and to-night she screamed so, that I was very uneasy. The enemas don't seem to relieve her as they should. I had to stop writing here and take her up. She had a severe crying spell that alarmed me. I had to walk her some time before she was quieted. Tell the doctor her food agrees with her perfectly or he might say change it. Tell him I boil her milk sometimes and sometimes only scald it. I know something ought to be done, for she will have the piles or something worse if things go on this way long. See Dr. G. and tell him all about it. Don't fail baby. . . .[2]

Father has just come in with your letter. It came on Narrow Gauge. How my heart thrills when I see my boys handwriting. I know he tells me he loves me and calls me "darling" and "little wife" and many other loving things that makes me so happy. I've written to you every day since you left and I can't imagine why you failed to get my letter. I'm sorry darling. My baby blue and homesick? If I could hug you and kiss my dear boys face (you know where) he would feel better. This is Thursday night. I don't feel like I can stand things much longer for I want to see you so bad. I can't possibly hope for you to come before Saturday morning and maybe not before Saturday aft.

Baby has had another crying spell. I tried to give her some whiskey but she would take very little of it. Her lips turned blue and she cried so hard. I don't think it was anything more than pains in her stomach caused by constipation. She is sitting in Hattie's[3] lap now playing with her doll, looking as well and pretty as ever. She has shown more temper this week than ever before. She ate some peppermint candy today. It might have made her sick. Clock has just struck eleven and I must try to get baby to sleep. We enjoy our hickory fires. I keep a good one all night.

I'm sorry you lost your case, but don't get blue any more, my precious husband. Baby is fretting. I must take her.

> Your devoted wife,
> Ina

Baby had me up twice last night, but I think she's all right this morning. O, if you could only come to-night! This week has been so long. I love you, I love you!

1. Although Winder's name had been officially changed at this time, the postmark on this letter's envelope is still Jug Tavern.

2. There was a doctor in Winder, Dr. Charles Almond, but Ina felt he was too young and continued to use Dr. Gerdine. She planned to return to Athens for the birth of her second child.

3. A servant.

To Hon. Richard B. Russell, Monroe, Walton County, Georgia

Winder, Ga., Feb. 19, 1894

My darling one,

When the train came in to-night I could not keep from listening for your footsteps. I didn't really expect you, but then I love to listen for you to come, even if I am disappointed sometimes.

I've been real sentimental to-day and have lived over the past, when we were off by ourselves and loved each other—O, so much. I wondered if you had our same old room where we have spent so many happy moments.

We were fresh married then, but I'm sure we would be just as happy now, even if little Mary Willie is here to share our love.

I've been smart to-day & almost completed four gowns for Mary Willie. I have felt real stupid too on account of my late hours last night. I got real nervous when the storm came up this afternoon and left the machine and took Mary Willie in my arms. I was glad it was not severe as I was in the humor to get frightened. The baby has not been as well as usual to-day. I gave her two doses of Castoria and think she will be all right in the morning.

Darling, I was silly to tell you of my feelings last night. You see I love you so much and its so seldom that I can do anything for you. I feel the same way now when I see Mr. Quarterman's handwriting on your papers. I wish I could be your little lap dog and follow you around and do thousands of things for you every day. . . .

Ina

To Hon. R. B. Russell, Homer P.O., Banks Co., Georgia

Winder, Ga., March 19, 1894

My own precious sweetheart,

You will never know how dreadfully bad, sick and lonesome I felt yesterday when the train left Athens. It was the first time I had ever left you,[1] and O, how I longed for you to be with me. I am too dependent on my husband to make even a short trip without him. It was so warm on the train that Mary Willie got restless, but she slept some. Just as the train left the crossing, the handsome Mr. Cohen came and offered to help me off the train. I thanked him & said that I thought I could do very well with the conductors help. About that time that horrid red faced conductor came & grabbed up my satchel without saying a word or even looking at me & made for the car door. Mr. Cohen picked up my little brown bag and the baby's cloak, then put them down and asked me to let him take the baby. She went right to him, smiled and put her little hand on his collar. He seemed much pleased and said, "This is a fine boy." I told him she was a girl and he blushed. It was a pretty picture to see him holding her. She was so white & her eyes so blue and he was so different. Jno. [Brother John] met me at the train door & he took the baby. When we got home he spoke of how sweet baby looked in Mr. Cohen's arms. I was surprised that she went to him, but you know how she walked towards Sarah Stern. The little minx is learning fast to show a preference for brunetts.[2]

As we came on home I was real blue for I felt like it would be a perfect age before I saw you again. To-day I got real happy when I remembered that the Vestibule went on to Elberton Sunday night if the Accommodation did stop in Athens.[3] I know you can come to Athens Saturday night & come on to your wife and baby soon Sunday morning. We will be here with our hearts overflowing with tenderness and love for our own darling papa. We will feel the sweetest pleasure of our lives when he holds us in his good strong arms.

Darling, I suffered the greatest agony of my life last night. It was worse even than when Mary Willie was born, for I hadn't a minutes rest from pain. My face pained me until I hadn't my right mind. I started ever so many times to get Jno. to go for some doctor to give me morphine, but was afraid.[4] I took a real strong drink & that didn't seem to help me in the least. I was desperate and got up and took a drink as strong as I could stand it. Without sugar & with very little water. That eased me some & I went to sleep & slept about 2 hrs.[5] I awoke at two & was in as great pain as ever. About three I happened to think of my hot water bag. I got up, made a fire & heated some water. When I got well fixed in bed with the hot application to my face I soon felt just a little better and got some rest before day. My back has been paining me a great deal to-day. I am almost too weak to walk about the house & have kept very quiet. It is a trial for me to write this letter, for I feel wretched. A larger abscess is coming on my tooth and when it bursts I'm sure I will be relieved. I sent uptown for some Carter's Iron pills but couldn't get them. I feel like I need something to strengthen me. Could you get me some when you come through Athens. I hope to be well when you come home and am going to get something to cleanse my stomach.

Didn't you forget your night shirt? I hope you & Judge H. didn't room to-gether in Mayesville. Jno. said he saw in the last Jackson Herald that Col. Pike would be a candidate for Judge. . . .

By-by my precious boy. I love you, I love you so much.

Your devoted *wife.*

Your precious letter mailed at Mayesville has just come & O, how happy it made me & little Richard![6] I feel better now & think I can sleep some to-night. . . . How I wish you were here to-night. I want to see my Richard so bad.

1. As opposed to his leaving her.
2. Richard was also brunet.
3. Names of trains.
4. Because she is pregnant.
5. Although Ina abhorred drinking whiskey for pleasure, she used alcohol for medicinal purposes, such as in this battle against toothache.
6. Ina refers to the unborn child as little Richard. Richard refers to it in his letters as his Ina Dillard.

To Hon. Richard B. Russell, Carnesville, Georgia, Franklin Co.

Winder, Ga., M'ch. 27, 1894

My own darling boy,

Have you received my letter that I wrote you last night? It seems to me that weeks and months have passed since you kissed me good-bye over the banister Sunday afternoon. This is Tuesday night and I'm a little nervous and wish you were here to hug me and pet me. We had a little excitement to-night about half past seven that made my heart beat a little fast. The chimney caught on fire and it was right bad for awhile. [Brother] Jno. had just gone back to the office. I heard the roaring & went out in the yard to see about it and everything was bright as day. The blaze was at least three feet high and sparks were pouring out of the chimney. Jno. saw the light and came tearing back, much to my delight as I had tried to send Hattie for him, but she was perfectly crazy. Jno. went on top of the house. Some men from Camps store brought a ladder and I guess the danger is all over now. I tried not to get too scared, but the house was so dry, and the sparks were so thick. I don't think I can sleep much to-night. Just then I thought I heard something hit the ceiling and Jno. has gone on the house again.

I have been real busy to-day, but found time to take two nice little walks in the bright sunshine. I have something nice to tell you. Do hurry on home.

All of our rosebuds are dead and the garden looks miserable.

I'm afraid you got very cold Monday morning going to Carnesville from Bowersville. I hope you can see the Constitution or some daily to keep up with the proceedings of Colquitts burial.[1] When I read it I think of the piece you read me from Tom Watson's paper.[2]

I must close now for I'm a little rattled. I will add a line in the morning to let you know how we passed the night. When Jno. was scrambling through the trap door that he had reached by means of your *two little shelves* I thought about you & how I fussed when you put them there. . . .

     Your fond and loving wife

1. Alfred Holt Colquitt, from Walton County, former governor of Georgia, was a United States senator at the time of his death. He was governor during Richard's first term in the state legislature, 1882.

2. *Georgia Populist.* Watson, a former U.S. congressman and newspaperman, served in the Georgia legislature with Richard in 1882.

To Hon. R. B. Russell, Carnesville, Georgia, Franklin Co.

                        Winder, Ga, March 26th, 1895

My dearest darling,

How I longed for you last night! Mary and Walter[1] were here and we had such a nice time, but it would have been so much pleasanter if you had been here. We spoke of you so often and wished for you. I miss you just as much when I have company as I do when I'm alone. There is no time in my life that I wouldn't be happier if Richard was by my side. No matter where I am or what I am doing I want you with me. Our babes are getting to be the same way now. Ina[2] calls "pap" and Mayne[3] calls "papa" and my heart longs for "papa." You make us love you because you love us and are the best papa in the world. You are so precious to me and I love you first and best of all. . . .

I was just crazy to go on to Farm Hill with Mary & Walter. I know they are going to have such a nice time. George is a sweet smart child and the three babies seemed to enjoy each others company very much. . . .

Our dinner is nearly ready and Ina is squealing for me to take her. I hope you can come home early next week. I will be so glad when you can be at home with me longer than one day. My darling I love you so dearly. I will write again.

>   Your true and loving wife,
>   Ina—

1. Ina's brother Walter Dillard and his wife.
2. Born June 22, 1894, the second daughter was named Ina Dillard Russell.
3. One of Mary Willie's many nicknames.

To Hon. R. B. Russell, Carnesville, Ga. Franklin Co.

Winder, Ga., March 27th, 1895

My precious one,

I say precious one because you are *so* precious to me and I want to tell you to-night that I love you with all my heart and you will never know how much I do love you. I have thought of you to-day so often and wondered if you had had time to think about your three little girls in "Winder, Ga., Jackson Co."

I am feeling so badly to-night. Almost too sick to feel like writing, but I said, "I must tell Richard that I love him." My visitor[1] that I've been look-ing for so long came to-day about twelve o'clock and I have had the head-ache & backache ever since.

This morning I planted a long row of beans and two rows of beets. I am perfectly delighted with the work I've done in the garden. Henderson has ploughed the field between here and the R.R. beautifully and planted it in corn. I wanted it planted in grain but he had the rows all laid off before I knew anything about it.

I heard this afternoon that Dr. Geo. DeLaPerriere had withdrawn from the church. Mr. Hamby preached a very forcible sermon that made the bit dog howl, I guess. I expect the church will do better now, eh?

I went up town [to the dry goods store] this morning and bought me a beautiful dress. I almost know you will like it. If you do, then I will like it better. Mr. Strange showed me a lovely suit of clothes and asked me how I thought "it would suit the Col."[2] I bought Ina some little dresses too. . . .

Our old black hen is laying in one of the new nests. I'm going to let her set. Eggs are 8¢ per doz. now.

All of my little rose bushes are sprouting so nicely and my tomato seed are coming up beautifully. I am enjoying life now working with all my things. I do love to keep house and have things of my own and you are my darling, precious husband who is so good to me and lets me have what I want and I love you *so* much. More than you can ever know.

Ina & Mayne have called you to-day and they love "papa." Come home darling soon. . . .

Your devoted little one

1. Her period, likely the first since her second baby's birth.
2. She is buying cloth to make these garments.

To Hon. Richard Russell, Lawrenceville, Georgia

Winder, Ga., Sep. 9, 1895

My darling husband,

We are still in Winder and I guess will not leave before you see us again. Dr. Almond[1] came this morning and said he thought it would be perfectly safe for me to go home and then asked me how *you* felt about it this morning. I told him you hadn't said anything about [it], that you were waiting for him to say. Then he said the reason he asked me was that yesterday afternoon you didn't seem to want us to go. That decided me in an instant, and I said well doctor I wont go this morning, that's sure.

I felt awfully hurt that you should express yourself to doctor Almond and not to me. I couldn't understand it and don't yet. I had noticed that you had never seemed anxious for me to go, but didn't think you objected to it or you would have told me. I feel like I cannot live through another week here by myself but will try it. This morning I feel like a ten pound weight is hanging to each foot, but cooking, cleaning, nursing and everything must be done and I'm the one to do. I didn't eat a mouthful of breakfast this morning before half past eight. I guess I'll get along all right though and will try to make the best of it. . . .

I love you better than anything in this world, but baby, why didn't you tell *me* that you thought best for me not to go home? I had my heart set on it and long for the rest that a trip home will give me. It is miserable to be here without you and by myself all the time. I know Father is here but he never understands anything I say[2] and then I'm in the room all night by myself. I have never left you here by yourself. But when you are away I get so tired of staying here by myself. I'm sure you don't understand anything about my feelings. Dr. A. said I might wait until to-morrow & see how the children get through this afternoon. . . .

Mayne is fretting for me to take her. I'm awfully nervous this morning. I'll try to give the little baby a lesson in self control, but am afraid I'll fail.

I love you Richard, but I am so disappointed this morning I had to write you this terrible letter. Please destroy this one. I won't write any more like it.

> Your devoted wife,
> Ina

1. Ina is about two months pregnant and has decided not to return to Athens for the birth of this baby, as she had for Ina Jr.'s birth.

2. She is probably referring to his deafness, not his inattention.

To Hon. Richard Russell, Carnesville, Franklin Co. Georgia

Farm Hill [Oglethorpe County], Sep. 24, 1895

My own dear Richard,

This is Tuesday afternoon and we are fairly melting. I don't think there is any difference in Ina's condition—though I'm sure she is no worse. I am disheartened about her. Poor little thing! She says "mama" two hundred times a day, I'm sure.

Maynie continues to get fat and seems perfectly well and is full of life.

I am suffering agonies now with neuralgia and feel perfectly dreadful and good-for-nothing. I do wish I could get well. I must see Dr. Gerdine when I go through Athens & see if he can do anything for me.

Sister Pinkie[1] is begging me to leave Maynie with her until she comes the last of October. Be thinking about it. I'm almost tempted to do it just for Maynie's good. I know I would miss her sadly, but if I keep sick & Ina goes back home sick, I can't see after Maynie much. If you don't come home (I mean to Farm Hill) Sunday or Saturday night like you did this last time, I think I will go to Athens Monday morning & then go on to Winder Monday afternoon. If you find out that Court will not adjourn this week please let me know. I don't want to go to Winder before you are ready to come, but I want to go the minute you are through. I dread going back too, for my breath is so short I can hardly breathe sometimes. Especially early in the mornings. If I could just have twins I would feel paid for all this trouble I'm having. Nothing short of twin boys will satisfy me this time.

We listened in vain for the train Sunday night. I took a notion you got left & looked for you to come back & wouldn't go to bed for ever so long. I wouldn't take anything for your sweet little visit to us, even if the people did pour in & I couldn't have you all to myself as I wanted to. I would always have you to myself if I could. I love you better every day of my life and you get more precious to me.

I hope Court will get through this week & then we can have a few days at home all to ourselves. As I write this, I remember that it is a matter of impossibility for us to have any time all to ourselves for there's old Mrs. Jackson & Joe to come along & make our lives miserable for awhile.

Spinkie[2] is very indignant to know that I've written that Ina is no better. She says she is much better than she was Sunday.

I manage to eat a good supply of scuppernongs every day, even if I don't feel well. I believe I'll go crazy if this neuralgia keeps hurting me.

I read some in Blackstone[3] this morning. I read a sketch of his life first & was struck with a statement made by the author, that young Blackstone was much benefitted by the death of his parents when he was very young. That if they had lived he would never have made such a great man. I didn't like that. I hope I won't have to be taken from my children in order that they make brilliant men & women.

Let me hear from you once any how & tell me if you still think Court will adjourn this week.

Ina is sitting in my lap & pulling at the pencil. . . . She says she loves papa. Maymie sends love too.

I love you & send a wealth of love to you.

>   Your own devoted
>   Wife

1. Ina's special name for Pipey.

2. Contraction of Sister Pinkie/Pipey.

3. Sir William Blackstone, English judge and jurist, (1723–1780), whose greatest work, *Commentaries on the Laws of England,* influenced the creators of the Constitution of the United States of America.

To Hon. Richard Russell, Carnesville, Franklin Co, Georgia

Farm Hill, Sep. 26, 1895

My own precious mate,

. . . I wish I knew how you were this morning. I think about you all day long & your face is right before me and I do hate for you to have to sit in that stuffy old Court house these fierce days. Do make Judge Hutchins get through this week.

I don't think Ina is any worse, but I can't say that she gets better very fast. Mrs. Arnold, a neighbor with a baby and lots of milk, came yesterday to spend the day & she nursed Ina three times. Ina enjoyed it immensely. I do think I am the poorest mother that ever lived. Am perfectly disgusted with myself. Ina has begged me for "tittee" this morning until I almost cried.

I thought Tuesday night that I would either die or go crazy. I never suffered so with neuralgia in my life. Mama & Pinkie stayed up with me until after one o'clock and I was crying, groaning & walking the floor all that time. I took antikanua, paregoric & laudanum. I finally got easy & rested right well after two o'clock. Was in bed all day yesterday and am not able to go to the scuppernong arbor this morning. I do wish I could get well for Ina's benefit & for the sake of my twin boys.[1]

Maynie keeps so well and continues to boss everything on the place. Ina takes more interest in things and seems to enjoy herself more than she did a few days ago.

I hope you will write soon about when you're coming home for I don't want to go to Winder until you are ready to go home. We love you my precious darling & will love you always. Our precious papa!

[no signature]

1. Twins from this pregnancy would even her daughter-son ratio.

To Honorable R. B. Russell, Watkinsville, Georgia.

Farm Hill, July 29, 1896

My precious husband,

I have looked so hard and long for a letter from you. Surely you received mine written last week. I am anxious to go home, but I think we had better make the trip in the night and not stop in Athens. It is so fearfully warm.

The children are all broken out thick with heat and fret from it. I think we had better leave here some night about twelve o'clock and take it while its cool.

I've been real sick ever since you left. Was in bed Monday and suffered agonies with neuralgia and backache. I can't sleep at night. I long to be able to drop off to sleep as you do. I still ache in my bones. Dixie[1] is getting to be too much for me. I have a darkey helping me to-day, but she is not much good.

I wrote to you at Winder, and have looked for an answer. You know I think about you all the time and love to know where you are. Did you & Father go to South Georgia.[2] This weather is so warm. I hope you have your linen clothes. The children seem perfectly well, but suffer so with heat. I dread to go back to that sunspot or sun target in Winder. But I must go back. . . .

I still give plenty of milk for Dixie, but she is so hard to nurse. I'm just crazy to see you. Do let me know what to do. I think I ought to go home to be there when you come. . . . The children talk about you. I'll send this off if possible this afternoon. Hope I will hear from you. I feel like you have had a hard time since you left me. It has been *so* warm and you think so little of your welfare. Do plan the best way for us to get our family home this hot weather.

Write to me & come as soon as possible. I want to see you *so* bad.

Your true & devoted wife,

Ina

1. Born April 11, 1896, this daughter was named for her father. The spelling is soon changed to Dicksie.

2. To visit William John Russell's people at Walthourville, Liberty County.

To Hon. R. B. Russell, c/o W. W. Braswell, Esq., Decatur, Georgia, Special Delivery

Winder, Ga., April 27, 1897

My precious darling,

I mean every word of that—My precious darling! This is your birth-day—such a pretty day. I do wish you could be here now so I could put my arms around your neck & hug you tight. Hope you are feeling well today & are in good spirits about your case.

I think I am much better this morning. This is the first time I've ever felt that I was really better. Haven't tried to get up yet.

Father came on Vestibule to-day. Mother made him come after Mary got my letter.[1] He said he went to brother M's for Pinkie & she would come to-day. Jessie[2] stayed with me last night. Yesterday Mrs. Kelly sent me such a nice waiter, & Mrs. Stanton sent a pitcher of cherries.

I am sitting up in bed writing this before breakfast. The children are crawling out of bed one by one, & Jessie is dressing them. I felt so much better last night I ordered a ham & will have some for breakfast.

When you come thro' A[thens?] if convenient, get my gowns. I'll need them on my *bridal tour* to Savannah, when I leave my 3 babies at home.

Your four or must I say *five*[3] babies, send you lots of love & want to kiss you this morning.

    Lovingly & devotedly,

    Ina

1. Richard's father, mother, and sister were keeping an eye on Ina, who was pregnant again and having problems.

2. A servant.

3. Ina is again hoping for twin boys.

Although Ina's fourth pregnancy proved her most difficult in the early months, on the cold and blustery morning of November 2, 1897, word reached Richard that he was now Richard B. Russell Sr.

Richard Sr. raced home as fast as a horse and buggy could carry him, and when Dr. Almond held the newborn son up for inspection and admiration, the ecstatic Richard slapped the doctor so enthusiastically on the back that he almost dropped the precious baby. Then Richard, unable to contain his elation, rushed into the front yard with his shotgun and fired off several blasts. Everyone in Winder knew the Russell baby was a boy. Some time later—the exact date is unknown—Dicksie's name was changed to Frances Marguerite, a name chosen by Mary Brevard (Auntney), Richard's sister. She chose Frances because it was Ina's mother's name and Marguerite to satisfy her love for daisies and for the French language.

Life seemed so satisfying at the birth of his son that a few weeks later Richard came to Ina with a proposition. He was, he said, delighted with his wife and children, and would not wish for a finer family. He had in his possession an object that would allow them to continue to enjoy their conjugal bliss and limit their family at the same time. Did that not sound like a good idea to her?

Ina declined. She intended, she said, to have all the children God meant for her to have. The hired man was digging postholes in the backyard. Would Richard like to take this object and drop it in one of those holes, or would she do it herself?

1898–1910

I've Been Nursing *Regular* Nearly Sixteen Years

*T*he years 1898–1910 were both fruitful and sorrowful. Ina gave birth to Harriette Brumby in May 1899 and to Robert Lee in August 1900. Ina became so ill with mastitis after Rob's birth that she was unable to care for a new baby and the others, so Sister Pipey took Harriette to Farm Hill. She would stay there four years, the favorite of Pipey and Grandmother "Mec."

In 1902, Patience Elizabeth was born, and in 1903, Walter Brown arrived. In 1905 Susan Way, born April 15, lived only three months. Grieving over the loss of this little girl, Ina prepared for the birth of Lewis Carolyn on June 7, 1906.

That Ina in motherhood was growing in wisdom is evident from these lines in a birthday letter from her sister Hattie, February 18, 1903: "I am so glad that you are my dear sweet sister. I love you better since I saw you last. While I have always loved you (you know I have), I have a tenderer feeling for you now. I dont know whether it is me growing better or you growing sweeter. I think it is the latter. You are so lovely and gentle with your children, and are wise enough to accept them as gifts from God, and you show a willingness and pleasure in doing the best you can for them. I dont often hear women express themselves about their children as you did. It made me very proud of you, and thankful that there was one common sense woman in the world."

Meanwhile, Richard was pursuing his career in public service. In 1896 he had left the Western Circuit as solicitor in order to make more money in his law practice and better support his growing family. However, in October of 1898 he was in Atlanta campaigning hard with state legislators for a four-year term as judge of the Superior Court of the Western Circuit. On October 23, 1898, he wrote to Ina: "I will certainly try to do right as you ask me in your letter. I don't know how long I am for this world, but I want to leave the legacy of a good name to my precious little boy who bears my name. My faults I hope he will avoid, but I want to do some good at least which he can emulate and imitate, conscious always that he possesses in an unequalled degree the tenderest affection of a loving and devoted father." On October 28, 1898, he proudly wired his wife: "Your husband is judge by overwhelming majority."

At the turn of the century the city of Winder occupied a unique spot— literally. The town center was at the meeting place of three counties— Gwinnett, Walton, and Jackson. Some of the small town's citizens lived in Gwinnett, some in Walton, and some in Jackson. As the time for Richard's reelection to the judgeship drew near, his political enemies in Winder circulated a rumor that he was, in fact, ineligible to be the Western Circuit judge because he did not live in Jackson County.

Indeed, the Russell home on Park Avenue was in the Jackson County sector, but because of the unique structure of the town, Richard feared people outside Winder would believe the rumors and his reputation would be smeared. His solution to this dilemma: Start his own town, one clearly located in Jackson County. He bought two hundred acres of land about a mile and a half outside of Winder on the Seaboard Railroad line, and on December 8, 1902, the City of Russell was chartered by an Act of the Georgia legislature.

After this confrontation, Richard had little use for Winder. His brother Lewis was practicing law there and shared a home with their maiden sister Mary [Auntney], and his cousins the Quartermans lived there. Except for visits to these relatives, Richard remained aloof.

There were four or five houses at the settlement so grandly called the City of Russell. If Ina had thought Winder a cultural desert, what must she have thought of Russell? Yet when a black hired man arrived at her front door with a two-mule wagon saying Judge Russell told him to take some furniture out to the Gresham house—the first she knew of the exact moving day—Ina packed up her children and her furniture and soon set up housekeeping in a five-room bungalow a quarter of a mile from the railroad tracks. This was July 1903. She had given birth to her eighth child, Walter Brown, on June 18.

In Russell, Richard leased his land to tenant farmers and provided seed, fertilizer, and groceries for them. Ina kept the books on this farming business, with occasional help from Richard's brother Lewis. As they grew older, R. B., as Richard Jr. was called, and Rob, had to help unload supplies and keep track of disbursements too. Richard also started a hosiery mill, hoping to profit from the fact that Winder was developing in the textile direction. On the advice of his good friend and classmate from the University of Georgia, Dr. Joseph Jacobs, a well-known and prospering druggist, Richard turned down the chance to buy stock in Coca-Cola. Dr. Jacobs noted that the beverage ate away the metal under the fountain from which it was served, and thus he was sure it could not be good for the stomach. Richard decided to invest instead in his own bottling works in Russell.

In 1904 Richard ran for chief justice of the Georgia Supreme Court and was defeated. He was not discouraged but felt instead he had gained important statewide recognition. In 1906 he ran a vigorous campaign for governor in which he gained a reputation as a formidable debater. During the summer reporters came to interview him at his home in Russell and photographed him with his wife and nine children. One such article and photo appeared on the front page of the *Georgian*. Ina held the baby, Lewis Carolyn. The *Georgian* reported Ina had sent out several hundred campaign letters, and the children had been putting their own posters along the roadside. There were five candidates in the race, and although Hoke Smith easily won the election, Richard, a dark horse, came in second. But Richard and Ina had little time to rejoice in this showing. The baby Lewis Carolyn died on September 9, 1906, following a swift, unidentified illness.

In November 1906 Richard was elected by the legislature as one of three judges on the newly formed Court of Appeals, and his commuting to Atlanta began. Sometimes he stayed in the city, keeping a room in the Kimball House hotel, and sometimes he came home on the train. The train stopped at a crossing near their house, eliminating the necessity of using the station at Winder. As his case workload increased, he was away from home more and more.

Another of Richard's activities was membership in fraternal organizations such as the Shriners and Masons. He was particularly active and popular in the Royal Arcanum, an insurance society. He was frequently chosen as Georgia's representative for national conventions and received expenses-paid trips. An enthusiastic and capable orator, he was a favorite after-dinner speaker. He loved these gatherings for they gave him a taste of the acclaim he so desired. From one he wrote Ina of the success of his speech and concluded: "I feel like the lion of the hour." Ina accompanied him in these travels when possible, and as the children grew older one or two of them were always taken along.

On August 21, 1907, Ina at last had her twin boys, named Fielding Dillard and William John, after her father and Richard's. Since the twins' father, now papa of a dozen children, was an eminent judge of the Court of Appeals, they were announced in the Atlanta papers, and congratulations poured in. Ina saw her "twinnies" as sent to replace the babies she had lost and hoped her family was complete.

When Henry Edward arrived on September 26, 1909, his birth made national headlines. It was happy human interest news that he was not only the seventh son of a "distinguished Georgia jurist" but also the thirteenth child of his mother, herself a thirteenth child. The *New York World* ran a front-page article on September 28, 1909, on the subject, and the *Washington Herald* covered it on page 2 on September 29, 1909. Congratulations came from all over the country as Richard's friends in Royal Arcanum and Shriners read of another baby boy for the Russells. Richard gloried in the acclaim and found time to write effusive answers to several of the telegrams and letters.

Although few of Ina's letters survive from this period, those extant show the growing complications of her life and her improving ability to adjust to them. One of her methods was to "give" each new baby to one of the older girls, no doubt thanking the Divine Wisdom that sent her daughters first. Bill, as Mary Willie came to be called, had early adopted Rob of her own accord, perhaps because of her mother's illness at the time of his birth. Ina Jr. was given Walter, probably at the time of the move to Russell, and when the twins arrived, Ina Sr. designated again. Fielding became Marguerite's charge, and although William was encouraged to call Ina Jr. his special sister, Ina Sr. recognized that this son needed the devoted attention of his mother.

Although she needed her older girls at home, Ina insisted they be sent to school when old enough. Mary Willie went first to Agnes Scott in Decatur, but by the fall of 1909 Richard had determined the tuition at this private girls' school too high, considering the number of scholars he anticipated, and so Mary Willie and Ina Jr. were sent to Georgia Normal and Industrial College at Milledgeville, thus beginning a long tradition of Russell daughters at the school that Richard had helped to bring into existence in his early days in the Georgia Legislature. Ina Jr., ill with asthma, was unable to keep up the stringent work routine required of all girls at GN&IC and eventually had to be brought home.

By the spring of 1910 Ina Sr. was pregnant with her fourteenth child. Although she admitted in later years that she did not welcome every pregnancy, Ina's letters and her life prove beyond a doubt she welcomed every baby. In spite of her new expectation, Ina went ahead with plans for her older girls to go away to school in the fall of 1910. Billie returned to GN&IC, and Ina Jr. and Marguerite went to live with Aunt Hattie in Washington, Georgia, to attend school there.

Ina's regard for Richard was growing with her maturity as well. Although his frequent absences—not always strictly work-related—were sometimes irritating, she appreciated the difficulty of being dutiful breadwinner and beloved father of their brood while struggling to satisfy his tremendous and tormenting ambition. Letters from her sisters and later witness of her children testify that she made every effort for his homecomings to be moments of rejoicing and his time at home peaceful. She continued, too, to welcome every opportunity to travel with him.

To Russell Chicks, Winder, Ga.

May 19, 1908
On Pullman "Imperial," Flying thru Georgia
on the "Dixie Flyer." We are just a little ways
from Chattanooga.

My Dear little brood of ten!

How are you to-day? I guess Walter B. has rec'd his letter. I'm still think-ing of, & can so plainly see each of my little ones. My precious twinnies! Kiss them for me, you big chicks.

We are on a nice sleeper. Each seat has a large nice white pillow. Mine is to my back now & is so much help. The porter has given all the ladies nice white sacks to put their hats in. I don't think they would quite hold a "Merry Widow." The coach is full of passengers. Nearly all the ladies are nice looking old ladies & wear their hair fixed as I do mine. We left early & I have been amused watching some of the passengers eat breakfast. One lady & her pretty young daughter, who wears a brown coat suit & has her hair all puffed & a big brown bow, had such a nice tin lunch box. It was all red plaid on the outside & fastened with a strap. Another couple, a man, & lady, had their lunch in a big wicker suit case. They had a quart fruit jar full of tea & ever so many jelly tumblers. The man ate jelly & butter on bread and finished up by eating 3 apples. Another old man & lady had their lunch in a box & before the man began to eat he tied on a big white bib. He had a long beard & put the bib over his beard.

We are seeing mountains & flying over rivers. We have been thru one tunnel about ½ mile long. . . .

It is raining & very cloudy. I couldn't see Lookout Mt. very well, but I could see Point Lookout house & Lookout Inn, where papa & I stayed on our *first* bridal tour.

I can't write much now for looking at the lovely mountain scenery. I say like Walter B. "Ain't that bee-tee-full." We have just been thru a tunnel & over a very high trestle. Part of the way we were going right along the Ten-nessee River, with a big high mountain on the other side of us. It was so grand, so beautiful. I think we will cross the river directly. I won't write any more now. Will try to let you all hear from us every day. If you can, call for mail Saturday aft, as something may be there. We have crossed the beautiful Tennessee. R. B.'s boat would do fine on it. We went over one river & a little island & then crossed the Tennessee. It was so beautiful. I wish you all could see it. We saw steam boats. One a two-story. Just think children! Mama seeing all this & we haven't been from home 24 hrs. . . .

Love & be good to each other, & to dear Pipy & aunt Hattie. It is so sweet of them to take care of you all. My twinnies! Sweet things! Keep well for mama's sake. . . .

Your loving mother

To Robert Lee Russell, Winder, Ga.

[Chicago] May 23, 1908

My Dear Robert,

I wish you were here with your wheel [bicycle] this morning. The streets are so smooth & level & the little boys & girls just seem to ride all the time. I can see two little girls now who are having a fine time. You must not have your heart too much set on a tent and an air gun. They are big things & cost so much money, but we will bring you something from Chicago. I'm glad you are being good. Of course my Robert is good, for he loves his mama too well to act ugly.

If I could, I would bring you all the cutest little flying Jenny. Just like the ones we see in the papers. I would love for you to have one.

I wish you could see the automobiles here. Every color, size & shape, & some go so easy you can't hear them. We are going to have a ride this afternoon & I will wish for my Robert to be with me.

Your loving Mother

To Richard Brevard Russell, Jr. at Farm Hill

September 22, 1908

My dear R. B. Russell, Jr.,

It made my heart glow & swell with pride this morning when I read Pipey's card telling me that you were proving yourself a man & were faithful in nursing our darling twinnies. I had hoped that you would do this and expected you to do it. Some people don't think there is much good in boys, but I know there is "heap much good" as the chinamen say, and I want people to see it in *my* boys even when they are way off somewhere.

Yes, darling boy, help care for our babies—the strong must always help the *weak,* and you are stronger than Ina and Harriet[1] and even Pipey, Granny, aunt Annie & aunt Hattie, when it comes to nursing. *Nursing* regular is *hard, tiresome* work but our love for twinnies—bless their sweet little souls & bodies—helps us to stand it. You see your mother knows all about it, for I've been nursing *regular, nearly* sixteen years. Just keep up your good work a few more days & I hope by the first of next week for us all to be together again. I'm feeling very nearly well.[2] Poor Marguerite is laid up today but not bad off. The doctor had to treat her throat yesterday & he said she must be quiet for two days.

O, the "hall room" girls are doing well. The doctor will have to see Marguerite again Friday. Then I suppose we can find out exactly when we can leave here. I want to have two of my teeth fixed before I leave, if possible.

Your papa wrote our teacher a note & told her our school wouldn't begin in another week.[3] I believe it is October 2. I'm sorry we are late, but don't suppose it will make any difference . . .

Be a good boy. Don't forget to drink your fresh water every morning before you eat breakfast. Help everywhere you can & be sweet to everybody. Never forget your grandmother or dear aunt Annie, Hattie, and Pipey. . . .

Good-bye my darling old freckled face boy. I would love to see you this morning.

      Your fond Mother

1. Ina Sr. was in Atlanta nursing Richard Sr. through a bout of pneumonia. Marguerite had also come to Atlanta for medical treatment, leaving the other children at Farm Hill. Ina Jr. had severe attacks of asthma, and rheumatic fever had left Harriette (sometimes spelled Harriet, as here) with a weak heart. Since Mary Willie was in Decatur at Agnes Scott School for Girls and Marguerite was ill, R. B. was the next in line to help with the younger children. He was not quite eleven.

2. While nursing Richard, Ina suffered a miscarriage, believed to be twins.

3. Richard had secured public funds for a school in Russell, and the children were eager for it to open.

To Miss A. P. Dillard,[1] Winder, Georgia U.S.A.

      May 18, 1910

My Dearest Children,

We have just reach[ed] Montreal & in a *pouring* rain. Papa & Mr. Simmons were so afraid they were late & hurried on to answer roll call. *We children* [R. B. and Rob] walked slowly up the hill to the Hotel & are waiting in the ladies waiting room for papa to find us.

A desk & one round table just *full* of paper, pens & ink tempted us to write our dearies at home. We had *such* a lovely ride today. Almost in view of Lake Champlain & Lake George all the way. Lake C. is beautiful. On Lake George the track went *so close* sometimes it seemed we were going right into the lake. We were always wishing for some of you & all of you. . . .

I am real tired, but I have stood my trip better than any I've ever taken.[2]

I put on my old slippers yesterday when we left Washington. We didn't know we would have to change cars in N.Y. until we got nearly there. So I went flying around under the ground and up & down steps for about 7 miles with those old slippers on. I said to myself: O, if my children could only see me now!

I will kiss you all good-by & write a short note to Bill. Mother loves *everybody* at home so dearly. Kiss Edward & my twins. Hug Walter & Patience & my three big girls. Tell Bell[3] her crackers were so good & we ate some after reaching King George V ['s] dominion. The officers came in & looked thru our satchels. He didn't see anything in mine but my kimona, slippers & the jar of pea-nut butter that was right on top.

Heres loving & hoping each one well. You can see how we are thinking of you. Having been here ½ hour & *this letter*! after riding 1800 miles!

Mother

1. Pipey wrote to Ina, letting her know how each child was faring. "We are not afraid to be alone at night," she wrote, and "Nothing will come between me and your children, Ina." She also supervised letter writing for the children to their mother.

2. Ina is five months pregnant, but it is doubtful that her children know this.

3. A black cook and housekeeper.

To Miss A. P. Dillard, Winder, Ga. U.S.A.

May 19, 1910

My Dear Children,

We are just in from a *fine* street car ride *all over* Montreal. We have seen the handsome buildings, beautiful parks and the many churches and convents and Catholic schools.

This morning *we ladies* were taken to see the Grey Nun Convent where poor little babies and pitiful old people are cared for. R. B. could hardly stand to see them and begged to be taken out. We saw about 150 babies under 2 years old. Some not a week old. They were tenderly cared for by good nurses. The old people were pitiful, but they were cared for & everything so nice & clean. This building is over 200 yrs. old & the Nuns there dress as they did 200 yrs. ago—brown skirts & waists, calico aprons of black & white and the black bonnet. We have seen so many priests and they wear skirts like a woman. . . .

Everything here is in mourning for King Edward. He will be buried to-morrow & all R.A. business has been suspended until Saturday. We are going out to see a big military parade to-morrow. Will see 20,000 soldiers drill & see & *hear* 101 minute guns fired. R. B. is wild over the prospect. . . .

I do hope you are all well, & happy & good. You are all *sweet,* I know, just the dearest children in the world. We wish you could all be here & each of you shall have a trip this summer. I didn't intend to say *this* summer, but *sometimes.* You know we will have to take it "*turn about.*"

How are my twins & Edward? How thankful I was this morning that I could care for them in our good, sweet home.

It does me good to see Papa so popular here. The men gathered around him & seemed so glad to have him back. When we went in to dinner the first evening, I had to stop at every table & *stand* while different ones said: "Hallo, Judge," "So glad to see you Judge," and "We haven't forgotten your jokes at St. Louis," &c, &c. When Papa would introduce me, so many would say: "Mrs. Russell, we are so glad to meet you for we think so much of the Judge." . . .

The boys have had *spasms* because we haven't found post cards to send you all. We saw some this morning, but didn't have time to buy.

> Love to Pipey and Miss L[ula] & Mrs. M[urphy] [1]
> and a heart full for each of my *chicks.*
> Mother

1. Miss Lula Fowler and Mrs. Murphy were teachers. Miss Lula lived in with the Russells, and Mrs. Murphy lived in a cottage nearby.

To Miss Marguerite Russell, Washington, Ga.

Sep. 19, 1910

My Dear Child,

Your letter came this morning. I was expecting one from *some of you* & it was so nice not to be disappointed.

I am very glad you are studying hard & that you think of papa & me when you begin to study. We do want you to do well, & are *expecting* you to do well. I am so glad you like your teachers too. It makes study and school so pleasant when teachers & scholars like each other. We are doing very well at home without my three big girls, but I do miss you—I tell you I do.

Harriet is so smart and faithful and R. B. has the milking for his job, & he does it *well.* I never have to remind him of it & he takes good care of the cow. Rob still feeds, & he dries the dishes nearly every day. He helps me cook, too. Says he wants to learn how. Sunday he peeled & sliced the sweet potatoes to dress, put them in the pan & I let him put in the sugar, butter & water & he felt very proud of them when we ate dinner. Patience & Walter help too & we do very well, but O, the sweeping! R. B. is trying to learn—you should have seen him sweeping the hall this morning. This time of year, spiders & dust keep you busy. Both are so ugly in a house. I don't suppose or I'm afraid my parlor won't get cleaned again until you & Mary Willie come home Xmas.

Saturday morning I had every thing in "Miss Tavie's room"[1] torn up— sunning the beds & cleaning everything, working as hard as I could, and who do you suppose walked in & came right on to the back porch before *any body* knew it? Just guess! Why *Sister Murphy*!!!!!! I was busy and didn't look up for an instant, trying to think what to say & do. I treated her all right, but we talked affairs over & I told her I was on papa's side, but was sorry things had turned out as they had. She wept a little, and said *I* had always done my part & if it hadn't been for me she couldn't have held out &c. Well, we got that trunk out & those pictures & her box from the ware house. She has a position in the City school in Atlanta. Teaches 2nd grade at Walker St. school & gets $50 per month this year & $60 per month next year. [Mr.] Murphy has his same old place back. I invited her to eat dinner with us, but she had promised the Morris' she'd come back there for dinner

& she went on back after searching the house over for her elocution book. Harriet found it on top shelf of book case. So much for Mrs. Murphy! I don't suppose we will ever see much more of her—& I say: "Peace go with her & joy behind." [2]

I'm sitting on the swing writing, William on one side of me & Fielding on the other. I told Fielding I was writing to Sister, to be still so I could write. William said, "Now mama, you got to write to Ina." You know how they say: "you *got* to."

Just as I finished writing the sentence about sitting on the swing, &c., Mr. Huff [3] came in & we have thoroughly discussed Mrs. Murphy. . . . Now, I'm all broken into & don't know what I wanted to say. . . . & will have to close. I will look up the [dress] patterns & send soon. Aunt Hattie is sweet & kind to make you all *anything*.

> With a heart *full* of love,
> Mother

1. Miss Tavie was a former live-in teacher.

2. Mrs. Murphy had quarreled with the judge over his pay schedule. The pay was delayed because the money did not come from the state and Richard had none of his own with which to pay.

3. A neighbor.

To Miss Ina Russell, Washington, Ga.

Home—Oct. 3, 1910

My Dear Ina,

If you and Margo could have seen the pleasure your letters gave us this morning, you would not regret one moment of your time spent on them. We did enjoy them & I read each one. The twins enjoyed theirs, and the pictures were a great *hit*. Rob & Harriet found suitable books and soon had them pasted in, & the dear little boys were very happy. The twins are very amusing these days. They are *so* smart. I know they were sent for my special pleasure, for I enjoy them so much. The other night at supper Fielding was asleep, but William was at the table and in one of his high glees. I called him a monkey, and then I asked him if he had ever seen a monkey. He said: "Yes." I asked him where. He said: "On front porch." Well, that surprised me, & I then asked him what the monkey did. He said: "Strike match." Of course, we were all surprised that he should remember[1] & every body felt like eating him up. I wondered if Fielding remembered as well. The next morning I asked him just as I did William & he said the same thing. I thought it wonderful in them. They don't forget you & Marguerite at all. If F. gets into any great trouble he still cries out *"Sissie,"* & William cries out "INER." You know how they drawl it out.

Edward is not walking, but he grows fast & is so sweet and smart.

I especially enjoy the school news you all send in your letters. I like to know what your themes & compositions are about & your teachers names & what hours you have certain studies, and anything about school. As I always say, I'm counting on you two to do well in everything, and to be model girls in every respect. You both know well what is right & what your father & mother expect of you.

I told aunt Hattie to tell you how much I enjoyed your letter & I would answer soon. You know that was your first letter to me. Of course you know aunt Hattie must be joking when she says we don't love you as well as we do Margo, for you know your mother loves all her children alike. I'm willing for aunt Hattie to have you for her girl, but you must know we all love you as we do the rest. Margo had written so many letters home & you hadn't. . . .

Bell came in this morning & we all hailed her with delight. That is, we felt it, but kept our feelings inside. I told the children they dare not tell her anything about how we had missed her or anything we had been doing while she was gone. She seemed very glad to get back.

Toler seems to be over her lameness, but doesn't travel quite as well as usual. Edward, the twins & I still go to meet papa, but its almost dark now when the train comes. . . .

Bell has rushed in & wants to have soon supper so she can go to a church entertainment at "Mr. Guss Griffeths." Their Conference is going to meet at Bush's Chapel & they want to fix up the church. Emory has just come by & stopped at Bottling works & got 2 crates of soda water to take over to Gus'.

I'm always sorry of an interruption for it causes me to forget some of the things I want to write. My mind is a blank now, and I guess I'll have to "draw my letter to a close."

I wanted to tell you one thing William did. Both of the twins amuse us talking about the Black Manorca chickens. William in his funny way began call[ing] them "Black Maniggers." He seems to think it a good joke, & it does sound funny. . . .

>With a heart full of love for you & Margo, and aunt Hattie &
>Cleo, too,
>Mother

1. A gypsy organ grinder with a monkey had paid a visit to Russell the previous summer.

To Ina Russell, Jr., Washington, Ga.

Nov. 17, 1910

My Dear Ina,

Here I come with my letter to you, as I promised yesterday in Marguerite's letter. And how did the circus please you? . . . I hope you enjoyed it all & I trust the dust under the tent didn't make you wheeze. We have been very dry here. Not one rain since the baby came [October 19]. . . .

My nurse stayed with me three weeks. When she left I cared for the baby, and he is real good—rarely gets me up more than once or twice during the night, & he sleeps well in the day time. But you know there is *plenty* to do for *any* baby, no matter how good he is. Mrs. Austin nurses him every afternoon about 3:30. Mary Pope[1] nurses him occasionally. I would like to be near Mrs. Huff. You know her boy—John D. Rockefeller they call him—is just three days older than "Little Dick."[2]

The Huffs are building a new "two-story" house for themselves—over behind the brick school building. It is built with the lumber from the church [that blew down in the tornado]. I imagine it will look like a crazy quilt when completed.

Papa's stenographer boards at Mary Popes and she has a graphophone. You can imagine the neighborhood going wild over it—especially when Miss Adair goes to Atlanta and brings new records. Our children are crazy over it, & they go down & listen by the hour.

As I wrote Margo, I think its impossible for me to make you all a visit— but, O, my, wouldn't I like to! I think Pipey is liable to go home any time now, & I'm not feeling very strong. Poor Pipey is very sad, sometimes, over breaking up, and I wouldn't feel good to leave her in charge of things.[3] This morning Walter, Patience, the twins and myself, just for fun, made a fine plan. We would get Dee Jackson to take us to Washington in his auto. We had a good time talking. William's eyes were big as moons. . . .

I've just got off our whole household—except "Little Dick Russell" & myself to Winder, to see a Minstrel parade at twelve o'clock. I thought Edward & the twins would like to hear the band.

I've been occupying the spare room since the new baby came. I walked into the hall just now—first time I've left the room since Oct. 19th. . . .

O, I will be so happy to have my three big girls at home again! I've missed them so much. Tell aunt Hattie of course she must come. To remember she promised to spend every Xmas with us [when Brother Arnold died]. Wouldn't it be nice if Pipey & aunt Annie are in the Mealor House by that time? . . . [4]

I am writing too much. You will get tired reading & just now, I dipped the handle of my pen in the ink instead of the point. I was in such a hurry.

Bell has just come in to get dinner & she said she wanted to have soon dinner as "it was her day to take a music lesson." Think of it!

I know you want me to do something about those pictures. Now listen! You must give *me* the one of Mary Willie. Won't you? Its so sweet & just like my big girl. Let me know. I enjoy looking at it & showing it. You know she doesn't take a good picture, but that one is *good.* She can see it Xmas.

It was so sweet of aunt Hattie to give you & M. the hats. Tell her for me not to spoil you *too* much. I'm so glad she enjoys having you all with her.

Tell aunt H. to read your letter & excuse me for not writing to her. I do love her so dearly. . . .

Take care of yourself. Drink water before breakfast—*hot* water is best. Let me know how you are these days.

> With a heart of love,
> Mother

1. Ina's cousin. She and her husband, John Moseman, had come to Russell to help manage Richard's businesses.

2. All the women mentioned in the paragraph were wet nurses.

3. America Dillard and her eldest son died in December 1909, creating dramatic changes in the lives of Pipey and Annie, who had lived under their protection at Farm Hill.

4. Pipey and Annie were planning to move to Russell.

To Marguerite Russell, Washington, Ga.

November 29, 1910

My Dear Marguerite,

Just as I picked up my pencil & paper, the baby began to make his funny little fuss, & that means he may cry out any time & make me stop writing. He has a funny little way of grunting & stretching just before he wakes.

Your letter came yesterday morning & Inas this morning. I'm always so glad to hear from my chicks. Tell Ina I will answer hers right away— to-morrow if I have time—and I will look up the things you & she wants & send them right away.

You & Ina had better buy some shirts. I can send Inas, but you know you haven't any. Papa said last night he would send you a check today. If he doesn't, just get Aunt Hattie to get your shirts, or borrow some money from Ina, if she has any, for papa will send it sometime this week. You & Ina must not take cold. It is so much colder today than it has been.

You will be surprised, I expect, to know that I let Harriet & "old Jebs"[1] go home with Pipey Saturday. He was beautiful when we got him ready to start. Pipey wanted him & I didn't see how I could fix bottles through the night for both babies. "Little Dick" is good & never cries in the night & Jebs cries sometimes & I thought he would be more than I could manage. It is sweet of Pipey to be willing to care for him & Harriet promised to nurse him faithfully, if I let them go. I don't know how long they will stay. I'll send Harriet's card that came this morning.

I was so glad uncle Lewis[2] went to Washington. He 'phoned me about seeing you and Ina, & about how he wrapped Ina up on the auto ride.

Tomorrow is the last day of Nov. & then our Christmas month will be here. Get the *glad* spirit on you & don't think of getting homesick. Don't worry about presents. You are in school & studying hard & thats excuse enough for not having presents. I feel sometimes that I can hardly wait for you all to come, for I do miss you & want to see you *so bad*, but I don't have much time to *brood* over it, for I keep so busy. I'm real busy now, since Pipey left. I miss you & Bill [Mary Willie] about the cleaning up. My house is *awful—dirtier* than I ever saw it. I got Bell to give it a raking over this morning & told her she need not cook any dinner. You know she wont clean up & cook too.

What do you think about us moving into the Mercer Jackson House.[3] Its all the talk now. The Moores move out soon. We would have more room & lots of nice fruit in the summer. That is, if we had a good fruit year.

The baby has been so good to let me write this hurried letter. I must fix his milk.

R. B. went to Atlanta this A.M. with Papa to bring home something for papa. Papa is going to a *swell* dinner tonight. I fixed up his dress suit & shirt.

We had a nice Thanksgiving. Mr. & Mrs. West, Mr. & Mrs. Jim Perry & Auntney. Papa invited all the guests. I didn't intend to have a soul, but I had planned a nice dinner. Mrs. West, Pipey & Bell fixed things so nice & I didnt do a thing but sit in parlor. The baby slept all day. He was so good. He went in parlor & amused himself looking at every body. I mean when he awoke I carried him in the parlor. He can't quite walk yet. . . .

Give Aunt Hattie bushels of love for us all. She is sweet & lovely to want all of you until you graduate. Ask her if she will take R. B. next year if we don't have a teacher. Tell her she may send him home the first time he disobeys her. He must be in school. He is growing so fast.

> With a heart of love for you & Ina,
> Mother

1. *Jebs* and *Jeb* are nicknames for Henry Edward. He was Harriette's "boy," and since Harriette had been Pipey's favorite charge since Rob's birth, both children became Pipey's special children.

2. Richard's youngest brother.

3. Ina was not delighted with the idea of moving into this two-story structure because it was in poor condition, but her housing situation was desperate.

1911–1922

I Can't Have One of You
a Failure—Not One

*I*n the summer of 1911 Richard took a step he had been contemplating since 1906. He felt the time was right to run for governor again, and this time he expected to win. He faced an autumn of rigorous campaigning, and Ina faced supporting him and sending four of her chicks away to boarding schools. R. B. was sent to Gordon Military Institute at Barnesville. Almost fourteen, the lad was growing fast, and his parents felt he had ranged a wild prince in the fields and woods of Russell long enough. Ina also believed Ina Jr., seventeen, and Marguerite, fifteen, had received maximum benefit from the Washington school. Consequently, Margo was sent to GN&IC, where Bill, eighteen, was a junior. Margo was admitted as a freshman. They each were following teacher training programs—the "normal" course.

Ina Jr. was sent to Lucy Cobb Institute in Athens to be nearer home in case her asthma worsened. There were only forty young women at Lucy Cobb that year, and they were the closest thing Athens had to coeds. They enjoyed a lively if carefully chaperoned social life alongside an academic program less serious than that at GN&IC.

Richard's hosiery mill and bottling works were not doing well, yet with only his Court of Appeals salary and uncertain income from his tenant farmers, he was undaunted by the task of finding funds to pay school fees for four and money to fuel his campaign as well.

As the campaign began Richard was considered a top contender in the race. However, the issue of local option on liquor sales turned out to be a divisive and deadly one for Richard Russell. Although his position that each county and municipality choose for itself whether to allow liquor sales was ultimately adopted in Georgia following Prohibition, in the warm-up to Prohibition, temperate Methodists and members of other denominations as well branded him a Mephistophelian miscreant. It was rumored that somewhere a Methodist bishop had said Richard Russell ought to be tied to a whipping post and every church member in the state be allowed to take a whack at him. Ina's brother Miles Dillard, a Methodist minister, had died in 1898. Her beloved brother Walter, also a Methodist minister, felt he had to stand against Richard's candidacy, but he did so with less vehemence than the bishop.

This was an era in which politics was totally a man's world, an arena in which women were rarely seen and more rarely heard, but it was also a time in which women of stout religious faith and determined prejudice against strong drink crusaded into man's domain. Women's Christian Temperance Union members followed Richard's campaign from time to time and made speeches against him in towns where he spoke. Ina's sister-in-law Lella Dillard, widow of brother Miles, was active in the WCTU statewide and was among those women who spoke for Prohibition on the courthouse steps of many Georgia counties.

When a rumor rumbled that the Methodists in Winder were going to ask Richard to leave their congregation, he left to avoid a confrontation. Ina followed. She could not attend a church that refused to accept her husband.

In spite of strained family ties and four of her precious chicks off at school, Ina brought enthusiasm and optimism to the gubernatorial campaign. With touching naïveté, she waded in wholeheartedly, determined to do her best to help her Richard achieve his lifelong ambition.

In 1912 Richard went back to the Court of Appeals and embarked on further plans to promote the City of Russell. He wanted a train station and a post office, and he was considering plans for a hotel near the proposed site of the train station. Ina, hearing of hotel plans, said if Richard was going to build a structure of that size, she was going to live in it. The hotel plans became house plans.

Hoping to encourage a growing community, Richard again secured public funds for a school in Russell, and when it opened in January of 1913, for all eligible students in the area, the response was almost overwhelming. Trying to keep foot-dragging scholars such as Ina Jr. and R. B. actively in school continued to be a problem, as well as what to do with eager scholars such as Harriette and Rob. All suffered severe homesickness from time to time, but Ina always advised them to "fight the feeling" and do their best with their opportunities for education.

As the years passed, Ina's mothering tasks became more complex. While guiding her six older children without interfering where they needed to take responsibility, her work associated with teaching and nursing those at home went inexorably on.

Richard left the Court of Appeals in 1916 to run for Congress and to practice law. There was plenty of law work for a former Court of Appeals Justice, but much of it involved travel. Richard was away from home for days and sometimes weeks at a time, so life at Russell still carried on without papa.

World War I and the automobile brought sweeping changes to Ina's daily life as Winder became more accessible. It was, with a "flivver," possible for the young children to go to school in Winder, and soon the idea of a Russell school was abandoned.

To Marguerite Russell, Washington, Georgia

February 21, 1911

My Dearest Margo,

. . . You must get some medicine & heal up your little boils—But first drink just lots of water, especially at night & soon in the mornings. Buy 5 cents of cream tartar, & about 2 cents of sulphur & 2 cents of salts—mix all to-gether, *well* & take ½ spoonful once every day. As you are in school, take yours at night. Do this. You know I always give you all something in spring of the year. *Don't you fail to get this right away and take regularly.* Let me know.

My birthday was a great success. In the mail of the 18th aunt Hattie's sweet letter came. A card from aunt Mamie, & a lovely hand-made jabot from my Bill. Then Pipey sent me a can of figs & a can of beans—Next day

I rec'd a card from aunt Mattie. Papa didn't give me anything. I told him not to, as I wanted every cent I could rake & scrape to fix the inside of my awful looking house.

Tell aunt Hattie I enjoyed her letter & will answer right away. I just couldn't do without her birthday letters. I look for them as I do my birthday.

I can hardly write. I never have a spare, quiet moment. Ellen, Laura,[1] the school children—mine, Uncle Bens & the Huffs generally—coming in & out—talking, asking questions & wanting various things. You know how busy my life is & I'm busier now than ever. No one helps much but Harriet & the boys. But I didn't mean to tell you all this. I just had to stop writing twice & it worried me. I'm so thankful for Laura. She is just what I've needed all the time. She is so kind to the children & so firm too. She is a *fine* cook, & helps feed the children & waits on the twins. Gets Papa's breakfast in time for early train. She will be great this summer when you girls have your company. She doesn't mind anything that is reasonable. She made me a beautiful white cocoanut cake for my birthday.

I will or expect to send M[ary].W[illie]. a box Friday.[2] I've made her a beautiful kimono, & will make candy & Laura wants to make her a caramel cake. I enclose a card for you to send Bill if you want to.

Mrs. Huff has just been over & gave little Dick all he could drink.

Its getting late & I must hurry. R. B. will take this to Winder. We are nearly frozen here & I've been busy getting up wood &c.

Did you hear that Miss Lucy Jackson (Mrs. Niblack) was dead? She left a little boy one week old. Miss Laura Arnold & Edgar DeLaPerriere are married at last.

Our school is splendid. I'll see that the children write soon & tell you all about it. Cousin Annie Zu [the teacher] is a fine, fine girl. She [is] a great treat to have around.

Pipey is keeping house [in the Mealor house] & Rowena, James & Francis[3] seem to be doing all right. Aunt Annie will come Friday. . . .

Mr. Logan Bleckley gave papa a *wind*coat. Its perfectly splendid & I love him for doing it. Its made of fine leather, something like chamois & covered over with fine corduroy. . . .

> With a heart full of love for your dear precious self, & for
> aunt Hattie.
> Your fond Mother

P.S. I have a little book about person born in April to send you. I want you to read it every day for a week & then every other day for a month & study your self. These books are wonderful & true. Yours & papas are the same. . . .

1. Servants.

2. Ina sent each child who was away from home a birthday box. It was filled with gifts and good things to eat. Mary Willie's birthday was March 1.

3. Children of Ina's brother Ben Dillard, whose wife died in a buggy accident in 1908. Because he was a traveling salesman, what to do with his children was a problem that Pipey and Annie were called on to solve. Rowena, the oldest, was about Margo's age, and the boys about the same ages as R. B. and Rob.

To Miss Marguerite Russell, Washington, Ga.

April 3, 1911

My Dearest Child,

Your letter rec'd Friday. I was glad to hear from you, and glad to have your marks for last month. Study hard & do better your next two months. . . .

We are torn up here now. Painters are here, fixing my ugly old house & we are doing just any old way. Yesterday Harriet fell off the bicycle & almost broke her ankle. Couldn't get Dr. Almond until this morning. I was up trying to doctor & relieve her pains nearly all night. She is on my bed now & at times suffers very much. Don't suppose she can use her leg for a week or ten days. She is so much help. I miss her dreadfully, & I am sorry for her to miss school & I'm so sorry for her to suffer . . .

Edward spent the night at Pipey's & the twins ate dinner there. . . .

I am worried about the dress Miss Bramblett[1] made for you and wouldn't take pay. I believe you said you were to clean her room on Saturdays. Let me know if you are doing this. You must keep up with your little expenses & not let aunt Hattie be worried with your bills. Jinsy[2] will make a dress like the one Miss B. made for 50 cents. If you can't do her cleaning to suit her, just pay her 50 cents & let it alone. I'm willing to let you do these things, but I don't want people to think you can't pay for having your dresses made. . . . Learn to manage things so no wrong impressions will be made. . . . I know this is not all I want to say but will have to close. Aunt

Annie, Ina & Rowena are ready to go to town. So much commotion going on *all* the time I don't have time to *think*. . . .

Take care of yourself in this wet weather & don't take cold. Study & do your *best* in *every way*.

        Mother

1. A boarder at Aunt Hattie's.
2. A black woman living nearby who was a seamstress.

To Miss Marguerite Russell, Washington, Ga.

                                      April 10, 1911

My Dear Child,

After much commotion I got your hat to the Ex[press] office this morning. Annie Zu went to Atlanta & as Rob took her to the depot, I thought best to send your hat on. Since moving out here we have to watch our chances to send to town. It takes so much time. When I got ready to send your hat, I found I hadn't a cent of money. Monday morning always finds me dead broke. Ellen & Laura both had got money to go to At[lanta]. . . . Papa is so busy to-day, I won't trouble him by asking him to write your check. But I'll send it *sure* this week. When I send checks off, I like papa to write them.

Papa is working the street in front of the house to-day.[1] He has 5 or 6 men, 2 or 3 teams & all the shovels & wheel barrows & scrapes. He has dug down the hill in front of house & is filling in in front of house & below making a nice road.

About your old hat: . . . I don't think your black hat will be needed. Suppose you give it to aunt Hattie for her little colored girl. She can give it to her, or maybe she could pay her off with it. It might help a little. Give it to aunt Hattie & tell her what I say. Remember you are to give her the shoes, & anything else you have that you can't use. O. yes, be sure to let her have that lilac Mary Jane. I don't want you to wear it in Washington any more. Give it to aunt Hattie and let her use it in paying off Susie. Now, don't misunderstand me, & don't let aunt Hattie misunderstand you. If aunt Hattie can use the dress & hat in paying off Susie, give them to her and let her use them just as I would. I don't want you to receive anything for them. I want them to benefit aunt Hattie. If aunt Hattie can't use them, you give Susie the hat *now* & when you come home, if Susie is still with aunt Hattie, you give her the dress as a parting gift. . . .

Mother loves her little "Dicksie"² & wants her to be very happy on her birthday.

Mother

1. Richard enjoyed moving dirt. He used a wheelbarrow and shovel when working alone. It was his way of keeping fit and of improving the City of Russell at the same time.

2. In spite of her name change, both Richard and Ina often referred to Marguerite as Dicksie.

To Russell Children, Winder, Ga.

July [no day] 1911

My darling "kiddies"

Here we are in Eastman. Have eaten supper and let me tell you: papa & I both had two pieces of fried chicken—all white meat! What about it, R. B.? And we had eggs, roast beef, fried potatoes, grits, biscuit, ice tea, peaches & cream & cake. I'm just telling you this to let you know we are not starving.

Well, we reached Dublin [Georgia] this morning at 9 o'clock. Ever so many men were at the train to meet us. They seemed glad to see me too. I met so many kinds of men. One man didn't have any thumb, but he has a vote all right. The New Dublin Hotel is right at the station & when we walked up, the first man I saw, that I had ever seen before, was cousin Cam Brumby. I was introduced to so many and can't remember many of their names. . . .

I went to my room & rested & papa *mixed* with the people & arranged for his speaking. A brass band had been engaged for the occasion, & when papa & I walked up the street to the Court House the band was playing a lively tune. People were looking at us, & so many were passing around and about, and I had on my pretty blue dress! I felt *almost* as if a carnival were going on, and I was a "Peerless Mamie," or something on that order & it was time for me to perform.

We went on in the Court House & a right big crowd was waiting & watching for the Judge. I mean your father. The band came in side & played one piece, & the court room soon filled up. One lady beside myself was there. Papa brought up about ten men & introduced them to me before he began speaking. A Mr. Hawkins introduced papa. He said some very nice things & introduced him as "Plain Dick Russell." Ralph Smith would say: "The building shook with applause" as papa rose to speak, but I will tell you the clapping was very generous & unanimous. Papa made a very good speech. He seemed to make a good impression. You will see some of his speech in the papers. He spoke one hour & twenty-five minutes. Papa has a good voice & it sounds so sweet when he is speaking. His voice is clear. You can hear every word he says & it never sounds too loud or harsh.

A man from Winder was in Dublin & sat by me while papa spoke. His name was Tucker. Dublin is a large place—7000 people. Pretty, wide streets, three large school buildings & nice churches.

Papa received three telegrams in Dublin. One was for him to be in Edgehill, Gascock Co., to speak at a big picnic, Friday. That is where the man heard papa in "August & died in October." We don't want any fatalities this time.[1] We expect to go to Edgehill. . . .

Papa speaks here to-morrow. People seem to be for him all right, but there are so many people in Georgia & we are seeing just a few of them on this trip. . . .

Hope things are moving on all right. Be kind & good to each other. Be sweet to my twinnies. R. B. & Rob, see after selling our stuff in the store & keep acct.

Tell Laura & Doscia[2] to keep a sharp lookout to take care of every thing. I hope Laura & Marguerite are *jellying* & preserving or canning.

You can send my letter to Harriet & Pipey to read. Hope Dick & Jebs are well and happy. You might get Jebs some day & let him spend the day with you.[3]

I've written very hurriedly. I was tired, but couldn't go to bed without writing to my "dearies."

   With a hug & a kiss to each one of you
   Mother

1. It is likely that a letter or an oral report of this man's death linked his hearing Richard speak with his death in this way, causing the family to tease Richard about the lethal effects of his speaking.

2. Doscia is a new servant.

3. Harriette and Jebs were at Pipey's house.

To Miss Marguerite Russell and Miss Mary Willie Russell, Milledgeville, Ga.

Sep. 22, 1911

My dearest Girls,

Just guess where your mother is! This rickety writing will give me away, so I might as well tell: I am on the Central of Ga. train, with R. B. bound for Barnesville & Gordon Institute. . . . I feel timid going without papa, but I'll try to be brave & talk up to Jere[1] about our boy. I'm grieving myself to death over giving up my children, and if I ever am at home a whole day, I'll grieve "sho nuff." Do you know, I haven't been at home a day since you left.

After your train left, we hurried home & began a mad rush to get Ina ready. As usual, she would do a little & then run & play on the piano, or go to the apple tree with Rowena. Then she would come in & wish she had started packing a week ago &c. She finally had her things fixed & next morning we again went to the ten o'clock train & Ina, Auntney & I (and I carried the twins) went to Athens. . . .

In afternoon, we went with Ina to Lucy Cobb. Everybody was so pleasant & every thing so nice & home-like. Ina has a splendid corner room—three windows & three single beds, a big ward-robe, 2 dressers & one wash stand. Guess she has written you about her room-mates. The twins had a great time. Of course [everybody] noticed them.

We came home that night & hurried on to Atlanta next morning to have R. B.'s dental work done & go to Barnesville as I thought. Papa met us, so dressed up I hardly knew him. Wish you could have seen him! A pretty gray suit, new brown vest & new hat & a rose bud on his coat! He said if we waited until Friday, he could come to B[arnesville] with us. He had to go to Covington Thursday. Well, we went on home, & early next morning ordered Walter Stanton to come with a car. He & Ralph Sharpton[2] came in Mr. S[tanton]'s *case*. R. B., the twins & I went with papa. What a grand ride we had! We went to Oxford to see if sister Lella would let us in. She was very sweet, but told papa he had broken her heart. Annie Zu was overjoyed to see the twins. . . . Fielding is the best looking Dillard I ever saw. Miles is a dear boy. He & Annie Zu went over with me after dinner to hear papa speak. Well, we rushed back that aft. & got home about 8:30. Then this morning we rushed to Atlanta again with R. B. Papa was too busy & I had to come alone. Don't know exactly what I'll do when I reach Barnesville, but I expect to do the best I can & get our boy a good boarding place. . . .

Papa's pictures have been put on big thick cards & I'm crazy to send you one. R. B. is taking one for his room. . . .

Poor Laura stepped on a 20-penny rusty nail yesterday while I was gone. She suffered so much. It almost went through her foot. Dr. Almond was called. She was able to use her foot a little this morning. One of you or both of you write her a letter of sympathy & enclose with mine or send to her. Tell her a little school news. You all don't know what a blessing that old black soul has been to your mother.

I'm tired & will stop. I may mail this in B'ville. You girls must write to R. B. I hate to give him up. When I told Miles about having four away from home, he said: "I'm thinking you'll have lots of letters to write." I'll write once a wk. if possible & you all write once a week. Poor Pipey is holding forth at home. I know she is crazy to get back to her cottage.

With love,
Mother

1. Possibly a Gordon official.
2. One of Marguerite's beaux.

To R. B. Russell, Jr., Barnesville, Ga.

September 25, 1911

My dear boy,

The mail has just come & with it your nice letter. I was so glad to hear from you & so glad you are not home sick.

Joe Brown[1] has announced & now its up to us *all* to *beat him,* & to stand up for our side with *perfect* good nature, *good* judgement & *great composure.* Don't be upset by any harsh or bitter criticism you may hear & you'll be sure to hear some. Papa has a good start & I think, I mean I feel *sure* he'll win this time.

Saturday afternoon as I went to the station in Atlanta, four men with long ladders & ropes were putting up a tremendous sign on [the] corner of Kimball House,

State Campaign Headquarters of Richard B. Russell, Candidate for Governor,[2]

all red & black. You can see it now, can't you?

I'm busy this morning but am thinking about you, a *new boy* at school, & my 3 girls. I'm counting on you *all* to keep up our reputation.

Give my love to Mrs. Ely[3] & to Berdie Hall & the other two girls. Be sweet & good to the children in the house. Be a big brother for them. We'll send money for uniform when it comes & when it is accepted. . . .

We are few in number[4] & feel kinder lonesome—especially at night.

Lovingly,
Mother

1. Brown, son of Georgia's Civil War governor, had served as governor in 1908 but lost to Hoke Smith in 1910. When U.S. Senator Alexander Clay died in November 1910, Brown was still in office and appointed Joseph M. Terrell to succeed Clay, but Smith was elected senator by the legislature in July 1911. It was, of course, expected he would give up the governor's chair. However, he refused to give it up until November, creating an unprecedented situation that generated much criticism. Richard hoped Georgians were tired of this feuding pair.

2. The sign's message is in bold letters in the middle of the page.

3. The mother at R. B.'s boarding place.

4. She had eight children at home that night.

To Miss Ina Russell, Lucy Cobb Institute, Athens, Ga.

[Sept. 25, 1911]

Monday morning, and so busy, but I feel that I must write you a short letter, my dear child & name sake.

Yesterday when I heard that Joe Brown had announced for Governor, you were *first* in my thoughts. Now this may seem queer to you & you would naturally suppose I would think of papa first, but I did not. I thought of *you* & can you imagine why? Well, in the first place, I don't fear Joe Brown on papa's account, for I think papa's campaign is in such good shape now & he has such a good start that I feel sure we will win this time.

But this is why I thought of you: If you have any ambition it must show itself *now*. You are in school with Joe Brown's daughter—you are *Dick Russell's daughter*! Don't you see, Ina!! It's up to you, child! You are blessed with a good mind & fine intellect—*use them, child & keep up your father's name.* And watch your disposition & guard your feelings. You can't afford to be any thing but *pleasant, sweet, charming, composed, sympathetic, fair &*

square, under all circumstances, & with every body. You must act with good judgement, & if anything comes up about the Governor's race, just keep your senses & do the right thing. You try to make as many *Russell men* as there are *Brown men* among the girls. You can do this, Ina. Think over what I've written & keep these things in your mind. You have the opportunity of your life to make a reputation for yourself & for the sake of your father that will last a life time. These things are important. Be sure you don't talk *too* much, even to a friend. You never know what they'll say. The old saying "Silence is Golden" is certainly true. This thing wont last long & we *all* must do *all* we can. You have a great responsibility on you & I'm sure you are fully capable of working it out to your honor & glory as well as to your fathers.

When you read this you may feel that there is something awful & big for you to do this minute, but there is *not.* Just these things I have written for you to remember *all* the time, under *all* circumstances & then you act according to your very *best judgement* & the very best of all good there is in you.

Let me know at once what class you are in & what class the *Brown girl* is in. This situation is very interesting to me. I don't suppose it ever happened just this way before.

I'm afraid this fight will get very bitter before the race is over, but we must keep *sweet* through it all. I've decided not to let any thing upset me. I can talk with a person who is against us & keep perfectly *cool.* I've learned this from papa. It doesn't pay to do any other way. Mr. Pierce is against your father, but you be *so* sweet that Lucile can't see why he is.

Think of me going to aunt Lellas! Did you know it? Papa went to Covington in auto to speak & carried R. B., twins & me. They were so glad to see us, but aunt L. told papa he had broken her heart. Annie Zu went to hear papa speak.

Right here the mail came & I enjoyed your dear letter. I'll send the middy blouses right away, & I also have you a pretty vanity box with chain & some beauty pins. I'm glad you are not home sick.

Now Ina, make a rule to write to Auntney often. She is very sweet to you & she is interested in you & you must show your appreciation. . . .

I'm sending my heart's best love to you, my child.

     Your Mother

To Marguerite Russell, G.N.&I.C., Milledgeville, Ga.

Thursday [undated]

Dearest *Margo, bad-toe, so-so, ho-ho, well-toe, I hope so*!!

Bill's letter telling of your trouble came this morning. I'm *so sorry,* but think you did the wise thing. When you get well this time, I hope you'll never have any more trouble.

I'm sending stamps for you to keep up your Washington correspondence. Tell Samille about papa's good pictures & that mama says she is going to send her one & that I'm going with papa if he speaks in W[ashington]. Tell her how much papa appreciated her last letter & say that papa is so very busy &c. I haven't seen papa since last Saturday in Atlanta.

You all need not expect to see any news of our race in the papers unless the Journal comes out for papa. The other papers are *dead* against us. I'll keep you all posted if anything *important* comes out. The Constitution is wild for Joe Brown & a few of his supporters now are talking as if he is the only man in Ga. . . .

I bought two pieces of music in Atlanta. One was "That Mysterious Rag." The picture on the back & the words & music [are] too cute for anything. The other is "You don't know how you'll miss her, till you say good-bye." The music [is] very sweet, on the order of "Down by the Old Mill Stream," but the words very love sick. If you and Bill want these I'll send them. I can't play "That Mysterious Rag." I did wish for Bill to play it for me. All this reminds me of a piece I saw in paper yesterday about rag-time at Wesleyan. I'll send it for you to read. Guess that professor would think it horrible for a *Mother* to send rag-time to a daughter *any where.*

We miss you children a *whole lot.* Laura says she don't know how to cook for just *a few.* I read Bill's letter to Laura & she kept saying, "Po Chile, I knowed she'd have to cut that toe." If Bill could have seen Laura when she received her letter! She said, "Now just see what my chile thinks of me!" And she called in everybody to hear her letter. Her foot is getting well but she has to walk with a stick.

Walter is standing here & he says tell you he has made 50 cents picking cotton, & he sure is sorry about your toe. . . .

With a heart of love for you & Bill,
Mother

To Misses Russell, Milledgeville, Ga.

Sunday morning [October 15, 1911]

My Dearest Bill & Margo,

Mother just dreads to tell you what happened to our dear Pipey Saturday morning. Her "Cottage" & *everything* she had was *burned*. I know just how you are feeling now. We have been feeling this way for over 24 hrs.

Saturday morning about 4:30, Edward was restless. Pipey tried to quiet him, but he didn't seem to want to go back to sleep. He began to pet her, he patted her on the face & played with her so, she opened her eyes & began to play with him. Imagine her horror when she saw fire in her closet! She jumped up, ran to closet, then got water & tried to put the fire out—poor thing! All the clothes on left of closet had burned & were falling down in a heap, the flames must have been way up in the ceiling. Pipeys night cap was scorched on her head while she was trying to pull things out of the closet. When she saw it was so bad, she woke Rowena & told her to run on the front porch & cry Fire! Pinkie [Pipey] ran to the window & both gave the alarm, & George McB[rayer] & Mr. Algood were soon there in their night clothes.

You can't imagine the confusion! Pinkie running around wild telling them what to please save. You know how dear her relics were to her! She wanted the trunk with mama's things, & she wanted Stannies[1] trunk, her watch. . . . George McB. called to them to get Edward & the [other] children & he says he had a hard time keeping Pipey out of the fire.

Every body lost their senses for the hall ceiling fell through first & of course that shut them off from the rooms. We feel that some one *could have burst* through the windows & saved *something* but not one thing was saved except one trunk of aunt Annies & a rocking chair, two lap robes & a few pitchers & tubs that were on the back porch.

James Gresham ran up & told me. I dressed & hurried down. The whole roof was in & we could see piano, chairs . . . burning, going up in smoke!

Pipey & children were at Mr. McB[rayer]'s in their night clothes. Pipey did put on her kimono & slippers. Didn't have on her glasses.

We are so thankful no one was *lost* or hurt. When I think of my *Jebs*! Suppose they had slept on!

Aunt Annie was in Marietta. I 'phoned her & she & uncle Walter came on *our* train. Aunt Annie believes she could have saved many things, but I doubt if she could. Its all dreadful to think of! Poor Pipey & the things she has loved so long! Last night we happened to think of the "little red cradle" & a fresh lump came in my throat. Just think! Every garment they had & some of Edwards—except a weeks washing (which, [it is] very fortunate, hadn't been brought home) is all they have. School books, *everything*. Papa didn't have any insurance on house, so he's out about $800.00. Of course aunt Annie had her summer clothes with her, but every winter garment, including new cloak, furs, hat &c. were destroyed.

Friends have been very kind. Mr. Bell brought $5.00 & gave to Pipey. Mrs. Huff brought over a dollar. Laura, with streaming eyes, gave "poor Miss Pipey" a dollar & Doscia gave Rowena one. Mamie came right out & brought Pipey two new house dresses, a shirt waist & aunt Ellens black shawl—& some trousers for James. Mrs. Florence Bell brought Pipey a nice gown & corset cover & new waist for James. Miss Sunie gave Rowena a corset & Pipey a shirt waist & white apron. Misses Pearl & Dovie[2] gave the children a dollar apiece to replace books. Several say they will make waists for the boys. Aunt Mary-Walter[3] sent Rowena a nice coat suit, blue dress, some underclothes—jackets for boys & waist for Pipey—and some nice dresses for Jebs.

When I got to the fire, several autos & about 25 people had come out from Winder—too late to help. Warren brought us all home in an auto, & James got into R. B.'s old clothes, Francis into Walters, Pinkie into mine & Rowena into Ina's.

Just think of the nice bed clothes they had! Aunt Annie is grieving over cousin Josie's picture,[4] & many, many things.

Pipey has been raking in the ashes & finds ever so many things, but nothing good, of course. Her poor watch all black & ruined. The pretty frosted goblets every one, standing erect, seemingly whole—but break as soon as you touch them. *One* seems sound. They got it out yesterday, but it is smoked.

I don't know what they will do. Uncle Ben is coming to-day & I guess they will decide on something. I don't feel that I *can* have the children[5] here for any length of time.

I can't write any more now. I'll ask you to mail this letter at once to Ina. I just can't write another *detail* letter. I'll write Ina about it & tell her a letter will follow in a few days. I'll have to write R. B. & I want to write Annie Zu.

We are all right well, but feel pretty well used up.

Mother

1. Contraction of Sister Annie's [Stannies trunk].
2. Teachers at Russell.
3. Ina's sister-in-law, wife of her brother Walter, so-named to differentiate from Mary/ Auntney.
4. The picture of her dead daughter.
5. She means Ben's children.

To Marguerite Russell, Milledgeville, Georgia

Thursday night [October 27, 1911]

My Dearest Margo,

Mother is too sorry about you being in the infirmary again—and with rheumatism! It's too bad. I do hope you are well now. I had a touch of rheumatism several days ago & this morning I began my lemon water drinking. I want you to get some lemons right away and take the juice of half a lemon *every* morning in a whole glass of water. Begin this at once. It will help you in every way. . . .

I've been feeling all day that I just had to come to see you & Bill. . . . You know Laura had been sick & Ellen has moved off & this week I've really done all my ironing. My hands are blistered & I can't write well. . . .

Laura hasn't come back. Doscia, bless her! is here, but you know she is slow & I have over half the work to do. I can't leave home at night until Laura gets back, & she sent me word yesterday she wouldn't be able to come back until next week. Poor Laura! She has been on the verge of pneumonia. . . .

Ina is doing so well & seems so happy & satisfied. I know we all rejoice to-gether over this. I had almost despaired, for I was afraid she would never go to school again. . . .

Aunt Hattie sent Pipey & Aunt Annie a check to-gether for twenty-five dollars. Aunt Mamie sent them ten apiece. Aunt Annie is in Oxford this week with Aunt Lella. Aunt Annie is restless.

Tell Bill I say write Miles Comer a real nice school-newsy letter & just happen to remark in it that if papa goes to Ft. Valley to speak she hopes he'll go out to hear him. Just take it for granted that he's for him & don't mention local option or anything only that she hopes he is doing all he can &c., &c. I saw in the paper that papa was going to Ft. V. sometime in November.

I just [heard] the date for the election was fixed to-day & I'll be crazy to see Constitution in the morning. It'll be my luck for Smithy not to bring it. The Constitution is fighting papa to a finish. I feel like fighting some myself.

Dear child, let me hear how you are. If I could I'd come to-morrow. Tell Bill to take this letter as hers.

> With a heart full of love,
> Mother

To R. B. Russell, Jr., Barnesville, Georgia

Thursday P.M. [October 27, 1911]

Dearest Boy,

It has been a long time since a letter has been mailed to you, but when I knew papa had really been to *see* you, I thought that would take the place of *many* letters. . . .

Your gun is all right & your books are being cared for. Every body busy in school & not much reading done these days.

Son, you never write me about your friends. I want you to have them by the score.

You have never told me what you drink for breakfast. I'm anxious to know. And I want to ask you not to drink *any kind* of soft drinks—*ever*. Cut them out entirely & candy too. I want you to grow strong & be a *man*. You can't do it if you indulge in these things. Buy fruit when you buy any thing. 5 cents put into apples or bananas or even your *dear peanuts* would be all right. Mother is in earnest about this. Write me. . . .

Our children are picking cotton to make money to go to John Robinson's circus the 3rd. Rob has written you a dear letter. He speaks of you often & I'm sure he misses you. . . .

I'm so sleepy. "Goodnight, Pleasant Dreams."

> Mother

P.S. . . . . Do you go to church? What does the preacher say about papa? They are jumping on him so terribly. Guess we will know to-morrow when the primary will be. I'll be glad when its over. Do you want one of papa's buttons? Men come by & ask for them. A big Russell Club is being formed in Winder.

To Misses Russell, Milledgeville, Ga.

Oct. 31, 1911 [Brown House Hotel stationery]
Dearest "chilluns,"

I'm in Macon at the above hotel. The grand lodge of Masons, with about three hundred delegates, is in convention here & papa, our dearest papa, thought he'd stay over & "mix" with them.

Papa says he reached Macon at 3 o'clock last night & when my train came he was sleeping soundly. I just waited & here he came in a hurry, of course, telling me why he was late. I didn't mind for I was so glad he had been sleeping.

We came on over to the Brown House (it seems we are doomed to the Browns) and when our baggage was settled & I had looked to see if my hat was on all right, we went out to find some breakfast. Papa hadn't had a bite. I told them I'd had breakfast, but we went on to-gether to the Dindler Hotel Cafe & had a nice breakfast.

Papa has a *man* going around with him, to see after him in a general way—to attend to any business that might come up. He sees after papa's baggage and takes any thing into his hands that interferes with papa meeting & seeing as many people as possible. His name is Rufus Bellew, & he is a great big, rather handsome looking young man. He *would* pay for breakfast this morning. When papa objected, he said, "O, yes, I'll just take a meal with you when you get in the Mansion, to pay for it." When we finished breakfast, papa & Mr. Bellew went to the Grand Lodge meeting & I meandered back to the *Brown* (*O, Brown*) House. I had to *meander* in the rain too, but not a very *wet* rain. I don't know how long we'll be here.

Mr. Bellew told me in all seriousness that papa was "sure to be elected." I told him not to be telling me "just for fun" & he said "Well, Mrs. Russell, I really believe it." Papa says he had a great successful time at Hazelhurst. . . .

My chicks, I did enjoy seeing you. Study good now & get ready for Christmas. Not long now. Margo, papa was horrified when I told him you were out Monday night. Mrs. Elleson told me that a girl was almost killed at the Mansion frolic & that a rock was thrown at one of the girls & broke her shoulder bone. I'm so glad nothing happened to us. Didn't we have fun though? Papa laughed good when I told him I dressed up too.

I must "stop, stop, stop." Keep well & cheerful. Drink lemon water every morning. I leave you with this *new* advice.

Give my love to the girls. Especially Maggie & Margaret. I love them all.

Mother

To Misses Russell, Milledgeville, Georgia

> Nov. 6, 1911 [Headquarters, Fulton County Russell Club]

My Dear Girls,

Your mother is in Atlanta again. Papa couldn't come home Saturday night & he 'phoned for me to come down Sunday & spend the day with him. I got the message Sat. night about 12:30, so I hurried around Sunday morning & *just did* catch our train to Atlanta. Laura rushed after me with a biscuit & cup of coffee.

I had a lovely time with R. B. He looks fine in his khaki uniform. He & I stayed in the same room & he talked & talked before we went to bed. R. B. has a lovely boarding place. Mrs. Ely is so dear & sweet & loves her boys so. I fell in love with Tom Thrash. Tell Mary Sams I'm not surprised at her liking him. He's a great, big, brown-eyed boy & seems to have a lot of sense. He asked me if you & Mary S. were chums. I told him *yes*. George Hill is the tallest boy at Gordon. He is a blonde & he didn't sit in the room with us after supper like Tom did. Tom takes a general interest in *every thing*. He helps R. B. with his algebra. The boys told me they were coming to Milledgeville the 20th to play G.M.C. They play Tech here the 19th. R. B. says he is coming up. I'm going to see the game if I can. . . .

I reach[ed] home Thursday night. Left my baggage & coat in Atlanta. As the train was pulling out I saw papa & the porter coming with them. . . .

When I reached Atlanta [today] every body (almost) was talking about papa's speech Friday night. Papa's picture is *every where*. Every way you turn you see one. I hope you saw the Journal. Papa's speech was in full. I want you both to read it. The race is waxing warm now. Papa is going to leave Tuesday or Wednesday in an automobile & do all the speaking he can in next 30 days. He will be in Milledgeville the 13th. Wouldn't I love to be there!!! . . .

I must stop. Papa has gone for a shave & we will go right out for breakfast when he comes back. I may be here until to-morrow afternoon. I know I'll be busy to-day. . . .

Take care of yourselves. *Drink lemon water.* Lemons are just 20 cents per dozen in Winder.

Papa has come. Good-bye my dearies.

      Mother

To Mr. R. B. Russell, Jr., Barnesville, Ga.

                                        Dec. 4

[No salutation]

Here's your permit. Hope you'll get it in time. I was in Atlanta Sunday. Very exciting times were on hand. Nevin[1] figured we'd carry 104 counties. Walter Brown[2] says "not less than 87."

Write Miss Sunie[3] a short note & thank her for contributing the candy to your box. She made the nut divinity & some fudge. Write a little school news. Miss Sunie is so interested in you all.

Dick is the finest boy you ever saw.

Be sure to send Miss Hettie[4] a card on the 9th. Its her birthday. I'll enclose a card for you. Don't forget this.

Papa's working hard on his home run. Thursday will tell the tale.

      Heart of love,

      Mother

1. Richard's campaign manager.

2. One of Richard's closest friends.

3. R. B. and the girls received Thanksgiving boxes. Miss Sunie, a young Winder matron, was one of Ina's closest friends.

4. Miss Hettie, an early live-in baby-sitter, came when R. B. was born. After her marriage to a mule trader, she lived in Atlanta but was always a part of the family. R. B. and Margo were her favorites. Ina often reminded R. B. of his debt to Miss Hettie.

To Miss Ina D. Russell, Athens, Ga.

Tuesday, [December 5,] Wednesday,
Thursday

O, how near,
But do not fear
We'll blow our horn
As sure as you're born
On Friday morn.
Just a word, my dear Ina, at Lucy:

I enjoyed your long, diary letter so much. Don't care how often you write them.

I spent Sunday & Monday in Atlanta. Was in the thick of the fight. Things quite different from what they were when you went. Every thing alive & moving to & fro. We are still hopeful. Things are bright for papa.

You must tell your friend that I'm expecting my sisters (5 in number) to visit me Xmas. I don't see how I can have her at all. Not even for a day or two. You know, I'm always glad to have your friends, but at Christmas its different. We are so crowded & you never know who's going to crowd in. Arrange some way. Just don't say any more about it. Would that do? I'm sorry for her, so far from home, but you say her best friend will be in Athens. We must manage some way. Would it do (if she should still talk about it) to tell her you'd like for her to come & after you get home, if you find its convenient you'll write & let her know. Don't talk about this to any body. . . .

I bought black gloves yesterday to the tune of $3.50. Its awful. I didn't know they were so high. I need some too, but will send these on to you. They are 6¼. Be careful when you try them on—but they are guaranteed. If they burst in trying on they'll take them back. . . .

Guess if we are elected it will be joy enough for a long time, & I won't write right away. . . .

Mother

To R. B. Russell, Jr., Barnesville, Ga.

Saturday [Dec. 9, 1911]

My dearest boy,

Your letter[1] to papa came this morning. So glad you wrote as you did. Be game. Its *awful,* but be game. I'm having the struggle of my life & I felt *so* much for you all away from home. Dad is brave, but O, how it hurts! [He] is in Atlanta today.

Write to Ina. She is right there under the same roof with Cora B[rown].

I'm impatient for my chicks to get home. The days are flying & we'll soon be to-gether.

Write me something about Geo. Bosche. I *love* his father. I hope you love George.

      Heart of love,
      Mother

1. Following the defeat, Richard wrote comforting letters to all his children who were away from home.

To Misses Russell, Milledgeville, Ga.

Tuesday January 28, 1912

Dear "Chilluns,"

Your letters came this morning. I always feel like answering *immediately,* if not sooner, but find I can't always do it. This time I'm doing it, & using the only paper I possess [Georgian Hotel stationery]. Papa has promised to bring me some tonight. . . .

You should see old cute Dick walking over the house. His latest accomplishment is saying: "Kittie, kittie, kittie," when we tell him to call the cat. He refuses to say Patience any more. He fell off the porch yesterday. His hair was full of trash when we picked him up & he was yelling, but wasn't much hurt. I've bought the twins & Edward wheel barrows & shovels. They keep busy with them.

I'm glad you are keep[ing] well. Manage some way to eat at least two oranges or lemons every day. I'll send you some money soon. Oranges are the things (or lemons) to eat this time of year. They keep off colds & keep your digestion good. Wish I could send you a whole box. . . . I found a [dollar] bill I didn't know I had so send it to you. . . . Buy oranges & *eat them* at once. . . .

When Aunt Annie goes to Odessadale Thursday to take charge of the children,[1] I'll go far as Atlanta, and Bill, I'll see about getting you a corset. . . . It sounded right funny a few days ago when Papa came home one night & said he wanted me to go to Atlanta with him next morning. I asked him why he wanted me to go & was so surprised when he said: "Well, a wonderful *corset sale* is going on at Chamberlins & I thought you had better buy some & put 'em up for the girls." I was very much amused. I couldn't go, for it was before Pipey came back. Poor, precious dad! Who would ever have thought of him thinking of such a thing? But he is thinking about us *all* the time, in many ways we never think of. . . .

> With heart of love,
> Mother

1. Ben Dillard's boys, Frank and James. Rowena, who was about fourteen, had married at the end of December.

To Richard B. Russell, Jr., Barnesville, Ga.

February 19, 1912

Dearest Boy,

Your letter & key came this morning. I'll go right up stairs when I finish this & get your pictures. . . .

Cook hasn't been here since Christmas. Slow but sure Doscia has been cooking & of course that means more work for me. Your sarcasm about the cake did not amount to much. Your box was bum, but better than none—eh?

Look here, son! You must try to write a better hand & a better letter. Your poor dear daddy grieves about it & you know I've been after you a long time. I want you to write papa a nice letter. Mind about paragraphs & *everything*!

Mamie had papa & me to dinner yesterday [my birthday]. Uncle Lewis was there too. At the table Wm Henry asked about you & whats the latest from you &c. I said, well the latest is he wants $2.50 to buy an annual & Mr. Russell says I must sell eggs or something to get up the money.

Uncle Lewis said, "How much did you say it was?" I said $2.50. He said: "Well, I'll send this to him—I'll send it to-morrow." I thanked him most sincerely for you and everybody concerned, but of course if you hear from him, you write *at once* & write a *nice* letter.

Well, I stopped & got your key *myself*. The boys are playing with the mitt now. I smiled when I saw your mitt and your *thousand* other things in that box. I came very near taking that nice Nunnally's box out to put candy in, but I didn't. . . .

Two of the Braselton Bros.[1] spent last Tuesday night with us. "Smiling John" and "Henry Creatore" for doesn't John smile & doesn't Henry look like Creatore, walking stick, that black hair & all? I enjoyed seeing them. In speaking of you, John smiled & regretted that he didn't send "some of the boys" hunting with you when you were in Braselton. The telephone line is booming right along. . . .

Now this other news is *awful.* Call for Tom & George [room-mates] to come & support you in this hour of trial. Are they near? Well, I tell you your calf or is it Ina's was meandering on the railroad track & a cruel freight car, carrying about 30 boxes, came along & knocked the calf off the track, breaking one hind leg and otherwise injuring him. Of course he had to be killed & it sounds hard-hearted, but we have enjoyed veal for several days & more in the pantry. James Bell hurried over & told us. It happened in the cut, just as you come to the station. The cow was with the calf, but she had sense enough to get off of the track. . . . No chicken or rooster news this time.

> Mother

1. Richard Russell was establishing a telephone company with the Braselton brothers of Braselton, Georgia, a town located about ten miles northeast of Winder.

To R. B. Russell, Jr., Barnesville, Ga.

Sunday, March 3, 1912

My Dearest Boy,

After our little 'phone talk last night, I wanted to see you awfully bad. I had been wanting to see you anyhow, for I felt uneasy and sorry about you having sore-throat and a bad feeling in your chest, and nobody to see after you and doctor you a little.

You went to Barnesville with a bad cold & cough and it seems you've had it ever since. You were coughing some Christmas. I'm afraid you do something imprudent to cause all of this. Your clothes must be too heavy or too light or your shoes must be thin. Do you wear your good B[raselton] B[rothers] shoes? The weather has been *so* bad this year. Do you get overheated drilling & then sit in a draft? I want you to think about all this and try to get yourself well. It doesn't do much good to take medicine for colds. But if your throat is sore you ought to gargle turpentine & a few drops would do you good, to swallow in a little water or on sugar. You must take something if you are constipated. If I had you here at home I'd give you a dose of oil. I can put it in orange juice & you'd never know it. Sure enough, boy, you must do something for yourself. Didn't that doctor give you anything. Good-for-nothing! I bet he didn't!! Don't take calomel. Get you a bottle of Castoria. Shake it good & drink ½ of it. This is good. Do it & you'll see you'll feel better. . . . When you write, tell me more about yourself & why you think you keep this bad cold. We must remedy it some way.

Your report came in the same mail with your letter. We were very happy over it. Papa was so pleased & I was so pleased to see that you *had* made an effort & "pulled up" in your Latin & Algebra. I was glad to have it to show papa when he came home. Papa brought your letter home for me to read. I was pleased about your spelling. Hope you will beat the Sophs.

Papa says he sent you a check for $10.00. If you manage well, perhaps you can make this fill all your wants and buy your baseball glove too. Let me know, for I want you to have it & the annual too. I expect to enjoy that when you come home.

I love for you to have money, but I want you to learn to manage it well & get the full worth of it. You will be wanting some when you go on your camp in April. Had I better save the Bosche dollar until then?

I want to persuade you *not* to buy a Kodak. They are expensive to "keep" & I feel that you would enjoy your money more in some other way. Let me know how you feel about this now.

Rob & Harriet are doing well in their studies. . . . My class of *two*—Walter and Patience—are doing beautifully in their studies.

The twins are smart & good. Fielding is growing *so fast*. William is well, but doesn't seem to grow much. Papa measured them to-day & Fielding is much the taller & heavier. Edward is a cute, smart child. He amuses us every day with his funny talk & quaint sayings. Dear little Dick is the pet of all. He walks *everywhere* & gets into *everything.* We have a strip nailed across the door of the porch by my room. He plays on the porch when the weather is good. We put the big chairs down to keep him from going to the front of the porch. . . .

Write soon & tell me more about your cold & how you are feeling. . . .

        Yours devotedly,

        Mother

To Marguerite Russell, Milledgeville, Ga.

        Friday night—[early April]

Dearest Margo,

I'll write just a few lines, for I've been grieving about you wanting to go to the show to-night. I just couldn't write a request when none of your class were going. It didn't seem fair to me & I felt that Mr. P[arks] would hate to refuse you, but I thought he would *have to.* . . . Maybe your time will come real soon. I hope you did not mind it too much & that you were not unhappy over it.

I will get your note books & your powder, but Margo, please *swear off* on your birthday & never put another dust on your face. *Don't use powder,* you & Bill. It ruins your complexion. Just wash with good soap *regular* & look sweet & happy & leave the rest to luck. It is miserable to be depend[ent] on powder. I'm so glad Ina has almost quit using it. I never put any on my face.

I'll send your box next Friday, I think, & you'll get it Saturday. You may be looking for it. We are saying something now every day about Marguerite & her birthday and we hope you will be very happy all next week. You know how to be happy. Just make others happy, even Miss Moon, & you will be happy. You were such a big, fat-faced baby. Dick looks very much like you sometimes.

The woods are beautiful now. The children bring in worlds of flowers. . . .

        Lovingly,

        Mother

To Misses Russell, Milledgeville, Ga.

April 9, 1912

Dearest Girls,

Is it possible that two weeks have passed since I wrote to my dearies?

I was amused when Ina told me that one of the rules at Lucy Cobb is to drink lemon water. Every morning before breakfast the piece of lemon was put by each girls plate & a glass of water & she *had to drink it* before she ate any breakfast.

Well, we are preparing to fix up Margo's birthday box. Don't be disappointed, Margo, if it doesn't come until Friday or Sat. I expect it will be Sat. We are doing all our work. I'm cooking again and . . . I have really cooked breakfast three mornings before leaving for Atlanta. I find that almost *anything* is *dead easy* if you once set your head to do it. I went to Atlanta yesterday. It gave me an awful heavy days work (*next day*), for I cook enough to last all day & all the dishes & cook things are to wash & everywhere to clean. . . .

No, Margo, you must not stop music. Papa sent a check for your music.

Bill, I'm sending you a pink dress. You can call it "Mamas dress" for its just the kind I would have adored when I was nineteen. . . .

The R. stationery is for Margo especially. The other for both if you need any. Margo's kimono has been made some time. Ina begged to take it back to Lucy, but I said *no,* I'd make her one & yesterday I bought it—a green one. . . .

I'm sure I can't conveniently put your box in the Express office before Friday morning, but it will be a birthday box all the same & I hope you are happy over its contents. I'm trying hard to save a taste of ham for Margo. . . . Laura is cooking at the Granite Hotel. I hope to get her yet. Doscia was "too feeble" to lead our strenuous life. I don't mind cooking now, but it keeps me awful busy.

I have some gowns for you girls. Does Margo need summer gowns? Let me know. I'll put in two if I use a very big box & you can choose between you. . . .

I went in the back room to see if there was anything else I need to tell you about. While I was gone, *somebody* spilled ink all on my bureau scarf. . . .

I have two pieces of music to put in the box & I'll let you girls guess which one is for who. I may put a few members of the family in the box, or . . . the mule.

I may not write a letter and put in box. You will know everything from this one. & I may be too rushed to write. Does Margo still want violets? I've wanted to send some, but it seems I can't get at such things. . . . I hope Margo wrote at once to Auntney when she sent violets.

This letter must go to the office this aft. & its getting late. I've been interrupted so many times. I'm afraid I've forgot to mention something—but no matter—I'll be writing again. . . .

     Heart of love,
     Mother

To R. B. Russell, Jr., Barnesville, Ga.

April 18, 1912

Dearest Boy,

I know you have been watching the mail for a letter. Haven't you? I've thought of you millions of times—especially since your report came & I saw "*22 extra tours of duty.*" Now I did not know that you like this work so well as to bring *22 extra* tours on yourself. Write me about this.

We have been so busy. Especially since the nice weather for farm work. Arch & Rob are busy to-day building a fence around [Rob's] tomato field. We are expecting to make big (?) money this year on tomatoes. Our plants are fine & ready to put out as soon as we can prepare the land. Its too wet to plow now. We have had three hard rain storms. . . .

Fielding is layed up with a bad foot. He stepped on an 8 penny nail—old & rusty & it went in ¾ of an inch, or more. You know from experience how he suffered, for its the worst accident of the kind we have ever had except your experience with nails. He can't walk a step, but doesn't suffer any now.

Pipey is busy with her chickens. We have about 65 little ones, she says. Your Josephine wants to set & Pipey tries to see after her, but she is very cross & fussy & fights everyone who comes near. Pipey said today: "Josephine can fly like an arrow" & Harriet said: "Yes, & she can hurt like a cannon." I don't know that she was speaking from experience for I never knew her to be *hurt* by a cannon.

I've never "had the heart" to kill Taylor Wilkins yet, & he still enjoys the freedom of our chicken yard, without limit or bound. Our grove is beautiful now—and our station is a *reality*. You saw the place papa was fixing? Well, our little station building is "going up"—not rapidly, but *surely*—and better than that, we can flag all the trains on SAL[1] except the two Vestibules. Sunday afternoon the 7, going to Atlanta, stopped—2 passengers got on & 2 passengers got off. We were sitting on the front porch & enjoyed seeing it. The Quartermans were here. Mamie had brought Wm Henry out for me to see him in long trousers.

I am still without a cook, & O, how busy I keep. Walter can draw water now, & he & Rob keep me supplied with wood & water.

Dick is so sweet & smart & cunning & cute these days, we almost eat him up.

. . . We have received 2½ cars of guano. One of them was unloaded at night & it took two nights to do it. Rob had to keep count & he was a sleepy boy when he'd get in at 11:30.

Patience & Harriet are going to Winder & they are ready to start.

Write soon. You haven't written but once since you went back. I did *hate* to leave you that day in Atlanta. Times up & my paper filled up.

> With a heart of love,
> Mother

1. Possibly Southern Atlantic Line.

To Misses Russell, Milledgeville, Ga.

May 16, 1912

Dearest Bill & Margo,

. . . Now I'll tell my news, as I know you've been thinking & guessing since my card. Papa has sold our Jackson house to Mr. Niblack, Mr. Carl Niblacks father, & has promised to give him possession in 3 mo. from yesterday, the 15th. Now, what do you suppose we will do? We have had all kinds of fun planning where we will go & what we'll do until we can build. We have located ourselves in the brick store, the warehouse, the Moseman house & everywhere else—in the new station, too. We are talking about our new home every day. Papa says it will be of brick—and the prospect now is we'll build on the corner below Bells. Pipey will buy the first Huff house & Edward is in the last Huff house.[1] The Bells have acetylene gas now & we'll have it too & papa wants to get on that side [of the road] in order to put in a ram [pump] & have water from the branch & spring just below the narrow gauge track. We have a flag station on the narrow gauge now. I cooked dinner for the Supt. of the road last Thursday, & a flag site was selected.

Now the above is the *news*. Are you glad? The Niblacks are nice people. We'll like to have them out here. Miss India teaches an art class in Winder. We can have one out here, too.

Now here is one thing I want to discuss. I've been cooking since March 21st. We have things in good running order & I've learned to manage things without going to much trouble. I cook only two meals a day & as aunt Hattie would say: everyone seems satisfied. If you girls will help, I'll go on cooking & save the cook money to go in our new house. Harriet & Patience do a good part now. You know we need not *depend* on regular help from Ina, but she is *good help* when she tries. Rob & Walter draw water & bring wood & they help prepare vegetables & fruits too. The prospects are *grand* for a good fruit year. That will be a help in fixing food. O, by the way, the Niblacks got every one of our apple trees, but as the line runs just back of the summer house, we still have peach trees.

If you girls will keep the house clean (I've become a *crank* on keeping things clean) & the dining room nice & just *help*, I'll cook & wash dishes. I've put this before you. I don't know that I can get a cook, but I think I could get *some kind* of one. If Laura *should* come walking in some day & say she was ready to begin cooking, of course I'd open my arms & purse & say certainly, my dear cook, & maybe I might take Doscia, but she is *so very* wasteful in the kitchen & dear dad has to buy so many things for us. Seven families besides ourselves eat from our pantry. It takes a world of food, but papa is trying so hard to realize something from his land & we have to furnish these people food to get them to work. Now you think over this & let me know how you feel about it.

I have another matter to put before you. . . . Last year, 1911, was the happiest year of your mother's life. I can't exactly give any *one* reason for it, but it seemed that everything went on just right, except our defeat, & I was just happy the whole year round. I told papa before the election I was afraid we would be defeated for I'd had such a happy year in every way. Now this year has been all right too, for I want to be happy all the time. I have enough to be happy over, but you know sometimes little things come into our lives to trouble us *just a little.* I have something now that has been very hard for me to endure as I should. I've thought of the effect on my big children more than on myself. When you go through with 9 months of study, & staying away from home I want you to have a good time when you come home. I had hoped that Dick would always be our baby, but it will not be so, for another little Russell will come this summer. Of course this won't keep us from having a good time & enjoying being to-gether, but we can't have any company or house parties & it breaks my heart not to have our pretty Washington girls again, but *next* summer in our new home, it may be nicer. . . .

Now this is something else for you to think over. I haven't told Ina as I thought it might not be best. Poor R. B. has begged for Tom & George to be invited here this summer, but I knew they couldn't come this year. . . .

All the above is one reason I've been doing my work. I'm good for nothing else. Can't go anywhere, can't fix myself up any, & I thought I might as well do *something* to help papa. I'm heart broken that I can't go to LCI commencement & see Ina in her play & attend Senior reception & see Ina in her pink dress. We had an invitation from Misses G. & B. & it made my heart sick when I realized how *much* I wanted to be there. . . .

Well, my letter is written & you two dears can take it the best you can. I'm so glad I'll have you here to help move. I don't want a grain of old dust carried into our nice new house. Papa says he'll have 16 rooms. I want 14, counting closets, baths & all. That's as much as we can keep clean & furnish. . . .

I've written so hurriedly, but hope everything is plain.

    With heart of love,

    Mother

1. Edward Russell, Richard's nephew, had recently moved to Russell to become Richard's court stenographer. He brought his wife, Alice, and a baby boy.

To R. B. Russell, Jr., Barnesville, Ga.

May 19, 1912

Dearest Boy,

As the days get longer, it seems I have less time for letter writing. I'll be glad when you all get home and I will not have so much letter writing to do. I love to write to you & love more than anything to get your letters, but when I'm so busy, & so many things to see after, its hard to sit down just to write a letter. . . .

When you get ready to pack, be careful to put in all your things. I haven't said anything to papa about your board. Didn't have the "heart to." He has been so worried over this trade of the house. He didn't get any money, but got a house & lot in Atlanta & a lot in Athens. He has put the lot in Atlanta in the real estate agents hands & hopes to realize a small profit. He will need *"some money"* to build our new house.

How much of your fifteen dollars have you on hand? Papa said he hoped some of it would be on hand for board. Didn't he write you anything about it? It was good of dad to let you go to Macon. I wanted you to go so much. I know you have need of money, but remember to use it wisely. . . . Uncle Lewis has never said anything about the annual money. If you have spent your fifteen dollars, or most of it, suppose you write to papa & tell him what you spent it for & all about it. I think he would appreciate it & it would let him know that you hadn't just carelessly spent it without any thought of him or how hard he has to work for what he gets. You see what I mean, don't you? Papa is still holding his cotton. Buyers from Winder came out & sampled it & priced it last week, but didn't offer papa his price. He says now, its going down every day. I read in papers everyday that the Flood in Miss. will cause cotton to go up.

We are all on the porch by my room & dear, little Dick is amusing us by going up & down the steps. He has just learned to do it & is quite proud of himself. He is so smart & sweet now.

Rob killed a big snake in the yard the other day.

I send a dime for stamps. Write to Mother soon, my dear child. I'll be *so glad* when you get home.

      Your fond Mother

To Miss Marguerite Russell, Washington, Ga.

July 18, 1912

My Dearest Margo,

It seems that we do not think about you at all, but we do. We speak of you ever so many times during the day, & wish for you to be here. We don't write much, for we keep right busy. I told Laura this morning I'd be so glad when you came home for I knew you would get to work & help Laura make jelly, pickles, &c. Our fruit will be fine in two weeks. In that time we will be moving into our new house, I guess, & I'm afraid we can't do much. Our house looks as if its nearly finished. Pipes are all in for our gas, & we will enjoy our nice new rooms—especially our dining room. . . .

Your boy [Fielding] had ear-ache last night and had to be brought downstairs to me about two o'clock. About four o'clock his twin brother awoke with ear-ache & tooth-ache & he crawled in my bed. Mary Willie was sleeping with me as papa was away & we were well-packed in. The children have had terrible colds & look just a little bit sick. . . .

Write & tell us about yourself. We enjoy your letters. You must not say you "*hate*" anybody. Just be nice & pleasant & take things as they come.

With a heart of love,
Mother

To Miss Mary W. Russell, With Miss S. E. Russell, Monteagle, Tenn.

August 29, 1912

Dearest Bill,

As the children say, how are you & Harriet? Well & happy I hope & enjoying the mountains of Tenn.

We have missed you sadly, but have not really needed you. Things have moved along very well, indeed Margo very good & thoughtful about every thing.[1]

Had a letter from Ina. Her dress arrived all safe & sound. She will come Fri. or Sat.

Guess what? Marion Graham came driving up in auto this A.M. & asked to come on seven [train] this aft. for a few days. She knew Ina hadn't come but was "so tired of Lawrenceville" & wanted to come so bad. I told her she had better wait until to-morrow & come with Ina. She said, "O, Mrs. Russell, please let me come on to-day. I'll be home folks & just sit in here with you." So she'll come this aft. & Margo says she will take her in charge until Ina comes.

I sat up some yesterday & more to-day. Feel very well but not much on walking or stirring around. Margo has made one waist & Miss S. [the nurse] is kindly working button holes in it now.

Give lots of love to aunt Pheme & the others I know. I'm so glad you are where you have nothing to do but enjoy yourself. Don't forget to write to papa & Auntney.

> With a heart of love for you both,
> Mother

1. Carolyn Lewis was born on August 19, 1912, and Ina is no doubt assuring Bill that Margo is adequate postpartum help, a position Bill usually filled.

To Mr. R. B. Russell, Jr., Barnesville, Ga.

Tuesday Sep. 17 [1912]

Dearest Boy,

Your letter just received this A.M. Guess I'll have to break my resolution[1] & write you a *"few lines"* any how—especially as you have been appointed corporal, & congratulations are in order.

Daddy received your letter Thursday. He didn't go to Atlanta Fri. or Sat., & yesterday was such a busy day he didn't have time to write. But he said he would write to-day, & this morning as he ran to the train, I yelled out dont forget to write R. B.

Mamie [Quarterman] came out yesterday. Glooms sat thick upon her head as she talked of "William." You would have thought she had left him in the heart of Africa or middle of the Sahara. Tell him I say write his mother a *long* letter. She has had nothing but *one* card so far. I told her you & Tom were not barbarious I *knew*, & I *thought* the Humphreys were civilized. I didn't hear *one* good remark about Gordon from Mamie. She must have been very poorly impressed about everything. . . .

[R]ob was vowing yesterday he'd never make you any more chocolate candy because you hadn't written a word about it,—and Cook [Laura] rushes in after each mail & asks: "What did R. B. say about his chicken?" Now its up to you to write them both notes of thanks. Do enclose one to Cook. She took so much pleasure in fixing up that chicken. Cook is suffering with rheumatism. . . .

Carolyn is just the most blessed baby in the world. She is growing fast & is pretty & so good. She sleeps nearly all night. Never have to get up with her until four o'clock. Then she takes her bottle & goes back to sleep.

Harriet has found your Word book. I'll mail it this aft. I'm afraid we haven't the other two. Margo took a Latin book back with her. If I can't find the other two books, & you can do without them a day or two, find out from WmH. if he has them at home & I'll get them from Mamie, or maybe, you can get them 2nd hand at Gordon.

I'll see papa about your uniform to-night. You must have a new one, I think. I want you looking nice & clean all the time.

Ina leaves for Lucy to-morrow. Aunt Annie & Pipey expect to move next week. We will be a small household soon. I expect Miss Pearl will begin school soon.

Our fixtures were put off [the train] yesterday & I hope to have lights soon. William turned over a table yesterday & broke one lamp & two lamp chimneys. Its time we are getting lights, don't you think?

[Cousin] Edward brought a graphophone home last night. You can see the commotion it caused among the small Russells. They could hardly eat supper & then we had a time getting them in for bedtime. . . .

Give my love to Tom & Wm. H. Do your best & lets have good reports this year.

> Mother

1. Apparently Ina had told her children not to expect her to write often, but she was unable to keep her resolution.

To Miss Ina D. Russell, Athens, Ga.

Sep. 28, 1912

My Dearest Girl,

. . . I'm grieving over your room-mate being a C[hristian] S[cientist]. I was hoping so much you wouldn't be thrown with any freaks this time. But you can be very kind & considerate of her in her belief & remain true to your own. Its not right to denounce *anything* unless we know it is sinful. So be charitable towards "*Susie*" and learn all you can about her belief, but *don't* let it have any influence over you *what ever*. You are right easily influenced any how, you know, and when Susie begins to read her little book at night, you get your bible & read the 23rd Psalm. Susie's religion may be all right for her, but it wouldn't suit *me* at all. I know you are sensible enough to know what to do *any* time. I'm patting myself on the back. You are my child you know, & I'm *counting* on you.

Bless you child I hadn't thought of your coat-suit since you left! And I know daddy hasn't. I'll see about it *at once* & let you have it & maybe a little *Divinity* thrown in. Poor Bill left a whole lot of things & I've got to send her a bundle. I'll hunt your nail file.

I hope all those steps wont hurt you & I'm glad your fare is good. If you should have a *spell,* let Susie see if she can cure you. You know I'm joking. Call Miss J. *at once.* . . .

Before I write a permit for you to write to those boys, I want you to promise me that you will not write to any *one* of them oftener than once a mo. You see, it will not do, & a post card occasionally will do. I don't like letters at all unless they are *rare,* say two or three months apart. . . . Don't have a regular correspondence with any of them. . . .

What about those teeth that needed fixing? Would they let you go to Atlanta some Sat. I'd make engagement with Crenshaw. Brush your teeth regular.

Do, Ina, keep up your studying. It will do you so much good & please dear dad so much, & you know how I *count* on your doing it *any how.*

    Mother

To Mr. R. B. Russell, Jr., Barnesville, Ga.

Oct. 13, 1912

My Dearest Boy,

This morning I have three letters to write, or rather, I hope to write three to-day, and I feel as the old fellow did when he was about to face his first battle. The men around him were planning what to do when the firing began, & it seemed the majority of them were preparing to run. So the old man said as he was a "*little* lame," he'd start "*right now.*"

As I'm a little lame I had better start right now, or I will not get my letters written. While Carolyn is just the best baby I ever saw, still I have to see after her & it keeps me right busy. Then you know I have many, many more things to do besides seeing after the baby. My big new house keeps me busy. I like to see it nice & clean all the time & it will not stay this way unless I *work*. Harriet is developing into a splendid house-cleaner & she helps me. Patience sees after Dick, & helps about any thing that comes along. Since Pipey moved,[1] Edward stays with her or with us, just as his whimsical head chooses. Often he eats 6 meals a day—three with Pipey—3 with us. He is a very amusing piece of humanity. Since his 3 yr. old birthday he feels very big. When he describes anything to me that is very large, he will say: "Its a great big thing. Its big as me."

Rob, Walter, James & Frank have been picking cotton. They made money to spend on the Fair. By-the-way: The Woodruff-Tri-County Fair was a great success. Three or four thousand people were in attendance day & night. The Mid-way attractions were very good, so I heard. I went only one night & saw beautiful fire-works. I heard the exhibits were splendid, & spoke well for the farmers. Of course Woodruff had all kinds of machinery that was made in their Foundery. I'm sorry I did not enter our turkey gobbler as Laura & Rob said he was finer than the one exhibited.

I bought some beautiful Plymouth Rock frys last week. I have "turned out" five pullets & one rooster. Now you must decide which one of your roosters you can sacrifice for mine. We can not have so many. I don't like that spotted rooster of yours or that old red one. Let me make them into chicken salad. What do you say? Let me know in your next letter, for, honestly, it takes so much to feed so many chickens. Our chicken feed is all gone & papa says he can't buy any more now & I have to hunt up corn & peas to keep them fed.

Papa brought your letter for me to read. I'll send you socks some time soon & will send more towels. . . .

If I get my other letters written I must close this one . . .

Mother

1. Pipey moved into the house next door to Edward's house, which was next door to Ina's new house, making a close family compound.

To Miss Marguerite Russell, Milledgeville, Ga.

Friday Night, Nov. 8, 1912

My Dearest Margo,

Your suitcase, accompanied by your *"Navy Blue"* letter was received . . . when your dear daddy reached home from Atlanta. I'm not going to take your letter seriously, for if I did, I'd cry my fast-failing eyes out. I know you could not mean it *all,* for didn't I say in my last letter for Bill to slip you in her pocket & bring you on, anyhow? You must have known I was thinking of you & wanting you to come. You know what I've always preached to you children—that old saying "every dog has his day" is very true. That's what I tried to remember this summer when I had to wear such ugly clothes & stay hid around on the side porch when I wanted to be fixed nice & pretty and go around some with my girls & their beaux!

Right here a very funny thing happened & I must tell you. It is 11:30 at night & papa had gone to bed. I thought he was asleep when all at once he raised up in bed & asked if I had anything sweet in the house. I told him that Laura had made a big pan of gingerbread, but thought we had eaten it all. He then said he believed he would go get him some bread & jelly & sweet milk. I told him I would go & find him something. I put your letter down & went in the kitchen. I found 3 *small* pieces of g.b. but also some soft hoe-cake & I opened a jar of pear preserves & brought him a big pile of preserves, a big piece of hoe-cake & a big glass of milk. He got up & seemed to enjoy his feast so much. He has just finished & tucked himself back in bed.

I'm almost forgetting your blue-letter. Dearie, you know mother & daddy & all of us would love to have you here all the time, but you must go to school. You don't know what a blessing it is to be able to go to school. When I was your age I was writing off to every school in Ga. for catalogs, & just wishing I could go *off to* school, but as none of the schools were *free,* & my father didn't feel able to send me, I just *had* to stay at home—wishing all the time I *could* go. You'll be very glad some day that you could go, and you'll surely find that everything you learn now, no matter how useless it seems, will be a help to you *sometime* in your life.

I thought about you coming home as Bill came on through, but I knew daddy would have to send more money, & times get tight sometimes, when four children are off at school & nine at home to care for. Then too, I didn't think you'd lose the time from school. Sophomore year is very important & you want to enter Junior & Senior with a good record behind you.

Ina does expect to come home this month, but you know she is near. Less than a dollar will bring her home & take her back. R. B. is not coming until Christmas. So take heart, dear child, & clear those dishes with a vim & a good will. You have your nice aprons Pipey made you. Just think what a good time you had this summer getting ready and "come through" all right. Hurrah! for G.N.&I.C. Its a great school, & when you are an old lady or even a middle age lady—& who knows, you may be wife of the president of the U.S.A.—you will enjoy thinking of your happy days & laughing over what you thought were sad days.

Now, no more "navy-blueness." I'll fill that suit case *full* of something good & you must take something thats "awful good" to that "hateful Eng. teacher" & see what a beautiful smile she will give you.

Well, all my lights are all going out. I'm writing by the light of a *pine knot*, but as I'm not a George Washington or a Daniel Webster it "gets my goat" as you girls would say. I'm almost in total darkness, so I'll kiss you good-night & hope my letter will find you well & happy.

Your fond Mother

To Miss Ina D. Russell, Athens, Ga.

Friday Morning [November 29, 1912]

Dear Child,

I've just heard something *so funny.* Laura says she is going to Athens to-morrow & *must* carry your box. Now isn't that funny? Now you must not let Laura know I wrote you she was coming, unless she asks you. I think she wants to surprise you.

Laura has just come in & says she doesn't care if you know she is coming so you'll be looking out for her. Make her feel as welcome as possible. She is a great blessing to me. I told papa yesterday I was more thankful for Laura than any blessing. I *never* have to go in the kitchen. . . .

Laura will want to see your room. Tell Fedora & Miriam so they can see her. [She] will come on 10 o'clock train, get on car & come right to Lucy Cobb.

Mother

To Miss Marguerite Russell, Milledgeville, Georgia

December 4, 1912

Dearest Margo,

. . . I'm getting ready for Christmas with a *quiet* rush. Trying to do *something* every day. I have bought a little Santa Claus & will add to my piles each trip to Atlanta. When I meet you in Atlanta I don't want any shopping to do for myself. . . .

When Papa & I got off the train in Athens Saturday night, on our way to the West wedding, I saw a G.N.&I.C. girl and a nice-looking fellow hurrying to take the train (our train goes on to Abbeville now) & I called Papa's attention to them & we wondered what she was doing there this time of year. I guessed she was running away to get married. This afternoon I was at Pipeys & Annie was telling me about a girl from Comer who had been to G.N.&I.C. & had begged her mother to let her come home & her mother wrote her to come. She was the only daughter & very much humored at home. Annie said she came Saturday night. I told Annie about her. Joe Comer was the boy with her. Her name is Kathleen Taylor. Joe told Annie when they were crossing the river she took off her cap & threw it out of the window & said "Good-by to *you*." [1]

I know you keep busy & I know you get tired. It just seems a part of life—that is to people who do anything. I'm just hoping every day that you are feeling well. Mother thinks of you more than you have any idea. I hope you will have a long vacation and get a good rest. Don't worry a minute over Christmas presents. We can manage some way. . . .

Don't worry too much over that Geometry. You are young enough to try it again. . . .

> With my hearts best love
> Mother

1. GN&IC girls generally hated their uniforms, especially the hats.

To R. B. Russell, Jr., Barnesville, Ga.

Dec. 8, 1912

My Dearest Boy,

Just a word! Haven't time for much letter writing—especially when its sleepy time and papa snoring away & looks so comfortable over yonder in the bed.

Rob went to Sunday School this morning, and had the good luck to get our mail. Your letter came and I was surprised to hear from you, and was so sorry you were feeling blue about your marks, but boy, I was sorrier still that you had such marks. What can we do? I'm sure it is not your "block head" as you said. Maybe you ought to be in Fresh again. Go to work *at once,* & find out the cause of all this & remedy it at once. Surely *my boy* can learn his lessons. Think well & see if the fault lies in your teacher, your class, your books or what. I know if you *study* you can learn. That is, unless you are in a class too advanced for you & I *have* heard of boys studying extra hard & catching up & doing all kinds of smart things. Now get to work boy & see what you can do.

Quit school! Never by *my* consent. You are preparing yourself now to make a living, & to make a mark in the world & a *high* mark it must be. Think of the nice things in the world you'll want by & by. How can you get any thing unless you are educated & competent to *take hold* and win for yourself fame & money.

Keep a store in Huffs store! Think of it! I can see you with your case of soda water & jar of red candy & box of chewing gum & *you,* "R. B. Russell Jr." sitting on the "small of your back" waiting for a customer to come along with his *pennies* to trade with you.

Just close your eyes and think of what you'd like to be ten years from now & twenty years from now—what you'd like to be & what you'd like to have & then *grit your teeth,* & resolve that your dream *shall* come true. The better you are educated the more you know, the better you will be able to *make* your dream come true.

I'll leave the subject with you now, for I must close, but I'll beg you not to be discouraged. You just haven't studied as you should. You have seen what *bad* marks you could get, now go to work & see what *good* marks you can get.

No, boy, I didn't bring you into this world to be a failure or to ever *fail* in anything you might undertake. So *rub up* that *"block head"* & get good marks from *now on.* Our seven Russell boys must be shining lights in this world. You as the oldest must lead the way. O, I can't have one of you a failure—not one. I'm so proud of you all. Your father & I feel that our boys are our life & our hope. Our girls are our happiness & comfort.

I'll kiss you good night & hope that you are feeling all right & can soon see your way clear to good lessons & good marks. Every thing depends on the interest you have in your lessons & a desire to get good marks & to stand well in your classes.

> With a heart *full* of love,
> Mother

To Marguerite Russell, Milledgeville, Ga.

January 8, 1913

Margo, dear child, your letter received yesterday was such a dear, sweet letter, that I feel like writing you one "all by yourself" for it. You know it is hard for me to write *many* letters. As I go about my various duties through the day and night, I'm constantly thinking of my absent children & I form or write *in my mind,* perfectly grand letters to them. This occurs often as I sit before the fire, rocking our darling baby to sleep. When the opportunity comes for me to write, I find my mind a perfect blank & am disgusted with my letter. . . .

I was glad you enjoyed your stay at home so much & if you children could only know how much we enjoy having you! I was glad to know you felt so affectionate towards each one. As I've often told you all, there are many trials in a big family, but its very sweet to have some one to love & some one to love you and the trials we have & the sacrifices we make is what we have to pay to have a family & some one to love & some one to love us. We can't have our pudding & eat it too. Don't you see? We can't enjoy having the home & loved ones without a few troubles & trials. Its impossible. But we can learn to "put up" with these trials etc. & find happiness enough to last a lifetime.

R. B. & Wm Henry went off on same train. Mamie went down, too, to Atlanta. Our boys looked "mighty sweet" to us & we hated to see them leave. We saw several G.N.&I.C. girls at the station. . . .

I packed R. B.'s trunk myself this time and I did a good job. R. B. is a funny fellow & a grand one to me. I think he will succeed well in life on account of a few things I see in his "make-up." I will not tell you what they are, but will leave you to find out.

Tell my darling Bill that I enjoyed her letter so much. I'll answer in a day or two. I'm so sorry she had headache on the train. I'm afraid she didn't eat anything. I told you to make her eat something. . . .

I must say good-bye now & make the fires. Its been so warm & now its turning colder.

Daddy didn't come home last night & we missed him so. Guess he'll come tonight. . . .

> With a world of love for you & Bill.
> Mother

To R. B. Russell, Jr., Barnesville, Ga.

January 12, 1913

My Dearest Boy,

Your letter received a few days ago. It was just a *little bit* better than some of your letters have been, but that doesn't imply that it was anything extra. I am going to start a new rule, if I can, about your letters. I will write you letters according to the way & manner in which you write to me. For instance: If you write me one page I'll write you one & so on. Now that is fair, isn't it? Sometimes I just long for a long newsy letter from you, telling about your studies, your friends, your boarding house & any little incident that might have occurred during school hours or after school. I used to write Mary Willie when she was at Agnes Scott & ask her to tell me of her friends and about *anything* however small that came into her daily life. I want you to improve in your letter writing too. Study it. Remember your paragraphs, by all means. You never misspell a word & I'm thankful for it, but the way in which your letters are written, as a general thing, is very awkward.

I'm glad you like your boarding place. Hope it will keep good. I want your surroundings as pleasant as possible, so you can study—study hard. Boy, I think it is up to you now, to show us what you can do. Papa has been corresponding to Pres. Holmes about you. He read a nice letter to me last night that Holmes had written in answer to his letter in which your father asked him several questions. I'm sure your crucial moment has come, & as

I say, it is up to you, my boy, to show us what you can do. Holmes said you could pull up in everything, he thought, unless it was Latin. He said you could be privately instructed, & perhaps he could do it himself. Now, boy, write soon & tell me what you are doing & what you are going to do. We are just counting on you & depending on you.

Our school began with a boom. Think of it! 40 pupils in the old hop-stand. I've been over twice to see if my eyes saw true. . . .

Carolyn is crying & I am just hurrying.

Miss Hettie came last night. She was real sick—but I believe you heard that she was—during Christmas. Ina went back yesterday. Rob went over to Athens with her & ate dinner at Lucy Cobb. He is getting the "Lucy Craze" early in life, isn't he?

Carolyn is screaming! I must stop or papa will be running to see about her. . . .

      Mother

To R. B. Russell, Jr., Barnesville, Ga.

January 28, 1913

My Dearest Boy,

You don't know how sorry I was to go to bed Sunday night and no letter written to you for papa to mail Monday in Atlanta. Sunday was a very busy day. Carolyn wasn't very well either. Uncle Lewis is in Boston, Mass. & Auntney was out spending the night with us . . .

I've been wanting to write you in regard to your "drinking habit." Now that sounds awful doesn't it. You know mine and your father's opinion of the average Soda Fountain stuffs, otherwise known as "soft drinks." You doubtless remember when you first went to Gordon I've compromised on "chocolate milks"—for they may do no harm & if you *have* to have some-thing & happen to have a *nickle,* why maybe they—the chocolate milk, will do & do no harm. *Don't* drink the other stuffs! I mean it. Did I ever agree for you to have coffee for breakfast? Let me know. I do want you all, my girls & boys to grow up with good, sound bodies & good pure minds. Think about this boy. Write me on the subject. Sometimes when I write this way, I have an awful feeling that you may not read my letters, you are so reticent. You never mention any thing I put in my letters. You see we mothers are very much concerned about our boys. They are *very, very* dear to us. We are thinking constantly of their minds, their bodies & their souls. One life is all we have to live. Begin early to live your life with patience, temperance & moderation & perseverence & many more good ways that you know of & I believe you practice already.

I am writing with Carolyn in my lap.[1] I am by my bureau & I'm using a can of condensed milk for a paper weight. . . .

We are all so sorry for Mr. Leak Smith's family. Five or six of them have been stricken with typhoid fever for a long time. All of them are sick except Mr. S. and two of the children. Mrs. Smith & two of the little girls have died. Its awful to see the undertakers wagon going down there so much.

Do write Rob something about the gun. He asks every day if you have written. You know boy he couldn't hurt your gun & you know he doesn't hunt much. I don't let him go, you know. He has been trying to kill a hawk that's been wanting some of our chickens. Some days he flies real near the house. Everybody in the neighborhood has promised him (Rob) a chicken pie if he will kill the hawk. . . .

Now as I have some important things in this letter, I'll request you to read it over twice & ponder well on what I've written. . . .

Heart of love, Mother

1. Ina notes in many letters that she is writing with a baby in her lap.

To Misses Russell, Milledgeville, GA.

Jan. 28, 1913

Dearest Bill and Margo,

I did not intend writing you a "union" letter this time, for Margo, your last long, delicious, charming & unique letter deserves an answer all by itself, and Bill, I do think it is a shame that I have not written you a *real* letter since your return to G.N.&I.C. Margo, I intend to preserve your letter for future generations. . . .

Bill, I've never written you one word since you wrote about Etta. Isn't her job grand? I'm so glad for her. Hurrah for G.N.&I.C. girls! They can get good places when they really want to do something. . . .

Bill I have just *one* idea now & that is to come in June to see you graduate.

I told Auntney yesterday & she wants to come, & you know Aunt Hattie says she is coming & Ina too, if Dad can find travelling expenses for us three. . . .

Carolyn cried right here & I had to stop & fix her bottle. She is so cunning & sweet & grows so smart every day. She has had a bad cold. So much damp weather. Have you had much rain & many fogs in M[illedgeville]? We have to have the lantern to flag the train for Papa nearly every morning.

Girls, I miss your music more than you can know. If I could only hear that "Bump, Bump, Bump" & "Ragging the Baby" occasionally, it would do me so much good. I have been practicing diligently lately. I have given up all idea of ever learning "rag music" as I want to, so now I'm devoting my time to the sentimental. I can really play & sing "Absent" & almost play & can sing "Vale of Dreams." Bill, if you were only here to play for me! . . .

Rob has not seemed at all well & he looks so thin & weak. I'm trying to doctor him & I give William raw egg & sweet milk to make him grow.

Bill, I'm glad you have the gardening. . . . I feel as if I must have some flowers this year. I've wired in a little place by my side porch & Margo, the jonquils have been planted a long time & are coming up. . . .

Laura came back Monday morning & we all greeted her with much gladness. We are not having anything much extra to eat these days, & Margo, if you were here I don't believe you'd ever feel like popping. . . .

I must stop now. Carolyn wants me to take her. She has finished her bottle.

I haven't written anything like I wanted to. Some children are here & they are banging on the piano. It gets my "goat," I tell you.

The 10 cents [is] to buy oranges. . . .

> With a heart of love for my girls
> Mother

To Miss Ina D. Russell, Athens, Ga.

Feb. 3, 1913

My Dearest Girlie,

This is a miserable day to undertake writing a letter, but I'll make a beginning & see how my effort will end.

I rushed the children off to school this morning & in just a little while they were back saying "No school, no school." Miss Pearl was sick.

Rainy days are so trying to me on account of the keeping the little ones in. I dearly love a rainy day. I love to sit & listen to the rain & think nice easy thoughts, & I love to sew while its raining. But my, my! Keeping all these little hands busy & keeping all these little feet as still as possible! that is "*some* job, believe me," as Marguerite would say.

I have good fires every where. Patience & Harriet are in their room, playing dolls, I guess. Rob & Walter are up stairs in their room. I try to keep the twins in sitting room & just now they rushed in, in the midst of a big argument about when Lucy Cobb & G.N.&I.C. would close. Fielding insisting they closed at the same time & William insisting that "Ina got home sooner."

Dick stays with Carolyn & me, & I'm thankful that Jebs is at Pipeys. He stayed there last night.

Carolyn is such a darling we almost "eat her up" every day. She sits ever so long now, every day in Patience['s] little rocker. I tie her in & give her something to play with. She is still the smartest baby I have ever seen— I mean for her age.

All of you were such smart babies, its a wonder to me you are not more wonderful now. Whats the matter? You, *especially,* was a perfect wonder. Its too bad that we so soon out-grow so much notoriety. . . .

Ina, I am going to ask you a question & I want you to answer it in your next letter. I want you to think well before you decide, & after thinking over it a minute, I'll say, you need not be in a hurry, but just decide some time & let me know. Do you object in the least in having your letter taken from the Methodist Church? If you do not object, which church would you prefer to join? The time has come when some thing must be done about our church membership. As you know, papa has taken his letter from the church.[1] He says now that he never expects to belong to any church. He says we can stay in the Methodist Church if we prefer. Now you know all of papa's people have been Presbyterians for generations back. I feel that if *all of us* can go to the Presbyterian Church, that *some day,* papa may connect himself with the Presbyterians, for our sake & for the sake of his parents. As far as I am concerned, I could go to the Pres. Church all right. In fact, I feel that it is the only church I could join, besides the Methodist. You know, I was brought up in the M. Church, but for the last few years I haven't been as fond of it as I would like. I will write to the other children & we can be thinking & make our decision. It hurts me for papa not to belong to *any church.* I think his mind is fully made up never to connect himself with any church again, but we must not lose hope & if we can all be patient & good we *may* get him to come with us some time in the future.

You know I consider your father the *best man* I ever knew. He is *good &* *kind,* we know that, & O, how we all love him! But we will want him in the church with us. However, if any of you should not *prefer* the Pres. Church, I wouldn't try to compel you. Don't say anything about the church matter to any one unless you want to write Bill & Margo, or R. B.

The children are making such a racket. I just can't write any more. Daddy was worried about you last night. Asked when I had heard from you. He had dreamed you were sick. But I'm counting on you feeling well & fine & studying hard & using some of that intellect that was so prominent when you were a baby. R. B. writes that he is struggling on, trying to master Latin & Geometry. . . .

We all send hearts of love,
Mother

1. Because of the Methodist criticism of his local-option stand in the 1911 gubernatorial campaign.

To R. B. Russell, Jr., Barnesville, Ga.

Feb. 11, 1913

Well, boy, I do believe you are beginning to under-stand the kind of letters that your mother dearly loves to receive. I give you 95 on the one that came this morning & if you "keep on" I'm sure I'll have to give you a glorious 100 in the near future. Just observe paragraphs &c. & the best penmanship you can afford. . . .

O, let me tell you! Judge Pottle came out with papa Saturday night & stayed until Monday morning. We all like him so much & enjoyed his visit. He made himself entirely agreeable & at home, on all occasions, & he let the twins sit in his lap & play with his watch chain & look at his children's pictures in his locket. You know what a blessed & glorious privilege this is to children & how grand for a guest to be so patient & longsuffering. Really, he did seem to enjoy it, & he held our darling baby ever so many times & I know he just *had* to enjoy her. She looked too cunning & sweet for anything & showed her appreciation of his attentions in various ways.

Mr. Alex Stephens came out Sunday morning & spent day & night. We enjoyed this visit of both good friends. Judge Pottle has been such a help to papa. You know how he gets behind & this time it was worse than ever. Papa says he could not have pulled through if Judge P. hadn't been so kind. Papa is still threatening to leave the Bench. Judge Pottle says he can't make a living there.[1]

Judge Pottle is an unusual man, I think. He must be smart to have accomplished so much. He is only 38 years old. His son is 20. He has been going to Emory but couldn't hold on any longer. He is in Atlanta now. His father got him a situation with the Bell 'Phone Co. Judge Pottle has a daughter 11 years old. She is in a convent in Macon. Mrs. Pottle is in Atlanta. I've heard she is very pretty. I've seen her picture in the papers several times.

The latest craze among the children is making money for the church. You know they go to the Presbyterian Sunday School. The teachers have given Walter & Patience dimes to see how much they can make on them. Patience makes fudge & Divinity & sells it 1 cents apiece. 6 for 5 cents. She has made 50 cents. I furnish everything every time & only charge her 10 cents worth of candy. You should hear the clamor for pennies. Even Dick demands his & when he gets his candy refuses to give up his penny. I invested Walter's dime in gum drops at Kress'. He sold them 1 cents apiece. He had 30 in his pound. He cleared 20 cents, you see. Next, I bought him some of those enticing pink cakes at Kress. They sold all right, so his talent is much improved. Frank [Francis] bought pop corn & Pipey pops it for him. He is hoping to make 60 cents on his dime—at one time. Uncle Lewis says he is going to give his class 25 cents. Rob & Harriet are "raking their brains" to know how to invest. I think the whole community will be bankrupt if this sale continues—unless we put on old Mrs. Bells nerve & refuse *point blank. . . .*[2]

I'm paying Doscia to keep the children just for me to write this letter. My chances for writing are very poor & uncertain.[3]

I hope you didn't have indigestion. If you ever have it, drink water, water, water. The more the better & *hot* water is better than cold.

    Mother

1. Court of Appeals Justices and Supreme Court Justices made four thousand dollars per annum in 1913.

2. The Bells were by far the wealthiest people in Russell.

3. While Ina is writing another long letter to Ina Jr., Doscia loses patience and runs away before Ina finishes the letter. Ina Sr. declares to Ina Jr.: "I'll not pay her that dime."

To R. B. Russell, Jr., Barnesville, Ga.

Feb. 19, 1913

My Dearest Boy,

Your letter dated Feb. 18th came this morning. You didn't say anything about my birthday, & I don't think you intended it for a birthday letter, as you didn't mention it, but I took it for one just the same. . . .

I was so disappointed that papa didn't come tonight, so I could discuss your situation. If you feel that you really want to come home & *work* to improve your physical condition, I am perfectly willing. I had a plan I wanted to talk to papa about. Its very beneficial to cut wood. Papa has that big gully full of big trees that ought to be cut out to let the little ones grow. I think he would be willing for you to cut the wood—haul it with Rabbit [a mule] to our station or warehouse & when you have a car load, ship it to Atlanta. Of course you could have the money, as far as my way is concerned & I think papa would be willing too, for you to have it all. Then when planting time comes, which is very near, you could plow Rabbit & then you could chop & hoe & so on. I think a few months work of this kind would help you physically & mentally too, if you *studied* & had your mind on what you were doing. There are important lessons to learn about everything, especially if the work is with *nature,* trees, planting, watching things grow, studying the cause & effect of everything. There is a world of interest & information in everything if we will only study a little & find it. Now, you may be laughing in your sleeve at me, for perhaps you did not mean a word of what you said. But I'm writing all this anyhow, for if you do mean it, I want to help you. I want you to grow strong physically as well as mentally. . . .

If any of this should happen & you should undertake to perform any of this heroic & muscle making labor, you must recall our efforts to get that cotton chopped out last summer & resolve to "stick to it" better than we did to that. You must work & not stop to read the papers until you rest for dinner. Follow the old-time maxim to "work while you work and play while you play."

I just wonder what papa will think of all this. You see, boy, when papa was at home he could help you with your Latin & mathematics & you need not get behind in those two studies—And pardon me, but I believe I could teach you to *write.* I'd try, anyhow. If you could turn yourself into a B. Franklin, or D. Webster, or H. Greely or an A. Lincoln, & work in the day & study at night, we might have a president in the family some day, or to say the least of it, a *very smart, strong,* healthy boy.

I'll leave a space & maybe papa will send a line or two.[1]

I know you will be sorry to know that our good R.F.D. carrier, Truman Smith, is dead. He was buried today.

      Lovingly,
      Mother

1. Papa did fill in the space she left, and his comments were equally loving and firm. He agreed with Ina about the work, and concluded: "You are my oldest son and you carry my full name. You can have—and *you must have*—a future of *usefulness* and *distinction* in Georgia or it will break my heart. You know now what is my mind about your coming home and of course I *often* miss you and wish you were at home. So make up your mind as to what you think is best and act accordingly. God bless my boy."

To Miss Ina D. Russell, Athens, Ga.

          Feb. 25, 1913

Well, girlie, its a "powerful busy" week with me, but I must chat a while with you, and may be it will refresh me. You know this is "Bill's week." It takes almost a whole week to fix her birthday box. This time I want it nicer than ever, for its her last, you know. I mean as a school girl. I'll tell you what I've made for her. If you write, don't tell her, for I want it all to be a grand surprise. I made her two kimonos—a long & a short one . . . [and] a silk petticoat. Don't you think she will be glad to get these nice things, our darling Bill? Then the cake & candy & ham & chicken & we want to send jonquils too. I wish you could go to Atlanta with me & help select some little toilet articles to put in the box. You know what she likes.

Every day I think about going to see Bill graduate. You put nice things in your "Hope Box." I put mine in my "Bill Box," for I want to be feeling good & have some nice things to wear when we go to see Bill graduate. Bill's report came last week. It was *so good*. A's & B's in everything but one, & that was Poultry Culture. She got C in that & I said, O, that's only C for chicken.

Mamie gave a nice entertainment last Friday in honor of "Aunt Lou" & the ladies in Russell. She invited 16 Winder ladies to meet us & we had a good time. She first had us all try to take peas from a dish with two tooth picks. Then she carried us in the sitting room where she had pictures of celebrities cut from magazines & pinned around on the curtains, piano cover &c. She had papa's picture—the little funny one cut from Cosmopolitan. She cut the names off and we had to guess them. Next she had a contest with a *prize to it*. All of us had to work a button hole with our left hand, except Mrs. Starr & she with her right as she was left handed. She won the prize. Pipey & aunt Annie seemed to enjoy the party. Pipey was one of the judges on the button holes. I told her it was a shame she didn't give a prize to *one* of her sisters. My button hole was awful.

I have been sorry that I wrote to you about coming home to stay a week. Of course you should not leave school that long. You know I have spells of wanting to see certain ones of you, just awfully bad. That was my "Ina time." I want to see you all all the time, but you know how it is to have spells about certain ones. I have had an "R. B." feeling on me this week. I'll have the "Bill feeling" next week, I guess. I had the "Marguerite feeling" on me some time ago when she was sick & in the infirmary. Of course you are coming home, but you mustn't miss a week. . . .

Your note & report came this A.M. Papa didn't come tonight, so he hasn't seen it. It does very well, as you say, for Exam marks, but not so well as I thought my smart Ina could do when she was about 2 yrs. old. It suited me all right. Just try to learn all you can & be sweet, considerate & good to everybody. I am so sleepy. . . . It's past ten & the children are all asleep.

    With a hug & a kiss
    Mother

To R. B. Russell, Jr., Barnesville, Ga.

March 31, 1913

Well, my dearest Boy,

. . . Your Feb. report came & I wanted to talk to you about it. You made 20 in Latin. Son, this is awful. You only got 83 in History. That blow was *hard*. You had been doing so well in that. Geometry 55—Algebra 60— spelling 92, Eng. 90, Geology 55—I haven't had the heart to show it to papa. This report is simply a disgrace to R. B. Russell Sr. & Jr. I'm thoroughly *disgusted*. Must I show it to papa? I await your answer. . . .

Why don't somebody from Barnesville write something about Gordon for the Journal? I never see anything. Couldn't find anything about Founder's Day, Ball games or anything. You do it & they will give you free transportation to Atlanta whenever you ask them. Mamie writes the Winder news & I went with her to the Journal Office & they gave her a free pass. . . .

Lovingly,
Mother

To Miss Marguerite Russell, Milledgeville, Ga.

April 11, 1896-April 11, 1913

Well, my blessed Precious seventeen-year-old baby child! Here is the 11th of another April & here we are still living on for good or evil. We both must have been put in this world for something *special,* we may never know *exactly* what for, but we do know that while in this world, the one who lives the *very best life* possible in *all* things, will be sure to find his calling & make his election sure.

Right here, your mother must tell you that she is so happy and pleased with the great improvement in your disposition during the last six months. I know you have improved & you may wonder why I know, but we mothers who are more interested in our children than anything else, just naturally know these things. . . . I believe you are trying every day to live a happy, patient, peaceable life, controlling *yourself,* getting all the good you can out of life, seeing & appreciating the good in all around you, at the same time you see what is bad, but making yourself kind and considerate with it all. . . . When you came home Christmas you were so patient with the little children & with the big ones too. You have always been a help to me with the little ones. This gives a mother more pleasure than anything a child can do. To help keep peace at home. It means more for a home than anything else. All of my children are *sweet* and *precious* to me. I do not regret *one* of you. Sometimes I've felt that I had a "hard road to travel" with so many little ones & big ones demanding all my time, all my strength and all of my life, but these times have been few. I'm proud of every one of you—from our good *old* Bill, and Ina, and you my darling third, and R. B., and Harriet, & Rob & Patience, and our energetic hot-headed Walter and our darling twins, your boy Fielding and William, our pretty blue-eyed Edward & our own smart big headed Dick & our precious baby, Carolyn. I only wish our two who are gone were here. Isn't it sweet to have so many to love & so many to love us?

My, my I didn't intend to write exactly this kind of a letter. I've been thinking about you all the morning & began fixing your box early. I found Laura had not finished one of your cakes & as I have a habit of putting in the cakes first, I decided to write while the cake was drying. I teased Laura good about her cakes. They do not look to suit me, but I know they are good. Laura says she didn't have enough butter—we have had a butter famine lately & I expect that is the reason. Anyhow, I want you to enjoy everything. We have enjoyed fixing it all. I have had your silk petticoat made for a long time. I have made you only one brown one. Your long kimono is the nicest one I've ever made. . . .

Harriet & Patience enjoyed making your candy. I think its good, all right. I'm sending two pieces of music. "On the Mississippee" is a popular piece & very pretty. I heard it first on Edward's graphophone.

I'm sending some cocoa & condensed milk. You can make something to drink. I did want to buy some grape juice, but forgot it, until right now. We haven't any good nectar, or I'd send some. Laura says she thinks we have some & she's gone to see.

It was a great temptation for me not to come with your box. Papa wanted me to, but I knew I was coming to Commencement & I didn't want to spend money on two trips. I've always wanted to go along with one of our boxes & see you open it.

Laura has brought in the nectar. I don't like it much, but will send it.

Dick has pinched on your cake & Laura & Doscia are laughing. I'm ashamed of the cakes. But your other things are all right. Laura says she wasn't feeling well & for you to take her mistakes all for love. Doscia says you wouldn't think she had much love for [you].

I've had so many interruptions. . . . I know there are many more things I want to say. Everybody in the room is making such a racket I can't think. As Laura says, take all for love. I do love you and I'm proud of you & I'm glad you are my child. You are having a rainy birthday but that's all right. Rainy days are good. I love them.

Everything for your box is piled around in my room on the table, bed, &c. I'll close now and put the box to rights. You'll be ready for it, I know, & I can see my Bill & Margo having a good time & it makes me happy.

> Your loving & devoted
> Mother

To R. B. Russell, Jr., Barnesville, Ga.

April 12, 1913

Well, my dearest R. B., time flies so that I just *can't* keep up with it.

I received your letter Thursday telling me about the book, your botany. I intended writing at once—not to send the money, for I told papa, almost *promised* him, a long time ago, that I would never send you any money. Once when you wrote a hurried call for money to pay your wash & I rushed a dollar bill off in a letter to you, papa didn't like it. You know how easy & kind he always is—well, he didn't say much, but I knew he didn't like it and I told him I wouldn't send any more. I think papa felt that I would always be sending you money (when I had it) and he was sending you some every month, you know, & he wanted that to last you. Well, I just told papa about your book yesterday morning. Papa seemed very much hurt. He said it was disgraceful for you to be "sitting in" for such a thing, that you should have provided for your book long ago when you *did* have money. And boy, you should have been more careful & not let this thing come on. "Take time by the fore-lock" always. Just keep your *hands on it all* the time and you'll never get in such a fix about anything. . . .

This money business is a hard proposition to handle, but the sooner we learn to do it the better it is for us. *Learn to use your money wisely.* You will get so much more good & pleasure from it. . . .

I've written this "soon in the morning" for [Cousin] Edward to take to Atlanta. Daddy didn't come home last night. He's working hard now.

Write soon and tell me all about your *financial* condition. It's a pity J. Pierpont didn't leave you a million or two, but you just better learn to make it as he did—but stay better looking, please.

Mother

To Miss Harriet Russell, Washington, Ga.[1]

Sep. 22, 1913

My Dear Harriet,

. . . Things have gone on about as usual since you left. You know how busy I've been the whole summer & lately I've been busier than ever, trying to save my peas & goobers. We haven't pulled my goobers yet, but got our half from Bone & I think I have at least 4 bushels. They are spread on porch up stairs & are almost dry enough to sack. I want to get $3.00 per bu. for them.

Ina has put on her clothes to-day for first time in 3 wks. I'm afraid she was not able to do it, she seems so weak—but she says she feels better to move about a little.[2]

Cousin Edward carried Rob to Monroe this morning. He has just gotten back & has told me all about it. He says the school [Monroe Agricultural & Mechanical] is very nice. Over 100 boys & 28 girls. The boys have to do 3 hrs. work per day. Edward says they have quantities of fine hogs, cows & horses. The buildings are steam heated, electric lights & water—4 bath rooms & toilets in boys dormitory. Not but one servant on the whole place, 260 acres—a grown negro man. The boys & girls do all the work. Board $9 per mo. All the work you do over your time you are allowed 10 cents per hour.

Of course we don't know how Rob will like it, but Edward says he was charmed to-day. He went down a little uneasy, for R. B. had written such a description of Powder Springs—no water & no bath room—a ten inch tin pan to wash in.[3] Has plenty of bacon, bread, syrup & water. Has good vegetable dinners from the school gardens.[4] They do the same amount of work & board is on[ly] $6.40 per month. He is full senior & Rob full Soph. Mr. Walker has a special Latin class of 6 pupils & Rob was there in time for it as it began to-day.

All of you are settled now & I'm so thankful. You don't know it, but your father & mother do the very best they can for you all & each of you, I hope, will study very hard & improve yourselves & will try to grow better every day in every respect.

I am too disappointed for anything. I had planned for two months or more to be with aunt Hattie on her birthday [September 19], but I just can't come. I can't leave Ina in the first place. She is very weak & you know I've been sleeping with her & waiting on her all the time. I will have to stand my disappointment & trust to good luck to be better to me next time.

I'm very glad you like your school. I knew you would enjoy being at aunt Hattie's & I'm glad you like Miss Bramlett. Hope you are wearing your hat to school & not going too thin these cool days.

You misspelled several words in your letters. I tried to remember to tell you, but can't now. You must be careful. One was semin*a*ry, one was disa*pp*oint—two p's.

Don't fail to write to Auntney & sometime write to uncle Lewis & tell how you enjoyed the $2.00 &c, and write Pipey sometimes. She has loved you a long time. . . .

      Lovingly,
      Mother

1. Harriette was living with Aunt Hattie in order to go to school in Washington, Ga. At fourteen, she was too far advanced for the Russell school.

2. Ina Jr. was recuperating from a near-fatal case of typhoid fever.

3. R. B. had failed Latin at Gordon and was therefore ineligible to return. Powder Springs A & M was a big step down from his easy boarding house life in Barnesville.

4. R. B.'s letter to his mother describing the food does not put this positive note on the situation.

To Robert L. Russell, Monroe, Ga.

Sep. 26, 1913

My Dearest Robert,

Your letter received this morning. I am "peeved to the bone" to know you are so home-sick. I couldn't believe my eyes! Rob home-sick! My Rob who was so anxious to leave home! Home must not be so bad after all, if you want to come back so badly.

I see in Cat[alog]. that [Cousin] Edward brought they are very strict about the boys coming home. The parents are requested not to encourage the children to come home. You can talk it over with Prof. W[alker] & tell him you want to come home to get some things. I forgot to put in napkins for you. I want you to have some. At the Presidents table too and the Cat. says for each student to have 6. I forgot to mark your counter-pane & your cotton blankets. If you can come next Sat. you can get napkins & I'll have your name on strips of cloth & you can sew them on blankets & counter pane. . . .

Walter, Frank [Dillard] & Patience picked all of our cotton. Walter & F. have been picking 3 days at Moffetts. Cook [Laura] has soon break fast & fixes a lunch for Walter & you know aunt Annie gets F. off in time.[1] They leave at 7 & get back about 7. To-gether they have picked over 400 lbs. and are there again to-day. Moffett seems to have a great deal of cotton. Picks a bale a day. 18 hands in the field. James went yesterday—picked 116 lbs., got his pay & says he can't go back any more. Walter & F. are holding out fine. I'm proud of them.

Polk wrote you a note—you can see it now, can't you? to send him flour, "sugga" & meat. I fixed him up, of course, but had declared I wouldn't. . . .[2]

Try to be satisfied & contented. Learn all you can & make a *name* for yourself. Now is the time to begin. Be so nice & good & polite & be a "shining light" among those boys. Think about what you want to be & what your mother wants you to be & how your father *counts* on his boys. It hurts me to know you are home sick, but I can't begin to beg now for you to come home. I'm sure you can come soon. Papa will see to it or I will. I can't do anything now while Ina is sick.

You didn't write a "descriptive" letter. You know how I enjoy them. I want to know what kind of work you have to do. I'm crazy to run down to see you. Surely *my boy* can perform *any* task as well as any one else! . . .

This is a long letter for me to write. To-day is Edward's [fourth] birthday. He is very happy. Laura is fixing his cake. Pipey carried him to Winder. . . .

Well, boy, I'll close. Get busy now & don't be home-sick any more. Enter into every thing with a *will* & get interested in every body and every thing. . . .

Mother must close. I've been writing a long time.

Heart of love for Rob.

1. Annie Dillard Launius was known for her strict discipline, while Pipey was known for softer ways.

2. Polk (sometimes called Poke) Manders was a white tenant, alcoholic and unreliable. The tenants got their groceries on credit and were supposed to pay for them when the crops came in. Rob had no doubt dealt with Polk many times.

To Miss Harriet Russell, Washington, Ga.

Oct. 7, 1913

My Dear Harriet, and I must say my dear sister Hattie, too, for I do want to write to you & I want to write to her. As I hardly have time for *one* letter I'll let it be to you both, for arn't you both Harriets and arn't you both *very* dear to me?

I'm writing principally now to let you know how Ina is. The poor child has had a time since her last illness [relapse]. She has been so much sicker since this last attack. Her fever has not been so high but she is so weak & just lies in bed as if she didn't care for a thing in the world. She is much better now, though still too weak to even sit up. We thought of having a trained nurse, but decided Sunday that I could hold my job as she had better symptoms in every way. [She] is beginning to enjoy her nourishment now & I think will soon be able to sit up. I have certainly done my best for her. She has rested tolerably well at night & I haven't been up very much. I'm feeling a little worn out, but keep going & get all my sweeping done every morning & seeing after my fall gathering.

The children have picked nearly 800 lbs. cotton from my field. To-day (they & Laura) have pulled my goobers. I'm expecting 25 bu. James & Francis [Ben's children] help. Walter is the best worker I ever saw. Dear old Laura invited James & Francis to dinner & rushed in about 11:30—killed two chickens, "threw a cake in the pan" as she says, & cooked them a good dinner. I've promised the boys a pk. of goobers apiece to help & they are working good. I've picked my half of Spanish peanuts from Mr. Bone & made 6 bu. I will have about that many more of the large goobers from Bone. I want to get $2.50 per bu. & maybe I'll feel as if my work amounts to something. Harriet did you tell aunt Hattie I sold $9.00 worth of green peas. I'm so rejoiced when I can do anything to make a nickel.

I have some young chickens too, sister Hattie—about 25, and three more hens to hatch. I do want plenty of frys for Christmas when aunt Hattie and the children come home.

Ina was asleep when I began this letter she is awake now & I must hurry through. . . .

Harriet we were so pleased over your report. Papa simply danced for joy over the latin mark. You keep up the lick now & get good marks every month. I'm glad to know you are studying. Rob says he thinks he could lead his class if it wasn't for Alice Walker, the President's daughter, about your age & size.

Sister Hattie, this letter is partly for you "sho nuff." I've been thinking of you all day. If you were here, you would enjoy bustling around with these goobers. The children work beautifully. They have picked off nearly 3 bu. already. I don't leave Ina but a few minutes at a time. Pinkie has been busy this wk. & last putting up green pickle (chow-chow) & catchup. She has so many green tomatoes she makes on halves with me & I tell you, its lucky for me. . . .

    Lovingly,
    Mother and Ina

To R. B. Russell, Jr., Powder Springs, Ga.

Oct. 8, 1913

Dearest Boy,

I'm trying to shoo the flies off of Ina & I want to write to you too. . . .

When I heard [from Rob] how nice everything was at Monroe I was sorry you didn't go there. Mamie [Quarterman] has given me a terrible idea of Powder Springs. Said Mrs. Hunt had remarked to her that mothers with boys who had nice table manners had better not send their boys to P.S. for the boys there had no manners & no one to see after them. Perhaps its bad for me to risk this in a letter, but I do it to warn you to "keep up" your good manners & not forget your home training.

Rob has two Latin lessons a week & he says Prof. W. certainly can teach it.

I've been wanting to know what kind of work you do. Rob says he has to split wood after its sawed. Rob is having a hard time with a bad tooth.

We have been so busy with goobers. I made 6 bushels as my half of Bones Spanish peanuts. I've picked off about 13 bushels from my patch & have about 2 more bu. on vines. Arch will bring up my half of big red goobers from Bones to-night & we expect to have a goober picking. Arch brings a crowd & we light the back porch light & to-night Laura will cook some refreshments.

Walter, James & Francis . . . picked [cotton] at Moffetts last week & you know [Walter] nearly made his 100 per day. He made nearly $2.50. He is going to Leak Smiths next week. Laura & everybody will go. Laura has hired *me* to cook dinner for every day.

You should see papa in his new suit. He looks *grand*.

I want to know if you drink coffee. I hope you do not—& boy, don't drink soft drinks at that store. Remember how your mother abhors *soft drinks*—especially coca cola. . . .

Carolyn is walking everywhere. Too sweet & smart. Dickson is so smart, too.

> Heart of Love,
> Mother

To Mr. Robt. L. Russell, Monroe, Ga.

Oct. 23, 1913

Dearest Rob,

I have resolved all day that I would write to you before I went to bed to-night. Now listen while I tell you what difficulties I'm writing under! In the first place it is nearly ten o'clock & I'm real tired & sleepy. Next, the lights went out to-night while Laura was cooking supper & I'm using the lamp. I have been real busy all day. You know how trying these rainy days are & how the children dislike to be shut in.

Our carbide [for the lights] has lasted very well, I think. You filled it when you came home Sep. 26th and to-day is Oct. 23rd. We burn a light all night, turned low, since Ina has been sick.

Ina is beginning to get well now and we are so thankful. She went to the kitchen to-day but it made her very tired. Poor child! She wants to go back to school so bad & I don't think she ought to go before Xmas.

We had a fine treat Saturday night. R. B. & Marguerite both came home. It was this way: Marguerite's eyes have been giving her a great deal of trouble. She wrote papa & asked to come home. Papa wrote her to come

Sat. R. B. just wanted to come to Atlanta & asked papa to let him come. Papa said he could & that he could come on home if he wanted to. Of course he wanted to come & he & Margo came the same time. Margo had to get some strong glasses. R. B. enjoyed his visit. Laura cooked good things. Sunday was Dickson's birthday [3 years old] & of course we had plenty of cake. R. B. is looking so well. He seems to have grown an inch or two. I think his syrup & bread agrees with him.

You did well to go so long without spending money. Its good practice. Try it again. Your report came same day with your letter. Your marks are not very good, but I'm hoping its because you began so late. You must pull up next month, boy. Get better than 50 in History and 57 in Algebra & 40 in biology—and I'd like for you to do better than 73 in Arithmetic. 100 in Spelling is good & be sure you never get less. 90 in Eng. does very well. . . .

I haven't sold my bale of cotton. Its in the back yard. I know I'll get 1000 lbs. & hope to get a good bale if I can ever get it [all] picked. Walter & Laura were busy picking to-day when the rain began. Cotton was bringing 14¢ yesterday.

Arch has made the syrup at last. He made 13½ gals. & we made 16 gals. I never want to hear of any more "syrup cane."

Miss Pearl will begin our school first Monday in Nov. I hope by that time all the children will be through with their [farm] work.[1]

Your "Cootie" is too sweet for any thing, walking every where & getting into every thing. She is so smart & sweet. We just "eat her up" some times. . . .[2]

Laura's son Ed is with her now. She hadn't seen or heard from him in 14 yrs. She thought he was dead. He came very unexpectedly the other day. Walked up to Laura, put his arms around her & [she] called out to him in her loud voice to "let her alone" & he called her mother. She looked at him & said, "*Yes, I'll mother you*" & then she recognized him. She is so happy to have him with her. He has traveled every where, it seems. He has played base ball in big games. He looks just like Laura & about as big as she is. He picks cotton at Leaks & generally picks 300 a day. He seems so polite and is seeing after his mother.

We dug a potato to-day that weighed 4½ lbs. & Laura cut off part of it. It was a monster. The potatoes are bursting out of the patch.

James & Cousin Lizzie Hattie[3] spent Sunday with us. A new conductor was on & carried them by Russell & they were put off at the crossing. You can imagine how "peeved" daddy was. Papa didn't come home last night or to-night. Said he wouldn't come before Sat.

Boy, I'm so sleepy, I must bid you good night & pleasant dreams.

I had such a nice letter from Prof. Walker. He said some nice things about you. Of course my boy is all right. I expect you to be a gentleman under all circumstances & I want you to be good, Robert, & have a good influence on those around you . . .

    Mother

1. Schools did not begin when there was a great need for seasonal labor, such as picking cotton.

2. "Cootie" [Cutie] is only one of Carolyn's many names. Others are Coots, Cootsie, Ca-line, Carolina. The baby is fourteen months old. She is called "Rob's" because she was born on his birthday.

3. Dillard relatives.

To R. B. Russell, Jr., Powder Springs, Ga.

Dec. 13, 1913

My Dearest Boy,

. . . Look here, son! Why can't you get up a good report to send us once in a while? Your marks are dreadful & I can't understand. Surely you have the sense of intellect to do better. I want you to tell me sometimes why you don't make good marks. I'm worried. I like for my children to do well, & I believe you could do better if you tried.

Did you plant that tree? You must bring your speech home for me to read. I spoke of you that day & Ina & I wished to be at Powder Springs A&M to see that tree planted. . . .

I must tell you that your last letter was the nicest one you've ever written. The writing was nice & the whole letter was very neat. Your last one to papa was right nice too.

Laura has been busy this week baking cake. Her fruit cakes are grand. My! How good they smell! Just waiting for my children to come home— Mary Willie, Margo, Rob & Harriet will come Sat. the 20th. . . .

Coots is worrying me so, fooling with the ink & knocking against me.

Write me as soon as you get this & let me know when you get out. If you can come Friday night, papa will wait for the late train. . . .

I've had to stop several times but I'm so glad I have your letter written at last. I did not intend to wait so long.

Your devoted mother

To Miss Harriet B. Russell, Washington, Ga.

Jan. 25, 1914

My Dear Harriet,

. . . I thought about you a great deal just after you left, and I think it was because you had a hard time getting a seat on the train. Ina and I stood and watched you until the train pulled out. I saw you go in the smoker but I also saw other ladies went in there with you. I felt safe and thought perhaps the conductor would either put the smokers out or get you ladies seats in another car. We have to put up with a few discomforts sometimes, even on a short trip and its best just to "grit your teeth" and make the best of it. Of course I mean when things can't be helped.

Guess what happened here yesterday! Well, Ina has been wanting to take the twins to Atlanta for some time. Wm had a tooth that needed attention, so Ina volunteered to take the twins Saturday, Patience to go with her. Laura began begging to go and carry Dick. Of course that got him stirred up and papa said he must go too. So yesterday morning, you can imagine what a getting ready we had. If we had only known it, the train was an hour and a half late, and we . . . had plenty of time.

We had a lot of fun last night hearing the comments that were made on them. When they got on at Russell, one of papa's friends asked what good-looking lady that was with all those children. When papa said it was his daughter, the man said: "Are those children hers?"

When Ina was waiting at Dr. Crenshaws she heard a lady say: "What a patient mother. My two are more than I can stand."

Ina says when they all went in at Nunnallys, took their seats and each ordered a glass of milk and hot rolls, that the people around seemed much amused. . . . Dear old Laura tugging along with Dick and she was so glad of the least opportunity that came along to tell whose "chilluns" they were. They went to two moving pictures and went into a place and had pictures taken of the "*party*." Ina is sending you one and she says she will write to you soon. Ina's hair is getting pretty now. It grows very fast. . . .

I'm glad you have the leading part in Merchant of Venice. While you are reading it, make a real study of it. Don't just *read* it. Memorize the best parts and fix them in your mind. . . .

I do hope you are studying hard and above all things trying to improve your self in every way. . . .

> Heart of love,
> Mother

To R. B. Russell, Jr., Powder Springs, Ga.

Jan. 27, 1914

My Dearest Boy,

. . . I don't believe I congratulated you on being elected President of your literary Society. Do your very best and never miss an opportunity to speak & speak. . . .

I'm sending you Patrick Henry's speech "Give me liberty or give me death" and I want you to learn it for me. I mean it. I want you to *learn* it, every word. I'm not going to offer to pay you to do it, but I'm going to tell you that if you will learn and speak it for me when you come or when I see you, I'll give you a *dollar bill*. I'll give it to you just as soon as I hear you speak it. This is no joke. I mean it all, for I want you to learn the piece.

I am teaching William and Fielding speeches to recite at school Friday. Fielding is so much easier to learn and takes more interest in such things than William. I don't think its because Fielding is smarter, but he is stronger than William physically and naturally shows more interest in everything than William. Fielding has learned William's speech and corrects him when he says it wrong. Walter has learned his speech. I expect to go down to the school Friday to hear them all speak. . . .

I am having some land ploughed this afternoon. You and Rob never did tell me what you were willing to do about our cotton patch. Must I rent it out or must we work it? If you go to school next summer, you won't be here to work much, will you? . . .

Emory and Arch are digging in the well again & we are praying for water. Write soon,

> Mother

To Miss Marguerite Russell, Milledgeville, Ga.

Feb. 2, 1914

Dearest Margo,

. . . We had quite an exciting experience last week. Judge Pottle leaves the Court of Appeals to-day. He is going to Albany to practice law. You know papa is very fond of him and he wanted to have him out to spend the night before he left. So he invited him to come Sat. Jan. 31st. . . .

Papa invited ever so many to come out to dinner Sunday but only Judge Roan, Judge Bell and Mr. Derrick came. We had a turkey and ever so much good dinner. I could hardly enjoy myself wishing for my absent children. You know Mr. Derrick is Sheriff of the Court. Well, at the table he told us it was his birthday. Then we all came forward with good wishes &c. . . .

But the grandest thing, O, my child! I can hardly tell you, for I want you and Bill and Harriet and Rob and R. B. here to enjoy our grandest treat with us. Papa invited a Mr. Avery—a dear, good man with a heart of gold and a purse of silver. Well, this dear man couldn't come, but he sent—O, he sent us a barrel of apples, a crate of oranges and a crate of grapefruit. Did you ever know anything half so grand! Imagine our surprise to see these things pouring off the train one night. Edward got the wheel barrow and brought them to the house. We could hardly believe our eyes or ears. . . . This same man sent papa a fine box of cigars and a plug of his favorite tobacco. . . .

I hope you are through with those awful exams and are feeling all right. You must not let such as this upset you. *Be a man,* even if you are a female. . . .

Laura has just come in and announced her intentions of resting awhile. That means I'm to cook, but I'm willing to do it and let the old soul have a rest. She is my blessing.

I feel like writing more but must close now. Be careful how you write letters to people. Never write anything you do not want seen.

    Mother

To R. B. Russell, Jr., Powder Springs, Ga.

March 2, 1914

Dearest Boy,

    As I have a few quiet spare moments, I'll try to answer your nice letter received this A.M. Yes, we certainly had a snow. The telephone people came up about 12 o'clock in a yellow automobile, all full of snow, and the occupants nearly frozen. They brought a new phone and now we can *hear,* when we *talk.* They were so cold, and I had them come in my room to the fire. They seemed to appreciate it, too.

    Two of the Oglethorpe negroes[1] landed here in the snow. Next morning as Too-too was coming to his breakfast, he saw a rabbit and just picked it up. He brought it to the house and dressed it for me. About that time Arch walked up with one. My! What luck! Walter became wild and he & James, Arch and Too-too were out with Walter's gun and Arch's dog, but our luck was gone. No more rabbit. But I cooked the two we had. They were good, I tell you.

    March certainly "came in like a lion" yesterday. . . . When I went out to the kitchen about 8:30 to get breakfast, I thought the house would surely go to pieces, and in a few minutes I did see the top of the generator house go flying off. It struck the bell post and made the bell ring. . . . The wind raged all day and all last night and is still howling to-day. I know you A&M's were cold last night.

    Papa was in Oglethorpe last week and came in from Athens Saturday night. He brought some good walnut candy, some "weenies" and some loaf bread. You see I'm still cooking. Cook went to Atlanta Saturday. Says she is coming back Thursday and will take up her old job again.

    If it stays so cold I want to have Sam [the hog] killed. If I do, I know you will want some of his good sausage, won't you?

    Yesterday was Bill's birthday. Did you think of it? She is twenty-one now. I sent her a real good box and this morning I had two sweet letters from her. I think she and Marguerite are planning a visit home about the 27th. . . .

Ina did not go back to Lucy Cobb. She is a sight, isn't she?

> Heart of love,
> Mother

1. Men who worked at Farm Hill, which Brother Walter, Ina, and Pipey had inherited. Richard was having the land farmed.

To Mr. Robt. Lee Russell, Monroe, Ga.

March 12, 1914

Dearest Rob,

I heard something this morning that made me very happy. I might say *supremely* happy, for I knew I was the mother of a son who possessed a *heart,* and who knows what kindness is. Tennyson said in one of his beautiful poems: "Kind hearts are more than coronets, and simple faith than Saxon blood." You will want to know what I mean. Well, when you told me about the Jew at your school, who was required to attend prayer meeting and who was rudely treated by the boys, you remember I said that I hoped you were kind to him. This morning I had a letter from R. B. The "Wandering Jew" had been to Powder Springs. He said there that he liked *you* because you were *kind* to him and did not make fun of him when they called him Leo Frank &c.[1]

O, Rob, tears are in my eyes now, as I write, and my heart is so glad that you were kind. Cultivate your heart to be kind. Why shouldn't we be kind to a Jew? We are told that man was made in the image of God. A Jew as well as a Gentile—a *black* man as well as a white man.

I feel so sorry for your friend. You know I took an interest in him when you first told me about him. I believe Prof. W. did wrong when he let him leave. R. B. said he did not like Powder Springs because they did not have bath rooms and electric lights. I wish he could go some where where he could be taught and loved, regardless of his belief and birth.[2]

I haven't time to write much letter. A letter from Margo was forwarded to you. I just *had* to *read my childs* letter, Rob, and you'll pardon me for opening it, won't you? . . .

> Heart of love,
> Mother

1. An Atlanta Jew who in 1913 was accused and convicted of a murder that he could not possibly have committed. While his case was being appealed, he was taken from prison and lynched.

2. In R. B.'s letter the young man is called Isador and described as a twenty-six-year-old Russian Jew who had been a tailor in Russia.

To Miss Marguerite Russell, Milledgeville, Ga.

April 6, 1914

My Dearest Margo,

. . . Yesterday I thought of you a million times, more or less. Papa & I went to Athens and spent the day with John and Addie. They met us at the train and we rode around some and went to church. *Presbyterian,* and sat in the old Russell pew. Had a sweet service. I enjoyed the music. After service we talked to our friends & then went on out to Uncle Johns for dinner. After dinner we went to ride & what do you think? We went down to Farm Hill! I went in my dear old home and sat in the corner of our sitting room where my mother used to sit. I felt so sad and wanted to see mama so much that a terrible lump got in my throat but I had to keep talking and make myself agreeable. I saw Tom's little baby girl. The first Dillard girl born in the house since *your* mother was born. It made the little baby look very sweet to me and I felt that I loved her for that fact alone.

We hurried back to Athens and Uncle John & Aunt Addie brought us home. We had a lovely moonlight ride but it was right cold. . . .

Papa bought himself a pretty new blue suit with tiny white strip & listen! A *green hat with a bow* in back! Our daddy! Think of it! . . .

Heart of love for you & Bill,
Mother

To Miss Harriet B. Russell, Washington, Ga.

April 27, 1914

My Dear Harriet,

I have been trying to find your last letter, so as to re-read it, and see if I could answer your many questions and grant your many requests. I don't believe I ever read just such a letter. . . .

Let me see! I believe you began your letter by asking if I had made your drawers. I had not then, but I got right to work and made you two "Teddy Bears" and "patched up" a pair of Ina's drawers for you. You see you haven't more than five weeks at best, and then you'll be at home and we'll see what you need. . . . Write me exactly how many gowns you have. . . .

Now about the shoes: Just have one pair fixed and wear them to school. I believe you said it would take 80 cents to have them fixed. Take them to the shop and I'll try to see papa about getting you the money to pay for them. . . .

I believe the next thing is your corset. You surely haven't worn it *completely* out, for I got it for you Christmas. If you can't "make out" until you come home, I'll try to get you one. . . .

Harriet, don't get an idea that I don't want you to have clothes. I just want you to learn to do on as few as possible—especially when you are growing so fast and when there is a prospect of you going to G.N.&I.C. this fall. Of course you'll need underclothes, but I don't want you to be buying material and trying to make your things, neglecting your lessons and worrying aunt Hattie to death.

After I send your bundle read this letter over and write me *exactly* what you'll need—not what you *want*. . . .

It is late & I'm real tired. I'm farming on a bigger scale than ever & I'm selling guano and weighing out meat, lard, sugar &c, just as usual. . . .

Did you remember this was papa's birthday?

> With a heart of love,
> Mother

To R. B. Russell, Jr., Athens, Ga.[1]

July 13, 1914

Dearest Boy,

I guess this must be your letter, as I promised you one in a "day or two." . . .

I was so glad to see Mamie yesterday. I wished for all of you to be with her.

Your letter came this A.M. Are you studying hard as you thought you would? Mamie horrified me by saying that you and Wm. hadn't been home a "single night" before 12 o'clock. This seems like too much for me—& it means that you cannot do much in study if you dissipate all night. Can't you get in a little fun & do more study? You know how disappointed papa is when you all don't seem to want to improve yourselves. And it hurts me too. You will get into careless habits so early in life & it will be awful hard to ever "buckle down" to anything.

Don't start an account at Sternes without asking papa. You don't *need* anything specially. . . .

The grapes are turning & every body's picking on them. Its a shame! I made a fine lot of jelly this morning. Thought I'd secure some of the grapes. . . .[2]

We have had some good rains now. Rob, Luther & I planted the two upper oat terraces in peas. I sowed them, & then the twins & I piled rocks. You know there are a *few* over there. . . .

Son, mother loves you so, & I'm always hoping & wanting you to do the *right* thing. Be gentle, be kind, be polite, be thoughtful of others, practice patience, & unselfishness. Remember that all these begin *at home*. Be nice to your sisters. Be thoughtful of Mamie. Just be an all round good boy, such as you know your mother wants you to be. . . .

  Heart of love,
  Mother

 1. Although R. B. graduated at Powder Springs in June, Ina and Richard considered his diploma inferior to a Gordon diploma. Thus he determined to go to Georgia and make up his Latin so that he could enter Gordon again in the fall and graduate in 1915. Mamie Quarterman rented a house in Athens for the summer so that William Henry, her son, could go to summer school, and R. B. was living with them.

 2. The property on which the new house was built in 1912 boasted a thriving vineyard of Concord grapes on the main road. Neighbors, passersby, and others stopped and helped themselves to the crop.

To Miss Marguerite Russell, Milledgeville, Ga.

            October 18, 1914

My Dearest Margo,

 . . . I think of you & H[arriet]. so often and can see you in my "mind's eye" in Room 27 at G.N.&I.C.

 I know you enjoyed Bill's visit and the ride & nice lunch &c. Harriet wrote me a long nice letter telling me all about it.[1]

I told you in one letter that I had something interesting to tell you about our school. Well, Ina is going to teach it & she begins first Monday in November. Miss Pearl has a place in the Winder schools.

Ina is having a little house party this week with Susie Perkins & Miriam Haselton. We told them before they came that there would be no boys. R. B. seems to enjoy them & they seem to like him. I don't know what they will do the next few days for amusement. It seems "funny" to have girls here this time of year.

You will be surprised when I tell you that I am renting two of our upstairs rooms. The ones over kitchen & dining room. Cousin Lila & Gussie came back to Alice's to live & it seemed they could not be happy to-gether. Cousin L. tried to get rooms in Winder & I just happened to think that my two rooms were "just the thing" and I could do without them. She pays me $6.00 per month and they seem so happy and contented. They have an oil stove & do their own house keeping. We didn't have much trouble moving out & I am real glad to have Cousin L. & G. in the house. They are nice, quiet, & refined. Gussie has adopted me for her mother and I call her my daughter. She seems very happy to be here & is no trouble & never gets in the way.[2]

Mr. Walter Brown came out last Sat. night & brought his big basket full of good things. Aunt Ruby, Mrs. Riviere, was here too. She went home Sunday aft. Uncle John & Aunt Addie have made us a little visit, too. We are constantly talking about the war & hard times. . . .

My eyes are heavy and . . . I must kiss you good night & you must kiss H. for me. I think of you girls so much & hope you are practising the kind & gentle arts day by day. If the time has not come, it *will* come some day, when you will need to know the art & power of loving kindness & tender mercies.

I haven't ½ finished my letter but must close. Heart of love to you & H.
      Mother

1. Bill was teaching domestic science in Sandersville, Georgia.
2. Gussie was grown, but a head injury in childhood had left her mentally retarded.

To Misses Russell, Milledgeville, Ga.

October 25, 1914

Dearest Girls,

I have been wanting to write . . . of Ina's house party, so as to let you girls know how things have passed off. You must promise me that you will not let anything I tell make you blue or regret too much that you were not here. "Can't have your pudding & eat it too," so you must be happy in remembering *your own* happy times & rejoice that Ina has had a successful houseparty. . . .

To begin with I must say that I was filled with fear & trembling over this occasion. As I wrote some of you: A houseparty & not a boy in sight! Enough to strike terror to my heart, for I dread *disconsolate, mopey* girls & I feared my fate. Ina assured me that neither Susie or Miriam cared for boys, so I tried to look on the bright side.

Ina began her houseparty by meeting Sue in Atlanta (Minerva couldn't come) and going to the football game. They came in that night lively as crickets & reported a grand time. R. B. had been very *funny* it seemed & had "cut up" much. As they expected Miriam on "our train" they were up early to meet her. How we watched for the train! It didn't come however, for all our watching & about 10 o'clock we learned there was a wreck & the train would not come until sometime in the afternoon. Well, that sometime was four o'clock and Miriam finally got here. The girls retired early Sunday night, & were up tolerably early Monday morning. I had my eyes open to see what entertainment they would find. They played & danced, played setback, & then after dinner went to Winder in surry to say hallo to Mamie & Auntney. They came back, joyous & happy & said Uncle Lewis was coming out to take them to ride [in his automobile]. Well, this was not bad, & I was glad they had something to look forward too. They went to ride & of course enjoyed it. So far, so good and I wondered what Tuesday would bring forth.

They began the day as usual, after late breakfast, and R. B. still "cutting up" and the mail coming in, was some diversion. About 2 o'clock the 'phone rang. Some one, guess who—wanted to know who those girls were that Ina had riding with her yesterday in Winder. You know, I could hardly believe it was "Jimmie" G. and [he] wanted to come out that night & bring

Ralph & Hank. Of all things! Well, of course they came & you know what that means. R. B. suggested a candy pulling & you should have seen how the idea caught. . . . Laura had every thing ready for the *pulling*. The candy was soon on, and O, how I wished for my absent girls to enjoy the fun. I got out my three cook aprons for the girls & then a search began for aprons for the boys. You remember the pink apron Mary Willie gave Ina. Well, Ralph wore that and Hank wore another pink one that Ina had made and Jimmie wore one of those first white aprons made for Margo to take to G.N.I.C. & R. B. pinned a handkerchief on. Look at Jimmie in that apron! It fitted in front, but was pinned way out on his blade bones in the back. It took the candy a long time to cook & everybody had a turn at stirring. Hank & Miriam pulled together, Sue & Jimmie—Ina & Ralph. Papa came in that night on the late train and after he came, at 12:15, Jimmie suggested that it was "time to go." . . .

Thus the third day passed off gloriously. . . . Friday night they have planned a Hallowe'en party. Sue leaves Saturday. Ina goes to Atlanta with her. Guess Miriam will leave on the train. Then the houseparty will be over & Ina begins her school Monday A.M.

I'll send this on to one of you & then you send it on to the next one. Guess I'll send to Bill first. . . .

I must close now & see after my night work. . . .

      Heart of love,
      Mother

Monday A.M.:
Ralph, Warren & Jimmie called last night. They sat on the porch & the cigarette smoke made me sick. So disgusting for boys to smoke when talking to girls. . . .

To R. B. Russell, Jr., Barnesville, Ga.[1]

                                       Jan. 8, 1915

Dearest Boy,

I regret so much that I have not sent your gloves. I'm sending them to-day. I tried to wash them, but they don't seem much white.

I haven't had a cook since Monday night. Laura & Hattie both afflicted,

I guess. Laura has rheumatism & Hattie do-nothing-ism. . . . Walter has had an awful swollen jaw from a tooth, so the twins & myself see after our beautiful stock.

Ina has 23 pupils & she seems interested & happy and is sweet as can be, even if she is "at home with her mother." I'm sorry you left those farewell words with her, but I do believe she will *rise above* them, and make the *best* of her surroundings.

I don't know anything about your arrangements for board, but it seems if you share Fred's room, you & he both ought to come out cheaper. Let me know how you are situated. . . .

I'm sending 4 cents. Use it in writing to Miss Hettie & *be sure* to write Auntney a short note or a nice long letter would be better, & tell her how sorry you are or were, that you could not be with her New Year's night. Do both of these & let me *know.* I want to feel satisfied about it.

I hope you are well-fixed in every way and will do well in all things. I've tried not to worry *any* over you big children, but I love you all so much, I just *have* to cling to my high ideal that I've cherished so long for you.

The children are making such a racket. I must close & get this in the mail this afternoon. . . .

> Heart of love,
> Mother

1. R. B. was back at Gordon to earn a second diploma in order to get into law school at the University of Georgia.

To Miss Marguerite Russell, Milledgeville, Ga.

Jan. 22, 1915

Dearest Margo,

I have finished your four *covers,* and have them all fixed up, ready to send with this letter. I do hope they will fit to a "t" and will give you comfort and pleasure. When you need anything in the way of clothes don't hesitate for a moment to write and ask me to make what you want and need. . . . If Harriet needs any under garments tell her to let me know.

I *enclose* a small piece of fruit cake. You and Harriet get by yourselves and enjoy it. . . .

I want you and Harriet to study every day how to be smart, good sensible girls. There seems to be so much foolishness among young girls. They are so sweet and pretty, and mothers and friends are crazy about them, but somehow they will cultivate little foolish fancies and ideas, that takes so much of their time and hinders them from improving in goodness as they should. I have no special reason for writing this way. Only my desire for my girls to be as near perfect as possible. You are mighty sweet anyhow and a good girl, I think—but I just want you so good.

Don't worry over your story not being taken for the Magazine. I'll bet it was just as good as some that were taken. Don't be discouraged when your plans don't "pan" out. Just keep trying and you will "pan" out O.K. I laughed good over your poultry experiences. It seems so funny to me. Auntney laughed good over your letter. She was out yesterday—walked out—and I gave her yours and Harriets letters to read. . . .

Ina seems to be doing beautifully with her school. She doesn't grumble or complain one bit, and if it doesn't give her pleasure, she doesn't say so. I am so happy over her attitude. She is just lovely and I enjoy her so much. She helps the children at home and seems to take an interest in it all. Two of her little first graders have come to take dinner with her. One came to-day. Another asked to come but she told them she'd have to take them one at a time. Rudez came to-day. . . . Rastus Rudez Sellers. Isn't that a name? They have a speaking this afternoon. The children came all dressed up. Ina changed her dress. She looked sweet and pretty. . . .

Cootie is here playing with my ink. She is so pretty & smart. I enjoy her so much. I really believe I enjoy *all* my children.

Give Harriet a lot of love and tell her I enjoyed her letter. The writing was nice and the whole thing was better than I ever saw her do.

Heart of love from Mother

To Miss Marguerite Russell, Milledgeville, Ga

March 8, 1915

My Dearest Child,

I am *so* sorry you felt so badly over my letter and I am *so* sorry I did not wait a day or two longer to send the reports. Then, maybe, I would have written differently and you would have understood better. I *did* say that I liked your reports—read the letter over and see. I should *not* have mentioned Dad's name, but it just came into my mind & I did. He did not "rare" one bit. He did seem pleased over the report, but did regret that you did not take Latin. I wrote you I had been sick and was still sick, and only hurried those reports on for I knew you were *so* anxious to see them. And then you could *not* read enough *love* between the lines, and you just *had* to write that letter so full of bad feelings towards me and Daddy. It did not sound one bit like the sweet letter you wrote Dad last week. . . .

I [have] been real sick to-day. It seems that I am on the verge of *something* unusual for me. I have such headaches sometimes. Was lying down when the mail came & did not read your letter or any of the mail in an hour or more. Your letter made me feel very sad, for I did not intend to "put a damper" on your feelings. I'm sorry I wrote. You have done well at school. Daddy or myself have never found any fault with you. . . .

Try to cultivate *calm, patient* feelings. When you read your letters and when you think your thoughts wear your good, happy glasses that see things as *they are* and not as they *seem.* Mother knows you are hard worked but that is the *making of us.* How we wear out faster, doing nothing. . . . Try to rest all you can. Have your lemons all gone? I'll see if Ina can make you & H some doughnuts soon. Drink water, if you have good water and *don't* worry. Get to feeling good and read my letter over, and see if it sounds so bad. When I realize how much I love you children, I don't see how *any* of you could ever see *anything* but the fondest love in what I say and do. Tell H. I'll write to her soon. Hope you both will keep well. . . .

> With fondest love,
> Mother

To R. B. Russell, Jr., Barnesville, Ga.

March 9, 1915

My Dearest Boy,

Your nice long letter came yesterday morning. Also the filling from your tooth. When it rolled from the letter, I thought it was a bomb, and I handled it very cautiously until I found out what it was. I'm awfully sorry about the filling. Robert is in a peck of trouble about his teeth and I've promised that he can have his fixed right away. Wish you two could come the same time. I can't do anything until I see papa. Is Monday your best day to come? I think papa will buy a ticket to-morrow (the 10th). He said yesterday morning when he left that he would come home Wednesday night. . . .

Papa went to Oglethorpe and moved Ann Pharr and Dot to Russell. They live in the Bone house. Ann "bucked" about going over there.[1] Papa finally used a little *strong language* and she seems better satisfied. She wanted a house on the "big road" like Mrs. Glenn [Laura]. Papa has put them under Zack Moores[2] care and I think he must have been a chain gang boss in his day and time, for he seems to know how to work them. . . .

Hope you are well.

  With a heart of love,

  Your fond Mother

1. Dot and Ann were black laborers. The Bones, who were white, had moved, but "the Bone house" was far off any road, among fields and woods.

2. Unidentified—possibly a white tenant farmer.

To Miss Marguerite Russell, Milledgeville, Ga.

March 18, 1915

My Dearest Margo,

You will have to take a pencil letter this time. I just don't feel like pen and ink, for the children come around and try to play with the ink. . . .

We all feel so heartsick about Laura.[1] She has been such a comfort to me for four years and I feel that she came just in time to almost save me.

Laura hadn't been as well as she usually was for several months, but since her last bad spell, she had seemed very well, and I've never known her so kind and thoughtful, and she seemed to enjoy everything so much about the house and yard and everything about you children! She cooked supper last Wednesday night, Mar 10th, and I knew from the way she talked she was not feeling very well. Thursday morning she sent Eunice to make the fire and to tell me that she was sick and couldn't come. I was so busy all day and didn't get over to see her—Hattie had some things she was trying to get washed and ironed for me to take [on] my trip, so she didn't come to cook. Laura sent me word Thursday night that she or Hattie should "be over in the morning," but when morning came, she sent Eunice to say she was "not so well."

About 10:30 Hattie came over and said Laura wanted the doctor. I phoned for him and he came right out. He examined Laura and left a lot of medicine—Laura told him to get her well, that I wanted to take a trip and she had to take care of her "chilluns." Dr. A[lmond] told her all right, that she would be in the kitchen "*to-morrow*," but when "*to-morrow*" came poor Laura was put in her grave—she died before Dr. A got back to Winder.

She was sitting up when the doctor came and when he left, she told Hattie she had to "cough again" and to come hold her head. She coughed and had a hemorrhage—I think she [burst] a blood vessel, and died. Ellen was there, and she ran over and asked for camphor, that she believed cook was dead. I gave her the camphor and followed as quickly as possible with some whiskey—but when I reached the house, she was dead. I felt so terrible about it and rubbed her wrists and temples, but the man who had run in to put her on the bed kept telling me she was dead. Poor Hattie was in terrible distress of course, but she conducted herself well and kept her presence of mind.

We sent word around and Laura's colored friends came in to fix her for burial. When Laura died her clothes and her bedding were so nice and clean. You know how neat she always went. We had her best under clothes put on her—some I had made—and we put white on her—white stockings and white gloves, and Ina made a little white cap, of lace that Laura had washed for me. It was nice and Ina put it on her. I 'phoned papa at once and he notified her son and sister who live in Atlanta. Papa bought a nice coffin for Laura and a colored friend paid for the grave and two buggies from the livery stable. Ina made a beautiful cross of evergreen and jonquils and several other designs were sent in by colored friends.

Sister Annie, myself and all the children except Ina & Cootie went to the funeral. I felt so grieved to see my good, faithful friend put in the ground. I could not do anything but weep, and I did weep. You know how good Laura has been to all of you—especially to our little children and we were a sorrowful crowd. When I go in the kitchen now I can see Laura in everything. I was hunting some sacks yesterday and I found them right where Laura had put them. Laura came to me at a time in my life when I needed help so much. My 14th child was just a baby, and I felt that she was a Godsend—and I believe so yet and appreciate her that way. She studied my likes and dislikes and tried to please me in all things. More than all I loved her for getting papa a nice hot breakfast before he would leave for Atlanta and in the winter time the train came so early. Can't you hear her calling now for "Judge" to come and eat?

Hattie is cooking—she says she is going to stay with me. She is a good cook and is nice and clean and so good to the children. Eunice takes care of Elizabeth while Hattie cooks. . . . I know I have suffered a terrible loss, but I try to make the best of it. I expected to go to Knoxville Tenn. with papa, but I just couldn't go after Laura died. Papa would hardly let me off, but I felt that I would not be happy at all. I've had neuralgia so bad, it's a good thing I did not go. . . .

Let Harriet read this letter. I owe her one and this should be to you both, so let it be. . . .

> With a heart *full* of love for my two sweet girls,
> Your Mother

1. Ina had sent postcards to all the children away from home to tell them about Laura's death the previous day.

To Miss Harriet Russell, Milledgeville, Ga.

March 28, 1915

My Dearest Harriet,

I've been wanting to write you a letter all by yourself for ever so long. Time flies so fast and I have so much to do that I find it so hard to write just when I want to. I think about you girls so much. I lie awake at night and wonder how you are. I'm always hoping you are well and happy and that you are trying to be bright and cheerful and helpful with those around you. School girls have a good opportunity to do a great deal of good, and I do want my girls and boys to study the art and practice it of being kind and considerate with those you are thrown with most constantly. Its hard sometimes, I know, for we say certain ones "peeve" us, or get on our nerves &c. Maybe we are the same to some one else, and maybe they are kind to us. I do want my girls nice and sweet and I want them to learn not to give 'way to thoughts and actions that are not in keeping with their precious souls and bodies. . . .

I don't want you to have much sewing to do. Your eyes are not very strong, from what you say, and until you finish school, I don't want you to use them too much on tedious sewing. . . .

Aunt Hattie had a bad spell not long ago—you should write to her occasionally. Did you get Pipey's letter? She said she sent you some stamps. Poor, dear Pipey! She works real hard. She is not looking well to me.

Walter and Patience have learned to skate so well. They can fly around the front porch. I can't stand the noise sometimes.

Hattie is cooking for me. She is a good servant and tries hard to do everything just right, but I miss my good, old Laura. Hattie made the tea cakes I sent you and Margo. . . .

This makes my fourth letter to-day and I want to write another before I go to bed. Write and tell me how you are and tell me all about every thing. . . .

> With a heart full of love for my child and a heart felt wish that she is very good and sweet.
>
> Mother

To Miss Marguerite Russell, Milledgeville, Ga.

March 28, 1915

My Dearest Margo,

Here goes my fifth letter to-day and as its late and I'm tired and sleepy too, I feel like singing a short metre tune and being dismissed. But I have thought of you girls so much. My Margo and my Harriet and I love you so much! I can't bear to think of you being disagreeable with each other. You are too sweet to do that way. O, I have the highest ideals for my girls. You will have these things to meet all through life—even if you are married to a man whom you dearly love and honor and strive to obey,—and the more *love* you cultivate in your heart and the more you strive to control yourself while young, the sooner and easier you can meet and overcome greater difficulties later on. I want my children kind to each other. I know a sister now, whose body is weak, and her purse *empty,* who left her sister's house because she was so unkind to her—and she went away off, and is trying to find work to do. Learn to be kind and to see things as they are. Practice the Golden Rule.

I don't blame either of you so much, for I know both just "flew off" and didn't think—but don't do it any more and study to avoid these things.

I'm in a fix about the gown. Harriet seems to want to work it so bad and you know I wrote and said we were willing for her to work *one* garment. I haven't been to Atlanta yet to get it. See if you can't decide to feel good, and let her work it. You know how hot headed Harriet is. She is young, and *you,* my Margo, a dignified senior.

Now let H. work the gown and you not care what her motif is. I hope you are both feeling sweet with each other. Life is too short to cherish these disagreeable things. We can forgive and dismiss them from our minds if we *Love* enough. Sisters and brothers are so *near.* They are our own flesh and blood. We should love them first and last and all times. Try to see all the good you can in them and try to help them overcome the bad. Let me hear from you and let H. work the gown. . . .

> Your fond & loving
> Mother

To Miss Marguerite Russell, Milledgeville, Ga

April 11, 1896-April 11, 1915

My Dearest Margo,

The 11th of April has come again. Another year of your life has passed. My third little baby child is a big girl now—almost grown—and nearly ready to graduate. Now all this means a great deal. You must have a place to fill or you would not have been sent into the world. You have been a fortunate girl, I think, born with a good little body, a *fair* amount of good looks, and a bright mind. Also, you found a fine father and a loving mother waiting to receive you with out-stretched arms—and two sweet sisters for your good companions.

You are nearly ready to begin life sure enough now, and in a few years you will begin to realize what you have done in the past years that is a benefit to you and what has been to your disadvantage. I can see so clearly *now* what I wish I *had* done, and what I wish I had *not* done.

Cultivate a good understanding of things, and always follow your best thoughts and feelings—practice love and kindness, and you will have less to regret when you are older. The better we train our minds, the better we train our hearts. I've known since you were ten months old that there was a great deal of good in you. When you were ten months old, you crawled to the washstand, opened the door and began to pull at something near the bottom. The washstand was divided into two parts and I kept bottles, medicine etc on the top shelf. When you began to pull, something on the top began to *fall over*. You immediately put up your other little hand and held it back, but kept pulling until you got what you wanted.

Papa and I have been talking about you to-day. Papa says he hasn't forsaken you, he has just been too busy to write.

I hope the box reached you yesterday. I wanted you to have your things to "eat on" to-day. Hattie wants you to know that *she* made those nice little biscuit. Mrs. Perry made your cake. Patience made doughnuts and candy. Pipey boiled the tongue, and I really don't think it good done. She is awful sorry and I am too. . . .

Poor Ina had one of her bad spells and couldn't teach the last three days of school. Pipey taught for her. She had planned a little party for the close of school and it was in progress the whole of Friday afternoon, and I was fixing your box in the morning and busy with it until about 2:30, and the party began at 3:30. Ina said several times she wished she could have made something for the box. Ina has had a very successful term. She made *a good* teacher and the children are crazy about her. Her little bank book looks mighty nice too, and its a good feeling to be able to write your own checks. I want her to teach the school again next year. She is not able to get out and *battle with the world*. I just wish we could finish our brick building—get up about seventy-five pupils and you and Ina teach. My! but wouldn't I be glad to have my girls at home! . . .

I must close and write to R. B. I've written more now than you will read—eh? . . .

> With a heart *full* of love
> Mother

To Marguerite Russell, Milledgeville, Ga.

May 7, 1915

Dearest Margo,

Your letter rec'd this A.M. I'll hurry you a short reply, in order for you to receive permit to visit Mrs. B. Take care that you are feeling well, so you'll have a sweet *look* on you, or they may think you have a grouchy disposition. . . .

Marguerite, I do hope you are cautious about the way you act these last few days at G.N.&I.C. Don't be influenced by any one, but use good judgement on all occasions. The boy or *man* who sends the flowers, I do *not* like that one bit. If certain nice people in M'ville like you, what do they think to see you carrying on with a man violating the rules of your college as well as acting foolish and silly. You say you are careful. I just hope you are *sensible.* It is nice to be *noticed,* but its much better to have a perfectly *good* reputation. Mind what I've told you about C having an influence over you. I do not think she has as much at stake, as far as reputation is concerned, as you have. I expect you are mad at me now, but you'll see it all some day just as I do now. It's mighty bad to do things for pleasure *now* that we'll regret by and by. I regret every day that I have not been more firm and strict with my children. I have a great desire to let you all do as you please, but I do believe that *Mrs. Hills* method is better than mine. I *know* you are mad now—but I may learn to speak out yet, and let my girls *know* that I *know* what is best for them, whether I carry my point or not. . . .

Much love,
Mother

To Miss Harriet Russell, Milledgeville, Ga.

Sunday night, Sep. 19, 1915

My Dear Harriet,

I was very sorry indeed to get such a miserable letter from you. I was sorry for a good many things in it, but more than all I regretted the way in which you referred to Mary Willie. She asked you if you were willing to room in Atkinson Hall. You said you didn't know and then finally came back and told her you were willing and then she sent off the check for your admittance. You know I am helpless to a great extent about such matters. I *might* have my way more, if I *insisted* on it, but some how, I don't seem to know what is best for some of you.

I showed your letter to papa when he came home this morning. Neither of us wanted you to go back to G.N.&I.C. much, but just didn't know what else to do, I guess. Papa said several things he might do. I'll wait for him to write. In the meantime, can't you compose yourself, and adjust yourself to your surroundings and try to make the best of things? Always remember *one* thing: If it had not been for certain things that papa and myself both *saw* when we were at G.N.&I.C. Commencement, none of this would have happened and we would have no doubts in our mind as to what would be best for our child. You would have been in Terrell 27, right now, if these things had not happened. I am sorry for it all. I do want my children comfortable and happy. I want them to live conscientious and be willing to abide by the school laws, and to observe the laws of good behavior.

Just try to calm yourself. Write papa and tell him all these things and tell him, that is, if you think you can't stay in Atkinson, if he will put you back in Terrell, you'll try to be good and not behave in any way to make him sorry, &c. I don't know that this is necessary. I just suggest it.

As I said, I am so sorry you are so miserable. Don't blame your sister so much. I know she meant nothing but love & kindness. . . . Write me again and write to papa. We may not be *seeming* to be doing our best, but I believe we are. . . .

Ralph [Sharpton] and Margo are out in the swing. Ina has not come home.

Hattie is sick in bed and I am melting in the kitchen. The boys are still picking cotton.

It's late and I must close. I'd love to know that you were happier than you were when you wrote the letter I received a few days ago. . . .

Your fond Mother

To Mr. R. B. Russell, Jr., Athens, Ga.

Nov. 1st, 1915

My Dearest Boy,

I have been so busy all day, trying to fix you a birthday box and trying to see after my corn that Dot and Zack were gathering. Monday was a bad day to buy bread for your sandwiches, but I finally got some and to-night after supper, Ina and Margo helped me fix some nice sandwiches (I think) and I hope so much I can get your box off on the ten o'clock train. I hope you will enjoy your eats.

I've thought of you so much to-day. When I think of you *specially*, I always recall the time when we went to the mountains to-gether and you were my own darling, *little* boy, and seemed to love me so much, and nearly always seemed to think that what *I* did was just right, and you loved to follow along every where I went, and seemed satisfied to be with me. Dick often reminds me of you. I love you now just as I loved you then. I love to think of the time when you called me "Dear." There never was a sweeter *little* boy than R. B. Russell, Jr.

Sometimes I'm almost made to believe that you don't love me very much now—something is always wrong, some how—but I just will not dwell on it, for I couldn't stand it. I'll try to think that you do, any how.

I do hope you are well and happy on your birthday. Try not to think about your self so much. Some things may seem pretty hard some times, but try to be patient and try to find a *little* pleasure in *something*, even if you do not have all you want. I believe you have more to be thankful for than you realize. Make a joke out of some of your distresses and see how quickly they will disappear.

We reached home safely Sat. night and without any breakdown. About five miles from Athens we passed a buggy smashed all to pieces, an auto turned over, a man and a dead mule by the side of the road and several people and vehicles standing around. Walter Stanton tried to fly home, but we held him back some—Made the distance[1] in one hour and ten min. . . .

I am so tired and sleepy I can't write much to-night. I just wish I *could* write you a real good letter, and help you to see things a little different from what you seem to see them. The last times I saw you, you seemed all wrong some how. I was so glad to see you. I would enjoy just standing off and looking at you. You are my boy, you know, and I *do not* agree with the Prof who wrote the piece you gave me to read—but I'm afraid you do. I would love to see you happy and enjoy *something,* just *anything.* If you are really miserable, I guess I ought to regret that you were ever born, but I'm selfish enough to be glad and to be proud of the fact that I am your mother.

So you see, I have something very happy to remember to-morrow. I will be thinking of you all day, and as I said: I will still be proud that you are my boy. . . .

Write me sometimes. Be happy, be *kind,* be *considerate* to those around you. Follow the Golden Rule.

We all send hearts of love and many wishes for a happy birthday.

    Your fond Mother

1. From Athens to Russell—eighteen miles.

To Mr. R. B. Russell, Jr., Athens, Ga.

Dec. 1st, 1915

My Dearest Boy,

It is late and I am very tired, but I've planned all day to write to you, so I'll do it any how. I had my pig killed yesterday. He weighed 208, and my meat is *good* and *beautiful.* Sam Manders came last night and persuaded papa to buy a hog from him at 11 cents. Papa thought the price was all right and I did too. Sam brought the hog to-day and it weighed 293 pounds. It looked as big as a cow on the wagon. Just think! I have four hams, four shoulders and so much good rib, backbone &c—and I expect to have a lot of sausage.

Hat has not "shown her smiling face," so I'm still in the kitchen. She went to Atlanta last night and sent me word she would "be on the job" Monday morning. So you see, I will not get to Atlanta this week. Margo intends going in the morning and she will get your pajamas. I'm afraid the 98 cents ones will soon be gone. I will see about the shirts as soon as possible. . . .

We enjoyed your little visit home, and I do hope you have a sweater for the weather has been very cold. I want you to have an over coat so bad. . . . Ina began her little school Monday morning. She has fourteen, I think. Margo wants to begin hers Monday.

Zack, Charley and Dot have been sowing . . . oats to-day. Dot and Charley came Sunday night and brought eight rabbits. I wished for you to have some. They were so good. I'd like to send Dot once a week. He says he killed twenty rabbits while in Oglethorpe.

I have been so busy to-day seeing after my meat. Pipey and I made 6 gals. lard from my pig. We will make up the other to-morrow and ought to get nearly twice as much. We will have grand sausage for Christmas.

Hope your cold is better. I don't like to hear you cough. Take care of yourself . . . .

Your devoted Mother

To Robert Lee Russell, Monroe, Georgia

Jan. 11, 1916

My Dearest Robert,

Your dear sweet letter came this morning. I enjoyed it so much, but I was so sorry I had not let you hear from home more, for I knew you were anxious to hear from R. B. I am glad you remembered what I said. I told Bill and Harriette the same thing, and I've written them only one postal card—just as I did you.

I've been thinking of you a great deal and have wanted to write just to tell you what a comfort you were to me Christmas. I did know you could be so sweet, kind and thoughtful. It was a trying time with us all and it does me good—makes me happy, when I remember how patient and considerate you were. I was so worried about R. B. and you know I was not well my self, and I appreciated the way all my children behaved. It made it easier for me.

R. B. is much better than when you left, but he improves so slowly and I find myself feeling very impatient. He is so weak. Can hardly walk from bed to the chair we have for him by the fire and I or Miss Dovie has to support him. He complains a great deal. I feel so sorry for him. He eats very little food. I've been wishing for his appetite to come back *strong* so he could get strong. His frat brothers sent him a box of beautiful pink carnations—and several of them have written. He regrets so much to miss so much from his law. I don't think he can go back in a long time. . . .[1]

Guess what? The other day a new five passenger Buick came up our pike and went to Pipeys. Cousin Mary Hawkins, Mr. Hawkins, young Thad, James and Lizzie Hattie. The car was Cousin Mary's Christmas gift from Mr. Hawkins. Some nice gift, eh? . . .

I worry about your clothes. I think you ought to wear some winter garments. Please son, let me know if you feel the need of more clothes. Don't run any risk about taking cold. . . .

Hope you will "pull through" all those exams O.K. and send in a good report to Bill, to papa and to me. Write when you can. I have missed you so much.

Your fond, loving Mother

1. R. B. was suffering with pneumonia, and nearly died on Christmas Day. He seemed stronger on December 27, so Dr. Almond recommended a full-time nurse from the Atlanta Registered Nurses' Club. Miss Dovie's records describe a racking illness: The boy coughed blood and phlegm, and vomited his food. Pains in his chest and sides left him in agony.

To Miss Harriette Russell, Milledgeville, Ga.

Feb. 9, 1916

My Dear Harriette,

I have been wanting to write you a big fat letter every day, since Mrs. Cook wrote me about your chicken-pox. I have been so sorry for you. I knew you were well cared for and all that, but I was sorry you had a contagious disease. I hope . . . you can soon be back in school. I never dreamed of you taking chicken-pox from the children here at home. I thought they had been well too long and I felt sure you had had it long ago. I hope you will not have whooping cough now. I am constantly expecting the children here to get it. I am sorry about your finals too. It seems to me they would let you stand the exams in your room. . . . I'm anxious to know if you were broken out much and do hope you did not pick the places on your face. Fielding did not take it at all. I . . . don't want him laid up some day, away from home as you are now. . . . Write soon . . . and tell me all about yourself.

R. B. is still improving—so the doctor says. I can see very little difference in the last ten days. He has had an awful abscess right where his leg joins his body. He complains of something all the time. He sits up just a little every day. Miss Dovie still here. . . .

I must stop now and see after Carolyn. She is too busy these days. Gets into everything. Good old Dick is asleep. It was raining so I knew they could not go out and they make so much noise when they are shut in—so I got Dick to sleep, but couldn't do anything with "Cootie." . . .

Heart of love,

Mother

To Miss Mary Willie Russell, [Roanoke Institute,] Danville, Va.

Feb. 10, 1916

My Dearest Bill,

Your letter came this morning. R. B. is asleep now, and he is not so particular about me being in the room all the time as he was sometime ago. Miss Dovie or myself are always with him. Just think! Miss Dovie has been here nearly seven weeks. And I'm afraid she will have to be here eight, or maybe nine. R. B. is very much better in some respects. He does not have much fever now. His appetite is right good. He is looking much better in the face. His four limbs are nothing but skin and bones. He developed another abcess about three inches from the first one. It was lanced last Saturday. We keep warm poultices on it continually and it runs continually. My little oil stove never goes out, for the poultices must be kept warm. I don't see how I could do anything without our stove. R. B. coughs two or three hours and it makes him very weak and nervous. We try to make him walk and he does try, and takes one or two steps with his arms around Miss D's neck and she holding to him. It is so pitiful. One thing worries me so—I'll tell you—but *do not* mention it in your letter for he reads them sometimes—but his left leg is stiff and bent at the knee and I have an awful sickening, terrible feeling that his leg may never be straight again. Dr. A examined it this morning. He and Miss Dovie say that he must exercise it and try to straighten it anyhow. But it hurts so bad he dreads to do any of these things. We are going to begin to-day, have begun already—to see that he tries harder every day. Miss Dovie has been a great blessing—She is a good woman, with a good heart and a strong mind—and a world of energy. She is a blessing to the world. No foolishness about her. She seems to live for her profession. R. B. has been awful hard to nurse and she has been so good and patient.

. . . I've been kicked down so much lately that I felt that I could never rise again but some how I manage to get up and begin again. If I didn't have Carolyn and Dick to work with and the other children to see after and Margo to get off to school, her lunch to fix, and I try to save something good for her & Fielding to eat when they come home. It is right pathetic to see her leave in the mornings with old poky Maud and the ugly old buggy and then come back in the afternoons. Sometimes its rainy & cold—but maybe it will be the making of her or will help her to be more capable of meeting the trials of life later on. She seems very much interested in her teaching. She is a splendid teacher—so faithful and conscientious. I'd like to see her in a good graded school. I'll tell you some of her funny experiences before I finish my letter.

Poor old Ina still mopes and groans over her school—wishes she did not have to teach another day. It is awful to teach & feel as she does. She is enthused over her chickens now. Has hatched out 17 in the incubator. They are out in the yard in the Border, and Ina . . . has not shown any degree of being tired of them. I bless those chickens in my heart every day for giving Ina pleasure. . . . My rule has always been to *try* to find *some* pleasure in everything you do. I have preached it to Ina about her teaching but she never seemed to enjoy anything about it.

Ina & Margo went to a dance Monday night at Mrs. Cronics. Ina danced with the man Baxter who painted our house. Lee McElhannon, one of Ina's big boys came by and went with them to the dance—Walter & Patience went too. It seems that Lee is very much impressed with Marguerites beauty, and yesterday he told William that he was coming Sunday *"to haul"* Marguerite in his buggy. Last night at supper we ragged the poor child to death about this. Lee said they were having their surry *"cut down"* for a buggy and that is what he will "haul" Margo in. Margo wrote you about two of her scholars calling Sunday afternoon. They wanted to come back the next Sunday but she put them off some way.

This morning I read a piece in the paper about a girl in Kansas [who] gave up her school because sixteen of her pupils had proposed to her—when they raised their hands in school she was afraid they wanted to propose. I have the piece for Margo to read when she comes home.

Rob came home Sat. He is so sweet and precious. I never saw such a change in a boy. He was so lovely Christmas. I know he is doing better because you are helping him. I do hate for you to do it. It is awful good of you. Papa seems to be so hard run all the time. I can't see why unless it is because he tries to do so much outside. I begged him six years ago to stop everything but trying to educate his children. He didn't see things my way. He is so blue all the time. It nearly kills me. I feel that I'm to blame some way. He can't decide what to do about running for Congress. He hates his Court work so much I wish he had something else to do.

Rob went back Monday. I did hate to see him leave. I wish Rob could go to Tech next year or this fall, I mean. He must go on through. He is smart enough to learn anything. I wish you could get the place in Atlanta. Maybe you could help Rob more if you were near him. I don't mean financially. I almost rebel when I realize that every month you take ten of your hard earned dollars and pay them out for Rob—but for his sake, I try to forget it. I felt desperate last fall when papa said he was not going to send Rob back to school.[1]

I have written a long letter and I think R. B. is still asleep. I hope so, anyway. . . .

Aunt Hattie wrote that she had sent you some flowers. I was so glad. . . . Write soon.

>   Your devoted Mother

1. Mary Willie had paid Rob's tuition ever since her first job in Sandersville.

To Mr. Robt. L. Russell, Monroe, Ga.

>   March 22, 1916

My Dearest Rob,

It is late and I am *awful* sleepy and tired, but I will write you a short letter. I enjoyed your letter a few days ago. I had been so anxious to hear about the debate. I am glad you hold second place, but boy, study up, and practice up. You must not let Madison or Sparta down you. I want to go to Athens to hear you. Go off in the woods—have the trees for your audience, and speak your speech until you have it *pat*.

We are moving along about as usual. I am afraid every night the lights are going out, and I think of *you* and wish you were here to see after them. Hattie is sick in bed yet. This makes my second week cooking. I have a *fast* time every morning getting Margo off and fixing her lunch and then getting the others off. But I *do* it and that is all we want.

R. B. went to Athens Sat. He went over for his trunk. Some of the professors wanted him to come back in the fall and review and go on with his class. He is not able to go back I don't think. He is complaining some tonight. The wind has been blowing so hard. He tries to take exercise—cuts wood and walks. He rides some with uncle Ben.

Ina sold one of her chickens yesterday for 20¢. She has taken off another incubator full.

Papa is in Homer, Banks Co. He seems to be running [for Congress], but has not announced. . . .

Boy, I am too tired and sleepy to write any more. Take care of your self and keep well. . . .

Your loving, fond Mother

To Mr. R. B. Russell, Jr., Seabreeze, Fla.

March 31, 1916

My Dearest Boy,

I just must write you a line or two, and tell you what I did yesterday after you left. *Immediately* after you left, I got very busy, for I felt *very miserable,* and I might say I was happy too, for I had wanted you to go to Fla. *so much,* and I was so glad to know that you were really "on your way." But I was miserable to a certain extent, fearing that something might happen to you and then I just felt so bad, and so tired, and I felt like crying, or something of the kind. Well, . . . I got busy, for work is my salvation when it comes to diverting my mind. . . .

I am busy planting corn and trying to get my canna bulbs out. Just think! You are in the "Land of Flowers." How I would love to be with you! I must say good-bye, and get to work. I just felt like talking to you a little. Write me long, descriptive letters. Tell me everything and anything.

Mother

To R. B. Russell, Jr., Seabreeze, Fla.

April 10, 1916

My Dearest Boy,

It is so cold here that I have to sit right in the fire to keep warm. So that means, I will use a pencil.

We got back from our . . . most delightful trip Friday morning. I enjoyed our stay in Blairsville so much. Found Etta Colclough there teaching. She rides over those mountains horse back. Sometimes twenty-five miles per day. She is employed by the Government.

Every body seemed to be for papa. He has decided to resign April 17—the same to take effect June 3rd. Mr. Crooks is papa's stenographer now and will be until he quits the Court. Then *you* will step in [to drive]. We spent one night in Blairsville—came on to Blue Ridge for a night. We spent a few hours in Canton. Then to Jasper and spent the night with Addie who was visiting her father Mr. Day. Mr. Will Day has a beautiful Victrola, and boy, what do you think! I broke one of his records! I'll never recover from it.

From Jasper we came to Norcross for the night. Papa went into Atlanta. Mr. C. & I came on home in rain & mud—but the little Ford made it. We stopped about one hour in Alpharetta. . . .

Papa was at his best on our trip. I never saw him in such high spirits. He was so witty and quick of speech, that he kept every body laughing and those who know him well would say: "He's the same old Dick." Papa wore his new suit and *your* shirt that was too large in the neck. We stopped and talked to nearly every man we met. You don't meet many in the mountains but there are a great many cross-road stores and saw mills.

We got stuck on the mountain Sunday night and spent the night in the car. We had a grand trip. Mr. Crooks is fine to take along. Next Monday we expect to go to Dahlonega. Will take Marguerite.

Mr. Hiram Flanigan & Mr. Crooks came out yesterday in a *new* Ford, and Mr. F. tried his best to sell papa. Papa told him he would wait awhile. . . .

I am glad you ride the bicycle. I met a Mrs. Quillian on my trip. Her eldest son had a spell of sickness just like yours. She said the doctor called it undesolved pneumonia—and the doctor told them not to let him be still a minute—that he *must* keep going and have plenty of fresh air.

James Bell had a terrible smash up with his car the other day. Broke three of his ribs and one of Guy Jackson's big toes was cut off. . . .

Rob came home last Sat. He is on another debate and is going to Decatur to try in the "Ready Writer's Contest."

Be sure to give my best love to every body. I do love aunt Pheme and aunt Lila dearly. They are so wonderful to me. They take so much interest in every thing and you'd never think they have passed so many years. . . .

[no signature]

To Miss Mary Willie Russell, Danville, Va.

April 27, 1916 (Papa's birthday)

My Dearest Bill,

. . . The day your letter came . . . I was preparing to go to Lexington, to an unveiling of a monument the U.D.C. have put on the Court House Square—yesterday was Memorial Day, you know. Well, I went and carried ten of my children. You can see the old hen now, and her brood. Mr. Mathews has two autos—his old Buick, and his son runs a Ford.— Well, I got them both and sixteen people went in two five-passenger cars. I wanted Auntney to go—so I had to do some planning to place the passengers. I had all my plans made and who should get off the train Tuesday night but R. B. and then I had to fix him a seat.

And next morning (I forgot to tell you that Pipey and Aunt Annie went too) just as we went out to get in the cars, who should come up but Rob; I didn't know what I was going to do but was determined to take him, but he said he could not go. He had to go back on the G[ainseville] M[idland] at 10:30. He had come over to buy a new suit. Rob had won his debate and is going to Athens tonight to debate again. If he wins he debates in Monroe at the final meet. I'm so happy over his success, and do hope he wins again tonight. If he does, I want to go to Monroe to hear him. He is a precious boy.

Well, I am going to tell you how we packed in—Auntney, Aunt Annie, myself and Carolyn on the back seat in Mr. M's big car—William and Fielding sat on tobacco boxes at our feet. I forgot to say that Dick was on the back seat in Auntney's lap—Walter and Patience on the front seat with Mr. M., Ina, Margo Pipey and Edward on the back seat of the Ford and R. B. in front with Ephriam, Mr. Mathews' son.

We had a grand day. The children were so happy and were very good all day. I saw so many of my old friends and relatives and they seemed so glad to see me and my children. But Pipey and Aunt Annie were in their glory. They were brimful of happiness all day. Pipey had a dandy new suit and hat and looked fine. Aunt Annie had a new hat. Ina and Margo wore new blue silk dresses and looked good. Many of my old friends told me that Margo looked exactly as I did when I visited Lexington as a girl, and just as many said Ina.

The unveiling was very nice. The monument had on it the names of 2000 soldiers who went from Oglethorpe County—nine Dillards were on the monument.

We had the grandest dinner I ever saw and more of it. We had ever so many invitations but of course we ate with Lizzie Hattie and Mary [Dillard]. Lizzie Hattie was standard bearer—she looked handsome in her white dress, panama hat, and red carnations. But their dinner was the grandest ever. I want you to write and ask Auntney how much dinner she ate. She certainly had a good time and seemed so glad to go. I wish you could have seen Carolyn and Dick sitting down by a grand box of cake. They ate unmolested, no one told them to stop—and they had chicken, ham and grand tomato sandwiches, chicken salad, potato chips, pickle and everything you can imagine. R. B. and Ina tried to see who could out eat and you know Margo—I was so happy to have all my children with me and I wished for you, Harriette, and Rob.

I am going to send you some papers. . . . If I send a paper with anything in it about Papa, you cut it out and save it. Papa is off the Court of Appeals now, or will be after June 5th. He says he will still keep a ticket for the balance of the year, anyhow. He will run for congress but will practice law too. . . .

I have so much to do I must close and get to work.

> Write soon.
> Mother

To Miss Harriette Russell, Milledgeville, Ga.

May 4, 1916

My Dearest Harriette,

I was to sorry to learn from Pipey's letter that you had been or was sick. It seems this time of year we all have puny spells. I hope you are entirely well now, and will keep well the rest of the term.

I have had an *awful* foot for ten days. William accidentally hit it with a hoe. I've done every thing for it I could & Dr. Almond had to lance it.

Papa goes on a lovely mountain journey to-morrow. He goes to Rabun County to make a speech Sat. I am trying so hard to get my foot well enough to go—for child, listen! We have a brand new Ford! Can you believe it, and can you imagine my joy and happiness! I am too full for much speaking, so you can close your eyes and see your mother in her *own* "*Fliver*"—and happy to go some when she pleases and can return at pleasure. Ina, Patience & R. B. have gone to Oglethorpe with papa this aft. I experienced much sorrow because I could not enjoy that first ride. Papa has Mr. Crooks for his stenographer now, until June 5th. He is breaking [in] our car and R. B. is learning to drive. . . .

Carolyn has a rising in her ear and Dick is complaining. I would feel fine if it was not for my foot. I keep it stuck in a lot of *hot* flax seed meal, trying to reduce the swelling. Patience has been so sweet to wait on me, I insisted on her going to Oglethorpe this aft. I have got to hobble around and see after night work now.

R. B. has come back from Florida. He stayed one week in Valdosta with Mr. & Mrs. Perry. He is looking well, but he is not over his spell yet. Still has a lump in his side.

Yesterday Cousin Fannie Dean came to Russell in her big, seven passenger Cadillac to spend the day with aunt Annie & Pipey. She brought Miss Mealy Morton & aunt Mattie. I didn't want aunt A. & P. to worry over dinner, so I fixed up a good one, and had them over here for dinner. We all had a good time.

Write soon & tell me how you are. I've written very rapidly & have been interrupted. Wish I could see you.

 Much love,
 Mother

To Miss Mary Willie Russell, Danville, Virginia

May 10, 1916

My Dearest Bill,

. . . Yesterday morning at 8:30 I attended chapel at the 9th Dist. A.&M. Last night I attended the graduating exercises of the 5th Dist. A.&M. Truly a "fliver" is a great thing and dear to me is mine.

We had a grand time in Rabun County. Met one of your G.N.&I.C. acquaintances, Fay Brown, and met Maude Yorks father & mother and heard much of her ability to teach Domestic Science. Papa made some good speeches and every thing seems favorable for him. We spent Monday night in Clarkesville and I enjoyed going out to the 9th Dist. A.&M. School Tuesday morning. Papa made a fine speech. Of course I was anxious to get on back home so as to be on time for Robs graduation. We did get back, and child, I wished for you a thousand time[s]. Rob has been debating some lately and Prof. Walker had a debate at the closing exercises and Rob's side *won*. Child, I wish you could have heard our boy. He did fine & I was very happy. You know he won the medal in the ready writers contest at Decatur and he had that to show us. Rob is sweet & lovely. I am very happy over him. He will come home this afternoon at three. The question has been in my mind all day: What *must* we or *can* we do with him this fall? . . .

Margo, Ina, Patience & Edward went to Atlanta this A.M. in my Ford. Mr. Crooks driving. He is so pleasant & kind. I'd like to have a Cadillac or Packard & have Mr.C. always at my command. . . . [last part of letter is missing]

To Miss Mary Willie Russell, Russell, Georgia

[Summer 1916] Wednesday afternoon

Dearest Bill,

We have arrived at *Orange,* but I see no oranges. About twenty men are here, but it is early & I hope more will come. . . .

I don't know where we will be to-night. We will go to Alpharetta tomorrow. Papa is very much disappointed that Mr. Bell says he will *not* be there. No wonder! He is *afraid* to meet our daddy! (Don't say *anything* about T. B. not going to Alpharetta.)

Listen! If R. B. comes with the car, don't all of you jump on him at one time about it. You know what I mean. You remember I asked papa if you girls couldn't use the car. Of course I mean in a reasonable way.

I do hope Emory's wife came to cook. If she did, you please see after my things, and don't let her rob me. I do want you all to have plenty to eat. If we haven't any apples, get Patience to go to Mrs. Ashe and get some. You know she got peaches [from us] & said we could get apples. Baked apples are nice for supper. I think you can get some fresh eggs out of the nests in the chicken house.

Rob & I have just carried three little girls home who live near here. Papa speaks in the school house and school is just out. . . .

I guess I had better go up to the school house & see what papa is doing.

Sometimes I feel so happy over this race and sometimes I feel so miserable. I still believe papa can win, if he can only see enough people. He never fails to convert men when they hear him speak.

I hope you all got the Rabun Co. mail off. I do want papa to have a big crowd when he speaks at Clayton Monday. . . .

Tom Bell speaks at Ball Ground to-night. You see he is following papa. . . .

The balance of this letter is for Patience—Patience, please be smart and see after my things and the small children. Feed chickens and calf and don't forget to water your coleus you planted in the yard. Help in the kitchen and dining room. Keep Carolyn clean. Get up early. Wash Dick and C. in the afternoon and put on clean clothes. Tell Harriette to please help and *be sure* to feed the cats and Sport and *bathe* them occasionally.

I must close now as the flies have found out I'm here and are worrying me.

> Heart of love,
> Mother

To Miss Ina D. Russell, Thomasville, Ga.

Sep. 28, 1916

My Dearest Girlie,

Your letter came this morning. It is night now and I am very tired from a strenuous day's work. Edward Russell 'phoned me Wednesday night that Alice, Cousin Susie Curtis and her son Earnest, would be out to spend to-day with me. I was very glad to have them and did my best to have things nice and to fix a good dinner. They got here about 12 o'clock. Came in a Chevrolet, that Alice says rides very rough and bumpy. She says my jitney is much nicer. I invited Auntney and uncle Lewis out to dinner. We had a real nice time. . . .

I had three letters in mail this morning. I read yours *first* and before I read my others, I had read yours *twice*. I was just wild to see what you had to say. I am intensely interested in your undertaking. I am very anxious for you to be happy and . . . to feel that you are really *doing* something.[1]

I confess that I was a little disappointed in your letter. . . . I read it twice and tried to see exactly how things were going with you. You didn't seem exactly as happy as I wanted you to be. You see its something like getting married and going to a new home. You see their habits are fixed and they are fond of their things and its a blessed thing that they are pleased with them. I think 12 mi. per hour is fine speeding for *old* ladies (?) and of course they love their little car. I'd love *any,* that really *belonged* to me.

Its nice to wash dishes in cold water when the weather is so warm. Hot water heats you so. Miss Hettie uses cold water all the time. Its nice when you have plenty of it. I'm sorry the piano is old, but maybe it is sweet-toned.

Margo wanted to read your letter, and she did, but I told her not to say anything about it until you wrote again. I couldn't exactly tell whether you were pleased or not. I was surprised that you had to pay for your ticket. I thought Mr. Futch paid for it. But maybe it will be all right. I'm glad you enjoyed your trip down. I had a great many thoughts and feelings while I was reading your letter. You know Mrs. Futch said in Atlanta that she realized that it would require some sacrifice on both sides. You know they've lived a long time and having a new member to come into their lives and home as you have, and they are old & feeble. You must try to *cultivate* an *interest* in them—a *real* interest. Then you will find everything so much easier.

You know how fairy stories always go. The "little girl" has a hard time at first, but she is always brave, and sweet, and kind, and patient—and finally the Prince comes along. . . .

I will have to get up early in the morning. Aunt Annie, Margo, Carolyn, Dick, Edward and myself will venture forth to Washington if the weather permits, so I'd better hurry to bed.

Remember what I told you honey, and don't make any remarks about *anything* or *any body,* that you could ever regret. I hope you will keep well and will find a great deal of pleasure in your little daily tasks. . . .

Mary Willie is at 21 15th St. [Columbus, Ga.] [2] I know she has written. All send love.

> Your fond
> Mother

1. Ina Jr. had gone to Thomasville to become a live-in companion and helper for the Futch family. It was hoped the climate in South Georgia would help her asthma.

2. Dissatisfied being so far from home in Virginia, Bill had taken a teaching position in Columbus, Georgia.

The seven women who lived together at Cottage Content attended school and/or taught in Athens from 1888–1891. Ina Dillard is on the back row, third from the left. *Courtesy Richard B. Russell Library for Political Research and Studies at the University of Georgia.*

Ina and Richard Russell on their honeymoon, "an extended tour of the North,"
including Niagara Falls, June–July 1891. *Courtesy Richard B. Russell Library for
Political Research and Studies at the University of Georgia.*

Richard and Ina with their first child, Mary Willie, about 1899. *Courtesy Richard B. Russell Library for Political Research and Studies at the University of Georgia.*

Richard, Ina, and children with visitors and servants on the porch of the Russell home in Winder, about 1900. *Courtesy Richarda B. Russell Library for Political Research and Studies at the University of Georgia.*

This photograph accompanied an article about Richard Russell in the *Georgian*, at the time of Russell's 1906 gubernatorial bid. The baby, Lewis Carolyn, born June 7, 1906, died shortly after this photograph was made.
Back row: Richard Sr., Ina Sr. holding baby Lewis. *Second row from back:* Mary Willie, Ina Jr., Marguerite, R. B. *Third row from back:* Patience, Harriette, Rob. *Front row:* Walter. *Courtesy Richard B. Russell Library for Political Research and Studies at the University of Georgia.*

Ina with her long-awaited twin boys, Fielding and William, 1908. *Courtesy Richard B. Russell Library for Political Research and Studies at the University of Georgia.*

Ina's mother, America Chaffin Dillard, with her six daughters, 1909. *Back row:* Mary Antionette "Mamie" Comer, Ina Russell, America Patience "Pipey" Dillard, Martha Tabitha "Mattie" Morris. *Front row:* Harriet "Hattie" Arnold, America Chaffin Dillard, Anne Elizabeth "Annie" Launius. *Courtesy Richard B. Russell Library for Political Research and Studies at the University of Georgia.*

On the Royal Arcanum trip to Montreal, 1910: the New York City stopover. *Left to right:* Ina, Richard, Mr. Simmons (an Arcanum delegate from Rome, Georgia), Rob, and R. B. *Courtesy Richard B. Russell Library for Political Research and Studies at the University of Georgia.*

Ina Dillard Russell, about 1911.

The new house in Russell, 1912. *Courtesy Richard B. Russell Library for Political Research and Studies at the University of Georgia.*

Richard and Ina on the porch at Russell, about 1913. *Courtesy Richard B. Russell Library for Political Research and Studies at the University of Georgia.*

"100% American" declared this photograph taken for Richard Russell's 1922 campaign for chief justice of the Georgia Supreme Court. *Back row:* Walter, Patience, Harriette, Rob, Marguerite, Ina Jr., and Mary Willie. *Middle row:* Carolyn, Ina Sr., Richard Sr. and Dick Jr. *Front row:* twins Fielding and William, Alexander Brevard, and Henry Edward "Jeb." *Courtesy Richard B. Russell Library for Political Research and Studies at the University of Georgia.*

Ina with her daughters, 1926. *Seated:* Ina Sr. and Ina Jr. *Standing:* Marguerite, Carolyn, Mary Willie, Harriette, Patience. *Courtesy Richard B. Russell Library for Political Research and Studies at the University of Georgia.*

Ina with Richard and their sons, 1926. *Seated:* Henry Edward, Ina, Richard Sr.,
Alex. *Standing:* twins William and Fielding, Dick Jr., Rob, and Walter.
*Courtesy Richard B. Russell Library for Political Research and Studies
at the University of Georgia.*

Richard and Ina listening to the election returns of
the 1930 gubernatorial race. *Courtesy Richard B.
Russell Library for Political Research and Studies at the
University of Georgia.*

Ina Dillard Russell in the garden of
the Governor's Mansion, 1931.
*Courtesy Richard B. Russell Library for
Political Research and Studies at the
University of Georgia.*

Russell family reunion at the homeplace in Russell, July 2, 1933. *Courtesy Richard B. Russell Library for Political Research and Studies at the University of Georgia.*

Ina with her children, June 22, 1953. *Standing behind Ina:* Patience, Carolyn, Harriette, Ina, Marguerite, Mary Willie. *Seated on the steps, first row below Ina:* Rob, Alex, Dick Jr., William; *second row:* Walter, Henry Edward, Fielding. *Courtesy* Atlanta Journal and Constitution.

To Miss Marguerite Russell, Eastman, Georgia

Oct. 19, 1916 9:45 P.M.

Dearest Margo,

I just can't go to bed without writing you a short note. It is right late and I am all fagged out. Have gone through with all of W[illiam]'s and F[ielding]'s lessons and you know what that means. They had to write a *thesis* or something on any kind of grain they wanted to represent. Wm was a grain of wheat. Fielding went over in the woods & found some chestnut bark & two or 3 nice chestnuts and *he* was a chestnut. They have had more to do since you left or I just miss your help. They had to memorize three long verses & I had to "sit up" with them then. . . . Fielding learned his quickly, but I had a time with Wm but he finally got it. Wm . . . reads so much better than he did at first.

I missed you dreadfully coming home Monday and in Atlanta too. I stood on the steps at the station & saw them put your trunk on the train. . . .

The children were wishing to-night you had not gone. Dick came to me at the supper table and said: "I wish that old man hadn't written for Marguerite, so she could be here on my birthday." He has had a very pleasant day. He asked me to-day who made God. I said: "He made himself." "Well, how did he do it?" And I said: "I don't know," & I don't.

I forwarded four letters to you to-day. I wrote on the backs of them and almost felt as if I'd written you a letter. . . . I am too sleepy to write any more. I do hope you'll have a fine beginning for your school and a most successful time every way. I can't imagine why the man wanted you to come so early. Did the other schools in the Co. begin Monday?

I'll be looking for another letter telling all about your prospects. . . .

Heart of love from
Mother

To Miss Ina D. Russell, Thomasville, Ga.

Oct. 27, 1916

My Dearest Ina,

Your letter came this morning. . . . I was in doubt as to whether I should send the middy pattern to Thomasville or Valdosta. I think it will be so nice for you to visit Mrs. P. and Willie B. too, but Ina, I did want you to try T'ville a little while. I feel that the climate there will mean so much to you. You didn't say when you would leave, but spoke as if just any time. You know *I'd love* to have you at home, but I do wish you could stick it out a little longer. It doesn't matter about the silk hose.[1] Just go on & wear them or you could afford *not* to.

I just don't know what to tell you, for I do not know the circumstances exactly, but unless you are *mistreated,* I wish you could try it a little longer. Mrs. F. may have some queer ways, but you must learn to *manage.* You know a lot of nice sweet ways when you get your best self out. I just grieve over you feeling so miserable. Can't you kinder "jerk a knot" in something and renovate yourself and things generally? You know how I used to beg you to see the *good* side of your little school? You will have to be satisfied & contented and get the *good* out of your condition and surroundings before you can be happy. I can hear you say: "Mother, *please hush,*" but I love you so Ina, and you have so much good in you, that I long to help you some way. You are capable & smart and sweet and attractive.

If the money is the only thing, may be papa can send you some occasionally or he can pay your little debts at Braselton. Your little √ [from papa for $3.00] will keep you in spending money. I can send you some shoes from Atlanta. I can take one of your old slippers or shoes and send you some from Bycks.

You weigh matters well before you do anything. Now of course you can do as you please, but you have what I've written before you. You have your license & can teach or you can stay at home. I wish I had just *lots of money,* I'd have you right here & we'd have a good time.

Let me know what you are going to do. If you leave, when, and do darling keep sweet & pleasant to the end. You *can* do it, so *do* it, for your sake & for mine.

Don't get blue any more. Whatever you do, do it, but keep cheerful and feel that life is worth living, whether we are situated just as we want to be or not.

It is getting dark & I'll have to stop & feed my pigs and chickens. I think about you all the time. Kindest regards to Mr. & Mrs. F.

      Your devoted Mother

1. The Futches disapproved of young ladies wearing silk hose and reading anything except the Bible or other religious material.

To Miss Marguerite Russell, Eastman, Ga.

Nov. 2, 1916

Dearest Margo,

. . . The twins have just come & kissed me good night. They brushed their teeth, and learned their lessons well. Carolyn has been marking on my paper. She works as hard as ever when the others are studying.

I do hope you are feeling less dread of your work. You know what I used to say about "grit in your gizzard"? Well, you need it now, and you have it, I know. I wish my girls could all be at home with me & I had just plenty of money for us to do all the little pleasant things as they came along. But it seems this is not for us. Of course we could all stay at home and we'd have plenty to eat and *clothes* to wear, but we might miss our little pocket change. Papa is still getting work. He has made & paid about $700 insurance, but my! the other day someone wrote that his note for $4000 was due, etc, etc, and I just thought how awful that sounded. It would kill me, and I'm so sorry for papa. I have to go to him for so much and it hurts me. I sent Harriette a check to-day for E. E. Bell (ever hear of him)?[1] She says she is not going to get anything else charged, and I am not—not until all our bills are straightened up in Atlanta. So when all this is on hand, it is mighty nice for my girls to be making something. I do want you all to find enough pleasure in your work so you will not feel over-burdened. Just get up a certain amount of *interest* and you'll be sure to feel a certain amount of pleasure.

O, I did wish for you in Atlanta Tuesday. Just as we got in the Terminal station we saw so many soldier boys. Papa had to wait awhile to see a man & I waited to see the soldiers. It was a N.Y. company on their way home from the border. They were in fine spirits. Papa talked to three of the captains. They had a fine band and gave us a grand concert in front of station. One number they played was so soft and beautiful and familiar that tears came to my eyes. I was carried back several years and many sweet memories came to me. The piece was: "Some Where a Voice is Calling." . . .

I am still missing you, but I know it is best for you to be where you are. I think of you all the time, and hope things are going your way. Give my love to Annie Maude—I think of her too. . . .

Your Mother

1. Charge accounts at Bell's store in Milledgeville were familiar to all the Russell girls who went to GN&IC.

To Miss Marguerite Russell, Eastman, Georgia

Nov. 26, 1916

Dearest Margo,

When Walter and Patience came from S.S. this A.M. they brought that fine Dodge County gobbler [you sent]. He rode on the back seat of our Ford.

I had planned to put him in that little pen that Walter made for his pigs so Walter, Patience and myself hurried out to the lot with him. The other children were over at Pipey's. We had the gobbler in the pen when here they came. I did wish for you to see them. They were so interested and happy. You should have seen us all standing round talking about you and fixing the pen so the turkey could not get out. We gave him corn and put in water. He didn't seem very hungry and he acted as if he had known us all his life.

I have never had *anything* given me that gave me more solid pleasure than your fine gift for my Thanksgiving dinner. It was certainly sweet and thoughtful of you. We will enjoy it so much. I only wish you could be here with us to enjoy the turkey. He is a magnificent fellow. Did he grow out near your school?

This afternoon we were out feeding *our* turkey and Aunt Annie and Pipey came over to see him. They both told me to tell you how sweet they thought you were to send it and that it was so nice for the little children to have the turkey to look at and to remember. I invited them to have dinner with us Thanksgiving and I'll have Auntney and Uncle Lewis.

I guess you will go into Eastman on the 30th and have a good time with Annie Maude. I do hope you will have a pleasant day. Just think of us as we sit around our long table. You can see us now. . . .

I see your little papers . . . you used to write for those New Chapel [School] children. One copy was: "Be clean and neat in all you do." As I went about my days work I remembered it and it did me good.

Hattie was out to-day with one of her spells and I tried to cook my folks a good dinner. I looked for Auntney & Mamie out in the afternoon but they did not come. I will go to Atlanta Tuesday to meet Ina and Dr. Crenshaw will fill in two teeth for me. I do dread it. It is late now and I must be sleeping and resting some. Hattie may not come in in the morning and then I'll have to hurry sure enough. [I] have the children some meat sliced ready for their lunch. That is my greatest concern in the mornings—I want to feed them well. . . .

Be sure you wear enough clothes these cold days. Take care of yourself and keep well.

Your fond Mother

To Miss Harriette Russell, Milledgeville, Ga.

Jan. 24, 1917

My Dear Harriette,

. . . Dr. Almond came to see Pipey last week. I told him you would write to him for certificates. I also told him that I did not want you to give up physical training entirely, but was willing for you to stop basket ball. I don't exactly understand your pain, but Harriette, you must *avoid* the things that aggravates it. It is not necessary for you to *ever run* up those steps, and you can be more quiet about some things. It is right to ourselves and just to our loved ones, to take care of ourselves when we can . . . not just *to pull through,* but stay as well as we can.

Dr. A. was to see Pipey again yesterday but I did not see him. [She] had a very bad spell yesterday but she says she is much better this morning. I have been and am, uneasy about her.

Hattie did not come this A.M. I had to get busy and I hurried with a rush. I had breakfast by eight and at 8:15 they had gone to school. Eunice[1] got the Ford started and Patience fixed the lunches. Patience stayed with aunt Annie & Pipey last night & of course she was up early. . . .

Yesterday was my mother's birthday. I had been thinking of her so much. I always wrote to her on the 23rd of January. Now that I can not, I always write to sister Hattie who has been a second mother to me. It is so sweet to have these dear ones to remember. As I grow older, the more I can realize what a wonderful woman my mother was. Her life is a great hope and inspiration to me. I only regret that I did not profit from it more years ago. . . .

To-day is uncle Jim Dillard's birthday. You know grandma was sixteen the 23rd and uncle Jim was born the 24th. Wasn't she a young mother? . . .

Alec[2] and Carolyn are here in my room cutting out pictures and keeping busy. Carolyn has had a bad gum boil.

The ten o'clock train is going by, so you see I'm "taking time by the forelock" and writing to you on time. The children will be in early to-day, and I cannot write then. R. B. is hunting for a book. He *reads, reads* on rainy days. Yesterday he helped Emory cut trees for cord wood. He is looking better and doesn't cough quite so much.

Walter, twins & Edward got on the Honor Roll. Poor little Patience worked so hard & missed it by *one* point. She made 89, and they require 90. . . .

> Heart of Love,
> Mother

1. A black servant boy.
2. R. B. had decided he wanted to be called Dick Russell Jr., and he thought there would be a problem if there was another young Dick Russell in the family. Richard, thinking of his oldest son's political career, agreed; consequently, he changed Dickson's name to Alexander Brevard, in honor of his mother's grandfather, a famous North Carolina Revolutionary War patriot. *Alex* was ultimately the preferred spelling.

To Miss Harriette Russell, Milledgeville, Ga.

Feb. 14, 1917

My Dear Harriette,

It is late. Every one in the house is in bed, except my self. I have *cooked,* cleaned up, and nursed measles all day. Fielding is in bed to-day and he has been my *main* stay. He was awful sick to-night and I had a time getting him quiet. He said his bowels hurt and I rubbed and rubbed and gave one dose after another of spts. of ammonia, camphor, paregoric & soda and jamaica ginger. Nothing seemed to do him any good but finally *every thing* I had given him came *flying* back and now he is asleep, & seems perfectly easy.

Wm & Edward are too lively for anything and declare they are well enough to go to school or do any thing else. I have a time keeping them in and keeping them from using their eyes. They both suffered so much with their eyes. They (and Alec) have cut dozens of valentines to-day. Carolyn & Alec are complaining and I think in a day or two they will have the measles. . . . Wm & Edward cannot get enough to eat. I am doing my best to fix them good nourishing food and they certainly "make way" with it.

Hattie is still sick. I am getting on all right, but when Alec & Carolyn get real sick, I'll *have* to have somebody. Think now I'll get Doscia, if Hattie doesn't get well enough to come back.

I certainly do wish you were here to help me. The children love to hear stories & they keep me busy reading to them. Some mornings when I'm so rushed and hurry through with my sweeping, I say to myself: If Harriette was here she would sweep this hall for me. Patience is mighty good to help but she doesn't have much time before school to do anything. You see, Ina has to be at school by 8:30 and its a rush to get off in time.[1] Eunice has been very good & he generally gets here soon enough to make the fire in stove.

Your letter came this morning. I hope you are over your bad feeling spell and are your *own sweet self.* All of us—the whole human family—have these crazy spells occasionally, I guess—and you said you "restrained your-self to a certain extent." Now that is what counts. Controlling yourself. It is awful to feel so bad & sometimes we can't help it. You are a smart girl, more sweet and good than anything else, and you will have to *study* your self and find out the reason of these spells and learn how to avoid them & how to control your self. The lamentable part about these spells is, that the inno-cent generally suffer from them, and in the "long run" it makes the one who has the spell suffer.

I have often heard & read too, that people who have unusual spells are always specially gifted in some way, and if they can overcome these feelings and master themselves they make the most noted and splendid persons. So it is up to you and if you "work out your own salvation," you will make a grand, useful woman and be such a blessing to the world—and I will be so glad I brought you into the world. I think of you a great deal. I often wish I knew exactly what to do that would be the greatest help to my children. It is all I am living for, & some times *I* get blue & feel that I was a poor one indeed to be put in charge of so many precious souls.

I am glad you wrote me & I hope it helped you. That is what we mothers are for—The world has to be kept going and we mothers are here to help our children in *any* way that is possible.

I am glad to tell you that Pipey is much better. I am still uneasy about her, but do feel better over her condition than I did ten days ago. . . .

There goes our late train & I must close up & go to bed. The sick children sleep very good at night. Fielding & Wm are in my bed. Edward is in Alec's bed. So that sends me & papa . . . to the back room where I sleep with one eye & both ears open.

Poor old Jinsy's house was burned last Sunday night. She saved her machines & beds, but lost so much. She had about $40 worth of cloth in the house to make up. Several of the teachers were heavy losers.

You must excuse my fancy stationery. I write so much & I save everything that will do to write a letter on. . . . Good night & pleasant dreams.

> Your fond Mother

1. Ina Jr. did not stay with the Futches but came back to Winder and was again teaching in a rural school.

To Miss Marguerite Russell, Eastman, Ga.

Feb. 22, 1917

My Dearest Margo,

I was in the kitchen Sunday, the 18th getting ready to make graham biscuit, and hoping they would be good, so I could send you & Annie Maud some, when Walter came from Sunday School and brought my sweet letter, from my dear girlie down in Dodge Co. He also brought one from aunt Hattie and one from Uncle John. Of course I read yours first—you were mighty sweet to write me such a loving letter and to send me that check. I feel that I cannot get it cashed, for you need all your little money. I told Ina, if you had been teaching several years and had a big bank account, it would be different.

I had a very happy birthday, but was cooking and nursing measles all day. Carolyn & Alec were at their worst, but some how, I was unusually happy—You see, I knew I had so many dear ones thinking of me and loving me. The ones at home had been so thoughtful and sweet, & hadn't I got your letter? I had rec'd a letter from Harriette Friday and she said: "I'll be thinking of you Sunday." And on Tuesday I received letters from Bill, R. B. and Rob—all written on Sunday, and they were dear sweet letters. Papa gave me a five dollar gold piece and Patience gave me six handkerchiefs and dear old Pipey sent me some canned scuppernong hulls.

. . . Our boys seem to be so well and lively and they look so sweet and rosy I am thinking of letting them go to school tomorrow if the weather is good and get up their lessons for Monday. The teachers are very careful of their eyes, and see right after those who have had measles. . . . They have the Geo. Washington exercises tomorrow. Ina's grade is on & she has to announce the performers &c. I want the children to be there to see the exercises, and I have their nice clothes all laid out & their books, pencils &c, are all ready to jump in the Ford as soon as they eat their breakfast.

Carolyn and Dick [Alec] are getting well fast. I let them go out some today, the weather was so beautiful. Carolyn's eyes seem to hurt her & they look pitiful—Ole Alec seems all right. He was the best child to nurse I ever saw. Fielding helped me nurse Edward & Wm and they were well enough to help me nurse Fielding & all three of them were able to help me nurse Alec & Carolyn. They would tell them stories and do things to amuse them. Alec lying still, never saying a word.

Carolyn was a sight and kept us all busy. . . . One day Carolyn said: "Tell the boys to come here." I called them & they came immediately. She amused them so much & they were always wondering what she'd do next. She said: "Boys, I want you to speak for me." Wm, the ever ready for anything, began: "Sing a song of six pense" & she cut him off in a hurry with: "I don't want anything like *that*. I want a *speech*." So they tried to recall all their little verses &c, and she seemed satisfied. One night she was moaning & groaning so, and I tried to get her quiet—told her it was not nice to "take on" so—she said: "Well, this is the best I can do with these old measles popped out all over me!" I must tell you something else she said. . . . I heard her "taking on" and I went to the bed and she said: "O I'm suffering—I'm suffering—I just can't do anything but suffer." Fielding was in the bed with her & he was very much amused at her.

Not long ago, Carolyn asked her daddy to buy her a ticket so she could go to Marguerite. She said: "I know you haven't much money and you can just buy me a *little* ticket."[1] When she asked for the ticket, she said she wanted to go to Dodge County.

The deaths you wrote me of were very sad. Especially the mother who had to leave her little children. I do hope they will have some kind person to care for them. All children need *tender, wise, loving* care, but the motherless child needs it twofold.

I got a box of graham biscuit off to you & Annie Maud Monday morning I thought you could heat them in your little stove and they might taste good & save you both a little cooking.

I am certainly writing one of my old, long rambling letters tonight & I must stop now. . . .

        With a heart full of love for you,
        Mother

1. The ticket books the family used were bulky; Ina describes them as "fat."

To Mr. R. B. Russell, Jr., Athens, Ga.

                             March 5, 1917

My Dear Boy,

Guess you'll be surprised to hear from me so soon, but I am dreadfully worried about something.

The remark you made to me about "tobacco" being healthy went home to my heart with a sickening thud. I intended saying more to you about it, but you know how quickly our day passed. Well, I went up stairs and cleaned your room this morning, and as I was finishing up, I saw *tobacco* in your slop bucket. My! If I'd found a flask in the closet I *could not* have felt worse! I *do not* want my boys to chew. I'd rather they would not smoke, but *chew*! My darling, your mother can't stand it! You will regret it, if you form the habit. You need not say, "just a little now" and "I'll stop one day"—for it gets worse—and you *can't* stop it.

I know tobacco chewing has been a great hinderance to papa. I've wish[ed] a 1000 times that he did not chew.

Now all this may be a horrible dream, and I hope it is, but I just had to write you about it. *Some* day, *some* body, who *thinks* she loves you better than I do, will be wishing you did not chew—and *maybe* she'll make it so hot for you that you'll wish so yourself.

I can't realize that you could *deliberately* form this filthy habit, and I'm *insisting* that you think good before you do. Healthy! The idea! Do you suppose any one really believes that tobacco is healthy? I leave the subject with you, and hope in my heart, that not one of my boys will ever chew— or smoke to excess.

We all enjoyed your little visit home. Tonight the train stopped and Alec said: "I know its R. B. coming back."

We have been troubled with dogs prowling around at night, and to-night Walter went out and shot a big hound. Walter can certainly shoot. I was sorry, but this dog comes on *my* porch and then growls at me, when I go to the door. He investigates my hen nests & chicken yard, too. We are all grieving over the death of the dog. Walter says he'll never shoot another. He says the thing that hurts him is that to-morrow morning, some body will be looking for their dog. Patience & Walter dragged him away off. . . .

I have a big "last-go" trade for you. Aunt Hattie came over this morning & was talking about you. She said: "I never believed R. B. would be as handsome as he is. Why, Ina, he is actually handsome." I told her yes, I knew you were. . . .

> Your fond, loving
> Mother

To Miss Marguerite Russell, Eastman, Ga.

Mar. 26, 1917

My Dearest Margo,

. . . I haven't been to Atlanta this year. I haven't been in my Ford this year—so you see I'm not keeping up with much that's outside of my yard. I'm thinking a great deal about this awful war. In the paper today, I see they are advertising for 20,000 men to meet the deficiency in the Navy. If the 20,000 don't hurry up and volunteer I believe they'll issue a *call* and they might muster out some that we'd hate to see go. Secretary Daniels says no woman will be put on duty on sea, but places in the Navy on land will be opened to women to take the place of the men who go to sea.

Seven hundred German sailors are interned at Ft. McPherson & Ft. Oglethorpe. They were sent from Philadelphia Navy Yard. I am grieving & worrying over all of it. . . .

Ina is looking so well and she is mighty sweet these days. She seems interested in her work, and she is very popular among the teachers and pupils. She *will* talk about getting married every now & then and I don't know whether I'm "fallin" for it or not. Mary Q[uarterman]. was out yesterday and she is *so* miserable—she remarked that if God had made her "pretty" & "rich" she could be good. Now isn't that absurd? She said further that she never had anything she liked . . . she would like to have a big handsome husband and "just see what I have!" You see Mary grows *bigger* & Mr. Q. grows *smaller* in their old age and it gets her. I told Ina to think over what Mamie was saying & if she was going to "fall out" with Van because he was not *large* & *handsome,* to be sure to do it *before* she got married.

But it all sounded so foolish to me for Mr. Q is good & smart and kind and good enough for anybody. I'm sorry for him. He gave her (Mamie) a fifty dollar gold piece on her birthday. . . .

I must close now & see after some chickens that are crying & I guess they are hungry. I have 22 little ones. I want plenty of fried chicken & good vegetables for you children this summer. . . .

> Your fond
> Mother

To Miss Harriette Russell, Milledgeville, Ga.

April 18, 1917

My Dear Harriette,

. . . I'm a busy lady now. Mrs. Wilson (so I see by the papers) has set a pace for economy, but I have set my own pace—and that is to *cook,* until this war is over. I've been cooking six wks. now and I feel very good when I *get* my wages, instead of *giving* it to some one else.

The 9th District High School [Literary] Meet opens up in Winder tomorrow. We are very much interested & excited over it. We will have some delegates. I have made two big cakes and cleaned up, and washed Ina some silk waists, hose, &c, washed Carolyns & Dicks [Alec's] heads and put out cabbage plants . . . to-day—I am tired, but feel *well.*

Aunt Mattie has invited us down to eat birthday dinner with her tomorrow, ... Pipey, Aunt Annie & myself intended going, but poor Pipey has had another bad spell and she is not able. . . . I'm so sorry aunt A. &

Pipey cant go. Aunt A. says she will not leave Pipey. I'm so worried about Pipey. I'm going to get her off to Wesley Memorial Hospital right away— if possible. I'm so glad you sent Pipey the bread. She enjoyed it so much & appreciated it. . . .

The war *is* affecting us as it is every body. R. B. is liable to be in training this summer. Rob says he is going too, but we will not let him, yet. It is all awful to me. John Dillard & Walter [Dillard] [1] have enlisted. I have heard there was no sugar in Winder & R. B. said there was none in Athens & flour is $12 per [barrel].

Papa is in Savannah. Will come back Friday, I think. I'll risk putting a dollar bill in this & you make it do until papa comes. We must learn to make our money go a long ways. . . .

     Mother

1. Sons of her brother Walter B. Dillard Sr.

To Miss Marguerite Russell, Carrollton, Ga.

Sept. 17, 1917

My Dearest Margo,

. . . I have wanted to write, but I've been so busy. My last *boarder* left this morning (Harriette). R. B. left last night so Ina is all I have now. I forgot— Brevard [a nephew] is still here, but I think he will go Tuesday. . . .

Walter got a crowd—I mean several boys from Winder and all of our peas are picked. I payed off every body. Just payed for all and kept your weights. The weather has been beautiful for harvesting. The goobers are not quite ripe and we will try to see after them. Walter and the twins seem interested in seeing after your things. Walter is laid up today with a bad foot. He stuck the pitch fork in it & its giving him trouble.

I had such a grand trip to Chattanooga. Its fine to be chaperone. I'm crazy about Green.[1] He certainly is a fine fellow. . . . I think Billie wrote you all about our trip & it was so nice I can't begin to tell you all, but some time I want to talk to you & tell you about it. . . . You know I had to take Carolyn to Chat. as I had no one to leave her with. [She] was beautiful & lovely on her trip. It seemed to bring out all the best that was in her & she was so smart, good & cute and gave us all pleasure. She got off some good jokes on the couples. She said she knew "sister" liked Green better than she did Maddox, for she walked by him all the time.

Time passes so, & I just can't recall how long you've been away, but of course you know that Pipey is at home. She is very weak and pitiful. I try to see her as much & as often as possible. I'm still cooking & fixing those seven lunches every A.M. I keep just as busy as possible but I'm well & I'm thankful I am able to work.

I guess you are still at the hotel. Only you'll have so much board to pay, but you'll be well cared for. I guess it is quite a contrast to the way you lived in Dodge County. . . .[2]

I certainly appreciate the way you left your room.[3] Whenever I go up stairs I *never fail* just to open the door & peep in, and say in my heart, bless her heart! It means so much to the one who has to see after every thing. Harriette donned her G.N.&I. duds this morning and sailed away. She said she had never dressed grinning as she did this time.[4]

Poor daddy got Rob off last Monday—R. B. off last night & H. this morning—He said he had just one dollar left. . . .

It is late & I'm sleepy, & I know it will be hard to leave my warm bed in the morning. It is so cold tonight.

>   Your Mother

1. Samuel Gordon Green, an Army engineer from Gray, Georgia, whom Mary Willie met while he was stationed at Ft. Benning and she was teaching in Columbus.
2. Margo's new teaching job was in the "city" of Carrolton.
3. Margo was the only one of the children who had a room of her own.
4. Harriette was grinning because this was her senior year.

To Miss Marguerite Russell, Carrollton, Ga.

>   Nov. 14, 1917

My Dearest Margo,

Your "Hark from the tomb a doleful sound" letter came yesterday A.M. I have been thinking about my big, fat, white baby ever since. You know you and Alex were the only fat babies I ever had and you were fatter than Alex. I've been thinking how you looked going around over the house by yourself. Mary W. and Ina were at grandmother's and I was at home feeling *so sick,* and I'd shut all the doors (outside) and turn you loose. You would crawl all over that house. I remember seeing you find a big cork . . . from a pickle bottle. You happened to have a small bottle in your hand and you spent at least fifteen minutes trying to put that big cork in the little bottle, and one day you climbed into a chair and sat down and you had never walked a step by yourself. This was early in the summer before R. B. was born in November.

I almost laughed over your letter. I know I smiled, and I was sorry for you too, from the bottom of my heart. But your troubles are just imaginary—You haven't anything to make you so miserable. My big, fat, white baby must brace up. I'm afraid if you harbor such feelings too long and too hard, they will begin to show in your sweet, pretty face, and you will leave a wrong impression on those around you. You must make the best of your situation, and live down your blue feelings. I wonder if Miss Clark knows you are feeling so miserable. I hope you are cheerful with her and help to brighten her life which I imagine is not one of "flowery beds of ease." But I know you are just as sweet and lovely as can be and will not show your blue feelings when they just will come.

We keep so busy here that no one has time to think of any one thing long at a time. Keeping the children up to their school work and home work, and seeing after my affairs, completely fills every minute I have awake. I have had one bale of cotton ginned from my patch, and sold it for $105. I have bought a Majestic Range with $90 of it and gave the children $5.25 to buy a foot ball. They have been so smart to pick my cotton. You see I haven't much left of my cotton money, but I have my range & I've wanted one so long, and I'm doing my cooking, you know. . . .

Your peanuts are upstairs in your room. I'd say you had about three lbs and they sell for 12 cents per. I'll buy them if you want to sell.

I'm enclosing a dollar so you'll have a "nest egg." I just wish I had a twenty dollar bill to send. Nothing would make me happier than to send you a nice big bill.

You must start a sweater for some nice Sommie. I really think you ought to knit Ralph one. He has been awful nice to you. Ina has Charlie's nearly to the neck. I'm crazy to begin one. Aunt Annie is knitting a grey one for the Winder Red Cross. . . .

Our children must really be bone heads as not one [of] our six got on the Honor Roll. I've started a new management and hope to get some on next month.

Papa left Sun. night for Washington D.C. A woman is crazy to get her son-in-law out of the army and paid daddy $300 to go to W. to get him out. If he succeeds she'll pay him $500 more. I'm afraid I'd never be able to get one of mine out (If I ever have any).

I am distressed about your eyes. You come up for T'giving & go to see Dr. Campbell. You must take time to do this. It not only makes you feel so miserable, but it spoils your looks. You must see after your eyes. . . .

I don't know why I keep on writing so—I know your poor eye is hurting now, sure enough. I do hope your eye will soon be better. . . . I'll close up now and give you a rest. . . .

Did you know that Rebecca Hill was at St. Joseph's Infirmary training to be a nurse? She told her father that there was *no life* but a *useful* one, and she was going to make herself useful.

I've nearly finished my page and I'll kiss you goodnight now and tell you that I love you very dearly and have you in my heart all the time. . . .

Your fond Mother

To Miss Patience E. Russell, Athens, Ga.

Thursday night Jan. 4, 1918 [Patience's birthday]

My Dearest "Sweet-six-teen,"

I have a beautiful picture in my mind. It's you and your *new* Mary Louise[1] as I saw you last. You both looked so pretty and sweet in your sleeping garments, with your hair all pulled back, ready for bed. . . .

You surely know I have been thinking of you *all* day. Even before I left my warm bed for the cold, cold world, I was thinking of my dear, sweet child over in Athens, at Lucy Cobb. I knew you were comfortable. At least I thought so, and I felt that you had a good warm breakfast, and I hoped you were very happy. We miss you just awful. The little children were not too cold this morning to say ever so many things about you, and they were all something sweet & nice. I want you to know, Patience, that I've always been thankful for you. You have been a good child and sometimes we have differed on a few subjects,[2] yet I think we have been very congenial and I have realized that you had a great many splendid qualities and would make a fine woman.

We are very cold here to-day. Everything frozen stiff. It was so cold in the kitchen this morning. Jim came in and made some plans to fix up the house and so on. Doscia came over and began to work. I was so happy, for I was beginning to think they were going back on me. Doscia says she is going to stay, so I'm going to feel more secure about having some help. . . .

I am anxious to know how you are classified. I know you'll be able to handle anything they give you. I want you to take music so much. It is $7.00 per month. Dad told Miss Millie he'd let her know about it. . . .

I'll be looking for a long letter soon.

> With a heart *full* of love for my Patience,
> Mother

1. The "old" Mary Louise was a longtime Winder friend of Patience's. The "new" Mary Louise is her roommate at Lucy Cobb Institute.
2. Patience had objected strongly to changing Dickson's name to Alexander Brevard.

To Miss Harriette B. Russell, Milledgeville, Ga.

March 4, 1918

My Dear Harriette,

Your card came this morning. I was so glad to hear from you. You must have felt lately how much I was thinking of you. I wanted you to come home and see Billie's clothes and help us discuss the wedding and I wanted you at the wedding, too. You would have reveled in every thing . . . I thought of you constantly. Billie gave me her bouquet and I took three roses out and sent it on to you. The stems were so wet I would not tie the tulle & ribbon on but put them in so you could see what belonged to it. I knew the roses would be withered when they reached you, but I knew they would still be *pink* & *sweet* and you'd know they were on Bill when she became Mrs. Green.

If Gordon hadn't hurried us up two days, I think you would have come home. When he wrote and said he could get off in time to be married the first and urged us so, we forgot, in a measure, every thing, & got ready to leave Wed. night. If Green hadn't married he would have been ordered to

France the 4th, but he didn't know about it until his plans were all made. I call it luck for him—especially as they had planned to be married in March.

We reached Washington Thursday night. Gordon came Friday and the wedding was at 9. Aunt Susie[1] had every thing so nice. Had ferns & palms in her big window and we bought beautiful carnations. I put one in for you to see. Ina had on 1 doz. or 2, I don't know, when she walked in as maid of honor. Maddox looked fine. He & Gordon came in—then Billie & Dad. Miss Brown, who soon marries aunt Susie's brother who is in the aviation, played the wedding march. The ring ceremony was very sweet—Green gave Billie a diamond ring—and then *our* dear Billie was Mrs. Samuel Gordon Green. I am as crazy about Green as ever. He looked perfectly grand and he & Bill were as cool as cucumbers. Green was *radiantly, beamingly* happy and Billie . . . [is] a "plum fool," you know, about Green and I'm sure she has every right & cause to be. Greens father & brother from Macon was there and we were all so glad they came.

The bride and groom spent the night in Washington at Raleigh Hotel. They came around to aunt Susies about two o'clock next day and stayed with us until we left at ten. They left at twelve o'clock for New York.

I was so proud of the suit you sent Billie. It was beautiful. She was crazy about it, too.

Miss Hettie went to the wedding. I guess Billie will write you about her wedding presents. If she doesn't, I'll tell you sometimes. She received some nice ones. Her address is 744 State St., Springfield Mass. 4th Floor.

Poor dad! He is hardly reconciled yet,[2] but he has acted very lovely & sweet. Carolyn had *such* a grand time. The night of the wedding when she was getting ready for bed, she said: "Billie didn't ha!ha! When *I* get married I'm going to ha!ha!" I am not sure what her idea was.

Did you see Billie's picture in Sunday's Constitution? It is fine. I am hurrying this off 'cause I know you want to hear something about the wedding. So glad you are feeling well & getting fat again.

> Heart of love,
> Mother

1. Richard's brother Edward and his wife, Susie, had lived in Washington for nearly twenty years, where Edward worked for the Postal Department and Susie ran a boardinghouse.

2. Richard sat on the edge of his bed before the wedding, weeping, unable to put his shoes on. Billie came in and helped him dress.

To Miss Marguerite Russell, Carrollton, Ga.

March 25, 1918

My Dearest Margo,

It has seemed an age since I had the pleasure of writing you a long letter and it seems *more* than an age since I received one of your long, interesting letters.

We just get busier every day, I do believe, and we cannot find time to do all the little things that we want to do. Pipey got so much worse about ten days ago. We couldn't get anyone to come and nurse her, and I slept over there every night for one week. Three nights we sat up. Miss Minnie Bell & myself. We made Aunt Annie sleep, for she had so much to do during the day. Pipey is much better now, but she is weak, feeble and pitiful. Her mind is in an awful state. Miss Bertha Meadows is staying with her now and it is a great relief to Aunt Annie and me. I think Pipey is gradually growing weaker, and some day she will pass out right before we know it. She doesn't take much interest in anything now. She never seems to *suffer* any and I'm so thankful. It hurts me to see her so pitiful. She has been such a good sister to me and certainly made my life much easier and happier.

I am so sorry you have been sick. Write a letter soon and tell me all about yourself and how you are—I don't like for my *teachers* to get sick. You were looking so well and I don't like to think of you getting sick. You see, not a day passes that I do not think of *you* specially, and I kind o'go'long with you—walk by your side, as it were, and *live* with you. Sometimes I kind o'see you *struggling,* but I also see that fine, healthy looking face and body, and seldom see you *sick.* But I know we all come to it, sooner or later, and have a few sick days. . . .

Sunday Papa had to go to Carnesville, Franklin Co. Ina drove the Ford and I went, for old times sake, and Walter, Wm, Fielding and Carolyn went for the fun of it. We left home at 11:30 — Got back home at 7:30 — Made 104 miles without any trouble except a lot of bumps & jolts. I enjoyed the ride. The woods and fields are beautiful. . . .

With a heart *full* of love,
Mother

To Mr. R. B. Russell, Jr., Athens, Ga.[1]

Oct. 21, 1918

My Dearest Boy,

Your letter received last week. . . . I'm so sorry you are worried about your choice of the Navy. I believe things will be better as soon as this Flu epidemic is over [and] maybe you will like things better. Papa says he thinks you can get transferred. I have some things I'd like to talk to you about. As soon as your [flu] quarantine is lifted I'm going to come over.

No, we have not killed our hogs, but Patience read your letter and immediately got on the war path for some chicken. I hope you received the box she fixed. I was busy and she did it all. She wanted to make a cake, but I had no eggs, and not much sugar. Our syrup crop is fine and may be we can have syrup candy when we want something sweet—and the goobers are good *all* the time. I have just heard that we will have no school next week. Walter is planning to pick 700 lbs. of cotton.

I do hope your fare will get better. Rob writes that his is good.[2] He has nice rich sweet milk. You wrote as if you have no meat. I do hope things will get better with you. Gordon says he is glad you are in the Navy. He seems to think it is best.

We are all moving on as usual. Dad very busy. He was in Athens last Monday and tried to see you.

Your fond, loving Mother

1. R. B., in the naval reserve, was stationed in Athens for training.
2. Rob, in the Army, was in camp at the University of Georgia.

To Mr. R. B. Russell, Jr., Athens, Ga.

Oct. 30, 1918

My Dearest Boy,

Your letter received yesterday. You just can't know how glad we are to hear from you. The little boys crowd 'round and get me to read your letter aloud to them and drink in every word.

I am so disappointed that you can't come Sat. night or Sunday morning [for your birthday]. You know how hopeful I am and if you find out that you can come, 'phone me by 12 o'clock Saturday, for if you *can't* I'll send a box to you Saturday afternoon and put on a Special Delivery, so you'll be sure to get it Sunday. I do want you to be here, but these war times we have so much to stand and this is a very small matter compared to what some others are standing. I hope you'll be feeling "fine and dandy" and can have a real good time, even if you are so closely confined. . . .

I heard from Bill yesterday. Gordon has been moved to Washington and they are very happy. I know Ina is just too happy for anything—but they may not be there long. Gordon has been wanting to go to Washington. He is so wild over making drawings of those machine guns.[1]

Ina likes her place. Her boss told her last week that her work for that week was perfect—not a single mistake. You know she is in the War Risk Insurance Building. She wrote us of seeing eight aeroplanes flying over Washington, demonstrating all kinds of stunts &c.[2]

I've been thinking of you and Rob so much since the rains have been on. Speaking of papa having Flue: He dug dirt every day last week and stayed soaking wet. I was scared to death he'd get sick, but he went to Atlanta yesterday morning feeling well and in good spirits. Said he had enjoyed his vacation. He has worlds of work to do and keeps very busy. . . .

The children are playing marbles in the hall and are making plenty of racket.

> With just *loads of love,*
> Mother

1. Gordon Green developed several guns and early gained recognition as a small arms expert.

2. Ina Jr. took the Civil Service Examination and received an appointment as a government clerk in the Bureau of War Risk Insurance, later the Veterans Administration. Her salary of one thousand dollars per year, compared to fifty dollars per month for six to eight months of teaching per year, seemed a fortune. She lived with Uncle Ed and Aunt Susie at first but later shared an apartment with young women friends who had also come to work in the capital.

To Miss Patience E. Russell, Athens, Ga.

Jan. 29, 1919

Dearest Patience,

Your letter to Harriette came to-day. It is late now and I'm awfully tired and sleepy but will write just a short note.

Now about clothes: If you have the satin skirt of course you'll need a nice waist. *Don't* get one *too* thin and too much of a nothing. You know they soon go to *nothing* any how. As to buying a dress I'll say this: Unless you find a grand bargain in quality and price, I would not buy one. . . . I think H[arriette]. mailed those slippers to-day. Patience, I do not want you to wear those awful high heels. You are too precious to me to be perched all out of plumb on heels like that. Don't buy the spats. I'll get you some nice pretty shoes for spring. . . .

[Try to] improve yourself and fit youself to be something in life. It is *awful* to see a girl go through several years of school life, and when she gets home to be so idle, dissatisfied with everything, and wholly unfit to do anything. I have had my heart set on you. My efforts to put you in a good school and in pleasant, refined surroundings has turned out so different from what I thought and it makes me heart sick and I feel like having a big cry sometimes. God knows I had nothing but your best interest in my mind. It hurt me to give you up at home for even if you were not here much, you were a great deal of comfort and pleasure to me. It seems sad you cannot understand my motives. You know when I had your tonsils removed and had your eyes examined, you seemed to think I was just trying to treat you bad, when really, I was concerned and just wanted to remove anything that might be in your way of growing into a well, healthy girl. I regret that so much goes wrong. But you'll find many obstacles as you go along. I just wish you saw things differently. Sometimes I've felt that I could not bear for you to feel so about me. It hurt me more because I felt that I was doing such a grand thing for you. But it can't be helped now. Mothers have to stand a great deal any how. I know you'll understand it all some day, and I'm feeling that you'll not always blame me. . . .

Papa is here and I'll get him to send a check. Write me why you do not like your teacher (music). I did want you to like her, and I do hope you practice a great deal. How much do you practice per day?

I didn't expect to write exactly this kind of letter when I began, but its been on my heart so long, it just had to come out. I do love you so much and want you to improve yourself and be a happy sweet girl.

     Your mother

To Miss Patience E. Russell, Athens, Ga.

Sunday afternoon Feb. 11, 1919

My Dearest Patty-whack,

. . . There is a wild rumor on foot here to-day that we are going to buy a car—a Dodge. I have been talking car ever since Rob bought the Ford and I talk big and strong. I feel that we *must* have a car and I tell papa so, just any time. R. B.[1] has taken up my theme now, and he said to-day, that we were going to have one. I think the car they want belongs to James Bell. James is married, you know, and he wants a lot to build on. I don't know tho' that they will trade that way. . . .

I want you to tell me sometimes if you are taking Domestic S[cience]. I hope you are. Papa told me a few days ago that I'd ruined a smart sweet girl by sending her off to school. That you know how to do *everything* and when you came home you would not know how to "pick up a pan." It seems that my good intentions have been misunderstood all 'round. . . .

I was awfully glad you made 100 in your Geom. exam. Do it again, child. Dick said a girl told him that you were a "Shark" in Geom.

My new smokehouse and store room is nearly completed and I'm so delighted.

Aunt Annie & Pipey are well as usual and precious as ever.

Patience, if you want the guitar and can learn it all right, I want you to have one. You can't help it that the others didn't have one. If they had had the opportunity to learn and had asked for one, I think they would have had it. . . .

Do you ever wear your hair down? *Don't* use too much powder and *very little,* so very little color (paint) you can hardly see it. . . .

You must write papa another letter sometimes. He is awful busy. He & Dick are getting along fine together. Rob seems to be doing O.K. in his "Hark! from the tomb a doleful sound" business.[2]

Auntney said you were looking so well. I've been wanting to run over to see you and will come soon if possible. . . .

Excuse pencil. I'm sitting up by the fire. Have been teaching the children the 1st Psalm.

> With heart of love,
> Mother

1. She uses both R. B. and Dick for her eldest son in this letter.

2. Dick Jr. was practicing law with his father, managing the Winder office, while Richard Sr. worked mainly in Atlanta. Rob was selling tombstones in Atlanta.

To Miss Patience E. Russell, Athens, Ga.

March 24, 1919

Dearest Patience,

. . . Walter brought your letter in Sunday morning. I was in bed with one of my old time spells. I had a real bad one but am feeling about over it now. I'm glad you liked the dress. I thought it would suit your type of beauty. . . .

Carolyn is sweet bad and cute as ever. She is going to school regular now. The weather is so good. She is up with her class. She told me the other day that she was the most "ignorant fool in school." It tickled me. She came in the kitchen the other morning and said with a sigh: "I am in a terrible condition." I asked how. She said, "Well, I just can't make this satchel feel good on my shoulder." Alex came in to-night with another A report. He's the same old steady. Edward is wild as ever. I don't see how he will pass as he never studies. William has a garden and is very much enthused. Fielding made 96 in a History test and is the same good old faithful worker.

You just can't know what a strain I've been on since the 7th of January. Thats when aunt Hattie was taken so sick. Every time the 'phone would ring I'd know it was a message from her. And you know I went when I could and stayed as long as I could. She suffered so much and died a horrible death. After she was buried I had to stay over and pack up all her things and see Laura (Mrs. Binns[1]) go into all her things. It was very trying on me. . . . I wanted to come home, for it was not aunt Hattie's house any longer and I didn't feel like staying there. . . .

I have your letter before me and have tried to answer every question. I have just reached the place where you said, if you asked 15,000,000 questions I'd never answer one. Now Pat, you are from a big family and you know you are not the only pebble, &c. I told Harriette ever so many answers to tell you to questions you had asked. I keep busier than ever, Doscia was not here a day last week. I'm trying to garden and get our home in good shape for spring and summer. Our grape vines are clean and look so nice. The porch boxes need attention. Sometimes lately I've felt like throwing up my hands and saying: I cannot go another step. I'm trying to raise a yard *full* of chickens and they keep me busy. . . .

I wrote you *long ago, I know* I did, that we wanted you to have guitar. Just buy it, case, and all, and have it charged to papa, and tell them to send him the bill. I am very anxious for you to learn to play.

I'm glad you got to the game. I want you to *take in* as many things as possible as well as learn a great deal while at Lucy Cobb, and cultivate a sweet, gentle disposition, and be honorable and truthful about *everything* and never forget the Golden Rule.

If you should get to come home, you'd better write Doscia a note & put it in some of the home letters and encourage her. She came back to work this morning in a fine, lovely humor and did wonders, but said she'd have to stop off every Sat. at 12 and not come back till Mon. I knew it was useless to argue, so I told her all right, but if I had company she'd have to come on Sunday. She seemed willing, if I'd let her know in time. . . .

You will have to get a day off to read this . . . .[2]

 With a heart of love,
 Mother

 1. Hattie's husband's daughter by his first wife.
 2. The unedited letter is twenty pages long.

To Miss Patience E. Russell, Milledgeville, Ga.

Mar. 6, 1920

Dearest Pat,

Your letter came to-night. . . . I believe you write to me oftener than any girl I've ever had from home. . . .

We have had some awful weather & I just can't do anything but cook & make fires and sweep just enough to keep all the big trash up & you should see me make the beds! I just *throw* the cover up & away I go, and I'm certainly glad there is no matron to come along behind me & *inspect.* . . .

Wm., Edward & Alex have cut a lot of wood, and Fielding & Walter have hauled a lot of rich dirt in the garden & you know that pleases *me.*

It was awful about Jeanette [Quillian]. H[arriette] wrote you about her leaving the little baby and the baby died the day she was buried. Poor Joe is left all alone. His little boy is in Gainesville with Jeanette's aunt and the little girl is in Madison. Joe is staying here for awhile. He said he could not stay in Winder. His little home was broken all to pieces. He has packed up all of his things. . . .[1]

Papa has two very important cases now—and he may have to go to Montgomery Ala. next week and then go on to Washington D.C. on some important business. He says if he wins this case he will not have to work any more. Papa is begging me to go to Washington with him, but I'll not go. I'm in for saving all I can to put in my house. I do want to fix it nice. I know we can't be so awful swell, but I think we can fix up real nice and comfortable. I want the wedding to go off just fine and I believe it will. . . .[2]

Carolyn was so glad to get your letter & got to work at once to write you another letter. She read it [your letter] over ever so many times & every time she would say: "Why didn't Patience keep writing till she filled up this letter?" You know you left a space & she wanted it filled up. . . .[3]

I'll try to send some eggs soon.

Mother

1. Joe Quillian, a young lawyer in Winder, was distantly related to Ina. Mary (Auntney), Richard's sister who lived with their youngest brother Lewis, died of pneumonia in December 1919, and Ina had taken Lewis in then. Rob had left the tombstone business in order to come home and read law. He passed the Georgia bar exam before he was twenty years old. Thus, including Richard Sr. and R. B., Ina had five lawyers living under her roof.

2. Marguerite was engaged to James H. Bowden, with the wedding set for June 24, 1920. Ina was spending some of the two thousand dollars she inherited from Aunt Hattie on her house and new furniture.

3. Ina always filled up every space in her letters!

To Miss Patience E. Russell, Milledgeville, Ga.

Mar. 17, 1920

My Dearest Pat,

. . . Doscia worries me to death about sending you a chicken.[1] She came over Monday morning and said she was going to fix that chicken any way and cook it and send it to you by herself. I told her I would send it to you sometime this week, if possible. . . . I never was so busy in all my life. Some days I feel like running away.

I'm certainly sorry I've never sent you any eggs. I think about you every time I gather up the eggs and then forget to send them when I get in the house, or rather I forget it when I get through with my cooking.

I think Marguerite is coming Sat. & maybe we can make some plans for our wedding, and I'll write you about them. Take care of yourself & keep well. Hold yourself *straight* when you walk and when you sit down.

   Your loving Mother

After supper:

All of our big men—lawyers all! have gone to town. Papa came from Atlanta on our train. I fed the gang—and I just can't cook enough some-times—then they all went to town to look up points in a big case—and I hope they get some money out of it. . . .

Harriette says she is going to the office in the morning.[2] She has washed her hair to-night.

I'm about to nod out of my chair. I have to get up in the mornings to get my crowd off in time. Just think! Twelve[3] leave and just one poor little me stays at home. Then dinner to get & then supper and so on, every day, just the same—but be not weary in well doing.

   Mother

 1. Patience adored fried chicken. When she was ten years old, she bet R. B. that she could eat a whole chicken, and although he required that she also kill it, clean it, and help Laura cook it, she won the bet.

 2. Harriette was working for the law firm occasionally.

 3. The five lawyers, plus Harriette, Walter, the twins, Alex, Edward, and Carolyn.

To Mr. Walter B. Russell, Monroe, Ga.

                 Oct. 5, 1920

Dearest Boy,

You bad old thing to write & ask me to let you come home Fri. You know you ought to ask papa. I want you to come on the afternoon train & not miss a whole day from school. Now arrange to do this and you can go to the Fair Friday night and have a big time. Sure enough boy, don't miss all day Fri. . . .

I didn't go to the [football] game. Sunie, myself & all the little boys &

Carolyn & [little] Sunie, & uncle Ben went [to Athens] for a little trip. When we got home it was dark. We stopped out on the road for the little boys to get out & do the night work. I was going to town to take Sunie & get bread &c. We saw a car coming and I told every body to be still until the car passed. Edward didn't seem to understand & ran across the road right into the car. It struck him & sounded just like a ball when a good player hits it. Of course we were terrified.

Papa was on the porch & came running. The car stopped & Mr. *Florence* Bell[1] got out and came back in a hurry. William had picked Edward up & Mr. Bell took him and tried to get him to the house. We all screamed & Carolyn, little Sunie & Alex were crying. It was awful! The house was dark. I ran in & tried to turn on the lights. Papa was saying all kinds of things about E. never being able to walk . . . or he might die &c. Mr. B. was crying like a child. Papa took E. after Mr. B. got him in the house and he & Sunie carried him upstairs.

Mr. B. *flew* for doctor Almond. Dr. A. soon came and examined Edward and said he was not *seriously* hurt. His head and neck were so bloody and he looked so pale. A gash was cut in his head & doctor A. had to take 9 stitches. It was all so terrible. Doscia & Jim were here & I had a fire in stove to heat water. It took a lot of water. Andrew West had brought H[arriette]. home from the game and he helped Dr. Almond.

Edward stood it like a man . . . and was able to get up next day about twelve o'clock. He limps some, but Dr. A. says he will soon be all right. He will take the stitches out Sat. Edward went to the Fair to-day but he had to stay with me. He rode on the Merry-go-round twice.

You be sure not to lose all of Friday from school. The Fair is just the same old thing. Nothing new. I am certainly glad you are studying. Go to it! I'm counting on you. . . .

    Mother

1. Of the prosperous Bell family who lived near Pipey and Annie.

To Patience E. Russell, Milledgeville, Ga.

Friday Night [April 15, 1921]

Dearest Pat,

. . . I think you all have to be having a big time this spring. So many nice lunches at the river and going out to Miss Lanes &c. I'm always so glad when you girls have these little outside pleasures . . .

Patience dearie. . . . Please don't make your dresses too short. It is out of reason for a girl to have her dresses to the knees. A few in[ches] longer would look so much nicer and I'm sure you'll feel much nicer when you wear them. Girls are making themselves *too common* in so many ways. The *extremely* short dresses is one way. Don't say I want them to your ankle. I do not, but I want my child decent and *reasonably* dressed.

Papa saw something on the train last night that astounded him. Two girls in the smoking [car] with two boys, *smoking* all of them. I guess they were going to Athens to Little Commencement. . . .

I'll try to write you a long letter soon.

With a heart of love,
Mother

To Miss Patience Russell, Washington, D.C.[1]

Friday night [Autumn 1921]

Dearest Pat,

Dad has given me your letter to address. Poor us! So many new city numbers & we can't remember them. I have them all put down on my stationery box, & I'm about to memorize them. Dad said I could read his letter and I have just done so. Poor Dad! He is so anxious for his children to do certain things & I'm afraid none of us will *come up* to his expectations. It is a beautiful, sweet letter and dad does love his children. He just has so many & he doesn't know what to do with them.

I rec'd your letter to-day—just as I was starting to the Fair—and you don't know how humiliated I've felt this week. No car—just the kindness of the Robertsons has gotten me to the Fair & of course I have to go when they say go & *come* when they say come & you know how I *hate* to trouble people. To-day was old people's day & aunt Annie & Pipey went with me & *all* of us got in *free*—all over 50 & you know that's *me*. . . .

I'm glad dad sent you a ck. You get Ina paid up for board. I know its hard on her & I hope you make yourself useful & a support to Ina for she is out working all day & all the responsibility is on her. . . .

The little boys worked & made nearly all the money they have spent at the Fair. Wm won 1st prize in poultry—$4.00 in cash. Pipey put in a counterpane that your great grand mother Patience Elizabeth wove over 100 years ago & she won the blue ribbon on it & she won 2nd prize on a quilt that your grand mother made the year she married—and she was just 16 yrs. old.

You will have to think good over dad's letter. He may insist on you coming home. I don't see what progress you could make in [taking] music in two or three months. It takes years to do any thing in music. . . .

Uncle Ed came in to-night on the local from Athens. He made me *absolutely sick,* talking about you all & my baby. Why can't I see you all? *Everybody* sees you all but me! Boo-hoo! . . .

Papa, uncle Ed, Joe & Carolyn are all in the dining room talking, talking & I can't hear my ears. Papa is telling uncle Ed. what he wants you to do. You are to learn to play & sing to amuse him in his old age. I'll have to stop writing as every body seems to be on a "high horse" and I can't collect my thoughts. . . .

  My love to Ina & to you,
  Mother

1. After graduating from GN&IC, Pat went to Washington in July to help Billie following the birth of her first child, a son called Richard Russell Green. Marguerite had given birth to Marguerite Russell Bowden in March.

To Miss Patience E. Russell, Washington, D.C.

Sep. 28, 1921

Dearest Pat,

. . . I ought to be writing to my Ina to-night instead of you, for I've owed her a letter a long time, but I thought I'd write you *one more time* about coming home. I thought I made it clear enough in my last letter, but don't suppose I did. *I said:* if you really *want* to stay in W'ton I'd ask papa to please let me stay until I could find a job. *I said:* I thought it would be pleasanter & more profitable for you to stay in W'ton than to come here to absolutely *nothing.* So much doing in a big place & you could improve yourself. I wish you could get so busy and interested that you'd *forget* to paint your face & pluck your eye-brows. There are so many nice things for girls to do these days. Sometimes I almost wish I could *start over* and try my hand. Couldn't you find some branch of Ina's nice school that you could attend? I don't know what else to tell you. You know I'm always so happy to have you at home, but I've found out that home is not always the best place for grown children—especially when its in the country as we are—so much thats useless & worthless—and nothing that really teaches you to live, or rather inspires you to *get out* & do things.

Now you do just as you think best & just as you'd rather do. Papa keeps saying he is coming to W'ton but I don't think now he will. He has not been very well. He has been at home a whole lot lately & moved enough dirt to build a city. He went to Homer with uncle L[ewis]. & Mr. Chandler & the car hit a bridge and bumped papa up (like you did me once) and cut a bad gash in his head. He suffered with it. Its most well now.

Mr. "Nick" Rainey died last wk. in Atlanta & was buried in Winder Tuesday. I had never seen a millionaire funeral so I went.[1] The church was packed. The flowers were beautiful. He was buried in an $1800 casket and his two children had a floral design "The Gates Ajar" most as large as my garden gate—that was simply magnificent and cost $1000. Mrs. Rainy [sic] had a blanket of flowers—mostly pink roses—that was beautiful. I carried aunt Annie & Pipey to the cemetery this A.M. to see the flowers. . . .

You asked about Walter. . . . We got him ready & sent him to Oglethorpe U. and he stayed two nights and came home. Didn't like it one bit. I felt so mortified. Had never seen one of my chicks do so. He says he is at his rows end, but as soon as papa can, I expect he'll get him in Ga. You see Walter ought never to have gone back to A.& M., for he had finished there. Athletics is the only cause of all these crazy doings. He would have wasted his time at A.& M. as far as lessons were concerned. Papa had every plan made to take him right over to Ga. Dick butted in & suggested Oglethorpe for one year. Walter consented and then didn't like it, for the dormitory he was in didn't have any boy who wanted to go in for athletics & there was no other place for him to stay, so he came home. Dad is worried some. But I suppose he will let Walter go on to Ga. His trunk is at Oglethorpe now. Its a mess & I'm disgusted with Walter for being so unsettled. . . .

I'm sending my love to my darlings in W-ton. Kiss my precious baby for me. . . .

Your fond Mother

The morning has come & I don't feel quite as stupid as I did last night. Dad said this A.M. at breakfast table that he was going to Washington to-night. . . . This is about his 'steen threat to go to W-ton. I don't know what he will do. He is not in a good physical condition at all. I wish he would go, and try to forget himself and get to feeling better. He said if he went he was going to bring you home with him. If he does, I guess you can help me cook and iron and get the children off to school and keep the living room & front porch in decent order. How does that strike you? You see these things have to be done—but I hope you can arrange for the best and my child will be happy and can improve herself.

Doscia has just come in & asked "which one of chilluns you're writing to?" I said *ole* Patience. D. said: "Well, she didn't look *old* when she left here—she looked young & pretty."

This reminds me: I carried Pipey & aunt A. down in Morgan County to see Cousin Jane Lewis. I hadn't seen her in 40 years. She looked at me & said: "Why Ina, is this you? The last time I saw you, you looked like a beautiful rose." I said: "And now I look like a withered collard leaf." She never *did* say I did *not*!

What would Henry Ford have *on his hands* if he married a widow with two children? You & Ina may know this joke. Of course Uncle Walter [Dillard] brought [it]. You may not know it, so I'll tell you: He would have a second-hand Lizzie & two run-abouts. I thought this was funny, so I pass it on.

I know you are ready to throw this letter down. I just felt like writing. I do want to see you all & my *boy* so much. If papa decides to bring you home, *sho nuff,* maybe you could get Miss Haygood's place in Winder—teaching *penmanship* & spelling. I hear she & Henry Hill will marry soon. . . .

We still haven't any water. We pray for rain & if it comes we catch every drop we can. Mrs. R. hasn't any either. We went to aunt A's & now a pesky *rat* is in her well. We go to Doscia's and the little boys fuss & grumble & I do too. Marguerite is crazy to move into her little home & it *hasn't water!* Excuse me! When I move to a city, I'm going to have water and lights. . . .

Really, I have waited a whole minute & can't think of anything else to say. Tell my Ina to please take part of this letter for hers and say I will send her one "pretty" soon.

    Mother

1. Richard had married Nick Rainey and Susie C. Randolph in a civil ceremony in 1901.

To Mrs. James H. Bowden, Atlanta, Ga.

Mar. 20, '22

Monday A.M. and so much to see after—But I just write a short note to tell you that I'm still enjoying the *perfect day* I had with you yesterday. You'll never know how I feel until our dear Marguerite is your age and maybe situated just as you are and you see how grand & fine she is—how efficient and capable—how lovely, sweet and everything! You & Jim & our baby are just *our own,* and we cannot find words to express how dear & precious you are to us. You fill in such a broad, beautiful space in our lives, that could not be so complete if we did not have you.

Can you realize a whole year has passed since I was hurrying to Atlanta to see my first grand child? Nothing in this world sweeter than a baby and *our* baby is just sweeter than any thing. . . .

When we *sat around* last night & talked over our lovely day, we had just as many sweet & loving things to say about Jim as we did you & our baby. Isn't that lovely? It just makes so much happiness in this world and we appreciate Jim and love him as our very own. . . .

    Mother

To Mrs. James H. Bowden, Atlanta, Ga.

May 18, 1922

Dearest Marguerite,

    . . . I had been expecting a Mother's Day letter from you. You see we mothers get spoiled. I had a telegram Sunday A.M. from Ina & a letter Tues-

day. Sat. I had a letter from Walter & one Sun. & one Monday & a box of
Martha Wash. candy. A letter Sun. from Rob and Monday a letter from
Billie. It is not such a bad thing after all to have a large family. I certainly
enjoy my children. Ina wrote a beautiful letter & told me how thankful she
was that she could wear a pink flower instead of a white one.

One little child wore a white rose in our S.S. Sunday. We had exercises at
our Sunday School. May & Grace had coached the children and they had
beautiful recitations and songs about Mother. Mrs. Mott has a beautiful
contralto voice & she sang Mother Machree. All of us cried. Mr. Potts had
been inspired & had composed a very sweet piece on Mother and Grace
asked Pat[ience] to dress like a Mother & sit out in front of the choir &
read it at the close of the service. She wore my mother's bonnet. I hadn't
seen it in thirteen years—and she put aunt Annie's switches on to represent
the gray hair & wore one of aunt Annie's black dresses & white collars. She
was an adorable mother & she sat in a chair that was all draped in white,
through the entire service. It was a sweet service, but very sad. I don't think
there was a soul in the house over 18 yrs. old who did not shed one tear.

As I wrote you, [the] little children all joined the church. We had had
two weeks of revival services at the Methodist & Baptist churches. Splendid
preaching and splendid singing. 115 joined the Meth. & 60 joined the Bapt.
& 17 joined the Pres. I put my letter in the Pres. as I told you I was. Two
ladies came from the Christian Church & two, Alice & Jack, from the Epis-
copal. The other twelve were children & joined during the revival. Uncle
Lewis, Cam [Brumby], Mr. Quarterman & Mr. Potts were so happy they
were ready to shout.

I wanted papa to join with me, but he said he could not. And I wanted
Rob to join, & I asked Dick to put his letter in, but he says he is going to
put his in the Methodist.[1] I do want us all to be members of the church.
I'm sure the church is a good safe place to be, and I know we need all the
help we can get to live here and to live hereafter.

. . . I'm sending my best love to you, Jim & my baby.

Mother

1. Dick Russell Jr. had actually never taken his letter from the Methodist Church. Rob
eventually joined the Presbyterian Church.

To Hon. R. B. Russell, Jr., House of Representatives, Atlanta, Ga.

[August 9, 1922]

Dearest Boy,

I am enclosing my letter to aunt Lella.[1] I hope it is satisfactory. As you know, or ought to know, I am *very fond* of aunt Lella. I met her the day she married my good brother Miles and she has been an inspiration to me and a guiding star. I believe I have always known how good and intelligent she was. She is not like a great many who are capable of doing things in public. She is sweet and patient and loving with her husband and children and never neglected them, for anything.

Now, I want to tell *you*, and *you* can tell Rob. *You* & *Rob* and *dad*, just you three, have made it very hard for *me* to go to aunt Lella this time. You speak in your letter of aunt Lella being "hostile" & "haughty" and Rob has always used the word *narrow*. She is too good at heart to be haughty or hostile and I cannot see that she is narrow. Now, here's where you've made it hard for me. When Sister Lella came to Winder & conducted her meeting and made her beautiful speech, I couldn't get one of you to go near. You all are not even nice to her children, my own blood kin, & those children are dear to me, for their father was my greatest help in many ways when I was young & wanted to go off to school and I cannot forget it.

I have grieved over Rob's *hostility* and haughty spirit and fierce criticisms—just because *somebody* didn't think as he did. Papa has been harsh & hurt me so, in things he would say about aunt Lella. Aunt Lella gave papa the opportunity of running on *her ticket.* He didn't believe that way. I don't see that she could well be for him. But I don't believe she ever said one ugly thing about him & many *men* did, that you *all* are friendly with now. You wouldn't go out to the W.C.T.U. meeting either and you have never been friendly to aunt Lella's boys and Annie Zu used to be so fond of you and you wouldn't go out of your way to see her. She is right out at Emory & has a splendid intelligent husband. I just want to remind you that if you all had been nice all the time, this would have been so much easier for me. I hope you will approve of my letter. I do love Sister Lella and love her children. I have often wished that my boys knew her boys. Rob thought, or seemed to think it grand, that he didn't know Fielding. Do destroy this, but I want you & Rob to think.

> [no signature; written on the back of Dick's letter, using every available space.]

1. Richard Sr. was running for chief justice of the State Supreme Court, and the Women's Christian Temperance Union, harking back to the 1911 governor's campaign, endorsed the incumbent, William Fish. Dick Jr. wrote his mother and asked her to ask Aunt Lella to use her influence in the statewide organization to dismiss such publicity because the issue of local option was "as dead as slavery," which of course it was, with Prohibition the law of the land.

To Miss Ina D. Russell, Washington, D.C.

Aug. 19, 1922

Dearest Ina,

. . . Papa and Walter leave to-morrow for a tour of South Ga. in a *new* Ford. *They* are very busy sending out literature & writing letters. People tell me that our dad is going to be elected. *I hope so,* for I don't see how I could stand it. I did not want him to make this race. . . .

Did you know aunt Annie has been very sick? For three days I was so uneasy about her. I stayed with her in the day & Pat at night. It was so pitiful over there—the 3 old, feeble people. Pipey seems very well but is feeble. You can't imagine what a fix uncle Ben is in.[1] He can hardly walk, and he can't talk. His throat is paralyzed & he is pitiful. Aunt A. is better now. She is up & cooks dinner. Pipey gets up & cooks breakfast. We help them all we can. You write to aunt Annie. She is so fond of you. . . .

> With my best love,
> Mother

1. Ben Dillard had suffered a stroke and had come to Annie and Pipey for help.

To Miss Patience Russell, Cochran, Ga.

Sep. 8, 22

Dearest Pat,

It is 9:30. My little crowd of F[ielding], E[dward] & A[lex] are fast asleep. Of course ole Carline is awake, but she will soon turn in. I am upstairs for

I just can't stay down by my self. I am too worn out to write much of a letter—have worked hard all day trying to get things cleaned up before next wk['s election]. I have ironed *all* my clothes for this wk. & I have had Arch cleaning up the yard all day. I have wished for my [porch] chair covers to be made. I got them out, but soon put them up. Didn't have the nerve to tackle them.

Your letter came this A.M. I hope you will not have headaches. Don't worry one bit. Edward has a teacher, Miss Donalson, who powders her nose and uses lip stick in school room. He seems very much disgusted & is always saying: "I hope Pat don't do that way!" Our Carolyn will say, "Don't be uneasy. I don't think she will." . . .

Joe K. is not at [campaign] headquarters any more & Harriette is in his place. I think she wants to come home. I guess everything will be over before I write again. Hope you have received my other letter, and I do want you to be careful of your health. . . . Wish you could be here Weds. . . .

Love,
Mother

To Mrs. S. Gordon Green, Columbus, Ga.

Sep. 19, 1922

My Dearest Billie, and my precious Bunny
and my dearly beloved Gordon—

I have wished for you to be here to enjoy all our good, happy occasions, resulting from our successful election. I have wished for you especially as certain things would come up. . . . Of course the good news we rec'd Wednesday night was the first. Alice & Jack were with me nearly all day Wed. We went to prayer meeting and stopped in town to get some news as we came on home, and Jack phoned the manager of the Athens Banner and we got it straight from the Associated Press that Russell was *sweeping* the state! We came on home, very happy.

Thursday, the Constitution verified the news and we were happy again. Alice stayed with me all day and I expected some of our people to come in from Atlanta, and they *did,* but it was nearly eleven o'clock when they got here. Dad, Harriette and Walter came. Mr. Cooper & Charlie A. were here

& I was glad for I had been by myself (except the children) since Alice and Jack left. We talked till one o'clock. Dad was so happy & we all were!

All day Fri. we heard rumors of an ovation that night from the people of Winder. I thought maybe a few ladies and maybe 50 men would come out from Winder, so about 7 o'clock I had dad fixed up (we had been trying to keep it all from him) & I was hurrying to get my *very* simple supper on the table and wishing that Rob had come on the train & wishing that *all my children* were with me. I was in the kitchen straining the milk & I heard somebody in the hall. I walked in the dining room to see who it was, and in walked Marguerite. Then uncle Lewis, then Rob & Mr. Walter Brown and Jim & little Marguerite. Of course, I was *dee*-lighted to see them. I had the house in very good order, so we placed them all around & I had coffee for dad & that was lucky for my menfolks. Everybody ate some supper & then about 8:30 people began to come. Soon the house was *full* of ladies from Winder & they all brought boxes and put them on the back porch. I was ordered to the front. Clio was commander. "Mrs. Russell, go right on out yonder and entertain your friends, we will manage things here!!" Believe me, Mrs. R. did go to the front and I was walking on air.

Soon a truck rolled into the back yard with tubs and big jars and boxes of cups. In the meantime cars were coming & going & people, men, women & children everywhere! Dad was on the porch shaking hands with every body & I was in the living room, receiving the ladies. At least one hundred ladies and about 400 men. Every body was so happy! Soon the ladies had two tables on the front porch & began to serve the punch and cakes & all kinds of sweet crackers. So many waiters & so many cups (tin) and so many nice little cakes and every body laughing & joking and I had *such* a grand time—just as I would at someone elses home—no responsibility, except to be pleasant and it was dead easy to be that.

In the midst of all our fun, we heard an ovation outside & soon found that the Gov. elect & his wife & all the Walkers from Monroe had arrived. Sunie was chairman of the refreshment committee so she introduced Mrs. Walker to me & to a lot of the ladies & she was very nice & friendly & easy among us all.

Of course we had some remarks from our successful candidates, and as it was Dad's ovation, he spoke first. Mr. Johns was master of ceremonies, & introduced the speakers. The lights were lit on the porch all this time of course & the people outside could see & hear dad perfectly. Dad made a lovely speech. The crowd went wild time and again when he brought out certain points in his campaign. Dear dad was getting just what he had deserved for so long, and I was so happy for him. After he spoke, the Gov-elect was called on & he said, that as he was only a guest & had come to pay his respects to the Chief Justice-elect, he didn't feel that he ought to say much &c, but he made a very nice speech. Mrs. Walker & I sat to-gether just inside the living room, by the hat rack.

Mr. Johns made the fact very prominent that on this occasion three distinct branches of our government was represented: the judiciary, the executive and the representative. Then he had Walker, dad & Dick to stand side by side as he pointed this out. As the judiciary and executive had spoken, he called on Dick to represent the representative & old Dick made a fine speech. Then Mr. Walter Brown[1] was called on & he was so happy and made a nice speech.

All this happened right on our porch & I'm sure it can be pointed out some day as a "historic spot." I was wishing for my absent children. Mr. Walker brought William over with him [from Monroe A&M]. I loved him for it. You, Ina & Pat and my Gordon & Bunny were the ones my heart was calling.[2]

I know all this will sound strange but you can close your eyes & see it, even if I can't write a *graphic* description. The house full of ladies did not impress me so much, but the sea of faces in our yard! Some of the ladies told me that cars were parked everywhere—about 150 cars!

Barrow Co. gave Dick a complete vote—1247—the total vote of Barrow Co.[3] Not a voter scratched him. Dad got 1100 of the votes. I don't care to know who the 147 are who voted against [him]. Jones Co. certainly stood by us. & Henry Co.

"There is no bliss without alloy" & in all our rejoicing I was regretting that we lost Muscogee on your & Gordon's account, but above all, I do not want Gordon to think harshly of sister Lella. I am sending a letter from her for Gordon. She is so dear to me.[4] I think dad got out very light for I was afraid the women would have it in for him on account of his local option platform. If it had been anyone else running I'm sure sister L[ella]. would have been *very* active. Columbus & Fitzgerald seem to be the only places that the women worked against us.

Marguerite & the baby stayed with us till Sunday. Miss H[ettie]. & uncle Jim came for them. Jim & Rob & Mr. B[rown] went to Atlanta Saturday A.M. in one of our Fords. You know dad bought two. He has given me one for the children to use for school. He wants to sell the other.

Dad seems well, but he is thin. Rob shows the effect of the election or rather campaign more than any one. He said he was going somewhere to rest. I immediately began to beg him to go & stay a week with you and rest up. I would never say anything definite about it.

Walter went to Athens yesterday to enter Ga. University. He seemed very much in earnest. Dick carried him over. He had been given an S.A.E. pledge pin, so Dick carried him to the Chapter House. He hadn't been in town long before his hair was clipped. Write him c/o S.A.E. Chapter House. I do want him to do well. He is so big & strong and is nice and good.

This is an awful letter. I've wanted to write, but had so much to do. Everything has been upset & in confusion. But I am so relieved over the success we have had and I am *thankful*. I had felt so blue & downcast, for I did not want to be defeated. . . .

I have Bunny's picture here by me. Kiss him.

      Mother

1. Richard's old friend who had worked so hard in his other campaigns.

2. In a similar letter to Pat, equal in length, Ina writes: "Two of the happiest souls here was Pipey & Annie. They looked so sweet in their white dresses."

3. He did not have opposition, but voters could and did scratch unopposed candidates.

4. Ina's letter to Lella and her reply have been lost, but the two women remained close and loving all their lives.

To Miss Patience Russell, Cochran, Georgia

                                    Sep. 27, 1922

Dearest Patience,

Our hearts haven't quit beating *so fast* yet, over the news we received this A.M. Just before the mail came Rob called me and asked if I had heard anything "from Patience." I said *no*—is any thing the matter? He told me then of the [automobile] accident. He had seen an account of it in Constitution. I immediately called Lella [Dillard Whipple].[1] She was out and I called Mrs. Jacksons. My heart was thumping terribly. While I was talking to Mrs. Mathews I heard some body come in the front door. I thought it was Harriette as she had been spending some time with Montine and expected to come home this A.M. When I finished my message & turned around, I saw it was uncle Lewis & cousin Alice. Uncle L. had seen an account of it in Constitution & had 'phoned Mrs. Jackson & he had hurried out to tell me before I saw the paper.

You should have sent me a message. Mrs. Jackson or Lella would have 'phoned me. You know that news travels fast & mothers don't like to hear things of this kind first from the news papers.

I wrote you of our meetings at the church and so many good prayers have been offered for each of our members every night & I feel sure that those prayers saved your life. I am thankful that you are not seriously hurt or will not be disfigured for life. You certainly had to suffer a long time [before getting treatment].[2]

I do feel miserable that it should have happened. I wish something could have been done to prevent it. You didn't say who was driving—or if the car was going *fast*, but I suppose it was. Rob regrets that it happened at night. It looked so glaring in the paper. . . .

I had been having such queer feelings about my children and felt that something was going to happen to some of them. The freshmen in Athens "took in" the town Sat. night, and Walter wrote Dick that he painted "26"[3] on the water tower. I knew he was safe then, but I had such a feeling in my heart & I still have it. I had not dreamed of him doing *that*. Now I'm thinking of *you*. I don't guess we [will] ever know who or what was the cause, but I regret it. I want my children to have a good time, but you know how I have preached and preached about fast driving & so much reckless driving—and how awful automobile accidents appear to me. Macon is 40 or 50 miles from Cochran, isn't it? A long distance.

Don't you think you had better come home until your arm heals? Yours is our first broken bone in our big family. I hope you are not suffering. I know you will be cared for, but I'd love to have you here. You come on home if you want to. You have always been so strong in your arms & I'd hate for you to have a weak arm now.

I should say the school [year] is broken into! I'm sorry for Grace and I know she feels bad. Alice stayed out here with me. You know how I am— I *will not* show my feelings before people—if she was not here, I believe I would lie down and cry, & cry, & cry. I just feel awful. I have hoped that nothing of this kind would ever come to me & mine. . . .

Mothers feel so terrible when their children are in trouble, or rather when they are away from home and are sick & suffering. I feel so bad about it all. I almost feel resentful against *somebody* for planning that trip for school nights, any how. . . .

I 'phoned Rob & told him the news after I talked with Mrs. Mathews. He said he had sent you a telegram. Poor dad was worried when he came to dinner. Uncle Lewis . . . came with him. . . .

I do want to do something for you. You are a mighty sweet child & I love you. I have missed you terribly.

Heart of love,
Mother

1. Aunt Lella's daughter, who lived next door to the home where Pat boarded.
2. Pat had to wait about five hours before her broken arm could be set because others were more seriously hurt.
3. "Class of 26."

To Miss Patience E. Russell, Cochran, Ga.

Thursday night [October 26, 1922]

Dearest Pat,

I have promised you a letter "real soon" and if I don't begin one to-night I'm afraid I'll be a long time writing one. . . .

Harriette has been in dear Atlanta since Monday A.M. She will be there until Sat. I think Ralph [Sharpton] is coming up, & they are going to a game. . . .[1]

Papa has a boy hired—He is 15 yrs. old & head taller than Fielding [also fifteen]. Of course he is hired to dig dirt, or rather *haul* dirt. Papa lets me have him when he is gone—and I have to give him dinner. When Trudie was away I made him help me in the kitchen. He is very bright & could do anything I wanted him to. I believe I could train him to cook, and I could have a "Clarence." I could let him drive the car too. I am thrilled over him. His father has moved in the house Arch lived in. Arch has moved into the house aunt Milly Ann lived in. I wish you were here to train "*Bob.*" (That's his name.) I have Bob hauling rich dirt for my flowers and helping me in the garden. I am going to have some lovely flowers next year if possible. . . .

I am glad you sent the ck. for church. Know you are glad too. . . . I have heard from Henry Ford & he says it is *impossible* for him to give me the car for our preacher. I don't like Henry any more. I was so disappointed. . . .

Do you feel real well these days? Is Grace's face looking better than you thought? . . . I'm glad you are going to make it easy on those children, even the little cocoanut-headed boy on that front seat. . . .

      Heart of love,
      Mother

1. Since Margo's marriage, Ralph Sharpton was courting Harriette.

To Miss Patience Russell, Cochran, Ga.

Dec. 7, '22

Dearest Pat,

    . . . I am so glad you enjoyed your visit home. I know you enjoyed some things about it, but I know you will always remember what a snivelling old mess I was & how I spoiled a great deal of your fun. It is so hard for us to understand our loved ones. I am not *generally* so weak and foolish, but I had had so much to stand that it got the best of me. I had anticipated so much pleasure in having you at home. . . . Then the Columbus trip came up & I was brave & said go to Columbus, & wanted you so bad myself.

Then you wrote you were coming home & my spirits revived & I even hoped that you would not go to the game (selfish mother) but would stay here with me. But I did not say anything, did I? Then you stayed in Atlanta until Fri. night. You did not seem natural somehow. You seemed so occupied in your mind and didn't seem thrilled over being here & came down so late Sat. A.M. & I had so much I had planned to talk to you about. When I came in & saw you sitting so quietly & looking away off, I couldn't understand. Then M[argaret] came & you seemed to revive & went to town. I hope you did enjoy that. Mrs. R[ussell] [1] said you were so precious & she had lovely salad for you. But you hadn't eaten my fried chicken & I had had so much pleasure in cooking it for you.

While you were away with M. I had thought of two or three things I really wanted to consult with you about & when you came in & said you & M. were going to Athens—well, it was the last straw that broke the camels back, and I was so surprised—I don't like to call myself a *fool*, but I *have*, every time I think of how I lost my nerve & I know you felt I was one too. I'll never forget it & I know you never will. I wish I had been seized with a sudden sickness or anything that could have prevented my acting so. . . .

But I did play the part of a *weakling*, & I'll never again. You & I had been having such a good correspondence & I had been loving you so. But I *will not do this way again.* I had been so upset over the accident of Williams & I was feeling pitiful. I have always kinder looked to you and Billie, especially for comfort—the others are sweet & good, but I have to treat them kinder like company but I feel so at home with you & Billie.

Mothers *must not* have feelings & they *must not* express themselves. As I say: I *will not* act so again. I am simply telling you all this to vindicate myself. I do not act this way often & I will not again. . . . Now burn this letter. . . .

Dad went out to dig this A.M. about 7 o'clock. He did not come in until 6 to-night. Had not eaten all day. I am not good enough to stand this without a groan. I had saved his food all day. . . .

    Mother

1. These Russells were not kin to Ina and Richard's family.

1923–1930

I Have So Much Before Me, Behind Me, and On All Sides of Me

*W*hile the Twenties roared toward their ignoble end, Ina found her world growing "larger and more beautiful every day." The isolated life at Russell took its place with other memories of the nineteenth century as the automobile and the telephone ascended. Consequently, she wrote fewer letters to the younger children when they went off to school, but she continued to use her pen to guide, exhort, correct, and praise. To the grown children she reported the family activities, keeping kinship bonds warm and strong. Grieving to see her youngest ones depart, she nevertheless urged them on. Walter and William disappointed her by not staying in school, but once their decisions were made, her ability to keep things in perspective enabled her to encourage their endeavors in the work world. She was especially anxious that Carolyn would not be spoiled and watched carefully to prevent the sapping of character that indulgence poses for any child but particularly for a "baby" in a large family.

Ina's social and intellectual life came to revolve around the Winder First Presbyterian Church. It gave her great pleasure to have church gatherings at Russell, particularly for women. She took teaching Sunday School seriously and considered study as much a privilege for herself as for her children. Her intensity about this work shows that the deprivation in spiritual and intellectual matters of her earlier life was deep but not damaging.

By 1929, with Carolyn a senior in high school, her three youngest boys doing well in college, and all the other children relatively settled in work and/or marriage, Ina might have been imagining a chance to slow down a little. She was sixty-two years old. But 1930 was to try all the endurance and love she'd built up in thirty-seven years of child rearing.

To Mr. William J. Russell, Walker Park, Ga. A&M School

Wednesday [February 7, 1923]

Dearest William,

Your letter came this morning. I don't mind you coming this week-end, but think you had better wait until the 16th or 17th to come home. You know the 18th is my birthday and its on Sunday and our preaching day too, and sister Marguerite and the babies[1] will be here. Now don't you think it will be best to wait until the next week-end and come Friday the 16th. . . .

We haven't received your report. Hope you made a good mark in your History test. . . . Some of the boys told me that Julian Smith said you were behind in your work 32 hours. I was horrified and wanted to come right to Walker Park to see you about it. You surely are not *behind* in your work, William. I know you can keep up with that. I want to know the truth about it. You must improve yourself in every way.[2]

Billie & Bunny left last Thursday night. We certainly miss them. Harriette is at home now. Wish you were here to go to prayer meeting with us to-night. . . .

     Lovingly,
     Mother

1. Marguerite and Jim's second child, Jane Mayo Bowden, was born December 22, 1922.
2. Ina understands that William may have trouble with arithmetic, but he should have no trouble doing the physical work required.

To Mary Willie Russell Green, Richmond, Va.

April 1st, 1923

My dearest Mary,

I thank you for my new grand baby [born March 27]. I've been wanting to write you for several days and tell you this—My heart is filled to overflowing with joy, praise and thanksgiving. I am very happy in thinking about you and my little Mary Nancy—most charming name, and I know she is adorable. I want grandchildren just as I wanted children.

I would have written you before, but Fielding has been real sick—has been in bed since last Tuesday afternoon—have had the doctor three times. I brought him down in *your* room and find it more convenient to nurse him and I sleep with him, or rather, I try to sleep. He has suffered so much and I am up a great deal at night. The awful cold is all in his head. His ear ached so much and we discovered a rising in his ear and his back aches and his stomach hurts. I'm busy rubbing with Vicks and Mentholatum all the time. His right eye is badly swollen and he hurts all over, *all* the time. For days he would not eat, but he has had 3 glasses of milk to-day and an orange, but he says he cannot taste anything.

I know you are so glad to be through with your *expectation* and as you are doing so well, I expect you'll be going home soon. It is a glorious feeling when you know your little baby is here, all safe and sound, and your greatest suspense is over.

Your fond Mother

To Miss Harriette Russell, Richmond Va.

April 6, '23

Dearest Harriette,

I wanted to write to you last night, while I was sitting here with Fielding and every body else had gone to the Glee Club, but I was too *scared*—now you'll wonder what *ma* was *scared* about, as I do not often have this feeling. But a great deal has happened to get me all out of my usual *even, calm* feelings.

First, you remember the Wall case—Henry Wall, who killed the Miller boy—well, you know Dick was employed to defend him. The case was

called this week of Court—began Tuesday, I think, and it took three days
to try it. Dick would come home every night & just sit down, & look so
miserable & would not eat supper. The second day Joe was employed to
help prosecute. Of course this put a terrible difference between Dick & Joe.
Joe was miserable, but stood it the best he could for he had been "offered a
good fee &c." Thursday was the final day & 100's of people were in Winder.
Thursday morning Joe & Dick would talk, talk. Dick would say something
about Mrs. Wall's baby & Joe would wail, "Hush Dick—that baby looks
just like sister." Of course, Dick would work on Joe's conscience all he
could. I was so wrought up over the case, for I was told the man would
either have to be hung or turned free. Dr. Almond has been coming to see
Fielding every day and he would talk about the case. He'd always say such
nice things about how Dick handled the case.

Now you see I was thinking about all this and worried over F[ielding]
too and was ½ sick from losing sleep too—and Thursday A.M. when Dr. A.
came, he told me about a burglary in Winder—two men stopped at the
Motor Inn filling station and raised the window, took the safe out—put it
in their car & flew towards Atlanta. A boy was asleep at the station, and the
lights on, and the Night watch man *somewhere*. Well, a man had escaped
from the Federal Prison in Atlanta—had been captured near Athens & had
been wounded & was carried to St. Mary's Hospital. He escaped from the
Hospital Wed. night and the Federal Officers were after him and just *happened* to run up on the burglars about two miles from Winder. The officers
were suspicious of the appearance of the car, overtook it, & found this safe
and a lot of toilet articles taken from the Prince Av. Pharmacy—Nunnally's
candy and a big quantity of narcotics. The men were brought to our jail.

You see, I had all this to think about—and then—Thursday A.M. a peddler—a genuine frenchman—came, selling lovely linen. This may not
sound exciting, but it was. He told his history (the best he could). He was
waiter on the steam ship Canada—Had just 12 days in America. He had
brought $100 worth of this lovely linen and was selling it for 75¢ per yd. His
ship was in Savannah & he had sold all but two pieces to "the wealthy ladies
in Winder." I bought one bolt and you can have a pair of pure linen pillow
cases off of it.

Now this famous Thursday was the day of the Glee Club, and Carolyn
was selling tickets, trying to get a prize. She sold 28 tickets and was second
in the race, but somehow-or-other "Coach Page" did her a "dirty trick" &

she didn't even get honorable mention & she came home crying—something so unusual for her. I tried to comfort her but felt they had not treated her fair—and then Edward had a grievance and a just one. Mr. Cash has simply cheated Edward & Ruth Wages out of their debate. You know Harold S. & Francis Hubbard spoke the same night E[dward]. & R[uth]. did & won, just as they did. Mr. C. seems determined that H. & F. will represent the school & has been coaching them & ignored E. & R. and has just acted unfair towards them. Ruth got very mad and expressed herself very freely to Mr. C. Edward was hurt. E. & R. both thought that Mr. C. would let them debate H. & F. in a fair manner and then if they lost, they would not feel so bad. You see, I was almost mad too, over this, but couldn't help myself or E. either, but I tried to comfort him all I could. I got the children off to the Glee Club in time to get a good seat. . . .

(I hadn't told you that I let William stay at home this wk. I had to have some body here that could drive and help me.)

So Fielding & I were left alone last night until eleven. The wind was blowing and we, or I, heard all kind of noises and I sat here, not knowing who might come in: Henry Wall—the peddler or the burglars—but finally Dick & Joe came. Joe had been to Atlanta on a hurried trip. *Dick had not been to the Glee Club!* Shades of Caesar! Could I believe it? But he had not. Henry Wall had been acquitted and went home in his own car with his wife & seven children & Dick was too happy to think of the Glee Club—and then too, those burglars had sent for Dick to come to the jail to talk over their case. When they asked about the fee & Dick named *said fee,* the man told Dick he could have his Buick car for defending him. In the meantime Sheriff Camp was receiving a wire that the Buick car had been stolen from some one in Chattanooga!

About 11:30 the children came in and began telling us about the fun at the Glee Club. They got off a lot of good jokes on Dick, Buck Radford, Cupid and the Winder Police force. . . .

To-night the children went to see a picture: "Where is my Wandering Boy To-night," [and they] have just come in and each one trying to tell about it until Fielding begged them to stop talking. F. has been very nervous. He has suffered so much. He has been in bed nearly two wks. He has lost flesh and is very weak. He has had very high fever, and awful night sweats. . . .

Walter went back to Ga. April 2nd. He was feeling weak in mind & will powder[1] & I'm afraid he will find it hard to study. He was well and looking *so well.*

Poor Pipey is still worrying over that knitting machine.[2] I am going to advertise for *some body* to come & show her how to use that machine. . . .

I'm sure you must have grown weary in trying to read all my letter—but F. was quiet & I just kept on writing. I enjoyed your letter. Pipey & aunt A. did too.

I forgot to say that F. could not declaim. Gibson House won. Mr. Cash has never inquired of *any one* about Fielding. F. was so disappointed & the night of the contest he tried to say his speech, lying in the bed & it made us all cry.

Give my dearest love to all my precious ones
    Mother

1. The entire family loved puns.
2. Pipey bought the machine from a magazine ad, but it proved difficult to operate.

To Mr. Walter B. Russell, Washington, D.C.

July 11, 1923

My Dearest Walter,

Your nice interesting letter came this A.M. You have been so good about writing to me and I have enjoyed your letters so much. It certainly is nice to be promoted [at the A&P store] and I am proud of you and rejoice with you. You see, it pays to be efficient and trust-worthy. I think about you so much as I go along, trying to serve my day and generation the very best I can. I have neglected you, as far as writing to you is concerned, but I've loved you devotedly and have always had a feeling that you were trying to do the fair and square thing in every way.

I have been so busy since you left—you know our wedding came right on—and I must add here that it is a shame that no one has written you about our beautiful wedding.[1] I know Ina told you all about it and the lovely trip they [Rob and Sybil] had in uncle Lewis' car. And the grand presents and everything. So glad you sent such a nice, well-worded telegram. I stood by at different times, and saw several people read it and comment upon it. The night of the wedding 27 slept in our house and of course they all ate breakfast here next morning.

I think it grand that you are buying the typewriter. I can see your little old nimble fingers now as they hit the keys. . . .

You ask what everybody at home is doing. Dad is busy as ever in Atlanta. Rob got back on his job Monday morning. He & Sybil are domiciled at 833 Peachtree. Dick is busy "saving the state." He was elected Speaker Pro Tem [of the General Assembly] without opposition. The other two candidates withdrew when they saw how popular he was. Us folks at home are living the same old life. Our little boys have made enough money to take their [Boy Scout] trip to Lakemont. They leave next Monday A.M. very early. The Ku Klux are paying for their transportation to camp & back. . . .

I don't know anything about dad running for the Senate. He has not said anything about it lately. . . .

Make Ina tell you all about the wedding and the honeymoon trip. Such a lovely trip in the car without any trouble with tires or anything else. . . .

> With my best love,
> Mother

1. Robert Lee married Sybil Millsaps on June 27, 1923. Sybil, daughter of a prosperous Barrow County farmer, was Pat's roommate at GN&IC.

To Mr. Walter B. Russell, Washington, D.C.

July 23, '23

Dearest Walter,

If I wrote to you every time I wanted to, you'd be getting stacks of mail every day. I enjoyed your last letter. In fact, I enjoy every one you write and you are *good* about writing.

I've been so busy this summer. To-day I haven't had any help except William and John Henry Barnes. The latter is very distinguished sounding, isn't it, but he is not very bright. I have missed my three boys who are off on a camp. They write as if they are having a grand time, and I do hope they are, for they have been so faithful and good to help me and do many things about the house & lot.

Yesterday was an unusual Sunday. Just one of my *seven* sons was at home. Dick was in Dahlonega. Rob did not come and the three boys in camp and you in W'ton. Uncle Rob & uncle Lewis were here for dinner, so with Dad, I had 3 of the *old* Russell boys. . . .

I wrote Ina about the lightning knocking me out while I was at the 'phone. You know how our phone explodes during a storm. Well, it got me that time, and I "awoke to find myself famous" or rather to find a great many friends who were very much concerned about me. I was fortunate to get out so light. My hair around my neck was badly singed and a burnt streak from my neck to my shoulder and almost to my elbow. I can't realize that anything happened, but my friends seem very happy that I escaped and of course my folks here at home are ready to start a Thanksgiving service just any time, and I am too, for I enjoy living and I try to be useful and helpful in this world.[1]

I love [cousin] Earnestine for being so nice to you. Tell her & give her my love when you see her and ole Dolly too.[2]

Uncles Lewis, Rob, & John had a trip to the mountains & saw our scouts. Edward wrote me that they gave each of them a dollar & you know how that act spread joy. . . .

Pipey has come over with a paper that tells us how to make $100 per wk—like the knitting machine maybe. I carried Pipey in the country to a lady who has one and she knit a whole sock for Pipey and showed her all about it. But Pipey doesn't do much better than she did before.

So much talking & Harriette & Pipey chewing on green peaches. So I'll get nervous if I sit here long. . . . Always thinking about you & loving you. . . .
    Mother

1. Ina was knocked cold by the strike. Dr. Almond arrived, expecting the worst, while the fearful news spread through Winder almost before he reached Russell. Many friends had come by the time she revived.

2. Earnestine Bealer was Richard's first cousin through the Brumby line. Dolly is her daughter.

To Mr. Walter B. Russell, Washington, D.C.

Sep. 5, '23

My Dearest Walter-Boy,

Your letter received this A.M. I'd give a great deal if this was dad writing to you instead of little old "Ma." She loves you all right but can't always give the advice.

Poor dad brought this very paper I am using and the very envelope this letter will be sent in, home Saturday night. He & I sat in the dining room after everyone else was a-bed, and he said he brought the stationery home just to "write Walter a long letter," and he gave me your grand good letter to read, and he was so proud of your letter for he said so. And I began to encourage him to write to you, even a *short* letter—and I thought he would, but he began saying how tired he was, and really, he almost went to sleep. (He had not dug dirt as he usually does.) So he went to bed and told me that I could write and that maybe he would write when he got back to Atlanta. He said he would send you the money. Now you let me know when you want this to begin. Dad seems awfully hard up. He will have $800 to pay before long. So you let me know when it will be necessary for the first check to come in and I will see that it is sent. I know dad will help you. I don't blame you for thinking dad has ignored you, but he has talked about you a great deal and seems *very much* interested. But you know how busy he is and he does have a heavy load to carry. All of us pulling on him all the time.

If I were you, I'd make *my own decision,* as you said, then trust to dad helping you, which I know he will. I think it would be awfully smart of you to work in the day & go to school at night. . . .

We had a time yesterday getting all the kids in school. And what do you think? Our old slow William is entering the eighth grade & says he is going to do wonders. All the teachers new but 4. I think we'll like them fine. The superintendent was out playing ball with the boys yesterday afternoon.

If you decide you want to come back to Ga. I know dad will be satisfied. He is anxious for you to hold on to the A&P as he seems to think it a grand opportunity. I do hope you can arrange things to your own satisfaction and do what is the very best thing for your future welfare. You are smart enough to do anything.

  With my fondest, best love,
  Mother

To Miss Patience E. Russell, Atlanta, Ga.

Monday A.M. [September 10, 1923]

Dearest Pat,

As you know, this, a Monday, is a busy A.M. My hands are trembling now 'cause I've been sweeping so much. The Living Room and front verandah had all the Sunday dirt, and then some more—and I swept & swept. Doscia was kind enough to do some kitchen stunts for me, so I tried to clean up. Billie is in the bed with a very bad sick head ache. Harriette, Doscia, Trudie & I have been trying to keep the kids in a good humor. . . .

William has entered 8th grade & seems to be in dead earnest. He is pestering every body to death to help him with his arithmetic. Edward is wild over foot ball. F[ielding]. is trying to make a triumphal entry into the 10th grade. . . .

Last night we had a grand Union meeting at the Christian Church. . . . Mr. Morton asked Dad to give the welcome address on behalf of the churches and Dad did it, and it was fine. O, you would have been proud of your dad. I was proud of him & thankful! The church was *full* and silence reigned supreme while dad was talking & after the service he was surrounded by his friends and warm words of congratulations flowed freely. . . .

I'm thinking about you all the time & I always *feel* that you are trying to do your duty.

> Heart of love,
> Mother

To Miss Patience E. Russell, Atlanta, Ga.

Monday A.M. [October 1, 1923]

Dearest Pat,

. . . I'm thinking about you hard this A.M. I've been up since 5:30. Got dad off on early train, & I've had your face before me all the A.M. . . .

I hurried & went to S.S. yesterday. Enjoyed it so much. . . . We had preaching yesterday. Mr. M[orton]. preached a fine sermon. Dad & I sat right to-gether & *held hands,* part of the time.

Yesterday was Christian Endeavor Rally Day at Statham and in the afternoon the Winder Endeavors went over. I went at 3 o'clock & stayed until the night service. The Statham Ladies served a lovely supper & everything was so nice. . . . The singing was good. I had all my little crowd. Doscia & Trudie stood by me all day milking at night for the boys. I enjoyed it all, & am more in love with this work for young people and will strive to help them more than ever. Its so nice to have something in our lives that we are striving for, that will *never pass away.*

Mr. Morton preached a short, splendid sermon at 7:30. His text was Davids words to Solomon, when he, David, was old & ready to die: "I go the way of the world. *Be strong* & *show* your self a man." Mr. M. preached to the young people on how to live mentally, spiritually & physically . . . and I was thinking about you much of the time. I can but think and believe that you were "cut out" for work of this kind, for you seem so capable. The big C[hristian] E[ndeavor] Convention is in Elberton . . . this wk. beginning Fri. Edward may go with Charles. All of them want to go. I'd *love* to. I believe if we could train our children better, we'd have better old folks. . . .

D[oscia] & T[rudie] say come on home. The chicken is here waiting for you.

Mother

To Miss Ina Dillard Russell, Washington, D.C.

Jan. 2, '24

My Dearest Ina,

I have thought of you so constantly. Your bright, sweet face and happy, sprightly manner has been right before me. I have wished for you to be with us. We have had a very pleasant Christmas and to me, it was a strenuous one, or I am getting older, or maybe, I was not quite as well as usual. This A.M. brings *to me*, the first *lull*, since, at least, one week before Christmas began and my *lull* will not last long, for Walter and Kinch[1] are up stairs in the bed and will be coming down about 12:30 calling for "chow, chow." The kids began school this A.M. Trudie is in the kitchen washing dishes. Marguerite, Jim & babies and my dear Pat left yesterday. Walter begged so for a dance last night, about 11 couples, and I had consented—feeling very pitiful with no one but Carolyn to help. I had just returned from the station to see Pat & Sybil off and had carried some food to my poor *Cranes* who had measles (6 of them). They live in the cotton mill village and the father is in the asylum. By-the-way—I ran across our friend Mrs. Camp and she went with me and carried a lot of nice groceries. I was so happy. I found they had no coal and Joe & Dick promised they would see the K[u]K[lux] Charity man & send them a ton to-day. Pardon my digression—but the Cranes are my pets.

Anyway: when I returned home from all this, the house was so still and I sat down by my good ole heater and thought I'd rest awhile. In a few minutes Ed Rowland & his wife drove up. Ed works in S.C. and they were on their way back to S.C. from Marietta. I asked them to spend the night & they did. I like Ed's wife & I really enjoyed having them. They seemed to enjoy the dance last night and I let Lois be chaperone. They left this A.M. at 7:30. Part rain & part sleet falling and a bad wind. They had a closed car.

The dance was a success, I guess. Walter, dear child, was so anxious to have it & then did not dance very much. I didn't like the dance much. I just had it to please Walter. I served hot cocoa & crackers. . . .

We had a prettier Christmas tree than usual. We had 20 at our Christmas dinner. I was not satisfied with my box I sent you & Billie, but I was "run to death." . . .

You should have seen D[oscia] & T[rudie] kissing those beads [you sent them]. If they had been pure gold, they could not have been happier. Doscia said she wanted you to know that when she fixed the chicken [in your box], she was loving you all the time. . . .

I hope & pray that my Ina will have a happy, peaceful New Year and as the days pass she will live so as to feel that her life is not in vain.

    Love,
    Mother

1. Kinch Carpenter, a friend of Walter's.

To Miss Patience Russell, Atlanta, Ga.

Oct. 13, '24

Dearest ole sweet child,

. . . We are enjoying aunt Pheme.[1] She is sweeter than ever, & seems in fine health. She almost "fell over" when I told her that H[arriette] had bobbed her hair. I think she is anxious to see how H. looks. She said she expected you looked "right well." Aunt P. seemed so happy to get here— said she had been crying & crying for me. Last night she asked us to sing some for her. None of us went to church. We sang & sang. Dick doing his best and F[ielding], Alex & Carolyn & myself. She enjoyed it so much. Said she hadn't heard any songs for months & months—nothing but cards &

frivolous music. She volunteered of her own accord to go to church with me Sunday. I couldn't get her to go when she was here 2 yrs. ago. Aunt P. asked who went to Washington with you this summer. We told her Margaret Russell. She said: "O, the child who came to the mountain with her father & mother." And then she said: "I hope she doesn't paint her face now, as she did then." None of us spoke, but I had to think of the many times I had seen her with too much on, and of my *own child,* when she had too much—on face & lips.

I attended an auxiliary meeting at Mizpah church, 6 mi. from Athens, in Jackson Co. A Mrs. Smith gave a splendid talk on our work among the young people. She mentioned the amount of paint & lip stick they use and deplored the fact that the girls used so much. She also spoke of girls drinking and smoking. She was a young woman herself & very good looking. Of course at the dinner hour, every one (almost) was discussing Mrs. Smith's talk. Mrs. Snellings (Dean Snellings wife) was talking to Mrs. Russell [Margaret's mother] & said: "I do not blame the girls one bit"—and before Mrs. S. could say any more, Mrs. Russell said: "*Now* you're right. I don't either," and Mrs. Snellings went on to say: "*I* blame their parents." Mrs. R. didn't have any more to say. . . .

Your fond Mother

1. Richard's elderly aunt, William John Russell's sister.

To Mr. William John Russell, Sarasota, Fla.

Nov. 12, '24

Dearest William,

We all rejoiced over your nice long letter that came this morning. We were late getting the mail and Doscia brought it in while we were eating dinner. I read it aloud to everybody and Doscia was as much interested as any of us. . . .

I enjoyed hearing about your trip and about Sarasota—and I enjoyed the Church Bulletin. So glad you went to church. We missed you and uncle Lewis Sunday. . . .[1]

Dr. Jacobs[2] married yesterday. Dad performed the ceremony. He married a Mrs. Smith.

. . . I heard to-day that Guy Thurmond killed Dick Bowman in Statham last night. Haven't heard the particulars.

Aunt Annie, Pipey and uncle Ben ask about you every day. . . . Fielding, & Alex were trying to make a list of fireworks last night & they were wishing for you. We all miss you.

Just drink the water anyhow & you'll learn to like it.

Mother

1. Lewis Russell had been appointed superior court judge by Governor Clifford Walker in 1922, and then ran unsuccessfully for the office in 1924. Hurt by the defeat, Lewis left Georgia to practice law in Florida. William went with him to try running a cafe. Joe Quillian was to be married in December, and he too would leave Ina's household.

2. Joseph Jacobs, pharmacist and developer of a drugstore chain, and Richard Russell had been friends since they were schoolboys in Athens.

To Miss Carolyn Russell, Winder, Ga.

February 8, 1925, Monday A.M. [From Atlanta]

My Dearest Child,

Of course Pat told me you had been sick and of course it made me sad and I wanted to cry. She said you were feeling better when she left. I want you to be real brave and hold out a little longer and I want you to stay at home or at Aunt Annie's. I think William and Doscia will fix some good food and F[ielding] will see after you too. Tell Doscia to cook some dried apples & tell W[illiam] and F[ielding] to buy some prunes. And you eat them and don't eat candy. I hope you get graham bread. Was so sorry you were sick at Aunt Mary [Walter]'s.[1] She has so much to see after. I felt like weeping, for I have been so homesick and I've felt like my "po" little chilluns needed me and I want to see you all so bad.

But we are so happy over Rob. He sat up just a few minutes this A.M. Sybil is feeling very well.[2] We still have one nurse. Rob has to have mustard plasters yet and he is very weak. . . .

Remember, my darling, I want you to stay at home from now on, unless something happens to cause us to change our minds—and want you to be a comfort to aunt Annie and Pipey and uncle Ben. I want you to do your "good turn daily" & be a *real scout*.

You may depend that I am coming as soon as I can. We are trying to save poor Bobbie money by helping all we can. It takes so much for nurses and doctors. Give my love to everyone at home. Doscia and Trudie too. Take good care of your clothes—and keep yourself clean. I can just see you, looking pitiful and neglected—but you are smart and can take good care of your clothes and can keep clean. I do hope you and the boys are not getting behind in your lessons. Remember, finals will soon be here and we will want a good report. . . .

> With my heart's best love,
> Mother

1. Ina's brother Walter Dillard was the Methodist preacher in Winder at this time, so Carolyn was sent to stay with Aunt Mary Walter while Ina went to Atlanta to help nurse Rob, who had pneumonia. Aunt Mary Walter had eleven children.

2. Sybil is expecting her first child, Robert Lee Jr., born February 21, 1925.

To Miss Carolyn Russell, Winder, Ga.

> May 1st 1925
> 71 Monmouth Ave., Cherrydale *Va.*
> Address—write to me.

Dearest Carolyn,

I have been thinking about you so much and wishing for you all the time. Billie's little home is in a beautiful place—reminds me some of the street that Marguerite and Rob lives on, only its not so near the street car line and theres more woods & flowers and the houses are much better. Billie has lovely flowers—tulips in bloom now—roses full of buds. Things do not bloom here as early as they do in our dear old Ga.

Ina & Walter came to see us Wednesday night. We went to see them last night saw uncle Rob. He asked me specially about the "universal favorite"—and that reminds me. I always want you to be a "universal favorite"—with every body. There is just one way to do this—always be *kind* in every word and deed. Remember the "Golden Rule." You are kind and sweet and I want you to *grow* more kind and sweet, every day you live. I have the greatest ambition for you to be an educated, refined, good person. I love you so dearly. I'll be thinking about you to-night. I'd love to see the May Festival. Hope you can do your part well.

Don't forget to help Mrs. Miller all you can.[1] If you can help anytime, let the tennis alone, for there will be another time to play. . . .

Give my love to every body at Mrs. Millers. See after your brothers. . . .
        Mother

1. The Millers are the family with whom Carolyn is staying.

To Ina Dillard Russell, Washington, D.C.

June 19, '25

Dearest Ina,

We are thinking about you more than usual these days. You see the 22nd is almost here, and then the 24th, and the next big day will be the day you arrive at "Home Sweet Home." We are thinking about you all and planning & getting ready for you. There is no joy in the world equal to the joy a mother feels as she goes about the home, getting ready for the children to come.

And I'll be thinking about you the 22nd. Dad is sitting here eating his supper (the clock has just struck eleven) and he has just remarked that "31 yrs. ago, Wednesday [June 24], Dr. Lane baptized our little Ina." Now, does it seem that long, or is 31 yrs. long ago?

We are having a warm summer but when you come, we can sit around in as few clothes as possible and we can always find a breeze some-where. . . .
        Heart of love,
        Mother

To Mr. Walter B. Russell, Washington, D.C.

Jan. 8, '26

Dearest Walter,

Of course I'm worried about Ina. Billie's telegram came this A.M. Edward & I had just been talking about our troubles &c, & Edward remarked that he hoped no[ne] of us would have to be operated on this year. Dick & I sat at table & talked about things in general & he said he wanted to write to "Ina to-day" and thank her for his Christmas gift. Little did we know that poor little Ina was in the Hospital then, ready for her operation! The operation [appendectomy] in itself is not so much—its the suffering afterwards—and O, I hope she will not have pneumonia! I hope you all have a special nurse, night & day. I started to send a telegram to insist on a *special nurse,* but I didn't know who to send it to. I'm just hoping that you all would use your heads & see after my child.

As I write now, I can see her suffering from the effects of the ether. I watched *you, Rob, Harriette* and *Edward*—its awful. I know these things have to come and I have to have my share, but this has caught me at a time when my spirits & courage are low. . . . Dad has been in the *bluest* condition—all through Christmas—Uncle John came with his tale of woe that would make a stone wall weep. I know dad did not smile for two wks or more—then William left for Fla. . . . Fielding not doing so well at Ga. Now my Ina sick & suffering. Do stay with her as much as you can. . . .[1]

My devoted love for my boy,
Mother

1. Walter and Ina Jr. had moved into an apartment together as Walter continued his work with the A&P.

To Mr. William J. Russell, Largo, Fla.

Jan. 19, 1926

Dearest William,

Your letter received to-day. I was so glad when I saw it, but after I finished reading it, I was terribly disappointed. I wanted to know if you were working or just loafing around. I have been so worried. Why did you & Aubry go to Florida so soon? It seems so foolish to me when you could have been making something here. I do not see how your money has held out. If I had known this, I would have *opposed* your going to Florida.

If there is no hope of getting a place in Largo, why don't you go some where else? I'd certainly move on. So many people say that Largo is about the size of Bogart. Uncle John would not say much, but he *sounded* like he was surprised that you settled at Largo. I have been trying not to worry about you, but I can't help it. . . . Really, William, what are you going to do? I don't see how you can afford to loaf. I didn't want you to go away, any how, & I have certainly been miserable to know that you had not gone to work. You have been gone three weeks. I want you to write me exactly how things are. . . . It just looks careless and unbusiness like for you all to hurry off & then *never* get down to work.

. . . I'm not fussing, but I do feel so bad to always say: No, they have not started up yet. I feel bad not only to *say* it, but to know that you are not doing any thing.

Write me *something* about your work. All of us are well.

> Much love,
> Mother

To Mr. William J. Russell, Clearwater, Fla.

May 31, 1926

Dearest William,

. . . I stay busy—but I go about my work thinking about you and hoping that things are going well with you. I missed you during Commencement. Every night when I got out of the car, up at school, I could just see you going in or maybe coming around the corner. We had a nice Commencement. Edward passed up in every thing and of course I was very happy. I think Edward will go to Davidson College this fall. That means just Alex & Carolyn here with me. Alex & Carolyn both drive the car now & take me any where, any time. For a long time I had Carolyn stop the car up by Mrs. Nowell's Boarding House & I'd walk to the stores. Now she drives me any where. . . .

I want you to write me some more about your work. I hope you are happy in your work. I want you to improve yourself—do something & learn something every day that will improve you. Do you ever go to church? Keep yourself nice and be truthful and honest. You don't know how I love you and how I want you to make a good, true man.

. . . The road commissioners are here to-day & Dad is trying to get his road fixed. . . .

> My best love,
> Mother

To Mr. William J. Russell, Clearwater, Fla.

July 3, 1926

Dearest William,

Your letter just rec'd—about 10 minutes ago. I have been looking, looking for a letter from you. The six months you have been away seems *very, very* short in some ways & *very, very* long in others. This has been a very busy summer for me. Have never worked quite so hard in my life—business with me is *never* dull. Sometimes the money part of my business is dull.

Some day I want you to write a diary of your days work & send to me. I'm always wondering what you are doing.

Dad's entering this [U.S. Senate] race has changed all our plans for this summer. Dick has given up every thing here & is in Atlanta working away. He is running too, you know, for representative & Speaker of House & we are hoping that Dick's race will not suffer from papa's.

Dad 'phoned last night for me to send Fielding to Atlanta in the old car—that he was going to get me a new car. F. left right early this A.M. & poor thing! he started off with a puncture. My old car looks almost as bad as the one the Saunders use to deliver milk. Dad says F. will have to stay in Atlanta to help with the mail. Walter wired dad that he would come home & help, but W. has too good a job & surely Dick, Rob & F. and "us" at home can do something. But Walter wrote last night that he & Ina would come in Aug. & be here for the election & thats the time for you to plan to come. Maybe we can all be to-gether again. Billie says she can't come until the fall, but now that the election is on, I expect they will come for the election too. All of us took it "hard" at first—but I believe we are more reconciled now or rather we *have* to be, for dad was dead set on running.[1]

I'm so proud of you for hanging on in Fla. I believe you will be rewarded. So many said, "I bet William will be coming home since Aubry left." I think Keith Quarterman has changed his job 3 times since he went to Fla. He was at home awhile. He is in Atlanta now.

Aubry has full charge of Rogers Store now. He told the managers he would not move, so they made him permanent manager. He makes a good one & he looks so well & clean & nice all the time.

Fielding has been digging dirt & is brown all over. . . . Have you grown any? Write to me. Don't wait so long.

> Mother

1. Dick Jr. had taken his father's decision particularly hard because he admired Senator Walter George and understood the futility of the race for Richard. Everyone worked hard, however, and Ina rejoiced that although Richard lost the race, election day brought all her children home and they had the first of many family reunions.

To Mr. H. E. Russell, Davidson, N.C.

Nov. 28, '26

Dearest Edward,

Sunday night and we are just in from church. We are very happy, for Mr. Morton announced to-night that he would not go to Columbus, but would stay with us. . . .

Fielding came [from the University of Georgia] last night instead of coming for Thanksgiving. He read 2 books on T'giving Day—Pilgrims Progress & Hamlet. He made 100 on one & 95 on the other. He seems to be doing well now. Dad told me of getting your report—said you had improved. I want to see it. I hope you show a great interest in your Bible study. Dad said something about it. And don't worry about church going being compulsory. Be submissive & gentle & learn to be patient, & do nicely & gladly what the authoritives say. Its miserable to always be feeling rebellious about something. I'll never forget the day you came to my S.S. class & acted as if you were so disgusted & didn't want to be there. I felt so badly about it & I was sorry. . . . We just have to learn to take things as they come & be patient & kind & submissive. We have so much to learn about *living*. Reading our Bibles is *undoubtedly* the best guide. We are told to "Take heed to our ways" that we sin not with our tongues. I have been reading the Psalms lately and they are so helpful. . . .

You be sure to write Mr. M[orton]. and tell him how glad you are he is staying in Winder. . . .

I've scribbled this off in a hurry but I did want you to know about Mr. Morton. If your board is due write dad a nice letter & tell him. How is your spending money coming on? Do you owe anything beside your board? Let dad know what you need.

Mother

To Mr. William J. Russell, St. Petersburg, Fla.

Dec. 2, 1926

Dearest William,

I have had a full, busy day. Most of it spent in seeing after the sick. Mrs. Morgan has had typhoid fever—able now to sit up some and Annie has just begun to have it & is very sick. . . .

I went to see poor ole Arch Barns.[1] He sent me word to come & bring him some post toasties and soda crackers. I carried them. He is too pitiful. Cannot move in the bed. His eyes are swollen & almost closed. He told me to tell papa that he wanted the Chief Justice to "lay him away"—for he knew it would have such a good effect on all the colored people. I don't think he can live long.

We have been in from prayer meeting about an hour—Carolyn & Alex up stairs sound asleep. Dick hasn't come in. He is in a big law case. Mr. Earnest Young & National Bank. I heard at prayer meeting that the Jury was spending the night in jail. . . .

You know dad says he is "dead broke" & I know he is, but he is going to try to buy the place Mr. Sanders is on, first Tuesday. You know, its where the McElhannons lived so long. "They say" its going to be sold for "almost nothing."

Alex has had one bale of cotton ginned. He is trying hard to get his cotton picked. Old Mr. Brown is so feeble but he picks about 50 lbs. a day. Green has picked out & ginned 5 bales & says he'll make two more. You knew old Mr. Fuller was dead, I suppose—& I guess you knew our mule died. When Mr. Green Smiths things were sold, Wess Hosch got a splendid mule for $12—& Mr. Bailey bought a beauty for $12.50. . . .

I hear Dick coming in. Its almost 12 o'clock. Let me have a letter soon. I'm thinking about you all the time. Do you go to Sunday [School] and Church. Take time to do this. We all need food of this kind.

Mother

1. Arch Barnes had worked for the Russells and farmed Russell land as a tenant for more than twenty years.

To Mr. William J. Russell, St. Petersburg, Fla.

Dec. 29, '26

Dearest William,

Our 1926 Christmas is about over and we find ourselves waiting for the New Year. . . . We are still missing *you.* All of us have . . . spoken of you every day. You, Billie, Ina, and Walter were our absent ones. And uncle Lewis. We always count him and have missed him . . . but we missed you most of all because its your first Christmas away from home. I am waiting to hear how you spent the day and do hope you were well and happy. . . .

We had a good time Christmas day—the only thing that happened sad was about uncle Ben. He went off about 11 o'clock in the morning—Aunt Annie kept watching for him & Edward would run over every few minutes to see if he had come back. We ate dinner. Rain began to fall and soon it was 5 o'clock & uncle Ben had not come in. I got every body out looking— Rob, Jim, Fielding, Edward, Alex. He had said he was going to town, so some of them had searched there. I felt all the time that he was in 50 yards of the house, but no one agreed with me. Finally, about 5:30, I was so worried & told the boys to go out by aunt Annie's chicken yard, for I was sure he had tried to go through the field to Mr. Bells. They found him under one of the pine trees. He had been there 6 hrs. He had on that Army Overcoat & his body wasn't wet but his legs & feet were wet & so cold. We made a big fire in his room & gave him some warm food. Edward bathed his feet in cold water & we put him to bed. He was all right the next morning— didn't have any cold. This made us feel very bad . . . Aunt Annie is real feeble & she has a time with uncle Ben. Pipey is feeble too, & the three are very pitiful.

All of my Atlanta folks went back Tuesday. Harriet went Monday. Jim has been transferred to Savannah and will begin work Jan. 3rd. Marguerite & the children may go in Feb. Marguerite hates to give up her school—but I know she ought to go on with Jim. . . .

You are an old settler now—been in the Land of Flowers a whole year. . . .

Lovingly,
Mother

To Miss Ina D. Russell, Washington, D.C.

Jan. 13, 1927

My Dearest Ina,

All day yesterday and to-day, I have been trying to carry things on, shove some things aside, and find time for a real good letter writing, just to you. Now the day is gone. I'm tired as usual—not half the things done that I hoped to do—but I have accomplished a few things. Wrote Edward a business letter, also one to dad and a business card to Fielding. I was thinking of you all the time. In fact, I've been thinking about you so much since Walter married. I'm just waiting to hear what arrangements you've made.[1] You had such a nice little place & all your *things* were so nice. You have been so smart in keeping up and *fixing* and arranging &c. Of course you feel broken up. I'm so glad you had such a wise head on you & made those kids do the decent thing. I'm so glad Walter listened to you and kept his promise about talking to E[arnestine] & Mr. B[ealer]. It would have been awful if they had run away. I never could look on a run-away marriage with any degree of patience.

I had a nice letter from Earnestine inviting dad & me to see them . . . but I knew I could not leave home now, unless it was very important. Carolyn & Alex need me all the time. Aunt Annie & Pipey need me. . . . Aunt Annie has a hard time with uncle Ben. Pipey can't & won't do much for him. We have hired a negro boy to come every morning & that helps some. Rowena sends money to pay for washing, tobacco &c. Frank & James send *nothing*. . . .

Getting Edward & Fielding off to College was some job. They are two sweet ole boys. Dad struggling along and thinking he can't possibly send them to school & he's buying land and assuming so many burdens. He has so much court work to do. . . .

H[arriette] gave Edward a lovely over coat & nice gloves. Sybil is fixing for her new baby . . . Marguerite says she is going to Savannah Jan. 28th. I wish she would make arrangements & go right on . . . & learn to be a real homemaker for Jim & those two lovely children. If she could only see the importance of doing this! So much depends on the wife & mother! . . .

Do you remember seeing a lady in our church this summer, with two little boys & the lady looked old and never wore a hat? Well, of course this same lady is in our midst & all of us in the church try to help her. I have been worried [ab]out her poor, "no-count" bed—Just a *straw tick* . . . & two thin quilts. I gave her a good thick quilt some time ago. Today, I had a load of straw carried to her . . . & when I went to town wondering if I *could* buy her a mattress, I found that a woman had *loaned* her a real good mattress to keep until summer. The bed looked so good & high & the two boys were wondering how they were going to get in the bed, "it was so high." I think of Maggie Videtto's pet expression: "Skunks of misery"—that's just what they are—they are so miserable—or rather, their surroundings are so miserable. . . .

I am asking all my children to join the bible reading contest that our whole church going people are carrying on. Read the book of Luke in Jan. & the book of Acts in Feb. . . . I love the book of Luke, especially the 1st— 2nd chapters. Write me what you are doing. . . . I'm loving you.

     Mother

1. Walter married his cousin Dorothea Bealer on January 1, 1927, in a hurried ceremony.

To Miss Ina D. Russell, Washington, D.C.

                    Feb. 28, 1927
                    Grandmother [Russell]'s birthday—
                    99 yrs. old.

Dearest Ina,

I did not want to be in a hurry when I wrote to you, but O, me, O, my— the older I get, the more I have to do and it seems that I am in a hurry *all* the time. But its a great life. I'm so glad that I am busy . . . with such worthwhile things. I do not believe that I waste many minutes. Your letter came and my birthday ck. You are too sweet. My first thought always is, that I *must not* have the ck. cashed for I know Ina needs this money—but . . .

Dad is groaning now under campaign burdens & I've never seen him quite *so low,* financially. I immediately began to plan several things to do with my nice five dollars—and I'll tell you what I did—I gave it to Fielding & he may bring the money right back to its original source—*Washington.* That's why I'm hurrying to write this.

You know F. has been boxing in school & won some fame. They go to Charlottsville, Va., in finals & F. wants to come on to Was. for a day or 2 & see you all and your big City. If he comes, he will wire *you,* I think, as Harriette & I both said it would be safer. He thought maybe Walter would come to see him fight—he has been writing to him. . . .

F. was here Sun. & he was asking dad for money & he did hate so much to do it. Dad finally said he would lend him the money—then said if he won in boxing he need not pay him back. Strange to say, dad is pleased over F's victories in this pugilistic line. Harriette gave F. $5 & I gave him my check, & dad gave him $15. So that will be enough & more to make the trip to Wash. His expenses to C[harlottes]'ville will all be paid. Poor boy—he had a bad finger. He had to box to-night & I'll be anxious to hear how he came out. . . .

I did appreciate the ck. for it let me help Fielding. You know we mothers do *love* to do things like that. I had such a nice birthday—H. & P. gave me a lovely eiderdown comfort. Dad could not come but wrote a beautiful letter & gave me a ck. for $36, one dollar for each year of our married life—but the poor dear told me not to get the ck. cashed till Mar. 10th—& he said I must not use it for household expenses. So you see it will not be long until I have some money. . . . My precious letters from my children were full of joy and I felt again that I had the dearest children in the world. . . .

My hearts best love,
Mother

To Mr. H. E. Russell, Davidson, N.C.

Sep. 15, '27

Dearest Edward,

Guess you think I'm very indifferent to your queries & requests—but I am not in spirit—for I have been hoping something would "turn up" that would help both of us.

About you staying at frat house. I did not want to say or do any thing until I could talk to dad. He has not been home since you wrote me. You must decide. You know how I am about frat houses. I can hear you say: "But what does *that* matter?" But things do matter & I am just heart sick sometimes knowing that my children are so indifferent to what is *best*— not in a vainglorious or spectacular way, but the very *best* way, to help them in every way for the *best*. We go through with so much that is *not* worthwhile, & time is *so* short, & we are ready to launch out in life before we are ready. If you were here, I'm sure we'd have a *big argument,* but as it is, well, I'm hoping & trusting that you can decide these things for the *best*.

I get so distressed that you & F[ielding] indulge in *tobacco*. O, it hurts me so—its so *useless*—so weak to let a thing like that have dominion over you. I have been & am so delighted to know Mrs. Morton [Taylor Morton's mother]. She must have been & is, a wonderful woman. Has 3 boys—neither use tobacco any way. Her husband does, but you see, she did not "raise" *him*. I haven't time now to say more & I know you are glad. . . .

Hope you got those scup[pernong]s Pipey sent.

Mother

To Mrs. James H. Bowden, Savannah, Ga.

Oct. 18, 1927

Dearest Marguerite,

To-morrow will be two weeks since [Harriette's and Ralph's] wedding. How I did wish for you & the children—especially the children. They would have enjoyed it all so much. They had been so interested in H[arriette]'s clothes, preparation &c, & had made so many smart, amusing remarks about things. If I had only thought, I would have insisted & begged that you let them stay. Missing the first few days from school doesn't amount to much. You see, this is still eating on me. I wanted them to be here so much and H. wanted them.

I do wish you could have been here to catch the spirit. The wedding was lovely and I feel so happy & satisfied now—if they had married 3 yrs. ago, I would have been hurt, but as it is, I feel that the time had come & every thing will be O.K.[1] Sybil stayed the balance of the wk. with me and I was so glad when she wrote to you & Billie, for I did not have much time for anything out side of what *had* to be done. . . .

H. writes that she has received several things. Of course she did not get so many but every thing was so nice. The wedding occurred exactly on the minute. Dad had got the train to stop & we did not have to go to Winder. Exactly 40 grown people were here, including everybody.

I enjoyed reading over your letter & seeing what you said about our children looking so well &c. when they got home. . . . Just to think I have 4 grand children in school. . . . Indeed it is worth-while to send our children to school & do our best for them in every way. But we have to be very patient in *waiting* for results. . . .

I hope William has written you. I think he is very appreciative, even if he does neglect to write. He is manager of a store now in Marshall N.C., & is making big improvements in the increase of sales & is striving for a reward, $20 in gold, for the month of Oct.

Today is aunt Annie's birthday—80 yrs. old & spry as can be. She has lived her whole life for *Others*—hasn't she? And still serving at age of 80 yrs. Dear ole Pipey 78—has been busy all day making Dixie Relish for me. You know, the good stuff made of big peppers & onions. . . .

I struck a big idea for you. I saw something in paper that gave me the idea. You are so blessed with a good servant & will have time for it & I believe it would be a great blessing to you. Don't you want to take a course at Columbia? Just read this paper & pick your subject. I thought of marking a few of these subjects that I would prefer, but I will not. I'll see what you say. You see, Jane & M[arguerite]. will soon be in High School. Time passes so fast. You take one or two, or more, of these subjects & be prepared to teach. You are a good teacher.

Give my love to Miss H[ettie], Jim & the children & your dear self.

Mother

1. Richard objected to Harriette's marriage because he did not have confidence in Ralph Sharpton's ability to make a good living. An unspoken objection to Ralph was also the fact that he had the misfortune to be from Winder. Richard never thought any man from Winder was good enough for one of his girls.

To Mr. H. E. Russell, Davidson, N.C.

Nov. 14, 1927

Dearest Edward,

. . . When I read your letter, my mind went to a poem Mr. Morton had in bulletin last week. I'm sending a copy & you memorize it along with your other gems. "Be brave to live"—"Make not of work a *labor*"—Its easy to be happy if we just try, and do try to be *interested—interested* in people, those around you & those far away. Just think how many you can help & benefit by what you are getting at Davidson! When I read from a reliable source that 328,838 Georgians cannot read or write, & when I read in Christian Observer about the Daily Vacation Bible Schools in Ky. & Va. Mts. how people come for miles, people ranging in age from 8 mo. to 75 yrs so eager to learn. Women learning to read & write after they are past 50 & 60. . . . I just want to get out & do something to help. Its so pitiful for people to be so ignorant. After I read all this, I turn a page & see that the women in America spend two billion a yr. just trying to make themselves beautiful. It makes my heart sick. I see this in one paragraph "$5,000,000 passes through hands of American beauty shops owners every day in the year." I can hear you say: What have I to do with this, & I see the bored look, but if some body could only be roused and quickened, & go forward, with one determination: to help some body. We can often do this & not move 3 ft. from where we are. Lets always be ready—always on the lookout. . . .

Mother

To Mrs. James H. Bowden, Savannah, Ga.

Nov. 17, 1927

Dearest Marguerite,

Dad is here to-night, and is really *sitting by the fire.* Just now he asked me if I had heard from any of the children and I said yes—from you & Billie—and I gave him your letter of Nov. 11 to read. . . .

Fielding came in for a few min. to-night & he said you had written & sent him the $2. He appreciated it & I did too, as I had promised to send him some this wk. Its all dad can do to furnish the *absolutely necessary* money & the boy doesn't have much spending money. Fielding is a fine old boy. He is a good boy.

I think its nice to write around to our brothers & sisters occasionally. We are all mighty close kin & we must keep close to-gether.

We are rejoicing over Dicks coming [home from Europe]. He is very refreshing. Sometimes people come home from a grand trip and just seem to go to pieces . . . seem all bored & tired out, but Dick is so happy and full of his trip, and is so agreeable & sweet and considerate.

I cannot see how or why you get tired of your routine of living. Suppose something just awful or very exciting happened about every other day. I believe we would soon go to pieces—and when you have served your household, the ones nearest & dearest to you, it is a great deal accomplished, if we have served well. . . .

Clock striking eleven. I'm sleepy. I think about you all so much & love you and want you to be so happy and thankful that you have so nice a part in carrying on the workings of our beautiful world. My love to Jim and my 2 big girls & a heart full for you,

     Mother

To Mr. H. E. Russell, Davidson, N.C.

Jan. 23, 1928
Grandmother Dillard's birthday. She would
be 102 yrs. old. The best woman I ever knew.

Dearest Edward,

. . . Now boy, I'm glad you like my little verse about visions. I saw it and thought of you—*everything* would come so much easier to you and you would be so much happier if you would only *allow* your eyes to open. You *can* do it, if you only will. Try to get interested in people and in things. Get your self *willing* to do, to see, to serve, to catch the *light* as it falls from so many places, around persons, places and things. Don't be reading books to find truths and get inspiration, unless you read the book of books. You can find it there. . . . [S]ee if Dr. Neal Anderson's book "God's World & Word" is in your library & read the chapter "Visions and visionaries." It begins with a verse from Acts 2:17. "Your young men shall see visions." Its with you to see. Don't be cheated out of yours by any rebellious thoughts or indifference or carelessness. You are my splendid *young man.* O, I want you to see, to know, to catch your gleam and get *your portion* of all that is needed to make and mould you into a *good workman,* that *will not* be ashamed. . . .

Dad came Sun A.M. He said he would get your money to you by the 6th. . . . Dad is looking well now. He has a room at Kimball. They let him have one across from parlors for $1.00 per day. I'm begging him to keep it until March any how. He has private bath & the Colgate Co. presented him with a *chest* of toilet articles, including a good razor & he shaves every day. . . .

I'll be anxious to know how your *marks* come out.

The weather has been so beautiful to-day. I had 2 Negro boys & we worked in the yard & I had a good time. . . .

> Devotedly,
> Mother

To Mr. H. E. Russell, Davidson, North Carolina

March 5, 1928

Dearest Edward,

. . . Now about that mark in Greek. If we had discovered a pot of gold on our place, I would not be half so glad to tell dad, as I am to show him this mark when he comes home. Isn't it a grand & glorious feeling to make 'em like that? Just get in the habit, boy, & it will come easy.

William came home to have dental work done—he is in Atlanta to-day, going through the tortures. William came to *vote* too. He is positively "batty" over all these politics in Winder. He is pulling for Ben Hill and Otis Camp. He is actually *intense.* Fielding came over Sat. & it makes him *weary* to mention politics. Such a difference in our twins!

Alex has done the usual in acting the unusual. He . . . is very busy helping Carlton N[iblack] mix stock tonic every afternoon after school. He can make the run from the house where they mix the tonic home in 12 minutes. He is looking well. Is taking all kinds of exercises daily. . . .

Poor Marguerite grew tired of *her place,* and she is visiting Harriette now for 10 days or 2 wks. The 7th is Marguerite jr['s] birthday. I tell you, its a great thing to rejoice in well doing and not *grow weary.* . . . I get a lot of fun out of planning something nice, even if it never materializes. Right now we are planning something very delightful. You know dad goes to W'ton every year to the Law Institute. Well, Rob has up a big scheme. Sybil is doing all her [house]work & Rob is smoking one cigarette less per day, & R. says he's going to buy a car & he, Sybil, dad & I will go to W'ton in April about the 27th & then I want to see Davidson if we have time. Isn't that a nice prospect? . . . So, I go about my daily tasks, doing them the very best I can, & I have delightful visions . . . & I believe some of it will come true, for "All things come to him who WAITS." . . .

Did I write you about Mr. Florence Bell?[1] The 16th of Feb. he ran away— Went in his car—took pillows, cover &c. off of his mother's bed. You know Miss Sallie died in Jan. A niece of Miss Minnie's went with him. Poor Miss Minnie—this is worse than death to me. He carried about $15,000 with him. You know Miss Sallie had a lot of money out at interest. James & Mattie have come to live with Miss Minnie. She is pitiful. William saw Mr. Bell in Marshall . . . so at night he went to all the hotels to see if he was registered—& a man *had* registered in Mr. B's hand writing as W. Johnson & Wife. When William saw that he did not investigate. . . . This is something terrible to me & every body is upset over it. You know every body liked Mr. Bell—& every body feels hurt, and especially sorry for Miss Minnie. Some think he is gone for good & some think he will come back.

You'll be tired reading all this. Write to me & boy study. Do your best in all things.

Mother

1. The same Florence Bell who hit Edward with his car in 1920.

To Mrs. S. G. Green, Cherrydale, Va.

June 27, 1928

My Dearest, *Neglected* Child,

You are having "er" time with those teeth! I do feel so sorry for you. It seems that this human body of ours is fearfully and wonderfully made and that *teeth* start early and go as long as possible with their trouble, but O, my, how much good food we have "*chewed*" and what a blessing teeth are—and right here, let me beg you to confine yourself to whole wheat bread & all kinds of food that build good strong bones, so your baby will "get by" as light as possible with tooth trouble, dear, little ole, sweet thing! I love him-her already! . . .

We are distressed about Pipey. For several days she has been on a de-
cline—just so weak & feeble. Edward slept over there last night & Carolyn
is over there now. Pat had to undress her & put her to bed last night. Her
bowels & kidneys act any time and she is not conscious of it. They are all
so pitiful—it tears my heart. Aunt Annie is unusually well, but at best,
you know she is feeble. Uncle Ben still helpless & pitiful beyond description.
I feel that it is time for Rowena to come back. She sends $5 every week to
pay the old man who cares for Ben and he is not very good & worries
aunt Annie to death. . . .

I should have written at first that dad has no opposition & we are all
so happy. Its just up to us now to fight Geo. Thompson. Dick must win
this time.[1]

We had a glorious 24th. Mrs. Millsaps invited us *all* to a barbecue dinner
and a grand one it was—*2 kids, young goats*—not [grandchildren] Bobby
& Betty—barbecued to the queens taste— 4 fried chickens, beans, beets,
Irish potatoes, squash, tomatoes, hot rolls, corn bread, tea & coffee, pickles,
ice cream, & 2 kinds of cake. 7 Russells there, beside Rob & family. . . . As I
remember, it is the only time in our 37 yrs. that I, or we, were invited
out. . . . To-day is Robs & Sybils anniversary. . . .

I'm so glad you are going to help with D[aily] V[acation] B[ible]
S[chool]. It will help you & it will do so much towards building up the
character & disposition of our *future child*. . . .

I've told aunt Annie not to cook any dinner to-day. I can help more that
way than in any other—sending them dinner.

I know there is more that I'd love to say—but this is a long letter. Rest
all you can & don't let the tooth trouble pull you down. My love to Gordon
& the children.

      Mother

1. In a letter to Ina Jr. she says: "It has never been known in history for a man who was
Speaker to have opposition. It took Winder to pull that stunt."

To Mrs. James H. Bowden, Savannah, Ga.

June 28, 1928

Dearest Marguerite,

. . . I enjoyed your letter of June 24. . . . You must not be feeling so badly
this early in the game, but I know from experience that sometimes you

do—anyway, enter into all you can with as much interest & animation as possible, so as to develop our baby.[1] Billie wrote that she was going to help teach in the Daily Va. Bible School & I was so glad. Read, study, memorize & do all you can [to] *build up* the baby. I hope you like your doctor better, but just let him alone & put your mind on something else. Of course if you are real awful sick you'll have to have a doctor, but I never did, only before R. B. was born & then I was sick in bed & did not eat food for about 5 wks.

I think its nice for you to go to McD[onough]., but you know you will not be "looking ugly" for a long time yet. I *hope* it will not hurt you *to ride*. You know I was never in a car with *any one* of mine—ole Hattie & the buggy was my joy. . . .

> My best love . . .
> Mother

1. Marguerite's third child was expected in January 1929.

To Mr. H. E. Russell, Davidson, N.C.

Sep. 18, 1928

Dearest Boy,

Your letter just received, just as I returned from Athens. You know aunt Annie's eye has been giving her trouble and Sybil carried *us* . . . to see Dr. Cabaniss and she feels better about it. Sybil will take us back in 10 days to see him again. We brought Alex home with us. He & F[ielding]. have just carried his trunk to the Ex. Office & A. will catch a ride back to Athens now in a minute. A. seems enthusiastic and interested—his address 290 West Clayton St. F. will go to-morrow. He has old "Victoria" all geared up & will start for Gainesville to see his *Lillian* & its *raining*. . . .

I've had a time getting A's trunk packed. He does not have to have sheets & pillow cases. He has a room 2 blocks from S.A.E. House & eats in house next to big corner filling station on corner in front of S.A.E. House. . . .

As you say, I feel that our *best* & *biggest* investment is in our 3 boys who are in College now. I am expecting *big* returns.

> Mother

To Miss Ina D. Russell, Washington, D.C.

Oct. 2, '28

My Dearest Ina,

The 12th was a great day for me—our success with the lunches & Dick's grand majority. George only got 449 votes out of the whole County. Dick is going right ahead with his race for Speaker and the representatives & senators are pledging him their support, right along.

My greatest joy now is that Rob & Sybil will soon be living out here. The garage & office overhead is almost completed. R. & S. will come here Thursday and stay until the house is ready for them to move in. Arrangements are about made to have the electric line brought out & then for water-works! *Electric range*—thats the talk now. Just watch us "dwellers in sticks" and see if we don't shine some day. . . .

Have you thought about our 3 *boys* in college? Alex is very refreshing. He comes home Saturday to see if his possessions are all here and tells me everything. He seems delighted with college life. He was laughing over the result of 2 tests he had in *math*—made 100 in one & 40 in the other. Fielding couldn't come home Sat. because he had to find a *cat* to dissect—he has graduated on frogs & tadpoles. Edward writes that he is very happy and has plenty of hard work to do. He has a job that pays him right well & that is a "*booster*."

Carolyn is struggling along in her Junior work. She is liking her French. . . .

Aunt Annie, Pipey & uncle Ben are still struggling along. Aunt Annie will be 81 on the 18th of this month. Pipey is *very* feeble. Aunt Annie is a wonder. My pen is awful and I have scratched along, any how. Carolyn says she can hear me up stairs.

> My love to my dear child,
> Mother

To Mr. H. E. Russell, Davidson, N.C.

Nov. 1, 1928

Dearest Edward,

. . . Dad seemed pleased with the row of Bs on your report. He said he was sorry for the E.[1]

I gave your letter to Pipey. Poor thing. She is pitiful. She comes over & talks to me about dying & seems so worried because she does not *know* more about it. Sister Annie says she was crying this morning & talking about it. I went over about 2 hrs. later. She seemed real cheerful—said she had been feeling real sick early in the A.M. but was feeling all right again. Poor uncle Ben falls out of the bed every A.M. about 5 o'clock & lies on the floor until uncle Mitchell comes. Poor aunt Annie goes in & puts pillows under his head & covers him up. Since the storm in Fla. Rowena writes that Carney's business was all destroyed. He hasn't had a job in 5 weeks. They were moved to Jacksonville & now they are in Miami with James. Rowena still sends the money for uncle B. but says she may have to stop.

To-morrow will bring a new birthday [31st] for Dick. He is creeping *on* now. . . .

Alex comes over to shoot jay birds & gather pecans. He is a funny boy. A good ole boy. He is anxious to see his report. Carolyn has gone to sleep over her lesson. She is pitiful when she flops. . . .

> Heart of love,
> Mother

1. E indicated failure. Edward was failing political science.

To Miss Ina D. Russell, Washington, D.C.

Nov. 14, '28

Dearest Ina,

. . . I've been thinking about you so much lately. Rob was taking every thing out of his house & your trunk was brought over. . . .

Rob's house is going to be so nice. Just think! electric lights right at my door! I do want them—it takes *cash.* Rob is paying for his. Dad is paying to have the house fixed over. Dad told me—when I asked him to have the line brought over—that if he did he would have to take one of the boys out of college. You know I'll burn pine knots first! but I'll be patient. My time will come, I feel sure. Our boys are so fine & doing so well. Its such a joy to think of having R. & S. & the children so near me. Surely "my cup runneth over."

Carolyn & I have been here 2 nights alone. This is the week for dad & Rob to work in Atlanta. . . . I've been looking for a telegram from Gordon. Dear Billie. She is so precious to me. I haven't written to her lately.

You see I'm writing so hastily. Got up early, made fire in stove & said: "I'll write to Ina, even if I have to hurry." I've been so busy trying to get my yard & flowers in shape before winter. Can't get any help. Doscia washes then hurries to the cotton field—lots of cotton & beautiful weather. Yesterday I had a white woman & her 2 boys to help sweep & clean up.

Now, my dearie, I'll go finish breakfast, get C. off to school, wash dishes, &c., &c. . . .

Yours
Mother

To Mrs. James H. Bowden, Savannah, Ga.

Nov. 26, 1928

Dearest Marguerite,

. . . When I heard about our little *Sam*[uel Gordon Green Jr.], I wanted to be the first to tell you, but I knew they would write from Washington—and the message came Sunday A.M. about 2:30 o'clock—a telephone message—if Sybil & Rob had not been here & sleeping down stairs, I don't suppose we would have heard the phone. Gordon sounded as if he was over-joyed. . . .

I intended telling you right at first what had kept me from writing, or rather what had delayed me. Besides the many things that arise every day, aunt Annie has been sick. She wasn't sick exactly, but just seemed to give out. You know every thing stops there when she gives out. I have to run over and bring in wood & coal. . . .

Sybil & Rob have moved and the house is nice & sweet. We had great rejoicing the night the lights were turned on. 'Twas like my Christmas feelings of long ago. And listen, my darling, and you shall hear of my great joy. In 2 weeks (D.V.)[1] I will have lights! Tell Jim & my children. Dick is paying to have them put in. Imagine me, if you can, with so much splendor! And I must say, convenience—an iron, for instance—always hot—no changing &c. I am so very happy about this, but there's no bliss without alloy—and I'm trusting that Pipey and aunt Annie will live to enjoy this with me, for we hope to get them some drop lights. . . .

Billie wrote me some time ago that she was coming in June to stay a long time. You must be here, too. I can't think of anything nicer than having my two babies here. If yours is *Jim,* he & Sam can have a great time—but if its *not,* we'll have a great time any how, for theres nothing sweeter than a precious girl. . . .

    Mother

1. Deo volente (God willing). In later years Ina often used this expression in her letters.

To Mrs. S. G. Green, Cherrydale, Va.

Winder, Ga., Dec. 4, 1928

My Dearest Billie,

    . . . You know I am one of the 7 wonders. I've never lived in a house with electricity. Rob's coming out here has put new life into everything. You know how progressive he is. Their little home is so nice. They have a lot of work to do—getting things cleaned up. Its such a joy to have them so near. Bobby & Betty are always around & they are growing fast & *so smart.* Rob has hired a negro man & his wife & we have fixed up Doscia's house for them. We have had good news from the ones the woman has worked for— very capable and good in every way. Rob says he will get a cow. You know when Alex went to college our cow went to the butcher. I'll get my milk from Rob.

    Dad is at home now so much. This is fine. He enjoys it. He will dig too much though. He has complained some lately of pains in his legs—and he will grunt around & say how feeble he is. I've almost been blue about aunt Annie. She got in such a queer condition—all at once—so feeble— couldn't talk—was not interested in any thing. She is better now—has been over here twice to-day, but I can see the big change in her. Pipey seems to be feeling very well—but she is feeble & pitiful. I went over this A.M. (Tues.) & Pipey said, "Ina, is this Fri. or Sat.?" When I told her it was Tuesday, she insisted I was mistaken—but was finally convinced. Uncle Ben pitiful as ever—or more so. I fix dinner for them every day. We hope to get some lights put in for them. If it was not for uncle B. I'd have aunt Annie & Pipey here for the winter.

    I was so glad Miss Hettie could go to you. Turn things over to her and don't worry over anything. I'm longing to hear how you & Sam are—if you give milk for him, if he is a good baby and just everything.

Every body up stairs & in bed *"but me."* . . .

You know my heart is with you, and tell R[ussell]. & N[ancy]. I love them & tell Gordon, too. . . .

  Mother

To Miss Ina D. Russell, Washington, D.C.

Dec. 10, 1928

Dearest Ina,

Your letter came Sat. A.M. I was utterly alone—every body gone to the Ga. Tech foot ball game. Dad went to Atlanta, but not to the game. He came home on Bus, getting here about 5:30. I cooked *all day* Sat. getting ready for Sun. Edward brought two boys from Davidson. William was coming, bringing 2 friends from Marshall. Fielding & Alex were coming. I always invite Mr. Morton. Dick said he would come in time for dinner & of course I had Rob & Sybil, and Pat came home with them Sat. night. 22 people ate dinner with me Sun. Doscia came to wash dishes which saved my life. 12 of these people were grown men with good appetites, and they *ate.* I had a good dinner. I counted aunt Annie, Pipey & uncle Ben in the 22, for I sent them dinner.

When your letter came, I wished that you could walk in after you left your work, and we could have had a good time. We hurried the man up, and had our lights going when the boys came. Every body so happy over them. I ironed aunt Annie's clothes the first night, with Pat's iron that she brought home. I want to work all night now, (so Carolyn & dad says) for the lights are so good.

Pat went to "Cicero-Bucks" (Sears & Roebuck) and bought fixtures. They are pretty & nice & cost only $35.53. We bought them on time, paying $5 down—and I have $5 more dollars to put on it and dad has promised to help. You see it was this way: dad is very antagonistic to the Ga. Power Co. At first he said they should not put a post on his land, but Rob got around him & they put the post right where he said &c. I did not know at this time that dad opposed it so. Then when I asked dad about putting lights in our house, he *still* didn't express himself about the Power Co. I really think the letter you wrote melted his heart, or *began* to melt it, for he did not give in entirely until the lights were put in. Now he seems to enjoy them more than any body—and I'm sure he'll pay for the fixtures. When I wrote you what Rob said I *did not* think that dad would be willing to do *anything*. He is a dear ole precious, but he has queer ideas sometimes.[1]

I hope to get aunt Annie's lights by C'mas. I do thank you for the check you sent, and Fielding, Edward, Alex & Carolyn are glad their names were included. . . .

Would you mind writing to Harriette & telling her what we are going to do, and see if she'll help. I'll tell you sometime why I do not want to do it myself. Aunt Annie & Pipey are all pepped up over the lights. Aunt Annie is better than when I wrote you—but she is *very* feeble—her right eye is very bad—the lid turns in. Of course the eye lash irritates the eye. We keep it pulled down with adhesive plaster.

I am trying to finish Harriette's Slumber Robe to send for C'mas. I've been longer on it than any of the others. Now, with the good lights, I can work on it at nights. . . .

Write to me soon. I love to hear. I'm *so glad* you are taking the law course.

> My heart of love & *more,*
> Mother

I must tell you something about little Bobby. He is a very peculiar child & smart. He has heard so much about *healthy,* eat this & you'll be healthy, see how healthy this boy is, and you know you want to be healthy. Well, Ina Ruth Thomas comes every Sat. to take music from Carolyn—you know how *robust* the Thomas[es] are & Ina Ruth is even more so than the ones you remember. She came in one day & Bobby went to his dad & told him we had company. Rob asked him who it was. He said, "I don't know, but I *think* its Mrs. Healthy." This has amused us all. He is getting off things like this constantly.

1. Richard had represented a client in bitter litigation against the Georgia Power Company in 1919. The suit asked for $150,000 in damages, a fantastic sum, but the courts decided in favor of the power company.

To Miss Ina D. Russell, Washington, D.C.

Jan. 15, 1929

Dearest Ina,

. . . I wish you could have been here Sunday. You may have heard of the death of Mr. Dave Barrow, Ex-Chancellor of U. of Ga. He was buried in Oconee Cemetery Sun. afternoon. Pat came Sat. Dad begged her to carry him over and she did. I went too. You know dad is Chairman of the Board of Trustees, so of course he sat on the stage. The funeral was conducted in the Old Chapel. Pat & I were fortunate enough to get in with the Barrow Co. delegation[1] and had splendid seats. As I was waiting, what did I see but dad marching in with Hoke Smith! The sight started me thinking. Dad looked so nice. He had purchased a lovely overcoat, and Pat had given him a Phi Beta Kappa Key & he was wearing that and he looked so nice and distinguished. Hoke has almost lost his mind. He is about what you call *imbecile.* He looks well, but no mind—just dumb. I was so thankful our daddy was in such good shape. It doesn't matter whether we were governor or U.S. Senator or millionaire!

Daddy spoke over Radio Saturday night. He has been made president of an American Agricultural Society and he invited anybody & every one in- terested to come to a big dinner & meeting at Biltmore Hotel Jan. 31st. Pat & I went to Judge Johns & heard daddy. His speech was good—every word clear & distinct. He thinks now he may come to Washington soon to see somebody in behalf of this Society. Daddy stays in good spirits when he has plenty of work to do. I mean something he *likes* to do out side of his Court work.

Carolyn was in a recital Fri. night. I confess I was scared. She did *so well.* She gave the "One-legged Goose"—the piece you sent her long ago.[2] She wore the dark blue dress you put on. She looked so pretty and gave the piece beautifully. . . .

Your letter to dad came to-night. Of course I had to read it. Dad will be home in day or two—will save it for him. Write & let us know how you come out on [law school] debate. Dick says you have a *hard side.* I've always thought they ought not to have *juries.*

Lovingly,
Mother

1. Dave Barrow was from Oglethorpe County, and his people and the Dillards were friends from generations back.

2. Ina Jr. sometimes gave comic recitations at social evenings in Washington.

To Mrs. James H. Bowden, Savannah, Ga.

Jan. 15, 1929

Dearest Marguerite,

. . . This was a most delightful Christmas to me, and a very unusual one. My three strapping college boys came tramping in 10 days earlier than I expected them. . . . All three left in a hurry—so many shirts, socks & ties left lying around.

But my Christmas was indeed a happy one. We kept well, and I am still thankful. William had flu—was in bed 3 days—the only one of us who really got sick. Rob was in bed one day & Dick was *almost* sick enough to go, but escaped. Alex went to Marshall to help William and those two left M[arshall]. C'mas A.M. at one o'clock and as I was making the fire in the dining room, 7:30 that A.M., William & Alex drove into the back yard. It was a happy time for me & they seemed so happy & tipped up stairs & caught every body "Christmas Gift." Alex went back with W. Stayed 4 days.

My Christmas cannot be described. I had been so happy over my lights, and I was showered with electrical conveniences—a floor lamp, waffle irons, toaster & a hot point iron—(I ironed last night until 10:30)—and I thought how fortunate. . . .

I am thinking about you constantly now. Know you are counting the days. So glad that you are feeling so well. You and Billie have been wonderful. Its marvelous to be a mother—to be blessed—to bring into the world a human being endowed with so much that is beautiful and useful. Your two girls are fine specimen[s]. I love them so much. Ina was just *full* of things about M[arguerite] & J[ane]. I was so glad for her to see them now, at this age. I'm so thankful they have such fine training at home, in church and Sunday School and School. . . .

I do not know what comment to make on our Jimmy & his Golf. I've heard & do hear constantly of how some men are so careless, drinking, running around, leaving home &c—and Jim is such a dear old boy—so sweet at home & takes good care of you & the children. Lets put up with his golf and be thankful its *that* and nothing worse. Jim is a good boy. He works hard and his work is confining. So maybe his health will be better and maybe it just takes golf to keep him going. . . . So lets not worry. We don't want our baby to be cross & fretful. We have a great deal to be thankful for. I'd be glad if Jim did not play on Sunday, but just let him play & let us be interested in his games &c.

Our daddy digging his dirt has hurt me. He has always dug on Thanksgiving Day, Christmas and many other times when it worried me—but I wouldn't *swap* him off for any body. . . .

Its past time for me to begin supper. . . . There is much in my mind *yet* that I'd like to write. . . .

> My hearts best love,
> Mother

To Mrs. James H. Bowden, Sr., Savannah, Ga.

January 28, 1929

Dearest Marguerite,

Your letter written Jan. 25th came this morning just about two hours after that grand telephone message from Jim. To say we are happy expresses it mildly. We are over-joyed. We are thrilled. Dick talked about it at the supper table. He said that he hoped the boy was *exactly* like Jim in looks and all.

You should have seen Doscia when I told her. She was in the dining room. She picked up a chair & went running around the table. Put the chair down & picked up another, running on the other side of the table. Then she came to me and said she "had to hug somebody"—as I was sitting down, she hugged my head & I hugged her legs. . . .

I'm *so glad* you are "over with it," and its a great privilege we women have—to bring forth human beings. I'm proud & thankful for mine. . . .

> Lovingly
> Mother

To Miss Ina D. Russell, Washington, D.C.

May 5, 1929

Dearest Ina,

I wished for you to be with us when we went to Atlanta to hear Carolyn *"orate"*—and I wish you could have seen how happy the beautiful pink roses made her. A friend sent a box of candy and she received so many congratulations—so many nice things were said. She did do well—so much better than either girl (2) besides Carolyn. We, Rob & I, thought a boy from LaGrange would get 1st place & he wasn't even mentioned by the judges. The boy who won is an Italian—a Catholic student at Marist. He did very well, but two of our own good *Americans* did better, I think. The boy who won 2nd place did better, *I* thought. He is Irish & a Catholic from Benedictine School in Savannah. Some said it was mean of me, but I said Atlanta judges & an Atlanta boy won first. His name so foreign I can't even call it—*Cefalu,* I believe. He is to represent our Empire State of the South. But Carolyn did enjoy it all & she *worked.* She did want first place *so bad.*

It was real funny, I thought—the 3 who won happened to sit right together. The boy from Sav. fell for Carolyn and made a date for that night. Carolyn stayed with Pat. When the boy came, the one who won first place brought him out in his new Ford Coupe and the three went to a show. Carolyn liked the boy from Sav. Don't let her know I'm telling you all this.

I had never been to one of the State meets & I did enjoy it. All the speakers & their coaches had lunch at the Henry Grady. Pat, Sara Pierce, and I had lunch at the same time & we enjoyed looking in on them. . . .

When I began this, I was all alone & quiet. Dick, Rob, Carolyn, Bobby & Sybil have all passed in—and out—discussing various things. . . .

I'm watching for news about you all coming. Harriette writes that she will come May 23—in time for Pipey's birthday the 24th. Poor Pipey. She watches and listens *every day* for H. to come. I tried to make her understand to-day that it would be 18 days before H. came. Aunt Annie is in Athens with uncle Walter. You see, we have the nice lady with them & she is taking good care of Pipey & keeps every thing so clean. Poor uncle Ben is still too pitiful for words. . . .

My heart of love,
Mother

To Miss Ina D. Russell, Washington, D.C.

July 12, 1929

Dearest Ina-Girl,

If you were only here to join in this rabble of words thats going on—and the radio giving vent also. We are just finishing supper. . . . I'm thinking about that nice coffee pot you sent me, and I've waited so long to write you. I used it first when Rowena, James & Frank were here for supper. I used mine too—and we had plenty of coffee with no agony of wondering if it would hold out.

We asked Gordon to tell you about uncle Ben. We had so much to see after and it was hard to write every body & Billie was writing Gordon—so she asked him to tell you. You may not know it, but uncle Ben in all of his helplessness never did make but one request. He never did ask for any thing—just took what was given him—but he *did* make one request & I was *determined* that *one* would be *granted.* He requested that his body be carried to Odesadale & be put by Matties. About 2 yrs. ago Rowena said this would be impossible as it would cost too much. Providence saw after uncle Ben. He did not die until the boys had good jobs. When Rowena came she said it was out of the question to take Bennie to Odesadale. I did not say any thing for awhile but I finally got the 3 to-gether and told them that their father only made *one* request & that was that he be buried by their mother & that I thought it would be best to put him in a very cheap casket and take him where he wanted to go—or not put him in *any* casket—but *carry him to Odesadale.* So, I carried my point & they agreed that it must not be otherwise.

Mr. Ferguson was very kind—let them have a $100 casket for $75. His shroud was $12.50—embalming $10—taking the body to Odesadale $50 (129 miles) and $1.50 for some underclothes and socks. They paid ½ of this amount & will pay the other soon as possible. Frank is manager of the 3rd largest A. & P. store in Miami. James travels for independent grocerymen—rides 500 miles a wk.—works on commission. He & Frank have friendly arguements—chain-versus independents.

Pat & I went with them to Odesadale. Mr. Harmon had a nice grave ready—with cement & every thing just as he had Matties fixed 21 yrs. ago. I was so happy over the way every thing turned out. Uncle Ben looked fine and distinguished—not a trace of the pitiful man you saw. Billie had trimmed his beard. Mr. F. shaved him, leaving a nice, close-cut moustache. I asked Edward how he thought uncle Ben looked & he said, "Like a French General" & he did. Of course aunt A. & Pipey miss him & they feel it more than any body.

Uncle B's body was carried to Ferguson's as soon as he died. Rowena & the boys came in about 36 hrs. We went up to the undertaking parlor & had a short service—the minister read the 23rd Ps. "The Lord is my Shepherd"—& I thought how appropriate for uncle Ben. The Good Shepherd had cared for him. He seemed so unfortunate to us. In the last 6 or 7 yrs. he has not had *one penny of his own*—but his table has been prepared for him and he has never suffered for the want of food. Aunt Annie was faithful & kind and did this for our Shepherd. He has no one but us to do these things for Him.

I felt that you would be interested in hearing about uncle B.

We still miss you. I *love* to think of our good time. . . .

Mother

To Miss Ina D. Russell, Washington, D.C.

Sep. 28, 1929

Dearest Ina,

. . . The gift for Doscia is splendid. Sybil & I look at it with envy . . . but we are so glad for our dear ole colored friend to have something so nice & I know her heart will beat long & loud over "baby Ina" thinking about her. The object for my "sweet tooth," like the ginger bread man, is "almost gone." My childhood days were brought to mind when a favorite cousin always remembered me with maple sugar.

Your "good luck"—just virtue and hard work being rewarded. I'm never surprised when things come your way, for you give out your best & then, of course, the best comes back to you. I'll just have to be coming to see you. I'll want to see those nice quarters you are moving into—that elevator? Is it the kind that moves all the time? *I've heard about 'em*—but my country *feet* and other characteristics haven't quite taken in such doings. Dad sat down last night and figured every thing out. He says you haven't as much room as our dining room. You just come on home when you want to stretch out.

I'm counting on you going to the top in your junior year in the law course. I'm so glad every day that you are taking this course. . . .

And you are a $2000 woman now,[1] so independent and courageous. I'm happy for you. Don't forget your spiritual side as your worldly part increases—grow evenly, you dear, sweet child of mine. . . .

Its late, as time goes, and I'm always tired & sleepy about midnight—but I just had to see you before another day dawned. I want to write to William too. He works so hard. He gives the best to his job. Did you know Fielding was teaching Eng. at Ga. U.[2] He was asked back as a scholarship. He was so undecided what to do. So we thought it would be beneficial to teach & study—get M.A. degree. He could have landed a job with A. & P. in N.C. William told him that he'd be a "fool" to take a job "like that" and he a *graduate*. He said it with so much feeling. You know F. is not "cut out" for that kind of work.

I'm rambling on & my paper most gone. Dad was real sick for a few days, but he seems so well now. I appreciate good health in my family. . . .

Dearest one, I love you & I'm proud of you. . . .

Mother

1. Ina Jr.'s salary for the year—double what she started with in 1918.
2. Richard had recommended that Fielding study medicine, but Alex took on the job of becoming the doctor that Richard and Ina wanted among their sons because scientific study appealed to him and partly because, as he wrote to his brother Jeb, "Fielding ought to be free to pursue his real love—literature."

To Miss Carolyn Russell, Winder, Ga.

Feb. 5, 1930

Dearest Child,

. . . We reached Raleigh to-day about 11:30. Bad roads from Athens to Hartwell & one puncture. We found that E[dward]. had been moved from the college infirmary to Rex Hospital [following his injury in a wrestling match]. Poor boy is in a bad fix but doctors say he will come around O.K. Must be still for 3 *wks.* Then *maybe* he can come home. He cannot use his fingers at all or move his head. He had two good nurses & 2 good doctors. To-day he had lovely flowers sent from Davidson. His frat. & the college and the nurse he had at the infirmary sent 14 gorgeous red roses. E's room mate Sam Coker has a sister living here & Sam sent her a wire about E. She & her husband came to see E. & insisted that I stay with them. I may do so when Dick leaves. Dick says I must not leave E. yet.

I'm worried about you all at home—*you, Pipey* and *aunt Annie.* See if you can get Doscia to stay there until I get back or maybe Callie will. Suggest to her to let her children stay with Annie until I get back. I'll pay her more if she sleeps there. Use the cot & take the cover I left on cot. I'm sending you a ck. Get it cashed—pay Doscia $1.00 for washing. Pay Callie $1.50 and pay Annie Lou $1.50 and if you can be at home Sat. have Annie Lou come iron, especially dad's shirts & collars. Buy any food you may need at aunt Annies or home. I do hope you deposited aunt A's money. I was almost *desperate* when I left. I tried to be quiet & sane—and did my precious Bobby get to his grandmothers. Do write to me c/o Rex Hospital, Room 84, Raleigh N.C. And *please,* child, take care of my mail and forward my letters. To-night I have written dad, Wm, Fielding, Harriette, Gordon (for birthday) and now you & I'm like the ginger bread boy, *"most gone."*

Please manage things at home. I am almost miserable over things. This money belongs to me, so use it well—& do as I say. Tell Mr. Morton about Edward so he can write.

Mother

To Judge R. B. Russell, Sr., Atlanta, Ga.

2-11-30 Monday night—[post card]

Received your letter and checks to-day. Wish I could write you a long letter, but can't to-night. Don't be worried about E[dward]. His mind is in perfect condition and his arms and hands are slowly improving. I could see to-day that he was so much better. He had a tray of solid food to-day—not much, but it was the first food he had had. I am so pleasantly fixed. Rob and Sybil couldn't be any better and sweeter to me [than the Cannons are]. We are going to Chapel Hill to-morrow to have lunch with [my nephew] Harry Comer and his wife.[1] Mrs. Comer has an uncle who teaches there and her sister is in school. Harry's wife is lovely. I'll write you a long letter if possible. Take care of youself. I do not want anything and I am so pleasantly fixed.

Ina

1. Harry Comer, son of Mamie Dillard and Henry Comer, was Methodist youth director at the University of North Carolina at Chapel Hill.

To Miss Carolyn Russell, Winder, Ga.

Feb. 13, 1930

Dearest Carolyn,

If you could have been here to-night when the jonquils came! They were fixed up perfectly, and in splendid condition. . . . E. is still improving, but cannot use his fingers yet—and he has to lie on his back, but his vocal organs are O.K. He whistles & sings sometime and jokes with every body— says the "sassassiest" things to the nurses. One nurse is Miss Byrd and he calls her "Commander" all the time. He is the pet of the hospital and re- ceives a lot of attention. This afternoon 7 boys from the college were in his room at one time. You & Inez should have been here. Later a preacher came (about young as Mr. Morton) and brought 2 pretty co-eds. One was just like Sunie. E. said he thought of Sunie when she came in. Both of the girls were pretty.

I intended telling you that I received a box of flowers to-night after yours came—1 doz. lovely carnations. The card on them read: Chief Justice and Mrs. C. R. Stacy. I had visited Mrs. Connor, Judge Connors wife. He is a Supreme Court judge and he came to see E. this aft. He is an S.A.E. Mrs. Wood had written to a Christian preacher about E. & he sent a Mrs. Hillyer to see him. She brought chicken soup & crax to him at his dinner hour to-day. She knows the Chief Justice & his wife and that is where I came in for the flowers. Mrs. Chief J. & her husband will call on me to-morrow aft. 5 o'clock.

I hope you get this letter and let Pat read it—bless her heart. . . . I do want to tell you about my visit to Harry Comer at Chapel Hill. How I love college towns and anything about schools and churches. I wished all the time for you to be with me. Edward often says he wishes Carolyn could come in.

So glad things are going on well at home. . . .

Mother

To Mrs. S. G. Green, Cherrydale, Va.

Feb. 14, 1930

Dearest Billie,

. . . I'd love to find words to describe the many kindnesses that have been shown to me since I came to Raleigh. My friend is the sister of Edward's roommate at Davidson—Sam Coker—he wired his sister to come to Edward at once. She did & found me and took charge of me. She has been married about 2 yrs. They moved into their little home about 3 mo. ago. The Cokers are very prominent people in S.C. Mr. C. has a wonderful farm & raises special cotton seed and has men from China, Japan, Eng., and many other places to visit him. This daughter reminds me of you & Edward said, "She['s] just like Billie." Her husband is lovely & they seem so happy—both of them about 30 yrs. old. She does her work, has woman to come twice per wk., & I help all she will let me. I call them my children. You & Gordon could not be sweeter to me. Two of Mrs. Coker's uncles teach at Chapel Hill, so Harry & Jane [Comer] knew them & the sister who goes to school there, so they were glad to meet each other and we enjoyed our day there Tuesday. Jane is a University woman & is a fine housekeeper. Harry so smart & nice & refined. My superintendent, 40 yrs. ago, when I first taught in Athens, is a prof. at Chapel Hill. Jane had him and his wife to lunch (Dr. & Mrs. Branson). Mrs. B. called me *Ina* and Mr. B. was so cordial and nice and we recalled old times. . . .

Later: I have come home from the hospital. Edward resting very well. His improvement is slow—he had a big day and it got on his nerves. He is so popular—is the pet of the hospital and receives so much attention. To-day he had 2 lovely pot plants to come in from girls he had never met. One lovely one from his best girl. . . . Carolyn sent me about 500 jonquils and I carried some to him. He received 14 valentines and 4 letters in the morning mail. Mrs. Josephus Daniels came in with a cute collection of funnies for valentines and talked awhile. He [Edward] said he was like uncle Ben—just had to cry when people were so good to him. Of course no one saw this but *me*—not even the nurse. Edward can't use his hands yet. He is eating some real food now. Mrs. Wood of Winder wrote a friend, pastor of the Christian church about E. and he sent a lovely woman, about my age, very rich, big Lincoln car, pompous chauffeur—she sent me home in her car one day—

Well, this lady, Mrs. Hillyer, has been several times & brought him nice chicken soup yesterday.

I feel that I am making my debut in Raleigh. I receive so much attention. If I stay much longer I'll have to have evening clothes &c. Mrs. Stacy, wife of the Chief Justice, called this afternoon, two Supreme Court wives came too. My friend Katherine insisted on serving tea and sandwiches. We had a lovely time. All seem to marvel at my 13 children & it seems that Katherine is so fond of telling every one.

This letter is so disjointed—has been written at different intervals. My friend is Mrs. Cannon. She was Katherine Coker. . . . A girl who saw Edward get his hurt was to see him & brought a bunch of lovely sweet peas & a beautiful red rose bud. She says she will never look at another wrestling match. . . .

I write letters for E. and read his letters to him. He gets 5 or 6 per day. Tonight he held a cracker between his thumb & forefinger. He cannot stand even a hair to touch his hands without pain.

I hope you can make some sense out of this.

Mother

To Miss Carolyn Russell, Winder, Ga.

Feb. 20, 1930

Dearest Sweet Child,

When we came in last night about 8 o'clock I found your precious letter. Never could a letter be sweeter. My heart overflowed with gratitude to God for you. We all blunder and make mistakes, but if the desires and aims are right and noble, all will be well with our souls.

I've been wanting to send you & Inez something. Yesterday I saw some pretty new dress goods and thought you'd enjoy a dress "just alike" . . . [because] my friend Laura Wilson & Vee Larson and I always had 1 or 2 dresses "just alike." . . .

Dr. made a good examination of E. yesterday. He is having him raised up in bed every day now, you know how they crank up those hospital beds, so he will get accustomed to sitting up and in a few days he will put the cast on his neck and then maybe he can walk around some. . . .[1]

Last night a kind, lovely lady brought a radio to E's room. Attach it to the springs & it gives all the Raleigh stations. Edward has been wild to hear some music. A pretty girl (like Annie Strange used to be) across the hall from Edward had a cute fruit basket that you wind & a nice tune was played. She let E. keep that every day for awhile. Yesterday she sent him some good food that her sister had sent her. . . .

Wish you could see E. this A.M. He is so much better. . . . [He] enjoyed your letter. I read it to him while he was getting a shave. Every body raves on about how good looking he is. E. has a mirror now, that I bought at 10¢ store. The nurse & I are constantly holding it for him to see himself. He held it one day. He can't turn anything loose that is put in his hands. We have to take it. He doesn't try much, as its very painful. . . .

Mother

1. Edward's paralysis was in his arms only.

To Mrs. James H. Bowden, Savannah, Ga.

March 2, 1930

Dearest Marguerite,

. . . I am all prepared now to leave here to-night. Edward still improving but its slow at best. Yesterday he had two nice rides in rolling chair. Walked several steps. He is very tired when he returns from these trips, but the doctor says he must *practice.*

I do not want to leave Edward. He does not need me as far as *attention* is concerned, for he certainly receives *that,* but I enjoy going every day and staying with him and sometimes he gets so blue over his school affairs. He does want to graduate with his class. . . .

You asked what you could do for E. I have been worried or concerned about how we would get him home. Dick has written many times that he will come *any time* the doctor says and bring him home. Now a lovely thing happened which made about 100 lovely things since E. has been hurt. Our friend Mr. Roberson [from Savannah] heard about it from a friend at Chapel Hill. He made it a point to stop over in R[aleigh] & hunt E. up. He stayed a long time. We were *so glad* to see him. *He is a fine man.* He says he will be glad to bring E. home for us. Now this seemed lovely to me. Mr. R. travels on passes, and he is *dependable.* He thinks he will be in North C. 14–15 of March. Maybe E. will be ready to come in that time. We are to notify him when E. can leave. Now, you see Mrs. R[oberson]. and tell her how much I appreciate this and say that we will do this, if things work out right. I'm leaving Mr. R's address with E's day nurse & she says she will write 3 or 4 days in advance so Mr. R. can be notified. This seems an excellent way to me to get E. home. Dick will come, but R.R. fare is $20 both ways. After other expenses it will cost Dick at least $75. If our plan works, just E's ticket. . . .

Another thing we can do for E. is to pass on kindness to people. I've never seen so much kindness as has been shown us since Feb. 1st. A notice was in the paper and the church bulletin and the kind people came & are still coming. Thats the surprise to me. Generally they come once. The same ladies and men have continued to come. Several bring something every time—a cup custard, some home made candy, some nice tea cakes, tomato aspic, beaten biscuit, angel food cake, & of course, flowers. 8 lovely vases in his room last night. Of course anything happening in school or college excites interest. One girl, not so young, she is Sec. at the College, saw E. when he fell. I've heard she cried all night. She has been every day . . . & she brings him the most beautiful flowers. She has a little radio set fitted up for him which is a great pleasure. She takes dictation sometimes from him and sends off letters for him. . . .

You did not say *one* word about *Jimmy* in your letter. I always look for *that.* I could [write] much more but must close. . . . My love to the girls. . . .

Mother

To Mr. Alex B. Russell, Athens, Ga.

March 5, 1930

Dearest Alex,

When I left Raleigh I made E's nurse promise to let me hear every day. Left cards and envelopes addressed so as not to take too much of her time. . . .

I am so glad that Fielding is back safe [from his boxing matches] and with only *one* bad eye.

The doctor thinks E. can come home about the 16th. Write him one of your good letters at least once before he comes. . . .

Alex, I've thought of you so much since I've been in Raleigh. I do hope you will make a *real* doctor and reach out and find some thing—just *one* thing—that would prove you were interested in the many ills that beset humanity. New things are being discovered every now-and-then. I thought of you when I read the enclosed clipping [about a treatment for pernicious anaemia].

Edward has a barber who is and has been an athlete. He talks about boxing and wrestling while he is putting on the lather and shaving. He can put his feet behind his head and sit in chair with his feet in his lap. He did all this one day when he finished shaving Edward. . . .

The boy who was in the wreck when the Oglethorpe student was killed has been in the hospital in Winder. His mother & father came from Cuba (Havanna) in airplane to Miami. Then to Atlanta on fast train, then to Winder in a Lincoln taxi—paid $30 for the taxi and tipped the driver $5. They have 6000 acres of land in tobacco in Cuba. I have been to see the boy—carried nice things for him to eat. His mother went to prayer meeting with me to-night. She is Presbyterian. The boy goes to-morrow. Dr. Mathews will take them to Atlanta & see how the boy stands the trip. He was thrown in the ditch and car on top of him. . . . The boy killed was his roommate. The boys name is Hedges. His mother is so nice. She went up to school and gave the French class a talk. They have lived in Cuba eleven years.

Dick said you were looking well. Fielding wrote Edward that you were growing and gaining in weight.

Carolyn has gone to bed and I must be going too. . . .

Your Mother

To Miss Ina D. Russell, Washington, D.C.

March 9, 1930

Dearest Ina,

If I had been keeping a diary to-day, I would have written this:

Sunday A.M.

Up very early to see after things, fires &c. Get breakfast, make preparations for dinner. Looking for Pat and Pete.[1] Get every body up. Fielding here. So thankful Annie Lou came to wash dishes and clean up. Ready for Sunday School when Rob came by. Back home at 11:30.

Hustle to get dinner by time Pat comes. Fixed a good barbecued pork roast.

Pat & Pete came about 12:30. I hurried up dinner, Pat *taking hold,* as is her custom.

Aunt Annie & Pipey had dinner with us.

When dinner was ½ over Mrs. Wood & Crozier came. I went out to see them, leaving my good bits of barbecue on plate & *all* my good dessert.

As Mrs. Wood was leaving Mrs. Harmon Williams and Miss Icie Smith came. They stayed 2 hrs. I was glad to see them, but of course I wanted to be with my folks. I was in the living room with my company. Every body else in dining room.

5 or 6 men came to see dad.

Girl & 2 boys came for Carolyn. They went for a short ride.

Elizabeth Kimball came in to see Pat.

I ate my dessert at 4 o'clock.

Soon after, Mr. Quarterman, Mamie, Keith & Nell came. Pat & Pete ran away and would not see them. Again I was left *alone* with *my* (?) company.

Pat & Pete left about 6 o'clock. I sat down for a few minutes of quietude. Another girl & 2 more boys came for Carolyn. (Of course, she was not here.)

After this a lady & her husband came to inquire about Edward. Fielding had to get on a bus for Athens.

Now this may seem foolish to you, but I just want you to know that I've had a hectic Sabbath. I had such a good quiet time in Raleigh and am convinced that I'm not naturally energetic, but just forced into [it].

I enjoyed my peep at Pat. She is our dear sweet child—so happy, and I love Pete as I do Gordon, Jim & Ralph. He is fine. Our Pat has a gorgeous ring. O, boy, its *beautiful.* Don't let her know I told you. Maybe she wants the pleasure of telling you. . . .

I have so much before me, behind me, and on all sides of me that I can't do all I'd like to do. I have to give aunt Annie & Pipey part of my time, & dad is at home for awhile, and Sybil & our new baby—he is *fine*—a beautiful baby. . . .

I may have written you. Dick spoke over radio Fri. Sounded good. He is invited to make speeches *somewhere* about every wk.

Well, darling child, good night. I can see you now, tucked away in your good bed that stands so nice & straight in your closet all day. Its 12 o'clock here.

Mother

1. Patience was engaged to Hugh Peterson. A June wedding was planned.

To Miss Ina D. Russell, Washington, D.C.

April 6, 1930

Dearest Ina,

Your letter came and brought great joy. I enjoyed it all and am so glad you have the nice room. I'd love to see the arrangements. I get home sick for Washington sometimes. Telling me about the cherry trees filled my heart with a longing to ride around the tidal basin. . . .

This has been a hectic Sunday. Dick has announced for Gov. at last. We had to answer telephone calls last night. Dick came in this A.M. from a trip off. He is all worn out. Some people have called today.[1]

I went to Sunday School and Church this A.M. Edward went too—his first effort since coming home. He is so much better, but still pitiful (*some*). He wants to go back to Davidson. . . .

We had a lot of excitement over the news papers to-day. Carolyn's picture and write-up about [winning the district] oratorical contest and Dick's picture and his announcement. I'll send some papers if I can get them. Maybe you can run across a paper in Washington.

I'm writing here in dining room. Dick & Rob & Edward discussing things in general. Sybil sitting here by me telling about a funeral she attended this afternoon. . . .

Our Presbyterial begins Tues. We are preparing to feed about 150 Tues. and 200 Wed. Tomorrow I am going to boil 3 hams and prepare 225 apples for Wed. lunch. . . . I'm paying for 2 delegates in town and taking 7 out here. Do you think I'm carrying my end of the load? You know I am Sec. of Lit[erature] & have to make an "attractive" report. I've labored over mine and decided to use a radio program, have a loudspeaker put up & perform behind a screen. I've written a song & Grace will sing for me.

I have also had to revise Pat's [wedding invitation] list & as Edward says: "We will let down the bars." Every body in Winder invited. If the church will not hold them, we can't help it. . . .

I'll try to write a better letter next time.

Mother

1. In a field of five candidates, Dick Russell Jr. was considered a third choice at best. Top spots were filled by George H. Carswell, who had served the state house and senate and been secretary of state, and E. D. Rivers, who had terms in the house and senate and was aligned with the powerful Commissioner of Agriculture Gene Talmadge. Defeated by Hardman in

1928, Rivers and others thought this time it was his turn. Russell had ten years in the state legislature and was Speaker of the House, one of the most powerful positions in state politics. However, John N. Holder, chairman of the state highway commission, was a candidate who had the support of many legislators who wanted highways in their districts. The fifth candidate was James A. Perry, head of the Public Service Commission.

To Mr. H. E. Russell, Davidson, N.C.

April 19, 1930

Dearest Edward,

We have just come in from Atlanta—and guess what! Our Carolyn won *first* place. She brought home $115 in *gold*. We are having a great rejoicing. . . .

Marguerite and children came Thursday night. We have been in a stir about Carolyn, and Dick and Rob were both away when your letter came. So I announced today that as soon as we got settled after Carolyn's speaking we would all get together and have a discussion of your situation. I'm up in arms if they do not give you a 1930 dip[loma]. I . . . have Dick writing a letter in your behalf. Harriette is here now too, and we'll do our best for you. . . .

Arnold H., Gibson House and Hugh Carithers came out to congratulate Carolyn. Mr. Stancil presented her with a box of candy. The boy from Marist gave her a beautiful rose tied with green ribbon to match her dress. He gave her the rose before the speaking. He carried her for a ride too. I'm yawning so, and will have to say goodnight. Will let you hear soon.[1]

Mother

1. With the help of the faculty at Davidson, Edward received his 1930 diploma.

To Miss Ina D. Russell, Washington, D.C.

May 13, 1930

Dearest Ina,

Your lovely, beautiful letter came today. I enjoyed every word. . . . My children are so sweet and precious and I am so thankful for them *all*—even if I do not show up with the Mexican mothers in numbers, I'll back the world on quality.

I am very proud of Carolyn. She is such a sweet child and her attitude towards things pleases me so much. You know she has planned her own clothes for years and she has selected every thing for her trip. . . . She *wants to look very Southern* when she goes to Pittsburgh—especially when she speaks. Carolyn is pretty. If one likes blonds they fall for her.

We intended leaving this A.M. via bus, spending first night in Knoxville, the second in Cincinnati, but Dick & Rob objected so much. I figured I could save over thirty dollars via bus. Finally we had a letter from Randolph Leigh, manager of contest in Pittsburgh. Among other things he said for us not to use a taxi, as there was a strike on and that "stones might be hurled at us." We must use street cars or private autos. Well, Rob suggested that the busses might be stoned too, so Rob figured again on prices, or rates &c. We leave Winder on 3:30 Vestibule tomorrow aft. Leave Atlanta 6:30 for Cin. Change cars & get into Pittsburgh Thursday aft. 5:30. . . .[1]

Pat's announcement comes out in Sunday's paper. She & Pete are coming down Sat. "No bliss without alloy." My alloy comes to me when I cannot be here with Pat Sunday—my bliss is going to Pitts. with my Carolyn. I hope dad will be here for Sun. Dick will be here & Fielding is coming over. Sybil wants them to have dinner with her! But Pat has planned to fix dinner herself & Pete so delighted at the idea, so they'll eat here. Annie Lou will be here to help. Pat is sweeter than ever. She is letting C take one of her beautiful dresses to Pitts and her lovely black silk wrap. Pat is very happy. When I get back from *this* trip, I'll settle down to work & think of our wedding. It *must* be perfect as possible.

I think, I know I'll have help this summer—not very efficient, but good strong help. I've never heard her complain any. . . .

I'm so glad you could stay with our dear daddy and I rejoice to know he is looking better. He needed a rest and I'm so glad he went on to W'ton [for the Law Institute]. I've been having such an awful time trying to get my mouth fixed up. Had to make 4 trips to Atlanta. I'm struggling now with a "partial plate"—very good substitutes, but hard on your nerves & pocket book.

I have worked hard today trying to get things in good shape before leaving & I've put up 7 qts. of strawberries to help with our punch for the wedding. I could put up more if I was not leaving. Sybil is going to help me while I'm gone.

I have so much I'd like to talk to you about, but I'm like the ginger bread boy, "most gone." . . .

Mother

1. Carolyn took second place in the national competition. She recalls that Ina had no fear of riding in a taxi while in Pittsburgh.

To Miss Ina D. Russell, Washington, D.C.

Sunday night Aug. 3, 1930

Dearest Ina,

Every body around here seems crazy—'cept *me*—You ought to be here and maybe there would be *two sane* ones.

Of course this has been a busy day with me. Sundays always are. I got up early 5:30. Edward was going to College Park to conduct services in a church that the pastor was away. He left at 7:20 via train. Fielding had an opportunity to go with a boy who was coming by at 9 o'clock and take F. to Conyers to see his girl. Well, I fed him & got him off. . . . Ten of us boarded the family chariot (Ford) and rattleded off to Church. Rob had 2 flat tires, so I took the crowd. Then dinner. Only 12 here today—uncle Lewis had plenty of fried chicken—& so did the rest of us. . . .

The crazy folks are Billie & Marguerite. They have decided to help Dick or *die*. They, with uncle L's help, have concocted a letter—and they are pouring over G.N.&I. now G[eorgia] S[tate] C[ollege] [for] W[omen] bulletins, and sending out these letters to classmates. I'll sneak one of the letters and send for you to see. I've just heard them say they will have to [have] 350 more letters printed.

Dick is all pepped up over his prospects. Really things are looking good.

In going over my busy day, I forgot to say that I nursed Jim & Sam for the mothers to fool with the letters, and Dick had to get off early for Savannah & I fixed some food for him, and Mr. Harlee Branch of Atlanta Journal came over to go with Dick, and the boy who drives for Dick, so I fed them and sent them on.

Marguerite is going home Wed. & will take Billie & family. I can do without M. & B. but it breaks my heart to give up Jimmie & Sam. They are two cute children. I've enjoyed them this summer.

I'll stop now, all this foolishness. . . .

Mother

To Miss Ina D. Russell, Washington, D.C.

Sep. 4, 1930 (Just 6 days till we know our fate)

Dearest Ina,

I was all set last night to write you a nice long letter. Something bobbed up, or my head bobbed down with drowsy feelings, and now I'm writing in a hurry while the boys, precious things, are getting ready to eat in a hurry and get to the office to help our ole "Dickey Boy." Things are tense here now—*just 6 days more*—X

Just to show you how things are going: right here at cross mark, I saw Williams car flying into the back yard. I had been up early, cooked breakfast, & eaten, was waiting for Ed., Alex and Carolyn to come eat. (To make this interesting I'll [say] that E. & A. had gone to the wash hole in pasture for a cleaning.)[1] Well . . . the car came flying in the back yard with 4 huskey men to eat. . . . Here they sit, eating & joking.

Can't write much now. I did enjoy your letter from Brooklyn. Write me more, you sweet thing. I know my southern girl was the sweetest & nicest in the whole bunch.

Carolyn is busy getting ready for Agnes Scott. . . .

I love you my precious.

Mother

1. There was no inside plumbing at the homeplace until 1934.

To Mrs. Hugh Peterson, Ailey, Ga.

Sep. 12, 1930

My dearest sweet child,

Instead of the long good talk, or talks, I had anticipated with you, I'm sitting here, all by myself in this big house, writing you a scratchy note. Carolyn has gone to Ann Hunters, with Hugh, to play a new game, and the men folks are at the office working on our final campaign. We are very happy over Dick. He has made a wonderful race.[1] I feel that he will come out victorious. He left tonight for Valdosta, where he makes a speech tomorrow. We have been up so much and going so hard in the meantime, that I'm most "whipped down." I manage to take a nap every afternoon, not more than 15 min., but its a help. I've had strapping men to feed and they come at all hours. I put the food on table when I feel that I cannot stand the kitchen any longer, and they eat as they come in. I try not to worry.

Uncle Lewis will be here until after the election. I heard today that Rob would go to Atlanta and conduct the publicity part and uncle L. stay here & see after this end of the line. Really, its very exciting and nerve racking. So many telephone calls and so many telegrams and so many people coming around. Of course most of this takes place at the office, but enough goes on here to keep me running. Edward went to Columbia today. Alex leaves next week. William may go to Marshall Sun, though he is crazy to stay here until Oct. 1st. These young boys have gotten a great kick out of the campaign, and they have been so dependable and willing. Alex, Wm & E. rode all night & put up pictures in Gwinnett Co., and you see that Dick did carry it about 40 votes over Jim Perry and took only county from him that he *thought* he carried. He had been so mean to Dick & our victory there was delightful. . . . .

Uncle Lewis got an idea of sending out missionaries in behalf of our race, and he wore his car completely out. It came "all to pieces" about 6 mi. from Atlanta. He was going to have a new body put on any how. So he had it fixed up & now its ready to go again, he says. Lewis had Fielding to drive & he would get a good man in Winder who had friends in mountain counties & they'd go work the counties. We got Greene, Elbert, Walton, Morgan, Madison and Stephens by using this method. I'd get up & fix breakfast & start off Fielding. Sometimes Edward would go. Wm made some trips too.

Our scuppernongs are fine now. I expect yours are most gone.

But speaking of the race, Marguerite wrote that Jim was wild and working day & night. Chatham did give a big vote for Dick, 2500—and *your* county! I knew some good folks had been working. 58 votes in Ailey & 54 for Dick! That was fine. I love 'em all, and you tell 'em for me! I hope you saw the lovely picture in Georgian of Dick, Rob and Lawrence Camp.

Dick, Rob, uncle Lewis & Alex were in Atlanta the night of election. Some of them told me (not Dick) that Mrs. Rivers & her son 16, & daughter 9, were at the hotel, and when they found they were defeated, they checked out, all three crying and into hysterics. The boy seemed beyond control, and Mrs. R. sobbing and crying as they left.

Its 11 o'clock. Surely some of my folks will be coming in soon. Dad is in Atlanta. Says he had a lot of court work to do.

Sybil had another scare on about her servant leaving. The cotton fields, $1.00 per hour, is too alluring. My Annie Lou is standing pat. I haven't heard her mention cotton and Doscia has been better than usual.

Addie & Wm[2] came over Wed. on train and were here until 1 o'clock. You know I always go to prayer meeting & I carried Addie. Wm stayed here with dad, in front of radio, with his pencil & tablet putting down every thing about the election. When Wm couldn't get the best place in front of radio he'd run to Sybils & get it there. He is a smart child—unusual. Carswell said in Athens that the Russells would be running for office 150 yrs. from now. Addie *clapped,* and Wm. remarked that he hoped so, and that they would be his great, great, great, grand children. . . .

Our boys were at the office all night answering phone &c. and I did not wake them this A.M. but got Carolyn up to take dad to the 7:30 train. I could say much more if you were here.

My love to Hugh & Marie and any of them.

Mother

1. Surprising the establishment, Dick Russell Jr. topped the five-man field in the primary, with 56,177 votes to second-place George H. Carswell's 51,851. Ina's early admonitions to watch his pocketbook paid off, as well as his experience helping Richard in low-budget campaigns. He ran the entire campaign on $3,848, of which only $600 was contributed by friends. Another great strength proved to be the statewide network of friends of his father and of his own friends from his early days at Gordon Military Institute and Power Springs A&M School.

2. Wife and son of William John Russell, Richard's brother.

To Miss Carolyn Russell, Decatur, Ga.

Sep. 16, 1930

Dearest Child—Carolyn,

Here we are back home and you, domiciled in Inman Hall, Agnes Scott, for a 9 months endurance, in good, hard, honest school work.

I was so provoked when I remembered that I had you some nice new hose and forgot to give them to you. When I stood by the table and gave you the money, I knew there was something else I wanted to do. I had so much on my mind. In Dad's office, when I tried to fix things up for you, Brewton and Dad would begin on politics and the phone would ring or someone would come in, and every time it was something about our race. I can send them or maybe I can *bring* them.

This afternoon, when we got on that awful piece of road, almost to the R.R. we saw a car coming and stopped for it to pass. The man pulled too far out and got stuck, hard & fast. He broke a set of chains to pieces. Alex tried to help him. The man told Alex he had a load of whiskey. Alex could see it. The man said he didn't suppose we would want to be found there. So, we moved on after Alex gave him some grandfatherly advice, as to what to do. . . .

Sybil had a good supper ready and Alex went for William & we all ate. Now Alex & I are here alone—both of us going to bed real soon. I will write our Pat a note. You be sure to write a sweet note to dad—*first thing*. . . .

> Mother

Wed. A.M. Last night . . . I felt like "crying for my Caroline," *but* we must not do that. Rob came on 12:30 train last night. He has told so much we did not know. Rivers speaks over radio tonight. Watch the fumes fly.[1]

1. E. D. Rivers was supporting George H. Carswell in the runoff.

To Mrs. Hugh Peterson, Ailey, Ga.

Sep. 16, 1930

Dearest Pat,

The deed is done. Carolyn is domiciled in Inman Hall, Agnes Scott, first floor, room 8—a large nice room, next door to bath room. Her roommate is Elizabeth Fulks, from Little Rock, Ark. She is a big girl—about Dolly's size. Yesterday we packed up every thing and thought we were ready, but you know how things go—a dress had to be altered and several things done and so 'twas 11 o'clock before we left. Alex carried us in William's Ford. We found things very much alive at Agnes Scott. So many girls going through with all the red-tape necessary to enter. Such nice looking girls and nice looking parents too. . . .

Carolyn got out at A.S. and Alex & I went in to see dad. So much politics kept us a long time. People actually seem wild. Telephone ringing—people coming in—every thing about our race.

Things in office in Winder is like a conglomeration. So many letters & telegrams. 7 stenogs work all day. Mr. Pratt's office, Frank Harris' office turned over to Russell—even Mrs. Spurgeon Williams and the dignified doctor have been helping. People are begging to help. The young people in Winder have made up $75 for a 15 min. talk over radio. Today a farmer came in and had $7—given by 7 different men—and said he would bring more when more cotton was sold. Two stenogs were sent out from Atlanta. They need some body to dictate. Uncle L. is going strong—gets to office in A.M. at 7. Williams stays in office till 2:30 or three. Alex leave[s] tomorrow A.M. will register & come back to help. William said 150 letters came today. . . . I hear the office in Atlanta sponsored by the Russell Club is a seething mass of letters and people. Rob is at that end of the line. He has been 'phoning Sybil tonight. Sybil is a good sport and is so kind to every body, and takes things so well. Of course we must beat this race now. Did you see Roy Harris's statement? Just never mind! We'll show 'em yet!

This is a disjointed letter. I began just to tell you of our child. She was so sweet. . . . Carolyn used Edward's trunk. We went by to see Edward for a few min. Its lovely out there [at Columbia Seminary]. E. said the church at Decatur was going to give a reception to the A.S. girls & the Columbia boys. . . .

Judge Wilhoit has been here helping with campaign. Paul Hunnicutt is working. Uncle L. has accepted a room at Miss Ruby Flanigans. He said it took so much time to go back & forth. Fielding came over Fri. and helped.

You see, before I know it, I am on the race, and I really wrote to tell you of Carolyn. We are all *"batty."* So many funny things happen. I'll tell you some of them when you come. (You see I dotted my t and crossed my i. I'm "batty" too.)

As I've said before, this is a "rambling wreck" of a letter, but Carolyn and I had spoken of you and thought of you so much.

My love to Hugh and bushels for you,
    Mother

To Miss Carolyn Russell, Decatur, Ga.

> Tuesday night—9:30 [September 23, 1930]
> *all by myself, the radio going*

Dearest Carolyn,

. . . Where *did* you get the idea that I was going to expect "grand" marks from you? I have only *one* request to make. *Please* don't have any summer school doings here next summer, unless you want to double-up like Alex.[1]

I do expect marks that will eliminate Summer School—the very time when we want to be free and easy—*going* to summer school! That doesn't appeal to me. . . .

Rob 'phoned he was coming tonight & bring 2 men. I sent word to office for Rob to bring them here. I have the spare room ready for them.

William has to make one of those [campaign] missionary journeys to-morrow—leave here at 6 A.M. . . .

The scuppernongs are so good and I think about you every time I go out there. . . .

When I started this letter I thought I had a *little* life in me, but I find I'm about *gone.* I did want to stay up until Wm came in. . . .

Things are raging at the office now. We have been hearing Mr. Rivers make some sulphuric speeches. Mr. Carswell too—but he is slow. Dick will speak again Sat. night. I heard he was going to call every ones name who contributed for him to speak. . . .

Well, honey—take things easy, study hard, and *avoid* summer school. . . .
        Mother

   1. Alex was finishing four years in three by going to summer school.

To Hon. Richard B. Russell, Jr., Atlanta, Ga.

                                                           Sep. 25, 1930
Dearest Boy,

I have just finished reading page 2 of this morning's Constitution. You wonder how I stood it? Well, in my opinion, its all "*straws*" they are catch-ing at *now.* You are making a wonderful fight. Keep it up with a *clear* head and a *stout* heart, and things will come out O.K.
        Lovingly,
        Mother

To Miss Carolyn Russell, Decatur, Ga.

Tuesday night [October 7, 1930?]
(10:50 p.m.)

Dearest Carolyn,

. . . I'm still living in a whirl. So much company! And Fielding in the hospital [for an appendectomy]! So many letters coming in every mail! and I haven't been quite as well as usual. I could have gone to Atlanta today . . . but felt that I could not get any further from Fielding. I asked uncle L[ewis]. after dinner if he couldn't find somebody to drive me over in Dick's car. He suggested I could go in his car as uncle Ed. wanted to go to his farm 4½ mi. from Bogart—and you know how torn up the roads are! He got Joe Allen Dunahoo to drive for us & he is so nice and thoughtful—says he will drive for me any time. I sent Lamar to town in *your* Ford today to bring out some groceries & mail some letters. I found Fielding "doing well," so says nurse & doctor, his room filled with beautiful flowers, and *Virginia*, sitting by his side. She was there all day Sunday & I guess yesterday. I like her.

Our excitement hasn't died down yet, as something is bobbing up constantly. I have received at least 50 letters—lovely ones and I'm congratulated too. . . .[1]

Annie Lou was *so* pleased with her note. She has been & is the best help I've had. She is always the same. . . .

Leman Anderson is staying here now.[2] Also uncle Edward came Sun. & uncle L. still here. Dick has stacks of letters and telegrams to answer. They are all busy as bees, dictating &c. Poor Dicky has a hard time doing any of it, for so many people want to see him & *will* talk.

I'm about worn out. Our men folks have all come in and have gone up stairs. Alex here tonight. . . .

My heart full of love for you my dear, sweet, baby chile,

Mother

1. In other letters Ina tells of hearing from people she hadn't heard from in over forty years.

2. Dick Jr.'s secretary.

To Mrs. Hugh Peterson, Ailey, Ga.

Nov. 1, 1930

Dearest Pat,

. . . You'd be amused to look in on us tonight. The "us" is dad and I, alone in our big ole house tonight & dad is really sitting here by the fire (we are using grate in Living Room now). I don't believe dad & I have *ever* been in this house alone at night! Or even in the day.

Sybil and I have had several talks about the trip & visit to you. Our last plan is to come Thanksgiving week. This is our best plan, but I'll have to "figger" on several things—just can't leave my old folks, you know, and Carolyn is planning to come home. She wants to be here one Sunday before Mr. Morton leaves. Miss Hettie said she could come and stay with Pipey & aunt Annie if we went *before* Dec. It seems she has some engagement in Dec.[1] It is a task for *me* to plan to leave home any time and here's *dad*! Sybil said get him to go with us—that would solve the problem of him. We will let you hear more about this. Both of us are keyed up to make you this visit. . . .

Ten minutes of twelve! Dad has gone out & I'm afraid he is *digging*, for the moon is shining. . . .

Fielding took up his work Wed. Did I tell you that Virginia came over for the week-end? She is real nice & sweet I think. I know I have much more to tell you but really ought to stop. My love to Hugh & to you.

Mother

1. As a nurse for new mothers, Miss Hettie was much in demand.

To Miss Carolyn Russell, Decatur, Ga.

Dec. 10, 1930

My Dearest Carolina-Lou,

. . . Yes, I've stayed alone about 6 nights. I have not been afraid one bit. I had Mr. Moore put a fastening on the door in Alex's room and you know my outside door has a good fastening. I go to bed and sleep well. I sit up as long as I want to. I write, read or work on *your* or *my* quilt. The funny, or strange, part is fixing breakfast just for myself.

I'm in no fix to write a letter tonight, or do anything but just *sit,* not even *think.* I've worked out doors all day. Lamar has been here and I tell you, we have worked. Planted sweet peas and moved some rose bushes, and planted . . . pink cannas and trimmed up things and cleaned up things dead after the frost. I thought about you and how you had spells of working. Yesterday I worked too. Lamar trimmed the scuppernong vines and dug up 1000's of those old Himilaya vines. Lamar cut up a lot of oak wood for me to use in heater to help out with the coal. The old heater has been giving out some good heat lately. . . .

I'm hoping the Ford holds out. James, Mr. Wise's bro., wants to sell his car. He is going to U. of Ala. Has just decided that he *must* have an education. He only asks $225 for it. I'd love to have it—but as you say, we haven't much money, but we have so much to be thankful for, and I'm so glad you feel as you do about it. Its terrible to be so dependent on money to carry you on, and nothing else. . . .

Surely I have written to you since we came from Pats. My, that was a fine trip. Pat knows how to entertain. . . . Annie Lou went to nurse Richard. She had a big time. She told me today that she had received two letters from "down there." One from Cleo, Pats cook, and one from a boy. . . .

Our [newly-paved] road is beautiful—just like a silver ribbon. The moon has been gorgeous. It and the road are magnificent together. . . .

Mother

To Mrs. Hugh Peterson, Ailey, Ga.

Dec. 26, 1930

Dearest Pat,

. . . Christmas Eve night I felt queer not to have you around, tying up pkgs. &c. Carolyn & Alex were in parlor playing & dancing. Dick & dad went to bed. I heard the Santa Claus bells outside just as I did 55 yrs. ago, so of course I had to look to *see* if I could *see* Santa. I got Alex & Carolyn & we went out to Rob's for a real C'mas treat. It was 11:30. We found them just finishing up their happy work. The cowboy suit with all its trappings, a nice desk, roller top, and chair and some other things. Betty's doll, according to order, bedroom slippers, bathrobe, gloves, &c., and some things for Richard on the pretty little tree. Next A.M. early, the cowboy suit was out in my back yard, capering around and the doll was brought over for me to see.

When I came home, I still felt that Santa Claus was just around the corner and I could hear the bells jingle. May my ears never be dulled to that sound! I came in & sat by my fire in dining room & got to thinking. I had rec'd your sweet letter and one from Nancy telling me that her mother was in bed again. This made me very sad. Poor Billie! I am uneasy about her. I cleaned off the dining room mantel, put your picture right in the center. On left end, I put Billie's. Then Inas. That sweet picture of you & Hugh was put up. Then Marguerites. Then Harriettes. I put out all the grandchildren and mine & dad's picture taken with Billie, when she was our only child. This was some comfort to me. Walter's picture should have been put up. He was the only boy absent.

William had begged Fielding to come to Marshall as soon as his school was out. He went and helped him with the pre-Christmas sales and came home with him. They left Marshall at 12:30—came by Walters & stopped awhile and reached home at 7 o'clock, just as I was getting up. Fun began then, for they brought fire works & they wanted to go up & pull E. & A. out of bed & "wake ole Dick." I fixed breakfast and had every body eat so we'd be ready to *talk to Pat*. I had told Rob & Sybil, so they were on hand at 10 o'clock. We have a negro working for us who plays guitar and he was here playing for us when you called. He said, "I'd be so glad to play for the mistress who is away." So that is why dad had him play. I wondered if you really did hear it. . . .

I had fixed almost all my dinner the day before, so I got busy to finish up and have every thing ready by one o'clock and I did. We decided to have our gifts immediately after dinner. Our dinner was not very elaborate, but it was good. 14 were at the table. Richard III was there just a minute to complete our circle. Then Annie Lou kept him while we ate. Sybil's girl got off at 12. We enjoyed our dinner and then went in to have the gifts. . . . William bought a lovely gift for Fielding to give his girl. W. has no girl, so he helped Fielding, for he certainly has one.

We cast lots to see who would go back with William. The lot fell on Alex, as Edward has to go to Covington Sun. to preach. Wm. let F. use his car to run to Duluth, 27 mi. to see his girl for a few minutes. Edward went with him. We went over to Robs after supper and shot fireworks. . . .

I know I have left out much that I wanted to say. I am up close to fire, writing on my lap. I'm keeping up fire for Carolyn. She has gone to a party. . . .

I have secured a girl to come live with Pipey and aunt Annie. Shirley Waters from Glenville Ga. I'm mailing her a ck. tomorrow for transportation. She is one of the girls that Billie looked over when she was in Sav. & advertised for a girl.

Its 'most twelve and my hand has about given out. One of my fingers has a broken vein, or something wrong with it. . . .

I know your dinner was a grand success and I'm *very* proud of you. I mean I'm *thankful* for you. Give my ardent love to Hugh. . . .

  Your Mother.

To Miss Ina D. Russell, Washington, D.C.

Dec. 27—[1930]

Dearest Ina,

 . . . I'm writing this to beg that you write me soon exactly what you think of Billie. I sorrow over her and I feel apprehensive. Do not mention what I say. But talk to Gordon and to Billie & let me know. I knew a lady, Mrs. Geo. Napier of Monroe, who had to stay in bed before her baby came, and afterwards for 7 mo., when she died with pernicious anaemia. The baby lived & is married & has children—but the mother!! So many people think, including *doctors* & *husbands* especially, that when a woman has 3 children, or more, or less, just so its *children*, that she can stand *anything*. Its a wonder I'm alive. Dear Dr. A. would say: "You can't kill Mrs. R. Just look how easy &c., &c." and I'd feel like throwing the book case at him!

I had planned to go to Atlanta & talk to Sybil's doctor. He is splendid—doesn't have *any* practice but mothers. I feel that he saved S's life with Bobby & Betty. Richard III came without any trouble. I have never been favorably impressed with Billie's doctor. Couldn't they see some one else? Don't let Gordon know too much I've said. He might think I'm butting in, but I am *so* concerned and uneasy. Christmas Eve night I was in agony over Billie!

I will write Billie a complete description of our C'mas and you see the letter, darling. I am so rushed every min. it seems. . . . I've thought of you many times, and I love you *all* the time.

Mother

1931–1933

All These
Such Good People

One of the criticisms leveled at Dick Russell's gubernatorial candidacy was his youth (at thirty-three, he was the youngest governor in the country), accompanied by the assumption that because he was not married the social side of the governor's duties would not be carried out. His reply to this was tantalizing: "When I am elected, I promise you there will be a Mrs. Russell in the Governor's Mansion to greet you." Since he was a popular young bachelor, fond of the ladies and they of him, this response produced curiosity and speculation, but there can be no doubt that he was counting on Ina to take on these duties. Everyone in the family knew well the story that when as a lad of nine he saw his mother crying over Richard's defeat in the 1906 campaign, he promised her he'd be governor some day and she his First Lady.

Winder pulled out all the stops for their governor. For this Russell victory there were parades and speeches and dancing in the streets. Before the throng of more than five thousand, Ina sat on the platform between the governor-elect and the chief justice as lavish speeches about the successful candidate flowed. When the crowd begged her to speak, Dick Jr. rose and explained she was too shy, but there were those who wanted to meet Mrs. Russell, and so, he said, "here is the best sweetheart I ever had."

Ina brought all her joie de vivre to her new life as First Lady of Georgia.

She particularly enjoyed the new Packard sedan, complete with chauffeur who lived at the Governor's Mansion. Her sense of humor and her extraordinary ability to maintain perspective, however, saved her from being unduly impressed with the trappings of high political office. In one letter, after giving a lengthy list of luncheons she is to attend—Dental Auxiliary, Woman's Club, Daughters of 1812 of Georgia, and so forth—she jokingly adds, "Fri. I am going to lunch with the sons & daughters of the pilgrims." When the Atlanta Woman's Club gave her son a standing ovation after a speech, Ina did not stand up. Not recognizing her, a woman next to her asked, "Don't you stand up for the Governor?" "No," Ina replied. "I'm not getting up for him. I had to get up too much for him when he was a baby." The story was in the papers next day, and Ina clipped it for one of her many scrapbooks. Nor did she let her duties as First Lady cause her to forget her first duty—seeing that Edward, Alex, and Carolyn, her last three scholars, had a strong support base for their labors. She kept after William, too, to improve himself.

To Mr. W. J. Russell, Marshall, N.C.

Jan. 7, 1931

Dearest William,

. . . I have been wondering if I had written you any thing about Billie being so sick. I'm sure I wrote Dolly and Walter, and I hope you heard from them—if I didn't write.

Billie was taken very sick and had to be carried to the hospital. She was in such a condition that she had to have two blood transfusion[s]. Her little baby, a boy, was born dead and Billie was, and is, very sick. I have kept in touch with her by letters, telephone and telegrams. I started to go several times, but Gordon and Ina advised me to wait. I felt bad to leave home, but I would have been alone, and I wired Ina that if any change occurred to wire me here and I would come at once. When Billie gets able to go home, I will go and stay awhile with her.

Patience and Hugh came up last Sat. and Pat was home for her birthday on the 4th. As the extra session [of the Legislature] opened Tues. Hugh [a state senator] and Pat left Monday for Atlanta. Alex left for Ga., Carolyn and Edward for their places, *and then I was alone.* Dick had gone in *early* Monday A.M. I felt like weeping and mourning. If I had not been so worried over Billie, I would not have felt so miserable. Dad came on the 5 o'clock bus and I was glad to see him. I looked for Walter and Dolly Sun. Alex said they told him they were coming. After you wrote of your tooth trouble, I did not look for you. . . .

Shirley Waters came Jan. 1st and is with our dear old people. I think she will be the *one* we've been looking for. Aunt Annie says she is "tough as whit leather," for she goes to the coal pile early in the mornings "*bare footed*" and in her *pajamas*! and she can pick up her heavy mattress and walk out with it! Then aunt Annie, so feeble and frail now, with her 83 years behind her, recalls the days when she could pick up mattresses at home and move them from one room to another. Pipey was the *strong* man though. She could take a 40 lb. mattress *up stairs*! Just see what time can do for us! we all have our day—let us live well while we are young—for the days do go—and as our *physical* parts grow weak, let our *spiritual* parts grow strong.

Write me how you are with your *mouth* trouble. . . .

My love, Mother

To Miss Ina D. Russell, Washington, D.C.

Jan. 9, 1931

Dearest Ina,

Your letter was delivered to me last night about 10:30. It brought much comfort to my heart about our Billie.

I want to tell you now about my feelings in regard to coming to Washington. I felt that I *had to be* nearer Billie. I was coming right on—get taxi and come to hospital and just sit quietly in reception room until I could see her if only for l min. Then, if I could sleep at your place, I'd come every day and do that same thing. I had some money Dick gave me C'mas, & I would use it in getting back & forth and for meals. I once thought of asking you to get a room for me near the hospital so I could walk. You cannot know how I have suffered. I had been so torn up over Edward last year. Dick carried me right to him. He had doctors and two splendid nurses. I sat in his room, when I could—and sat often in the reception room. I had never realized what a blessing this was and what a relief to my feelings until Billie has been sick. I went every A.M. about 9:30 to hospital and was *around there,* until 6:30, and occasionally those dear friends of mine brought me back after dinner. I feel relieved to a great extent over Billie, but I still have a feeling that it will take many days and skillful attention to get her even very-well-I-thank-you.

The ones in Winder who know about Billie seem very much interested in her. Two ladies have told me of some one who had a similar experience. One a mother of 5 had to be taken to hospital. When they brought her home she was feeling real well—but in another wk. she was dead. Of course I know she might not have had the attention that Billie has had. I thank God for capable doctors and efficient nurses, and *more,* for His care over us. When I am very miserable or very happy, I go to my bible. When I was oppressed over Billie I went to my bible. The psalms are my great comforters. I came to the 57th ps. and found my comfort in the *first verse*—and on through the short psalm. Get your bible and read it.[1]

Dad & I enjoyed your letter. It was your first letter since Billie's sickness. Gordon had written two letters and one card. Our 'phone conversations were very comforting. Dad was *wild* until he talked with you. Then he quieted down. His first wife died on the 6th[2] and he *knew* we would receive a fatal message about Billie on the 6th.

I feel so happy that Mrs. W[alshe, the housekeeper,] is "filling the bill" at 71 Monmouth. I know it is a comfort to Billie.

I have had a very pleasant stay in Atlanta [with dad], but I cannot enjoy things as I usually do, thinking of Billie. Pat & I have been shopping or rather, walking around, *looking.* The extra session is causing a lot of talk. You see, it was called for *political* reasons. I do not believe they will get our Gov-elect *balled up* in *anything.* Dad & I will leave for home Sat. on the Vestibule. I may come back next wk. He seems so glad to have me. I will let you know. I feel that I cannot stay alone as I did before Christmas—thinking about Billie & listening for 'phone all the time. . . .

The manager of Kimball does not make any charges for *me.* I have a *standing* invitation, so, you see, our expenses are not much. Carolyn called me last night. She says she is about straight after the holidays. . . . She said a bank closed in Decatur yesterday A.M. One teacher lost $10,000. The girls who manage the Agnes Scott Annual had the money in that bank—and all the money for the college paper, "The Silhouette," I believe its called. So many bank failures—not a bank is open in the whole of Walter's territory—or in William's town. 5 closed in Ashville in one week. William lost $125 in bank in Marshall. Our A & P folks have to ship all moneys.

I know there is nothing in this letter that you can read to Billie. I will write her one. Have been wanting to, but just couldn't, somehow. Precious child! she was the best I had to write to me. When she left to go home, she always wrote a card when she stopped for the night & then one as soon as she reached home. She has been a *good, satisfactory* daughter and sister, hasn't she?

You are all so precious to me. Of course *you* will hold down that place, and be the *outstanding woman adjudicator.* See if I'm not right!

Fielding's girl is not going back to Ga. on account of finances.[3] He is a dear boy—trying to hold up his standard and paying off debts for his operation. But we do so well. I'm thankful things are no worse.

I'm so glad the cake was good. The walnuts were under the snow & I had to use pecans.

My love,
Mother

Went to Mr. Walter Browns funeral. He was 80 yrs. [old]. Went to Patterson's to see his body. He looked sweet, calm, and about as he did when Margo married. His pink carnation on lapel of coat and his hair so white and long enough to lie out on the pretty satin pillow—all so natural. Dad says his friends are leaving. Dr. Jacobs, Alex Lawrence and our good friend Mr. Brown.

1. Psalm 57:1: "Be merciful unto me, O God, be merciful unto me: for my soul trusteth in thee: yea, in the shadow of thy wings will I make my refuge, until *these* calamities be overpast" (KJV).

2. Minnie Tyler Russell gave birth to three stillborn children. She died at the birth of the third.

3. Virginia Wilson's father worked for and had interest in a bank that failed.

To Miss Ina D. Russell, Washington, D.C.

Feb. 7, 1931

Dearest Ina,

I am living a strange life, for *me,* these days. Coming to Atlanta—then going home for the week-end, &c. But I am enjoying it. I enjoy my rest. Some mornings I do not get up until time for lunch. This, however, does not happen often. Pat being here makes my stay doubly pleasant. She and I enjoy going around, having lunch together, and *looking* at all the lovely things and wishing we could get *this* and *that.* Pat is saving, for there are a *few things* they want to do. For instance, buy a new car, build a new house, &c. And with *me,* its *Carolyn* ought to have this. Edward needs some new shirts. . . . So, I enjoy looking and am very thankful that my two eyes are still very good. I see so many totally blind, here in this city, and a group of deaf-mutes have been staying at the Kimball and very often I see people on crutches. Yesterday I saw . . . a boy about Alex's size, shaking violently *all the time,* and I was glad I could be *so* thankful that Alex was normal.

I know you wonder why I am raving on so, and I do too. But these thoughts and feelings were in my heart when I began to write and before I knew it, they were coming out on this paper.

Before I leave this subject, I must say again how happy I am over Billie. No one will ever know how I suffered. I am so thankful and I will endeavor to show *God* that I am thankful. . . .

My darling, I had just a few minutes and felt like scribbling off these hurried lines to you. I think of you and I love you. I wanted you at home to enjoy Walter's lovely children. Dolly is lovely too—just like my own child.

>   Yours
>   Mother

To Miss Ina D. Russell, Washington, D.C.

March 25, 1931

Dearest Ina,

. . . I have been planning in my heart to come to [your] graduation [from law school]—but can't be positive about it yet. I want to get my house in good shape to leave it in June. I want every drawer cleaned out and every crack and corner swept & dusted. I hope Billie can come early and spend as many days as possible with me, before I leave. We want to have our family re-union on Sunday, after the inauguration. June 28th, I think. The Inaug. is last Sat. in June. . . . I'm thinking of our Harriette so far away! No bliss without alloy! I do not think it possible for her to be with us this summer. Dad had a paper from Ralph. It really seems that he is "forging to the front" in the Gas business. . . .[1]

Now, about coming to your graduation. I have thought and thought. I wanted to come with daddy to the Law Insti[tute]., as he gets all of his expenses, and has had the wonderful offer to come to Johns Hop[kins] and have his eye examined, free of charge, and I am so filled up with a desire to go on there and get Alex into Johns H[opkins]. as soon as he graduates at Ga. Dad can do this, I think, through Dr. Hugh Young. Alex made such good marks and was accepted for the Gridiron Club. Its honorary, you know. Alex refused. We were all indignant, but he said he studied it over and couldn't see where it could be worth $20 to him ($20 fee). It was too late when we found out. Dad & Rob ready to get up the $20, but this is Alex. He is a queer child. He has made his four yrs in three. Dad is very happy over Alex—the only one of the boys who has been *almost* entirely satisfactory in school.

Now, about coming to see you grad. Suppose you write Dick and tell him how you'd love to have him present and for him to come and bring me. Tell him he will need a little rest, &c. Wait until May to write. This is about my only hope—unless I come with dad & stay over, and I do not see how I could stay so long. . . .

Aunt Annie is standing things very well, but she is very restless and I might say, dissatisfied. We do all we can for her. . . .[2]

> My love
> Mother

1. Ralph, newly employed by a gas company, was sent to California.

2. Sister Pipey died on February 28, 1931. Her obituary in the *Atlanta Journal* read, in part, "America Patience Dillard, pioneer Georgia woman and aunt of Governor-elect Richard B. Russell Jr. Born in Oglethorpe County, she had been a resident of Winder for many years and was one of the most beloved women in the community. She made her home with her elder sister, Mrs. Annie Launius, only a short distance from the Russell home and played an active part in the bringing up of the large family, one of the most distinguished in the state."

To Alexander B. Russell, Athens, Ga.

April 15, 1931

Dearest Boy,

When I say *dearest* I mean it. You are dear to me. I've been thinking about you more than usual. This is your last few days at U. of G. Make them your best. Don't be weak and do any thing, however small, that you will regret later. You have made a good record in *books*. We are proud of you and thankful for you. We may not have [been] exactly the parents we should have been, but we thought at the time we were doing our best, and even if you were our 14th child, we welcomed you with loving hearts and thanked God for you.

Dad mentioned last night that you were buying a Tux. Now, I know your age and I know you are a senior and ready to graduate—but you just don't know mothers! We feel a shock—my child, my baby boy! Well, I am so glad for you to have and to be ready to *Grace* a Tux. You will look fine and *I* feel that you will be a real *gentle man,* not only when you wear it, but at all *times*. I admit I have my uneasy moments, when I dwell on some of the things that are so popular. But I'm *counting* on *my* boys and girls to strive for the *uplifting* things in life, for their own good and for a good example to others. . . .

Alex, please promise me that you will read 8th chap. of Prov[erbs].[1] every day until you graduate. Then repeat it to me, with that good mind of yours. . . . Remember, Alex, I *love* you dearly. You represent *me* in your walk of life. I hope to see you soon.

　　　Mother

1. A hymn to wisdom and prudence.

To Miss Ina D. Russell, Sibley Hospital, Washington, D.C.

Winder, Ga., April 27, 1931

Dearest Ina,

My dear, sweet child! days pass and many strange things happen. I've been thinking about you so much. The lovely birthday rose is in bloom, and I was wishing you could see it, just this morning, before Billie's letter came, telling me of the operation.[1] If you didn't want us to know, its all right, just so you get well—but I felt very weak and almost un-done, while reading Billie's letter. I felt that I had *neglected you,* my dear, sweet child! . . .

We celebrated dad's [70th] birthday yesterday as he could not be with us today. . . .

I haven't known how to write, but I do love you, my child. It hurts me to know you have suffered so much, but I'm so thankful you are improving.

Mother

1. A hysterectomy.

To Mrs. Hugh Peterson, Ailey, Ga.

May 6, 1931

Dearest Pat,

. . . Yes, dad does get some money—$250 [for the debate with Mrs. Sanger]. That's the *why* of it—but you know he would not *mind* debating that subject.[1] Dad has a pile of books from the library and literature from Washington. I have seen the handbills & I'm thankful I was on hand and could have a part changed. They are little larger than this paper. Mrs. S[anger]'s picture on left & dad's on right. By dad's was "the father of 18 children."[2] I told the man to take that off & I've made dad *promise* that he will debate as if he had *no* children. The man, Russell Bridges, has paid dad $150 already. I went two days & nights with dad. I read & read, and I do hope dad will *impress* the young people of our Beautiful America how terrible it would be if the bill was passed in Congress to send the vile, dangerous doings broadcast over our land. We may go to Birmingham to debate, and the Lions Club in Augusta is begging for it. . . .

You come to the debate, May 14, & let us get in the gallery. Mr. Bridges offered me a box, but I refused. I think the crowd will be large. People seem pepped up over it. . . .

Dick & I have been discussing servants [for the Mansion]. . . . We may take Gus for a yard man and Folia for a laundress. I will see Millie soon and talk to her [about cooking]. . . .

Aunt Annie & Shirley have a time. Shirley has bought a puppy and it is more than aunt Annie can stand. She [Shirley] plays with the dog & then takes up the toast, without washing her hands. One night she put the dog in bed with her, & the dog stays in the house at night. She walks to town & carries the dog in her arms.

Aunt Annie came today & asked me who she must give Pipey's cuff buttons to. I was quick to say *Pat*.[3] She seemed glad to do it. I know cuff buttons are not in demand, but these are beautiful. She let me wear them when I was a girl. Every body wore them, who could afford them. These are pure gold. She gave $8 for them. Aunt Annie had a gold collar button & she put it in with the buttons, 'cause she said she wanted you to have it. I expect Pipey bought these buttons 58 yrs. ago with teaching money.

I must stop & get to my scrap book fixings. Used up 2 bottles of paste yesterday & last night. . . .[4]

> Yours
> Mother

1. Richard Russell was to debate Margaret Sanger, famous advocate of birth control, on the question of sending information about birth control through the mails.
2. Three by Minnie and fifteen by Ina.
3. Pat was named for Pipey (Patience) and Annie (Anne Elizabeth).
4. Ina compiled many voluminous scrapbooks over the next few years.

To Mrs. Hugh Peterson, Ailey, Ga.

May 23, 1931

Dearest Pat,

. . . I do not know what to say about the debate. The crowd was small. The manager said he was "in the hole" $700. Dad had gotten $150 before the debate. He is still due $100. Of course, *every body,* almost, was for Mrs. Sanger, 'cause every body who is *up-to-date,* practices and believes in birth control.

Dad made some good points and he was appreciated for *himself* and not his side. Some *women* sitting behind me called him "old fool" and they said, "he just doesn't know what he is talking about."[1]

I don't know much about Alex. He came over with Fielding Sunday. He is taking his graduation very indifferently—says he will come home and let them send his dip[loma]. I feel like spanking him. Of course this may all be *talk.* I didn't tell you about Alex's wreck. You know he used [his roommate] Jimmy's car to go for Carolyn. He was running fast and rain was falling and he tried to pass a moving van and ran into a man. The rail guard saved his life. It happened just beyond Auburn and he 'phoned Rob to send a wrecker. Damages about $70—all of Alex's savings act. gone & still owes some. The man is trying to make Alex pay for his car—$110.

Right here, Sybil tooted the horn of her *new car,* and I went to town to see Millie. She seems very much delighted, and I think she is going to try to go. . . .

But any how—about Alex. He bore up under this ordeal. The boy that was with Alex, going to Atlanta to get his car, said he would bring Carolyn out to Athens. . . . This left poor Jimmy without his car for Little Commencement. Alex said he was lovely about it. Alex got the car back to Jimmy by Wednesday—good as new. I was so thankful that no one was hurt.

I had a lovely letter via Air from Harriette. She was moving into her new home[2] & seemed very happy. . . .

Edward goes to Royston to preach Commencement sermon tomorrow. He & dad came in tonight. Guess you rec'd my card about aunt Annie. She is up every day, but she is very weak. I am trying to feed her good. She was real pitiful this afternoon.

Annie Comer wrote me that [sister] Mamie was very ill, and brother To[wnes] has been in bed a month and she feels that he will never be well again. He is about 76, I think. Mamie is 71. If you could write Annie a short note of love and interest. She has a heavy load to carry. She has been a noble daughter. I know Mamie is glad that she did not "space" Annie. That is what Mrs. Sanger says women ought to do—*"space" their children.* . . .

Carolyn is coming Thursday and bring 8 girls with her to stay until Monday. She said they *just couldn't* separate all at one time. She told them she would not have a car, and no boys here and they *could not* "flush the Johnny." I am going to try to feed them well and let them have a good time. . . .

Dick is reading your Emily Post. So you see it got here. Don't know why I always write you such long letters. I am *glad* I did not space *you.*

My love,
Mother

Monday A.M. . . . I might as well give you a big *ear full* at once. Edward, you
know, was left some money by Pipey.[3] He [needed?] a car so much & dad
got the money. He has a new Chevrolet. Went to Royston in it yesterday to
preach commencement sermon. He preached at Mansfield last Sun. He has
two regular Sundays at Winder, 1 at Danielsville and 1 at Center through
the summer, & he is going to Summer School at Ga. to get a degree in
history.

> My love to you my darling,
> Mother

1. Newspaper accounts of the debate bear out Ina's judgment. They report that although
Judge Russell was entertaining and his wit frequently made the audience laugh, the clear
winner of the debate was Mrs. Sanger.

2. Ralph Sharpton had been moved from California to Oregon by the gas company,
which had been taken over by Standard Oil.

3. After funeral expenses and four gifts of ten or twenty dollars to nieces, Pipey's remain-
ing estate consisted of her house, which she left to Harriette, and $600, which she left to
Edward.

To Miss Ina D. Russell, Washington, D.C.

June 6, 1931

Dearest Ina,

. . . I had two very strong reasons for wanting to be with you when you
graduated. First, because we are *so proud* of you, and feel so much interest
in you. Second, I felt sure you would come home with us. I wanted to rest
you up—and feed you up. Georgia chickens are beginning to get plentiful
now, and fresh eggs come to the back door. So I wanted the pleasure of
feeding you. Now you say you cannot come back with us! I am so sorry and
have lost some of my pep. . . .

My dear, sweet child—you have been so faithful in your work. I know
you will pass up that one subject and get your diploma.

Dad will leave from Atlanta. He wont make any definite plans. So I suppose he will just come and get out to your place or to Billies. He doesn't
like to notify any one. So, you can be looking out for him.

Dad is ready for bed. He has just come in to dining room & told me to tell you that *he is coming*. He hopes to get to W'ton Thurs. A.M. if possible and will 'phone Billie. You tell her, please.

I will see you in the imagination of my heart Thurs. night. I would love to be with you. . . .

My heart of love,
Mother

. . . I have a secret for you: Dad says every-now-and-then that he is *not* going to the Mansion with me. He says he will keep his room at Kimball. This hurts me very much. He may not carry out his threat, but you talk to him—just say how nice &c, and then if he says anything, you use your influence. Tell him how nice it will be for me not to have to cook &c—and how nice for him not to be paying grocery bills &c, &c. . . .

To Mrs. S. G. Green, Sr., Cherrydale, Va.

June 15, 1931

Dearest Billie,

I suppose this is my last letter to you under these same circumstances. I have just *fixed* myself for the afternoon—grabbed some scrap paper and my pen and made a bee-line for the swing on the east side of porch, and will endeavor to write you a few things thats been on my mind for some time. Every time we discuss or make plans, I think of you and Pat, specially, and then all the others. Harriette is coming! That will complete our family as far as we can see now. Walter writes *they* will get here about the 22nd— I think William gets in about that time. Marguerite writes that she will come the 25th. Pat will be in Atlanta ready for us. Ina wrote that she would get here in time for Inaug. The Com[mittee] on arrangements for the reception (one of them) was out yesterday. They will just have punch— 3 bowls—the orchestra, flowers &c, will all be ready. We have our list for punch girls and ladies to assist . . . the 6 sisters, Miss Lula Fowler, Sara Pierce, Miss Hettie, and sisters-in-law. . . .

Aunt Annie is at Mary Popes. O, I have been so concerned—could not feel good for her to go to uncle Walters—not now, any how. Julia is getting married this month, all young folks there. Mary Pope was so sweet to *beg* for her to come. She wrote two letters and then came. So, the dear soul is there with sister Mattie.[1] She is as feeble as aunt Annie—sometimes. The breaking up was very trying. Aunt Annie wanted to go and she didn't want to leave. I *had* to do something. I have been paying for Shirley and for the lights—and the time for me to go to Atlanta draws nearer every day. Aunt Annie was so dissatisfied with Shirley one day, and then seemed fond of her the next. I had a great trial—and I suppose sister Annie did too. I *know* she did. We let Joe Sanders move in the house—packed all of the things in uncle B's room and in the kitchen. Joe cooks & eats in dining room. This moving and packing up their little cherished possessions was more than I could stand at times. So much harder than to put Pipey away to her eternal rest. Aunt Annie . . . stood the ride to Mary Popes so well. I phoned next morning to see how she was. I miss her. I find myself hurrying through, so as to go over to see her. . . . Do write Mary Pope a short note and express your appreciation of what she is doing. It was my salvation & aunt Annie's too. . . . It is nothing but pure loving-kindness on Mary Popes part. I do hope if we can make *final* arrangements with her that she will be paid something if uncle W. will turn loose aunt A's little piece of land. I feel that I can never love M[ary] P[ope] enough or do enough for her. She just seemed to *see* the situation and was *filled* with sympathy for me. She said she felt that to relieve me of aunt Annie, I could enter into my new labors with more ease &c. Edward went to see aunt Annie Sat. He said she was feeling well & happy. I want to go to see her soon.

I still have so much to do. . . . You see, I will have to walk out of my house Sat. or may be Fri. and just *leave* things. Millie is going to be our cook. We have secured all the servants except a maid. I do want you to come & lets talk about things. . . .

Fielding has just come in from work. He is doing anything now to make some money. I get up at 5 & help him off—fix lunch, &c. He is working on the public road—building bridges &c. Goes out at 6, gets off at 6. . . .

We are looking for Pat tomorrow. Alex graduates Wednesday, and she is coming to see him finish up. I think Hugh has to be in Atlanta tomorrow. Dick's Committee certainly has been busy. Our pictures are beginning to come out now and news paper articles. A woman 'phoned me today and asked me a lot of questions. . . .

Dick is busy trying to get his Inaug. address written. He says it will be only 15 min. long. . . .

My love to each one. Tell Gordon he ought to be here to make punch—punch for 3000—some punch!

> Mother

1. Mattie was Ina's sister and Mary Pope's mother.

To Mr. William John Russell, Marshall, N.C.

[Atlanta, the Governor's Mansion] Aug. 17, 1931

Dearest William,

I have been thinking about you a great deal since I saw you last. Of course it is nothing unusual for me to be thinking about you—you and your twin brother. How nice and noble it was for you to let F[ielding] use your nice car. *They* have certainly had a lovely trip for their honey moon, which would have been impossible but for your kindness.[1]

Walter and Pierre came in Saturday night to take dad back. Dad had talked so much about it—was just like a child—had made little plans &c. I am so glad for him to have the trip & best of all, they told me that you and F. would be together on the 21st and have dinner with Dolly and Walter. I think that is lovely. I'm glad for dad to be there. I want him to enjoy it to the fullest. I am wondering when the *pair* will get back home and when you will have your car again. I suppose they will write us soon something of their plans.

This will have to be your birthday letter—though it may get in a head of time.

This last week of the Legislature will be a busy one for us. Dick 'phoned tonight that he could not come out to supper. Things have gone well for Dick. He is striving to hold up his part of things. I hope you see the Ga. papers. . . .

Write me if you have time. I'll be thinking about you on the 21st. I've always been very proud of my *twins*.

> Fondly,
> Mother

1. Fielding Russell and Virginia Wilson were married August 3. They were going to teach in Monroe, Georgia.

To Mrs. James Harris Bowden, Savannah, Ga.

Aug. 22, 1931

Dearest Marguerite,

Edward blew in last night about 10:30 on one of his rush trips. I say rushed because he always seems so rushed. He has had a full summer. Hasn't been idle a day. He has accomplished a great deal, I think—but it has not been best for his physical condition. Do not let him know that I am saying all this (Was interrupted here and now it is 12 o'clock. Dick hasn't come in. Some body said the folks at the capitol would still be talking when the morning came. . . .)

Now about E.—he needs a rest. If you will let him come for a wk. at least & go to Tybee and stay in the sun and Ocean breeze & salt water, he might be in better shape to start up his school work about Sep. 16th. I'm wondering if you have moved to Tybee. You let me hear from you about this. E's appetite is good, but irregular. Edward is nervous. His arms hurt every-now-and-then, and his hands are not steady. He has never gotten over the accident or injury. He is so young and may be we can help him build up. He ought to be absolutely quiet for awhile.

I told him I was going to write to you. He said he would love to lie in the sand &c. I'd love for him to eat *sea food* for awhile. I have worried over him all summer. He had a very strenuous program mapped out for the summer and has followed it to the letter.

The little pkg. came for Fielding. I am looking for the young couple to come in from the last round of their fine honey moon tomorrow. . . .

Give my love to Jim & the children. . . .

    Lovingly,
    Mother

To Mrs. Hugh Peterson, Ailey, Ga.

Sep. 19, 1931

Dearest Pat,

. . . So many things happen. I'd love to tell you about every one—but *one* was so glorious and so much happiness was shed abroad, that I *must* tell you.

Last Monday I had aunt Annie, aunt Mattie, Mary Pope, Margaret, Lizzie Hattie and Virginia to a spend the day party. O, I did wish for *you*. They had such a good time. Lizzie Hattie asked M. P. if she was going to the mansion or if she was going to see "aunt Ina." M[ary]. P[ope]. said: "Going to see aunt Ina." L. H. said: "Well, thats what I want to do." She walked every where—down the long walk & up the drive. When she left, she said she had enjoyed seeing the mansion *while* she was seeing aunt Ina, for the visit was just the same *in spirit* as it had been in Winder.

I had a good lunch—just what I knew they liked. My good servants treated them all as if they had been prize babies. Even Gus had to come up & talk to "Miss Annie." . . . Aunt A. was so funny in the comments she made. We were out on porch looking around & she said: "I never saw so many rocks in my life."

I have enjoyed going over to A[gnes] S[cott] with Carolyn and having such a nice way to go &c. Carolyn & Mollie White are coming this aft. for the week-end. They have dates tonight. I am going in town at 2 o'clock to meet them. . . .

Dad looks well and is well. I keep him nice & clean in his summer suits. He goes to College Park tomorrow to teach S.S. class. Miss Hettie has been with me. I love to have her. . . . [She] has made watermelon preserves.

Dick may go to Detroit. I think he *has* held 'em in the road pretty well.

Shirley [Waters] is married to a Winder boy, I heard.

My love to H[ugh]. Yours,

Mother[1]

---

1. Several letters tell of outings for Aunt Annie and Cousin Mary Pope with the governor's mother and chauffeur.

To Mrs. James Harris Bowden, Sr., Savannah, Ga.

Oct. 6, 1931

Dearest Marguerite,

. . . The boys [Edward and Alex] enjoyed their visit to you, and Alex told me that you were well situated at Tybee. I tried to get him to go into *particulars*—and he did try, but you know boys and men, too, on that. Alex is right down to hard tacks on his medical course at Emory. Came out Sat. night with 2 books, almost as large as W[ebster]'s unabridged Dictionaries—studied till 12 o'clock. Went to church with me at 11 Sun A.M. After dinner he studied for 2 hrs. He is *full* of his subject and delighted me by going into details about the professors and the bodies they work on &c. Every 2 boys have a body & work together. A's room mate is Jack Humphries from Moultrie. They named their body *Gandhi* he was so tall & thin. . . .

I often think of you and your two lovely daughters and the fine young son. Of course they will all 3 present new problems. They are each an individual with different thoughts and feelings. Just pray and try to be *just* with each one. I realize that I did not do enough *individual* work with my first children. I got on to it more, and I'm so thankful I did, with my last, beginning with Walter, I think.

I hope to visit you while you are on the coast. I know it is beautiful. I'm glad to know that you walk to school sometimes. It will do you good. . . .

Take care of your children & yourself and good old daddy Jim. Its fortunate to have a good daddy. My love to all. Kiss Jimmy.

Mother

To Mr. W. J. Russell, Marshall, N.C.

Oct. 7, 1931

Dearest Boy,

I have thought of you many times since you left here and have wondered if you had made your move, and were using the little electric [hot plate], and trying to keep your body and soul together by your own efforts at cooking.

I still do not feel that its best for you to try to live to yourself. Unless you have a nice companion—one that will talk and live as well and nice as he would if he was in a boarding house.

Its one thing I want you to guard against. Cultivate nice manners and refined speech, no matter where you are, or whether alone, with men or with a mixed crowd. It is so easy to get careless. Any way: you write me what you are doing. If you did leave Mrs. Hinkle. What she said—and if you are trying to cook all 3 meals or if you are going to the café for one real meal &c.

I am planning to go to see Fielding & Virginia tomorrow. Miss Hettie made some curtains for Va., and I want to take them. I want to go by to see Sybil too. Betty and Richard are both sick. Dick leaves tonight for the Yale game. He goes as a guest of the Athens crowd. Next Wednesday, he leaves for Yorktown for the big celebration. Carolyn is a sponsor & she has two maids and a chaperone. They are making plans for a big time. I have been appointed a chaperone, & Dick says he will pay my expenses, but I hate to leave dad. He is getting well fixed here now & if I leave him he will be sure to go down home and dig dirt. The doctor over at Grady says he ought *not* to dig any more dirt.

We are having lovely weather. The Fair is in full swing. Write to me and take care of yourself.

> Lovingly,
> Mother

To Mrs. James Harris Bowden, Sr., Savannah, Ga.

Jan. 6, 1932

Dearest Marguerite,

. . . We had a lovely holiday. Our Christmas Day was very happy. William came and stayed until Sun. afternoon. Alex went as far as Greenville, *so as to be company* for him. Poor boy—he left here *sobbing*. He feels so far off & alone. I wish we could get him out of Marshall. Alex came back next A.M. on train—got here just as we finished breakfast.

We had a very pretty C'mas tree on table in Sun parlor. The gifts were on the table. We went in as soon as Rob & Sybil got here. Uncle Lewis was here. I was master of ceremonies and called on Ina & Dick to sing some old songs—"By the Silver Rio Grande," "Poney Boy," "Fatal Rose of Red"—

You remember how they used to sing when we lived in the Jackson house. Then I called on each one for some little funny doing and all in all, we had a happy, jolly time. Uncle L. & dad got up a little "sob" stuff, but it was worth while. We didn't have so much on the tree, but we had a good time. . . .

Pat made us a flying visit one day during C'mas. Some body had to come to Atlanta and Hugh was coming, so she hopped in and we were so glad to see her. It made me sad to see our ole 1931 go by. It was a good year for me—brought me so much joy and happiness—but it had to go, and as joy and happiness is something you can never lose and can take *anywhere,* I've brought it *all* over into 1932. . . .

I know my children are sweet. I do love them. And dear ole happy Jim & you my precious child. May this 1932 be a very beneficial, well spent time of your life.

Mother

To Mrs. James H. Bowden, Savannah, Ga.

Jan. 14, 1932

Dearest Child,

. . . I'd love to come to see you. You held out very attractive reasons for me to come, [but] I can't leave now. This is dad's hardest season. He is working all day in banc [en banc] and then works some at night and has been getting up so early to "catch up." You know our dear daddy is nearly always behind in his work. Dad seems to be right well, but he has had a very bad cold and a terrible cough. Every day I am more thankful that I can be with him and see after him. I doctor him (when he'll submit) and I try to make things easy for him, or *easier.* . . .

I had a lovely trip with Dick yesterday to the wonderful Mount Berry School. I had never been and had never seen Miss Berry. When you want to take your children to a place of inspiration, *don't* go to Mt. Vernon, Arlington or any like place, but take them to *Mount* Berry. Some time when you are up here, lets go. Miss B. is a wonder. You should see the magnificent home she left to teach those 9 mountain boys. It has taken 30 years of *service* to accomplish what you see there now. We may not do *as much* but we can do as *well* as she has, if we do our part in life with the same vim and determination and build on *her* foundation. Yesterday, from everything I saw, I realized that God and the Bible had been her foundation—a foundation that cannot be moved. Let us look forward to a trip to Mount Berry.

I'm so glad you all had such a happy C'mas. I rejoice that you could say *this* was the happiest &c, and you were *contented.* I read some where that *contentment* is the sunshine of the soul. Think how good sunshine is for everything. . . .

I will figure around and I will come when possible. We did not do much C'mas but did try to send Harriette something. She is so far away. Give my love to each one and tell the girls I enjoyed their letters.

     Lovingly,
     Mother

To Mr. W. J. Russell, Marshall, N.C.

Jan. 15, 1932

Dearest William,

. . . I have a direct question to put before you: How would you like to be transferred to Washington D.C. and you and Ina have a nice little apt. together? We haven't done any thing about this, for we wanted to see how you felt.[1] I do not like for you to be in Marshall forever. You have done well and I'm so thankful that you have made a good record. If you would like this, let me know. You are the only one of us who is alone. Ina and Billie in Washington—Harriete and Ralph—Walter and Dolly—Fielding and Virginia, and our three youngest right here by us.

But the main point about you going to W'ton. Ina says you could take your choice of several *fine* business schools—*free*—just a little entrance fee to pay & your books &c. The A.& P. stores close on time in W'ton and you could have plenty of time at night to take your business course. Ina said she would be so glad to have you with her. She gets lonely too, for she has an apt. to herself. She said she would not beg you to come, but she would be so glad to have you. You saying that you might take a business course in Asheville put us thinking about this. Of course I've been wishing for a long time that I could get you out of Marshall. Look what Ina has accomplished after she was 30 yrs. old, working all day and going to school at night. She had to pay a lot for tuition in her law school. She says the business schools are free. You meet a good class of people in these schools—people who are really in earnest about things. You & Ina could have your apt. & divide expenses. You know Walter & Ina got along so well. Of course you would be further from home, but when your vacation came, you could get on that good paved road & be home in a little while. On Sundays you could run across the River to see Billie & family. Washington is such a beautiful place to live and a good place to *learn* and *improve* our selves.

You can think all this over and let me hear from you. Just decide for your self. Of course you could get as much in W'ton as manager as you do in N.C. and if your store should be far out, you'd have your car and that means *any where* is near.

Dick 'phoned for Clarence to come to the Capitol. He has just come back and brought a string of birds (quail), and says we will have three guests for supper (dinner). That means I must talk with Millie.

Now, my boy, I wouldn't do any thing to "set you back." I want you to *advance.* Going to the business school sounds like a *good opportunity.*

An automobile rolled down this incline out here & went right into the yard of that white house—missed the house a few inches.

Mother

1. Walter's wife, Dolly, had relatives in upper A&P management, and Ina was counting on their help to secure William's transfer.

To Mrs. Hugh Peterson, Ailey, Ga.

Feb. 6, 1932

Dearest Pat,

. . . Haven't time for much of a letter, but *must* make the attempt. This has been a *full* wk. for me. Know you have seen about the receptions &c. *Ours* was lovely. I had *all* the curtains cleaned and our old house was magnificent when the ladies got the decorations of flowers and smilax every where. I 'phoned Mrs. E. & she had a nice dress ready for me & it was soon fixed up & sent over. I wore it next day too. Too much trouble in the world for folks to be dressing up too much. Women seem (some) to be crazy on the subject. Yesterday the Committee to see about Alex Stephens' Liberty Hall went to Crawfordville to inspect. I've always wanted to go to C'ville. . . .[1]

I stopped on our way down and asked Sybil to have at least a bushel of jonquils ready for me in afternoon. We drove by our dear old Farm Hill and things were lovely there.

But the blow will *have* to come. Ralph has *no* job—just something on commission. Harriette wrote me about it. She is even answering ads to care for children! But is too old, she says. They want young girls. I'd send her letter, but want to answer in detail. Sent her a letter via air mail this A.M. Suggested she try to get place to coach children who are behind in class. Lot of that done here. Get $1.00 per hr. Its terrible, isn't it? Dad is down & out about it. The poor child is so far away. What do you think about them coming to Atlanta? If they were *of the type,* they could go to H's little house that Pipey gave her and make a living some way & theres my big house & no one in it! And poor dear Rob next door. I say poor, 'cause he is having a time financially—though he is off on a hunting trip this wk. All of us went to Russell Sun. to celebrate Richard III's birthday. Sybil is *so* sweet to us. . . . We had a great day—took pict. of the 3 R's—not so good, but want you to see them.

This will have to do this time, but I have much to tell you. Love to Hugh.

Mother

1. Richard Russell Sr. was invited to Liberty Hall when he was fourteen years old because Alexander Stephens had heard that the boy could recite the Shorter and Larger Catechism of the Presbyterian faith from memory, and Stephens wanted to hear this done. Richard spent two weeks with Stephens, and recalled many times that when he left, the old man, lying on his couch, pulled him close, and said, as his parting words, "Richard, never forget that the same worm that eats the pauper, eats the prince."

To Mrs. Hugh Peterson, Ailey, Ga.

Feb. 25, 1932

Dearest Pat,

. . . And *now,* I will get to my birthday. . . . My husband & children could not have been sweeter or more precious if I had been a queen. I made a list of my joys as they came. I mentioned the sunshine. Fielding & Va. sent a cute bottle of Coty's perfume & 'phoned. Marguerite sent a pink slip—& it *fits me.* These came the 17th. Your sweet letter & one from Billie came the 18th A.M. At breakfast table here come 2 doz. lovely red roses from Leeman

[Anderson]. In afternoon sweet letters from Jane & Marguerite. Towards night the *specials* began coming. Letter from Carolyn, Rob and yours & Hughs pkg. the lovely hose and a box of flowers from Sybil, cut from my yard—14 varieties. Then I began to almost *cry* & get homesick. The flowers, not one of the[m] *bought,* brought happy memories—some from aunt Hatties, some from Farm Hill, some Sunie had given me—some lovely pink roses from the vine on Pipeys house. Walter & William were the only ones who did not remember—but they love me just the same. Harriettes card—*postal*—written on the 18th of course was late, but I knew the child was thinking of me. Ina's letter was 2 days late. Mr. Morton sent a card. Miss Hettie 'phoned me & Lilla Brumby sent a card.

I'm trying to save space for I want to send a letter or two. I've had a long letter from Harriette. Sent it to Billie yesterday & asked her to send to you but *do not* let H. know that I sent it. I'm sending the Journal for 2 mo. Dad is sending small cks. Dick is trying to land Ralph a job.

Mother

To Mr. W. J. Russell, Marshall, N.C.

March 3, 1932

Dearest William,

There are two letters I want to write—one to you and one to Ina. Here I go, writing to you *first* and Ina has written me two letters right lately—and she wrote me a birthday letter and you did not. I wrote Walter a long letter today. Among many other things, I told him that you and he were the only ones of my family to forget my birthday. It was all right and I love you just the same and felt that you and he loved me. . . .

Fielding and Va. spent Sat. with us. The Wilsons[1] sent for them on Fri. and carried them back Sun. afternoon. Mrs. Wilson and Mrs. Mason came to see me when they came for F. & Va—first time Mrs. Wilson had been over. I'm so thankful that F. & Va. have good jobs and among pleasant people. So many people without work. Are you saving any money? Do put aside some every pay day. Really William, do this. Its not best to hoard money and to *love* money too well, but its a necessary thing—especially in old age. Right now I can call over some pitiful old people without any thing. Remember uncle Ben. I hear so much of this kind o'thing now and it gets oppressive some time. Do you know any one who has lost their job? So many are coming to Dick and dad every day and even come to me.

Yesterday I went to Crawford to see our kin people—the Halls. Lizzie Hattie and Mary Pope went with me. Mary Hall has a cancer—and she cannot live long. They have no money and can hardly hold on to their home. We had lunch with Sybil. Got flowers from my yard & stopped at Pipey's grave. When we came back from Crawford, I just had to go by *home* Farm Hill. Things are so pretty there—green fields &c. . . .

We hear from Harriette & R. They are still hoping and struggling. Dad has sent them checks (small ones) and Dick & Pat have sent some money. . . .

Aunt Annie is right well, but she is very feeble. Alex is studying hard—has passed two hard exams and has more hard study ahead of him. . . .

I could talk a long time if you were here. . . .

> Write to me boy,
> Mother

1. Virginia's parents, from Duluth, Georgia.

To Mr. W. J. Russell, Marshall, N.C.

March 31, 1932

Dearest William,

. . . Well, your curtains are on the way to Marshall, I suppose, as the girl promised to send them this afternoon. I think they are real pretty and hope you will like them. Hope you can get them fixed up O.K. They are the Criss Cross kind. The girl said they were all ready to put up and were no trouble to fix.

I have been and am very much troubled and upset about something I heard this afternoon. Bradley Dillard shot himself this morning. He was not dead at 3 o'clock. Doctors said he could not live. Its just too pitiful that his poor Father will have to suffer so for this deed that could have been avoided if B. had had a good sensible view of life. Bradley had had two splendid jobs—and lost both of them. He drank some too. He was so nice looking and so smart. He has missed his mother. She was so crazy about him. Just think of the sorrow he has caused them.[1]

Now, Bill, my William boy, write me a line and tell me how the curtains look, hanging in your room. Put them up at once.

Things are going O.K. here. Alex has started coming out at nights—he has all his bones, skull &c. in his room and Julia and Millie are very much on the look out for some of them to begin to rattle.

> Yours
>
> Mother

1. Bradley, son of Walter Dillard, died that same day. His mother, Aunt Mary Walter, had died in 1929.

To Mrs. Hugh Peterson, Ailey, Ga.

May 20, 1932

Dearest Pat,

When I saw Hugh's picture and the announcement in the papers last night I said: "I'll write to my precious child *first thing* in the morning." [1]

Dick said last night that he had to be up early (had me wake him 6:30) and dad wanted to get off early. . . . Dad is so sad and seems so upset over [the death of] Judge Hines. He is the one they will miss and dad says he knew more law than any "of us." . . .

I was glad they brought in extra copies of Journal carrying the good picture of Hugh. I'll send one to Ina & Billie. Have I written you since dad came home? He had a good time but surely I've written you about it.

¼ of 8—I hear Alex leaving for Emory. He was studying this A.M. when I went by his room at 6:30.

No one sleeps much here now. We are running on a strenuous schedule. [2]

Tell Hugh *I'm for him,* bless his heart!

Dick & Rob & Dad talking, all agreed that Hugh would make a "durn good" Congressman. Pardon the ugly word—but that is what they said.

My love to you both. . . .

> Mother

1. Hugh Peterson was running for Congress from the First District. Ina's own political situation had also just changed drastically. Dick Russell Jr. had proved an effective and popular governor, and "every serious political observer knew a second two-year term was his for the asking" (Gilbert Fite, *Richard B. Russell, Jr., Senator from Georgia* [Chapel Hill and London: University of North Carolina Press, 1991], 100). This security meant Ina would be able

to live in Atlanta while Alex, Carolyn, and Edward finished their schools. No one knew better than Ina how the best-laid schemes "go oft agley," and when on April 18, 1932, Georgia's Senator William J. Harris died in Washington, D.C., Ina's life in politics made her once again what she called "a victim of the unexpected."

The week following Harris's death was a tense one in Ina's home. Richard Sr. was hoping his son would appoint him to the seat and fulfill his lifelong dream to serve in the United States Senate, but Dick Jr. wanted the seat himself and knew he could not appoint his father and then run in the special election set for September. On April 25 the young governor announced that he had appointed John S. Cohen, publisher of the *Atlanta Journal*, to fill the late Senator Harris's seat until the election, and that he, Richard Russell Jr., would be a candidate for that seat.

2. On April 26, Congressman Charles R. Crisp of Americus, a twenty-year veteran of the House of Representatives and dean of the Georgia delegation, announced that he too would be a candidate for Harris's seat, taking for granted that election to the Senate was a "logical promotion." Crisp was well-liked and respected. The election was sure to be a thriller.

As Ina indicates, Richard Russell Jr. leapt into the campaign with a demanding speaking schedule. Congressman Crisp went back to Washington.

To Mrs. Hugh Peterson, Ailey, Ga.

Aug. 11, 1932

Dearest Pat,

Haven't time for much of a letter but must say a word or two—and I have a letter from Ina and one from H[arriette]. that I knew you'd enjoy. . . .

I feel that it would be a good thing for H. & R. to come back towards home. I feel that W'ton is home. When you & Hugh get there, I *know* it will feel like home. . . .

Alex went to Va. (Keysville) in the Long Green.[1] He had to meet Mr. M[orton]. there [for their trip to Los Angeles]. . . . Carolyn goes to the office every A.M. and files letters or clips clippings . . . [for] Dick's campaign. Its a busy place. . . .

Alex writes that he is having a wonderful time. He has written cards and *one* splendid letter. I may send it on to you if you *promise* to save it for me. . . .[2]

I miss seeing you so much. Its been an age now. After Sep. 14, you must celebrate & come up. I hope we will all have good news to discuss.

Rob has not been at all well. I begged for medical attention and Sybil did too, so she got a *real* doctor and had an exam from head to toes. Took 3 days. Sybil stayed right with him and would not excuse him from any thing. The doctor says he can pull him up if he's faithful, and he'll get through the campaign. After that, I think the method will be intensive training on diet, exercise and many things in general. . . .[3]

Dad is working hard and complains some, but he has a good appetite. I wish he could "lay off" for awhile. Aunt Annie is so pitiful & aunt Mattie has been so sick. Mary Pope faithful & kind. . . . Love to Hugh.

      Mother

    1. Long Green was the descriptive name of an automobile. Pat had bought the car but gave it to "her boy" Alex when she married.

    2. Alex had a reputation as perhaps the best letter writer in a family by this time filled with good letter writers. His defect lay in the infrequency with which he wrote. He was driving Taylor Morton, Morton's mother, and his aunt, across the United States, in order to attend the 1932 Olympic Games in Los Angeles.

    3. Photographs of the family following all of Richard Jr.'s elections leave no doubt that they were a great strain on his brother Rob.

To Mr. W. J. Russell, Marshall, N.C.

                         Aug. 21, 1932 [the twins' birthday]

Dearest William,

This has been a day of great upheavals and strain. In fact, it began yesterday—Read the enclosed clipping and see if you do not think we had great cause to feel distressed and terrified.[1]

I went to town yesterday aft.—heard the boy calling "Extra" and caught the words Russell and "auto crash"—I soon found out about the accident and got in touch with Edward and Fielding. They told me that Rob had talked to Mark and he said that Dick had been hurt, but had gone on to his appointment and had made one speech and was going on to Alamo and make his last speech. Of course I was worried, but tried to be sensible and hope things were not so bad. Sybil & I sat up and promised to wake Rob. Dick came in about two o'clock. He was looking real well and walking good, but was minus four front teeth.[2] His lip was cut some, but not bad. We sat up a long time hearing all about the accident. Dick has been up since 12 o'clock and looks real well. He has some adhesive tape on his

lip. He is going to Monroe tomorrow A.M. to make a speech. He is going
by Winder and head a motorcade of 100 cars and go into Monroe in
great glory.

We missed you today. Virginia's cake was so pretty & good & was deco-
rated with 25 pink candles. As you are coming soon, its well you did not
come, but we *did* want you here so much. We need you here now and
wish you could come *next* Sun. Fielding has to leave about Sep. 8th for
Statesboro.[3]

I intended sending you a night letter, but so much was going on & people
'phoning every two min. to find out about Dick.

Alex goes to Winder tomorrow in order for *one Russell* to be in Russell
headquarters. I hope you have been happy today and will have another
happy year.

> Lovingly,
> Mother

1. From the *Georgian:* "GOVERNOR RUSSELL THROWN THROUGH WINDSHIELD OF AUTO:
Front Teeth Torn Out in Crash." She wrote under the headline: "This looks awful and is
greatly exaggerated," but in another letter to Carolyn she admits she is feeling shaky after
getting the news this way.

2. The letter to Carolyn says that Dick was "joking and showing 3 of the teeth he had
picked up from floor of the car. They were not beautiful, but we were so sad to see them gone
from their place."

3. To teach at Georgia Teachers' College—today Georgia Southern University.

To Mrs. Hugh Peterson, Ailey, Ga.

Sep. 8, 1932

Dearest Pat,

You are the dearest and sweetest. You never fail to write to your mother,
even under stress and strain [1] and your letters have done so much in helping
me to "carry on." Your last letter was just in time and made a big bright
spot—not that things were dark—may be I was and did not feel as
sprightly as usual.

Of course you know whats in our minds now. William came Mon. and
added one more strong arm (or two, I should say) to our wheel. The boys
seem like *young folks* to me, yet they are working like *men*. . . . Every one

gets up early and if they do not, real early, the 'phone rings and its uncle Lewis wanting to know the whys & wherefores. Every one cheerful and full of vim. Virginia is so sweet and sensible. All this life is so new to her. You know how Sybil has always been so pleasant about turning over Bob [Rob] to such work and never making a complaint, even when she is left alone, &c.—but all is pleasant and sweet.

Alex has been in Winder since his return from his wonderful trip, for Rob said that a Russell had to be in Winder office. Then it was nice for him to be with Sybil last wk. Alex came in Sat. with Sybil and Sun. night he was rushed to Columbus with literature to adv[ance] Dick's speaking. So Carolyn went home with Sybil. Wm. & Alex are going down this A.M. and Carolyn will come back. Uncle L. & Rob have reserved some few *last words* for the last few days—so all will be ready for their part. We hear such good reports from every direction, yet as dad said this A.M. (early) he has a sick feeling, every-now-and-then and fears that *something* may go wrong.

I think and know this: If Dick and Hugh both go in, won't we have a happy thankful time, and we will have something to make us better in our living and demeanor towards *every thing*. If we do not *come in*, we must have that feeling any how, 'cause we have fought a good fight. We *must* be *good* and *better*, no matter what comes. . . .

> Mother

1. Pat, of course, is caught up in her husband's race for Congress.

To Mrs. Hugh Peterson, Ailey, Ga.

Sep. 20, 1932

Dearest Pat,

I will let my very first letter be to you. By the first, I mean the first since the 14th. I have mailed two business cards and a card to our dear Hugh, but no real letter.

I've thought of you many times. As the saying goes: *My heart went out to you.* Races are so uncertain. Many times during ours, my heart, or something inside of me, seemed to put me out of business entirely—then I would brace up and forget all about it. Now its all over. I had hoped so much that Hugh would win. Folks in the 1st dist. just didn't know what a *good* man was, did they?

We are beginning to settle down now to our old life. The house seemed empty last night. William and Alex left for Winder and I thought dad & I would be here alone—but old Mark [Dunahoo] came in about dark to spend the night and he would meet Dick this A.M. on 7:30 train. I was glad to see Mark. He & I drove to the Capitol to get dad. We had real early supper, for us, and can you believe it, I was in bed before 9. The phone rang twice after I got in bed.

I went to see aunt Annie yesterday and she seemed so well. Her right hand is badly swollen & give[s] her some pain, but she seemed very cheerful and could talk very well. I had not been home long before M[ary]. P[ope]. called and said aunt A. had had a real bad attack—found her sitting on bed gasping for breath and pulling at her collar. Mary Pope went right to her and bathed her face and had her to lie down. She slept a long time. M. P. 'phoned for the doctor . . . and [he] said he could not account for the attack, for her heart was in good condition. . . . M.P. is a wonder for patience and endurance. Aunt Mattie requires a lot of attention too. Aunt Annie has to be fed like a baby—has to drink coffee & milk with a straw.

I have been interrupted many times since I began this letter—started at 7 this A.M. Now its 6 P.M. . . . [and] I must stop this rambling wreck. Come soon as you can. My love to Hugh.

       Mother

To Mr. W. J. Russell, Marshall, N.C.

Oct. 30, 1932

Dearest William,

Today is Sunday and the time is real early in the morning. I have just gone down stairs and turned on the heat. Marguerite, Jim and two of their friends from Sav. came over for the game between Ga. & Fla. and they are here, and sound asleep, I suppose. Carolyn is here and dad and I. Dick made a speech in Miami, Fla. Fri. night for Roosevelt and hasn't returned. So you see our crowd for break fast this A.M. and I know it will be a late break fast. . . .

But any way: all this is not what is upper most in my mind this A.M. What I am thinking about is *you—You,* William—I still want to get you away from Marshall. You have passed your 25th birthday now, and its time we are planning seriously for our future. When old age comes, and it does come, it is so fine for it to find us prepared for it. First of all, our minds, our hearts, our habits and our attitude towards things, our way of living and a very important thing is the store, little or big, the bigger the better, that we lay by for our future comfort. This is a *necessity*, I think—I know its a necessity, unless we just go, trusting to luck, and may be wind up by reaching old age, helpless and dependent. I am not prone to be gloomy, you know that, but sometimes I shudder when I think of all my children— especially the boys, and this includes my sons-in-law. I think Hugh Peterson will accumulate and will be well fixed in the future. Jim makes a good salary and Marguerite teaches, you know. But they seem to spend a lot. Ralph, poor boy—I will not say. You knew R[alph]. & H[arriette]. were with Ina in Washington, didn't you? Ina of course taking complete care of them. They are trying to find R. a job. If Gordon lives and keeps well, he may have enough to do very well.

I'm afraid all this last I've written will spoil my letter, but it just came up and I wrote it down. Dick may save some. He will have many calls made upon him when he gets to W'ton. Rob, if he keeps well, will make a good living, and I'm not much worried about him. Now Walter, he may do very well, if he and family stay well. I say the same of Fielding. I feel that Alex and Edward *may* come out very well with their life's work.

Now *you, you* William—You talk to yourself in a good, serious, sensible manner. Do not be gloomy or feel discouraged—just think it over and talk it over with your self. I am not so worried about any of you, or want you to accumulate great wealth. I just want you to be frugal—not wasteful—careful of our time and money—taking care of our health and living a good helpful life and doing our part towards making the world better and happier because we are here.

I had a lovely letter from Virginia yesterday.[1] I hope you have written her a nice, sweet letter. I think she said none of the boys had written except Walter. Now you write, right away, and enclose a dollar bill for the little boy to start his bank account. He has had a lot of gifts, but don't think he has had any money given him. I expect to go to see the baby in the next few days. Sybil, Mrs. Wilson, my self and may be dad. Virginia wants to go to Statesboro as soon as possible. Miss Hettie will go to help with the baby.

Va. has gotten along so well. Marguerite says the baby is fine and splendid in any way. You must write to Va—surely you have written Fielding. This is a great thing in their lives and in ours. . . .

I must stop all this. Read some parts of this letter over twice and then destroy—the others might not like some of it. I am not gloomy but this A.M. I am vitally concerned about my children.

Mother

1. Virginia's and Fielding's first child, Fielding Dillard Russell Jr., was born October 14, 1932.

To Mrs. James H. Bowden, Savannah, Ga.

Dec. 7, 1932

Dearest Marguerite,

You know how I am about letters. I know you will enjoy reading this one from our friend Ruby,[1] so, I'm adding a few lines on the back.

I received your telegram. Thank you for phoning Fielding [about Aunt Annie's death]. I had so much to do and we have to wait so long when [we] phone Statesboro. Or I did the *one* time that I phoned. Heard from Va. this A.M. Its too bad about the bank. Do hope it will soon be going again. I believe the bank failures hit harder now than they did at first. They are *bad any time.*

I am very busy answering a lot of letters that accumulated when aunt Annie was sick—and some new ones too that had to be written.

Mrs. Nellie Wormack Huies came to see me and got a lot of dope for a piece to put in Magazine Sec. Journal. I know you have received your invitation to the [library] dedication.[2] You are coming and bring the girls aren't you? I have been invited to stay with the Beesons & the Allens. Mrs. B. wants to give a Tea for me Fri. afternoon. I don't think I can go then for Carolyn wants to go & she can't leave until Sat. . . .

My time here is so short. I have so much to do. What do you think of letting Miss Ruth Blair keep dad's portrait in Rhodes bldg. until time to hang it in Capitol? Just be thinking about this until you come. You see, I've got to leave *here.*[3]

So many are suffering with Flu. Hope your crowd keep well. Dick went to bed feeling so bad. He is coughing now.

Have just looked over your letter again. It would take a long time for me to answer it *in full*. Am glad you are collecting things for the less fortunate—and it does people good to *give*. Don't worry about not having money for C'mas.

Hope you find this—but am using these letters for you to see how nice your friends are to me.[4] But I was saying, don't worry about not having money for C'mas. Don't give *any* presents this time. Dolly writes that they are not going to give any, not even to each other. We all have each other, so lets not even *think* about *money*.

Edward failed to land the Rhodes S[cholar] S[hip] but he doesn't seem to mind *so much*.

I'll close this queer letter up, and find Harriette's last one to send. Dear child, they are having a time of it.

I went to Warm Springs Mon., shook hands with Roosevelt as he sat on porch of Little White House. The guard said, "Move on please." I started & Roosevelt took my other hand and talked to me about going to W'ton to see Dick sworn in. O, my, it was a thrill.[5]

I want the girls to go to Warm Springs. I saw some of the patients—three just Jane's size—in rolling chairs.

My love,
Mother

1. A sympathy note. Annie Dillard Launius died on December 2, 1932.

2. The new library at GSCW [GN&IC] was being named for Ina.

3. The family had had a portrait done of Richard to hang in the Governor's Mansion while they were there.

4. Ina has written her letter partly on her own paper and partly on spaces left in the letters she is sending Marguerite.

5. Ina had entertained Roosevelt at the Governor's Mansion, and they liked each other.

To Mrs. Hugh Peterson, Ailey, Ga.

Dec. 10, 1932

My Dearest Pat,

I know you have rec'd the invitation to the dedication of I.D.R. Library in M'ville. . . . Sybil is going—will take Bobby & Betty. I'm so glad, for

I want some of my grand c. there. Maybe Marguerite will bring M[ar-
guerite]. & J. or the 2 J's [Jane and Jimmy]. Haven't heard from her about
it, but I know she will want to be present. Mrs. B[eeson]. wants us at dinner
or luncheon at the Mansion [i.e., the former governor's home in Milledge-
ville]. I hope you & Hugh can come. I'm so happy over the Library. I do
feel grateful for the honor and will strive *always* to be *worthy* and will pray
for my grand children and children to *carry on* for me.

Dick has been real sick—not real bad flu but on that order. Doctor said
he must have a nurse, so one came out yesterday. The main things was to
keep him in bed and give medicine and mustard plasters regularly. . . . I
received your letters. I love 'em all. My love to Hugh & you.

Mother

To Mrs. James H. Bowden, Savannah, Ga.

Jan. 8, 1933

Dear Marguerite,

Guess *these* will be the last lines to you from the Mansion. I have been
on the go, trying to leave things in good shape for the new comers—every
curtain & rug clean, and the floors fixed as nice as its possible for these
floors to look. I have talked to Mrs. Talmadge about my departure & she
said she would love to send a few things over Monday.

Carolyn had her reception for Agnes Scott student body & faculty yesterday. It was a huge success. I think the whole crowd came. This is our last
Sun. We are almost ready to move out Tues. about noon. Providence
smiled on us. We found, or it found us, a lovely place, all *furnished,* just as
the Mansion, and as *nice*—the lady was going to N.Y. to visit her daughter—1198 Piedmont N.E. is our number. Telephone Hem. 1275. I can keep
her servant but have made Julia an offer. If she accepts, I will be fixed, but
the woman's servant is good. I will have every thing 'cept the *Packard,* but
am not worried over that. We will be right across from Piedmont Driving
Club. No houses in front. I'm afraid I will not want to leave in June—lovely
front porch and flowers all in the rear. . . .

We got the nice place to see after Alex[1] and for dad to be convenient to
Capitol. He has 2 car lines. I'm too rushed to write more—just sending

these last lines to tell my new address so you'll write to me. Hope every body will stay well and happy. My love to each one—

    Mother

If you can locate today's Sunday American see my picture packing up to leave Mansion. Julia, Sara & Helen came out Fri. evening & we took lots of pictures.

   1. Alex and two or three other Emory medical students had been involved in a shooting incident—one of the students wounded—at an Atlanta brothel, and the affair made the front pages of at least one Atlanta paper. Ina, although never speaking of her youngest son's tendency to play the wild rover, was acutely aware during this time of the importance of her own role as a stabilizing force in his life.

To Senator R. B. Russell, Jr., Washington, D.C.

                                 Jan. 12, 1933

Dearest Dick,

   It's 11:45 here, so suppose you are U.S. Senator from Georgia now. I've thought about you lots this A.M. In last nights paper, I read the article about Huey Long's *bibles* and I hoped *my, our* little bible had a part in your entrance into the work the people of Ga. have put into your care.[1]

   I am sending clippings from the morning paper that I thought would interest you. Of course you will see these papers. They have been such a part of us for so long.

   We are very happy and satisfied in our new home. Dad came in last night in time for 6:30 dinner and the two mornings he has gone to office before 8:30. I enjoy getting the breakfasts. I have Mrs. C[ooper]'s real good servant who comes at 1 o'clock. I leave all the cleaning for her and she gets dinner.

   We had a lock put on the garage door and I enjoy knowing the car is out there. Mark [Dunahoo] saw about the lock for me. He had dinner with us our first night.

   I'm sending this by *air* as I had a stamp already. I feel that you are off on a trip and will soon be back.

    Lovingly,
    Mother

   1. Dick Russell had used his mother's Bible when sworn in to the governor's office.

To Mrs. Hugh Peterson, Ailey, Ga.

Jan. 20, 1933

Dearest Pat,

. . . Well, we moved over to our new domicile. Walter brought me in the Packard with our suit cases and a few odds and ends—mostly *odds*. I had promised Dick that I would have the Packard in the garage *by 12 o'clock*. So, I came over by my self, feeling very *lonesome* and wishing for even *one* child to be with me.

Things were in such a stir and had been all day before. When I left the Mansion, all the Ansley Park *society* were there preparing for the reception. I held on to my room & defied any one to enter. My servants were feeling so forsaken, but remained at their posts, as Mrs. T. told me: "Of course they will stay there until I come. I'll have to have some body to start off with." So I gave them a good talk, & some cried. You know Millie. She *had* to cry & Gus was next. I was taking off all my leftover groceries, & Millie reminded me that they would not have *anything* for lunch, so I left enough for them until Mrs. T. could begin on the *hams*. I have heard that the Ansley Park ladies had a wonderful dinner for them [the Talmadges] that night.

Dad & I went to the reception. Rob & Dick were there, and I left by the sun parlor door at back & joined D. & R. & came on to 1198 Pied. with them. Dick wanted to see our quarters before he left. Dad & Edward soon came over and as I had employed Mrs. Cooper's help, we soon had a nice, early supper. . . .

Dick left his car for me & Marg. & I had a fine ride. Carolyn drove for me when she was here. Then Sybil & Rob came, thinking they were going back that night, Wed. I believe, but Rob had to stay. Syb. & I had a nice ride to 10th St. & round & about town. I am negotiating with a good boy to drive for me. Can't you come & drive? O, boy, we could have such a good time. I want to run down home for a few hrs. Dick had the car put in perfect condition.

Mrs. Cooper's servant is a good one—Josie. She comes at one & stays until 7 or later. Cleans up every thing & fixes the orange juice for breakfast. I hate to have the house cleaning done in the P.M., but I can stand it—the price is $4.50 for part day, $7.50 for all day. . . .

Of course you read in papers how many were present at [Dick's] induction into the Senate. One man, who had been in W'ton a long time, said he had never seen so many present at a ceremony of that kind. I did want to be *among those present*. Several things kept me from going. Dick said he would furnish the money so that was not in my way. I had not been feeling very well. The last three weeks of my life at Mansion were very strenuous— in fact, the time reached back before Dick's sickness. Then dad feeling as he did about going, and Alex studying so hard and moving into a new place and trying to start a home for us. I could not feel that it was best for me to go. Ralph has a real job now, so he could not be present. Gordon was hindered some way & was late—but the others were there with bells on. Senator Cohen's luncheon was swell and I can see our Ina & Harriette now. . . .

I've been interrupted so many times & this letter is a mess. The 'phone & door ring about as much as they did at the Mansion. . . . I believe Dick is home sick. He'd love to be at the Capitol hobnobbing with those men. I wish Hugh was there, don't you.

I have lots more to tell you. *Can't* you come to see me. . . .

Here I am, way after I wrote those last lines—Thought when I retired from public life, I'd have more time, but have not found it so. Give my love to Hugh. . . .

> Love,
> Mother

To Mrs. Hugh Peterson, Ailey, Ga.

1198 Piedmont Ave., Feb. 10, 1933

Dearest Pat,

. . . We went home Sun. as I told you we planned. Got to town in time for preaching. Edward had a Seminary (teacher) man to conduct service. I felt so good to go in the little church again. Just the usual small crowd, but so familiar like, and Mr. Graddick, Potts, Q¼man, Beck, Miller, and the women folks, all had tears, (not sorrowful) in their eyes when they came to speak to me. Mr. Potts just took my hand & said, "Mrs. Russell," his eyes full. Of course I had the moisture in my eyes too, but I tried to talk it away.

We went to Sybil's after church & had a happy time and a good dinner. Sybil is so sweet & good to us all and I came home very happy and thankful that Rob, my boy, had such a happy home. Alex played ball with Bobby. Carolyn carried her walking shoes and picked jonquils by armfulls, and violets, to bring back. I sent some upstairs to Mrs. Martin and she raved over them. . . .

I had wonderful luck in meeting Mrs. R[oosevelt]. Carolyn & I had stood up about 15 min. on 4th floor [at Rich's] listening by loud speaker. Then we went in basement to see about some bargains. I met up with the floor walker, Mr. Camp, Dick's friend & school mate at Powder Springs. He said, "You ought to be upstairs." I told him the doors were closed when I got in. He told me to follow him & he carried us up on the freight elevator and put us in the hands of Paul Jones, Dick's friend & school mate at Gordon, and he carried us into Mr. Walter Rich's office. Mr. R[ich]. was perfectly lovely to us. Told us to wait. There was her coat on rack & she would have to come back there. Several came in & out. Maj. Cohen, Chip Roberts, one or 2 women. Finally Mrs. R. came and I was introduced. She is fine, I think. Have admired her, even before F.D.R. was elected Pres. I asked her if she received the gift from Mrs. Brewer. She said, "Yes, its too beautiful." The woman had made it herself. It had lace on it made by a woman in Austell, who had never been out of the state. The cotton was grown & worked up in a mile of Austell. . . .[1]

Gus comes to see me. He still works [at the Mansion] & all of them. Millie sent me word by the bread man that she felt like a spanked child. Every time the *mother* comes in, she gets a *spankin'*. I must not write any thing. . . .

I went to see Doscia. Poor thing. She has cancer of womb & rectum. Can't get out of bed. She repeated the verse I taught her and tried to smile: "Be not weary in well doing," &c. Sybil & Rob have been so good to her. They send doctor & pay him $2 every time he goes & Sybil sends food. I'm going too fast now and my time is up. . . .

Mother

1. In another letter she describes a small rug or bath mat.

To Mrs. Hugh Peterson, Ailey, Ga.

Feb. 24, 1933

Dearest Pat,

Yesterday when I finished reading your splendid letter, I found myself watching the door to see you step in the room. I had a feeling that you were right here—and a queer thing happened last night. Sybil came in to do some shopping for Inaug. and came out here about five o'clock. I gave her all my good birthday letters to read while I ran in kitchen to stir the grits, & do a few little things. When I came back, Sybil said: "Mother, isn't this letter from Pat, "little old Pat," she said, "When I was reading it I felt that she was right here by me." . . .

I hear reports from our former place of abode. Gus has been fired. They come right to me to talk things over. Millie sent word today by our Camp Gordon friend that she was told another would take her place soon. As soon as they could all get *this nasty place cleaned up.*" As I said before, I should not have written that. Will leave blank at bottom & you cut it off.[1]

I really believe that dad & Ed. will come to see you soon. Poor dad has a time, trying to be reconciled to things, and get his work done too. He has worked hard this year. . . .

Just knew I'd have to get another sheet of paper. I always have so much to tell you. . . .

Dick stays at Hamilton Hotel. Said he might move later, but he'll be there till after March 4. . . . I heard that Dick & Leeman [Anderson] were coming home about the 12th for a flying visit. I think both have been homesick to a great extent. They have been very busy, & that has saved 'em. Dick wrote that he was hungry for some grits. Billie wrote me about Harriette making such good muffins out of meal you had sent & cooking some country ham Leeman had rec'd from a friend in Rutledge, & having grits & having Dick & Leeman out to dinner and Billie had nice sausage from Gray, Jones Co. [Georgia], and had cooked grits & had Dick out to eat. So he got cooking southern from two ole Southern girls, didn't he?

Alex is studying hard—made 100 on a test not long ago. I enjoy having him here. He is a queer body—but good as gold. . . . Alex has just come in for lunch. He does this occasionally and I must stop. A. has to be at Grady Hospital at 1:45.

My love to Hugh and a bushel for *you.*

Mother

1. The Talmadges did criticize the Russells for leaving the Mansion in a mess. Although Ina most certainly had not left the house in a mess per se (several letters attest to major cleaning and ordering), the building and furnishings were already deteriorating when she moved in, and during the Depression era, Dick Russell Jr. had felt house repairs were ex-

penses that could be postponed. Sixty years later Carolyn declared: "I *know* the Talmadges thought we were ragtags, but Dick wouldn't let us buy *anything!*"

To Mr. William J. Russell, Sylva, N.C.

Mar. 7, 1933

Dearest William,

Well, Well, well! and you are not in Marshall any more — only in mind and heart to a certain degree. . . . I know you will make good wherever you are and I hope you can manage your work in such a way that it will not be too hard on you. As I remember Sylva, its big piles of lumber and *black water* running under the bridge (small bridge) we passed over. We had to stop there once to have garage work done. . . . I know your friends in Marshall did hate to see you leave — that is nice. I would cry if they were glad to get you away from their town — and you will soon have good friends in Sylva, too, and the ladies who go to your store will be saying how nice you are, that new manager &c. You must use your head to save your legs and back. How much help have you? Is the store about the size of the one in Marshall?

I know Mrs. Hinkle did worry over your going. She told me that you gave less trouble and was more agreeable than any one she had ever had in the house, but you are away now, and I'm so glad you have so many pleasant memories of the years spent in Marshall.

Edward went to Washington. A friend who had a new car offered him a ride. Wish he knew you were at Sylva, for I am sure they will come back to Ga. via that route. He could stop to see you a few minutes. Sybil & Rob went to the Inauguration. Uncle John went with a friend. He will come by Sylva. Sybil & Rob intended staying a few days, but the banks closing and every thing looking so dismal in a financial way, hurried them home. They came in Sun. night. I was so glad to see them. They told us about every thing. Of course you have read the papers about the enormous crowd. They had dinner Sat. night with Billie and Ina, Harriette & Ralph & Edward were there. Dick was so busy with *folks,* he couldn't come. You know there were more than 2000 from Ga. and I guess *every one* knew Dick and made an effort to see him.

I think Edward & dad are going to make a little trip to see Pat and Fielding & Va. & may be Marguerite real soon. Edward is through at the Seminary. Will graduate with the class in June, *provided* he gets up the money he owes the seminary for his food he has eaten. I know he can do this. . . .

Dick expected to come home for a few days, but as Congress convenes Thurs. he will not have time. . . .

Wanted to tell you that I was enjoying the things you brought. The coffee is gone. Half of the prunes have been eaten. I like the Mello-wheat so much. Its like cream of wheat to me. I think of you & uncle Lewis when I say cream of wheat. I gave Sybil the box of oat meal, she says her children eat it so much & she doesn't have to buy milk. We like oat meal too, but dad just has to have grits & I don't like to cook both. . . .

You work away at Sylva now with a good will and heart and maybe you can come home sometime & we can farm at Russell.[1] When the banks closed I said I was going to Russell & farm. Sybil said she was going home & plant her garden. The thing is, we must never lose heart, or feel that things are utterly black.

When you have time, write me about your store—how large, what class of people buy &c. I hope you take time to eat quietly. If you had a heater or hot plate, and would cook Mello-Wheat for lunch—put butter in it & drink your good milk. . . .

    Mother

1. Because William was unhappy in his work and missed home terribly, this theme of his coming home to farm at Russell recurs in Ina's letters to him. She dreamed of seeing him "in possession of that 100 acres of land."

To Senator Richard B. Russell, Jr., Washington, D.C.

March 30, 1933

Dearest Dick,

This is a terrible time of night to be writing a letter. Its almost *one* o'clock—every body in bed but Alex and I—the every body is dad, Carolyn, uncle Lewis and a girl Buford some body, who is from West Va. and cannot go home for Easter holidays. Alex went to picture show tonight and now has to study. . . .

Uncle Lewis had a long case he will try tomorrow & he wanted to read it over to dad—so, they sat here and *enjoyed* the long case while we went to the show.

Last Sunday we went home. Dad's toe nails had been giving him so much trouble and we had Dr. Almond cut them off as he did the terrible ones aunt Annie had. Dad is much relieved. We enjoyed going home and I gathered up all the soiled bedding towels &c. and Sybil had her wash woman fix them up for me. As Carolyn has Easter holidays now we planned to go tomorrow and give the house a good cleaning. You know how bad it looked & it was worrying me. So we go tomorrow. I'll take Gus and he will fix the yard & trim up the rose bushes, and I'll get Millie to help me with the house. Gus wife, Folia, is working for Ike Hill, Ben's brother, who has a barber shop on Va. Ave. Gus gets 30¢ from me to buy his tobacco & a "piece of meat." I think he wants to go back to Russell. Of course they are doing right well now as Folia gets $5 per wk.

Of course all thats going on in D.C. now gives us a lot to talk about. Dad . . . raves over some of the things that happen in Washington. Dad is so grieved over Judge Pottle's death. I guess he has always been our friend as I've never heard dad make any statement to the contrary.

I put out the light in my room & came in living room to write & am using a stationery box for a desk and its not very satisfactory.

Billie wrote me that you and L[eeman] came out the Sun. you wrote me you were going and how much she enjoyed having you. I know you are busy and from all accounts you have plenty of callers. . . .

Edward is at Ga. U. studying for his degree. He & Alton are at Cherokee Hotel. Edward has two churches offered him—one at McDonough & one in Augusta. He said he would decide soon and begin Sep. 1st.[1]

I was so glad to get your good, long letter. You are so sweet to send the ck.

    Lovingly,

    Mother

---

1. Having finished his courses at Columbia, Edward continued work on a master's degree in history at the University of Georgia.

To Senator Richard B. Russell, Jr., Washington, D.C.

April 4, 1933

Dear Boy,

    . . . I began this to tell you about my trip home Fri. I think I wrote you that we were going to clean up. We did go, and things are looking much better there—especially on the inside. Millie and Gus and Carolyn and her friend and my self—we all worked. I worked most with the yard—dug so hard with my new hoe and thought I'd feel sore next day, but did not. Sybil was so good to us and gave us such a good dinner. A terrific rain came up in afternoon. Of course I was not through planting my bulbs & seeds, but the things I did plant got plenty of rain. Rain poured on us all the way home, but Carolyn drove carefully and we made a safe trip. Of course we are always mindful that if you had not been so good and kind to leave your car for me, we could not have so much pleasure.

Edward and Alton Glosure will be ordained at Hebron Church, Jackson Co. 8 mi. from Commerce, Apr. 12. Dad & I are planning to go. Alex thinks he can leave for one day.

Edward made his trial sermon at Augusta First Pres. Church, Mar. 25. Its a real city church, big organ, big choir, big congregation—real formal, compared to what he has been having. Dr. Campbell Morgan was the first person E. recognized in congregation. E. said this disconcerted him for a minute.[1] I had a letter from Walter Dillard and Ruth. They heard E. preach—said he did so well, and they were so proud of him. Edward went to McDonough Sun. for his trial sermon there. He had supper with your Reagan friends. Dad said a man from McD. came in his office yesterday and said splendid things about E. The session has to decide on whether they ask E. to take the charge.[2]

Carolyn asked E. what he wore when he preached in Augusta. He said "Dick's double breasted blue suit," and he wore it to McD[onough]. I told him I'd tell you that your inauguration suit was doing good work & giving good service. . . .

William came to see us Sun. . . . William sold over $1000 worth of goods last wk., he said. He looks well, but says his appendix gives him lots of trouble. He has only one helper in store—a young boy who suffers with a rupture. William seemed worried about him.

I know you have been "put to it," to know exactly what to do about all thats been happening so fast. We heard Huey Long last night. I liked him. He said he had done some things he never thought he would—that he had voted with the pres. in every thing except the veterans. He could not do that, he said.

Changes have to be made & right now seems to be the time & then adjust for the good of all.

Mother

1. Dr. Morgan was one of the best-known Presbyterian preachers of the era.

2. Edward received invitations to come from both churches and chose to go to McDonough.

To Mr. William J. Russell, Sylva, N.C.

April 12, 1933

Dearest William,

So much happened yesterday, April 11, 1933. To begin with, it was, & has been, Marguerite's birthday for ? years. Then next we have been looking forward for some time to the meeting of Athens Presbytery at old Hebron Church in Banks Co., 8 mi. from Commerce, and at this meeting our Edward would be ordained into the ministry—he and Alton Glosure who has been E's room mate at Columbia Seminary for 3 yrs. and who is E's very best friend. So that ordination carried us, dad, Alex, Carolyn & me to Banks Co. yesterday. . . .

The ordination of Edward & Alton was an impressive and beautiful service. Hebron is an *old* country church, situated in a grove of fine trees. Some kind of gas lamps hung from ceiling, but an oil lamp was on the pulpit stand. The boys had stood the examination in the afternoon and at night they both preached sermons, from texts a committee had assigned to them. Edward preached first, then Alton, neither sermon over 20 min. Then the boys were ordained. They were asked questions about their belief & then made vows to uphold & do for the church according to the vows they made &c. Then they kneeled down, & the members of the Presbytery came up, placing their hands on the boys heads and a fine earnest prayer was made by the moderator. Then the meeting was dismissed & a happy friendly handshaking with all those good, kind people—the very best on earth. Edward & Alton have preached at so many churches in the Presbytery and *every one* loves them, as so many said, "Just as if they were in my own family." They are fine boys, men. I wish you could have been with us last night. It equaled and surpassed, in some way, our inauguration 1931.

Have just heard reporter over Radio tell of Edward's ordination. How far is Sylva from Charlotte?

[no signature]

To Mr. Wm. J. Russell, Sylva, N.C.

July 11, 1933

Dearest William,

I believe I have written you one letter or card since you left here. So much has happened that I can't remember who or what about letters. Any way, I feel that you have not heard about the accident Ina had on their way to W'ton. As you know they spent the first night in Charlotte with Walter. As they were in 125 mi. of W'ton, they had a real bad accident. Ina has written us all about it and we are sending the letters around, and we have written Marguerite to mail the letters to you as soon as she reads them. Dad & I heard from Ralph yesterday. Harriette was hurt more than the others—in fact, the only one who was really hurt. Ralph stayed with her & the others, Ina, & Car—went on to W'ton. The accident occurred near Farmville Va. & H. was carried to a hospital there. Ralph wrote that H. had suffered a great deal. She will have to be in hospital 3 wks. & then may be she can be moved to W'ton, and it will be some time then before she can walk. We are all so distressed, and are hoping she can fully recover without any permanent effects. . . .

As Ina wrote details of accident I'll let you wait for the letters to learn of accident. I'm writing very hurriedly soon in the A.M. It's hard to keep the children inside. Had a hard rain last night and they want to get out with their guns.

You write H. a short little letter,[1] Community Hospital, Farmville Va. All of us are trying to write so she will receive lots of letters. Its so pitiful to think of her lying on a board, and may be suffering. Ralph said the doctor thought after first few days she would not suffer so much. The pelvic bone was broken and she will have to lie still for it to heal. The pelvic bone is the bone that holds the body together, & its so important for it to heal right in order not to leave one leg shorter than the other.

Of course we are all hoping for the best, but we feel very much concerned over Harriette. I may try to go to see her. Dick & uncle Lewis left Sat. for W'ton. They expected to go by F'ville to see Harriette.

Our breakfast is about ready & the children are buzzing around.

This is a messy letter, but I wanted to write you and had to do it in haste. Hope you are well, ole boy. Write me some times.

> Your mother

1. William wrote to Harriette and offered to lend her one hundred dollars. She refused at first but later wrote that she would have to accept the money, and William sent it.

To Mrs. James H. Bowden, Savannah, Ga.

Dec. 6, 1933

Dear Marguerite,

I have just finished going through a *candy bucket full* of old letters—some addressed to Miss Ina Dillard, but most of them are letters from you children when you went away to school or to teach school. Some were funny—all were sweet to me. I found one you wrote to Fielding. I think you were in Eastman. You were offering some little reward for him to brush teeth &c., and telling him to see that Wm brushed his &c. . . .

I wished for each one of you when I went to Crawfordville to celebrate for 100th yr. since Alexander H. Stephens *settled* at Liberty Hall. Dick made a splendid speech. Today we went to Crawford to unveiling a shaft erected in honor of Wm. H. Crawford. Dick made a good talk about him. Look out for pictures in news papers. When we get together next summer, we must visit these places. . . .

Edward will come some time, as soon as he can leave McD. Perhaps you do not know that we, dad, Pat, Sybil, Alex & I, went down to E's installation & met his many friends, or some of them, in McD. & made him a nice visit at the manse. He is nicely fixed, but he needs a lamp & he has not a single picture on his walls. I sent him one of our group pictures. . . .

As I looked over those letters tonight, there were reminders of aunt Hattie, Pipey, aunt Annie, uncle Ben, Auntney, all gone, and as I sat on platform in Crawford, my father, my mother and my home were foremost in my mind. All these such good people. I thank God for them. And I said, O, we who are living must show our appreciation and thankfulness by being better men & women in the future. . . .

> My love,
> Mother

Carrying On
the Work of the World

*T*he period from the fall of 1933 through the winter of 1936 was an unsettled time for Ina. She spent almost as much time with Richard at his
room in the Kimball Hotel in Atlanta as she did at her home in Russell.
Although she felt she was a help to him and enjoyed his company as much
as ever, living in two places at once was not a circumstance likely to suit a
homemaker like Ina. Nevertheless, she kept cheerful, while she waited to
see what might turn up or be encouraged to turn up.

In 1934 she saw Carolyn graduate from Agnes Scott and take up her first
teaching job in Blakely, Georgia. Ina wrote to Patience on September 14,
1934: "Carolyn must be at a faculty meeting Sat. Think of it! Our baby! A
faculty meeting! But time goes on, and these things will come. I'm so
thankful that I have children who can carry on the work of the world, in a
creditable and able manner. O, I'd grieve to *die out*!"

This new endeavor of her youngest child prompted letters of encouragement and advice. She wrote to her on November 23, 1934:

I read your dear letter & read it over & over and was so thankful for
you & for your attitude towards life. It caused me to remember a verse
I learned some time ago, that I found in a hymnbook that your great
grandmother Russell gave your dad. It was this: "Day by day, my Father, measure / All my changes yet to be, / And may each in thy good

pleasure / Bring me closer unto Thee." After all, its getting closer to our source of Life and grow[ing] into more happiness and contentment as we journey to the end. Its changes that tries our souls. Poor aunt Annie. I think of her as my changes come and I have had them. Aunt Annie cherished or harbored hers, until her memory failed.[1] I've thought of you so many times . . . what a change [Blakely] would be from your busy, pleasant life at A[gnes] S[cott]. . . . But I knew you'd be able to stand it. We must be prepared in a spiritual manner to take things as they come.

Hugh Peterson ran for Congress again in 1934, this time successfully. He and Patience went to Washington in 1935, joining the other family members there.

Because her far-flung family was generally well-situated, and grown children did not need instruction from her as they had when they were younger, Ina's letter writing became less frequent. To satisfy her need to communicate, she wrote postcards, cramming telegraphic-style news on a single card. Sometimes she sent two cards when she ran out of space on the first one. She wrote letters to those children she considered to have special needs or who were in a crisis, however minor. Among her active, numerous clan, crises were not lacking and multiplied as the years went on in the form of new babies, illnesses, operations, automobile accidents, marriages, and political campaigns.

William, single and unhappy in his job, continued to be a frequent recipient of her letters and cards until Richard bought the Bell place in 1935 and William came home to farm. Aware that Dick Jr. had actually "left home" for the first time, Ina wrote to him frequently, especially the first year he was in Washington. Alex graduated from Emory School of Medicine in 1935 (Dick Jr. made the graduation address), and Ina wrote often to her youngest son when he went away to a remote Civilian Conservation Corps work camp near Fort Eustis, Virginia, to finish an internship at Grady Hospital unhappily terminated for personal reasons. During the same period Edward, involved in missionary work in Brazil, needed letters from home, and she made sure he received his share.

The year 1936 promised the most severe political test of Dick Russell Jr.'s life, as Eugene Talmadge, after two terms as governor of Georgia, geared up for a summer campaign against Georgia's junior senator. Talmadge, a colorful and controversial figure in state politics, was enormously popular.

Early political forecasts predicted a bitter battle between Talmadge and Russell for the Senate seat. On January 26, Ina wrote to Dick Jr.: "With my meager knowledge and understanding of things, I can foresee tough times, but we can face 'em, can't we? Prepare now, *every* day, in getting ready for anything that might come—and I believe that would be by handling things as they come day by day in our most conscientious and painstaking way. To do this, we will be ready to handle the *crucial* times. You remember what you said long ago when you came home so sick, from a hunt down at Farm Hill. We must all be ready for the crucial times."

Ina kept a diary in 1936, a page-a-day type, the gift of her daughter Patience. Patience, an avid record keeper herself, knew that any record of her mother's life would be valuable. Ina was faithful to write daily. The diary bears the telegraphic, emphatic, and succinct style of her postcards, as if she is writing to an unknown reader. Although it lacks the involvement with the reader found in her letters, the diary provides proof that Ina's energy had not failed, nor had her role as the magnetic center of this great swirling family changed.

She moved back to Russell to stay during this tense time. Once again the family rallied to help Brother Dick win an election. Ina went on cooking and making beds for unexpected family members and other campaign workers who landed at Russell during the hot summer of 1936. Occasionally she accompanied her son on speaking engagements. On August 14 she wrote in her diary: "A most wonderful day. Dick spoke in Thomson. Conservatives estimated that 20,000 were present. I sat on platform. Dick introduced me. Flowers were presented to me. Dick made a wonderful speech. . . . 1000 went from Winder."

August 26 she wrote: "We have just come in from prayer meeting. Carolyn & I and 8 [grand]children went. Dick spoke at Griffin today and we listened over radio. Splendid speech. Great applause from the crowd." Russell's biographer Gilbert Fite writes that the Griffin speech may have been Dick Russell's finest hour in the campaign arena. Through brilliant strategy and speaking, Russell leveled the powerful Talmadge:

> Russell . . . began to verbally work over the governor in the best Russell style. Using a combination of humor, sarcasm and hard facts, he soon had the governor on the political ropes. Russell tore Talmadge's platform to

shreds. . . . Targeting Talmadge's disloyalty to the Democratic Party [Talmadge tried to unseat Roosevelt at the 1936 Democratic Convention], Russell said that now the governor was claiming to be loyal. . . . When Russell said that he still hoped to make a real Democrat out of Gene, a huge roar went up from the crowd.

Ralph McGill reported in the *Atlanta Constitution* that it was the greatest campaign speech Russell had ever delivered, and Talmadge's biographer, William Anderson, wrote in *The Wild Man from Sugar Creek:* "Gene had been drawn and quartered—his style and stomping, his demagoguery and showmanship all pared away."[2]

Ina was particularly impressed when people began to arrive in Russell looking for paved sidewalks. Talmadge had accused Russell of using state funds when he was governor to add such amenities to the tiny community. In view of Richard Sr.'s love for his wheelbarrow and shovel (Ina's diary records that he moved dirt all summer), this accusation prompted high glee in the family. Someone, perhaps William and Alex, put up a sign on the highway near the homeplace offering a one-hundred-dollar reward to anyone who could find paved sidewalks in Russell.

As the September election day neared, Ina delighted in the reunions as everyone in the family came at some time to the homeplace. For several weeks she had eight of her grandchildren with her. She was especially proud of the farm products donated to Dick Jr., noting that at a Warm Springs rally 26 bales of cotton were presented, "one of the bales ginned the year Dick was born. All the crowd has come in now. Its ¼ to one. We are all talking, telling of funny & good things that have happened today."

She took pride in the difference that emerged between her courtly son and the rampaging Talmadge. On September 2 she wrote: "A very busy pleasant day—things went well in the home. Nothing seemed to be lagging or hard to manage. We listened to speech made by Talmadge at Thomson Ga.—nothing to it but gall & venom. Went to Commerce to hear Dick speak. Big crowd, nice & orderly. 3 bales of cotton given to Dick."

On September 9, 1936, Dick Russell Jr. was reelected by an overwhelming majority to his Senate seat, receiving 256,154 popular votes (378 county unit votes) to Talmadge's 134,695 (32 county unit votes). Ina wrote in her diary that it was "a wonderful day & will linger long in our memory." The next day Winder again celebrated its native son as seven thousand people converged on the little town in a pouring rainstorm to congratulate the senator. Ina was again seated on the platform and introduced as his best sweetheart.

That was not the last major change of 1936. Two weeks later Alex married his nurse sweetheart Sarah Eaton, and the young couple moved in with Ina and William to begin a demanding rural medical practice. In addition to farming, William sometimes worked for the Barrow County Sheriff's Department transporting prisoners.

The year 1937 brought Ina's first serious health problems. In June she suffered a mild stroke, from which she recovered but with a loss of her former energy. With Alex and Sarah living in the house with her, she had good medical attention and supervision, but her health problems continued, and she had to follow her own advice about patience in healing. On December 11, 1937, she wrote to Dick Jr. following a happy visit to her Washington set of children: "I came home feeling so well and guess I forgot myself and did *something*. It wasn't work, for I had Annie & Modene in the house & Rich outside, but I guess I'm slated for a more or less life of an invalid. (I've always dreaded that word.)"

In March 1938 she was hospitalized for several weeks with pneumonia but was well enough to attend Ina Jr.'s wedding in Washington on June 4, 1938. Three marriages in the family were expected in 1938. Two weeks after Ina Jr.'s wedding to Jean Killough Stacy, the man who was attractive enough to make Ina Jr. finally give up her name (but not her job), Edward and his longtime sweetheart, Ala Jo Brewton, Hugh Peterson's first cousin, were married in Vidalia, Georgia. At the family reunion that took place in Russell two weeks later, Dick Jr. brought home Pat Collins, a young woman with whom he had fallen deeply in love, and it was expected their engagement would be announced while they were in Georgia. Perhaps they would be married as soon as July 15, with Edward officiating. Pat Collins was a Georgian, a graduate of Agnes Scott College and Emory University School of Law, who had gone to Washington to work as an attorney in the Department of Justice. According to Gilbert Fite, she was beautiful, intellectual, accomplished, and gracious. Ina Jr., who knew her professionally and personally, thought she would make Dick the perfect wife.

The match was not to be. Pat was a devout Catholic, and although Dick was not a devout Methodist, he could not agree to rear his children as Catholics. He was also apparently surprised that Pat wanted a Catholic priest to perform the wedding ceremony. Pat returned alone to Washington, and the engagement was never announced. Ina Sr., too discreet to mention any of this in letters, said little about it to anyone, even to Carolyn. "I'm always sorry for boys, or any one, trying to *decide* questions," she wrote about Alex's internship problems. How much she must have sympathized with Dick Jr. in making this difficult life decision. She believed in a happy marriage as a desirable state and wanted all her children to marry. She was never jealous of any of her children-in-law, but rather her warm, all-embracing nature welcomed them. Each daughter-in-law felt she was Ina's particular favorite, and as Sarah expressed it, "She wasn't my mother-in-law. She was my best friend." Ina's own children, sons and daughters, often jokingly accused her of loving their spouses more than she loved them.

Any grief over her son's failed love affair, however, was too soon supplanted by the greatest heartache she had ever known. On December 3, 1938, Richard left her for the last time.

On Sunday, December 4, 1938, the Atlanta papers carried the death of Richard Brevard Russell Sr. as the major front-page story. The *Constitution* headline declared: "CHIEF JUSTICE RICHARD B. RUSSELL DIES UNEXPECTEDLY DURING SLEEP AT HIS HOME: Brilliant Jurist Was Famed For His Penetrating Dissents: Death Brings Close to Half Century of Unflagging Service to Justice's Beloved Georgia."

Richard worked December 3 at his Atlanta office and came home in the evening, complaining of chest pains. He and Ina were alone; William was out, and by this time Sarah and Alex had moved into the cottage next door. The papers report that Ina prepared a light supper, and after the meal she helped Richard to bed. Thinking he had fallen asleep, she was reading quietly in a chair in the room when Rob came in, hoping to discuss something with the Judge. It was he who discovered that his father had, in Ina's words, "gone away."

As the scattered family gathered for the final tribute to their patriarch, accolades poured in. Georgia was ready to do honor to her fallen chief justice. In Florida on a tour with congressmen and senators, Dick Russell Jr. rushed to catch a train that was being held for him and was only slightly delayed when the car in which he was riding left the road and turned over. Although he suffered a knee injury, he insisted on getting into another car immediately in order to reach the train at West Palm Peach.

The chief justice's body lay in state at the Capitol on Monday, December 5, and government offices were closed between the hours of ten and three. In Winder, Mayor H. M. Oakley issued a proclamation that the city would be in official mourning for the late chief justice during the hours of his funeral on Tuesday. Schools, stores, and other businesses would be closed. "Almost as long as I can remember," Oakley said in the *Constitution*, "Chief Justice Russell was looked upon as the leading citizen of Winder and Barrow county. We counted him among us, even though his home was at Russell, adjacent to Winder." The old feud was gone and forgotten.

Newspaper articles highlighted Richard's service as a jurist and to the state's colleges, particularly the University of Georgia and Georgia State College for Women. At his funeral and later at the memorial proceedings in the Supreme Court in 1939, his numerous colleagues and friends, men of unusual eloquence, came to give testimony to the extraordinary life and character of Richard Brevard Russell Sr. Their praise of his work, their understanding of the originality, skill, and devotion given to it, would have swelled Richard's ambitious heart. Their sincere affection and admiration, their genuine appreciation of the man he was, would have stirred that deeper heart that sustained him when his ambitions failed.

Ina carried through this sorrowful period with dignity and courage that inspired her children, but soon after Christmas she fell ill with a virulent encephalitis. She was hospitalized in a coma or near-coma for several weeks. When her health began to improve, she also began to write a few letters. She wrote Dick Jr. on April 12, 1939, that William carried her to church on Sunday, and although it was her first trip anywhere the whole year, she "stood it very well."

Her legendary energy and strength were never to return, however. The great servant would have to learn to be served. Her epic task of motherhood was completed, and without the partner with whom she had worked so well in tandem, he in his sphere and she in hers, she rested. Nevertheless, she watched her children with her usual interest and ever-growing pleasure.

Richard Russell had written his will three days before his death, leaving everything to Ina. Although almost all his debts had been paid in full, there was scant cash in the estate. However, property was not lacking, and Rob, as executor, was a skillful and careful manager, selling off a lot or a few acres here and there, when Ina needed extra income. Dick Jr. continued to send her a monthly check and to pay for a practical nurse when necessary. It was never a problem to find someone in the family to contribute funds. Ina's children knew their duty, and it was prompted by the deepest love. There is no evidence that she ever worried about money for herself.

Although Ina was forced to live the life of an invalid or at best semi-invalid, she did not, by any means, bow out of life. She recognized and accepted the limits of her strength. During periods of good health, she enjoyed visiting her children in Washington, and when she was having problems that kept her in bed, she insisted on having her bedroom set up in the parlor, a front room downstairs next to the living room. In that way she kept up with all the comings and goings.

Her children came to Russell as often as possible, but this was never often enough to suit Ina. She continued to beg for reunions, and summers always provided long, satisfying visits with children and grandchildren, even when they couldn't all come at the same time and give her the pleasure of seeing them together. William continued to farm and to make his home with her. Rob and Sybil built a new home on one side of her and Alex and Sarah were in the cottage on the other side. Ina took to calling the little old house the Weaning Cottage because so many young couples had lived there as they started out.

In 1940 she rejoiced when Rob was appointed to the United States Circuit Court, writing to Dick that "it seems so natural to hear *Judge Russell.*" Because his office was in Gainesville, Rob was away from home often, traveling to the various courtrooms in the district. Judge Russell still wasn't at home as much as his women would have liked for him to be.

Although she wrote fewer and fewer letters in her later years, Ina kept up a lively postcard correspondence, and there were events that prompted her to write letters. Although she wished to write more, she found letter writing difficult in these years, a fact that shows how much energy and love she poured into each letter. In addition to heart and blood pressure problems, she was losing her eyesight, and by 1945 suffered days of almost total blindness. Nevertheless, when William, serving in the Navy, was shipped to Hawaii during World War II, she wrote to him every week, often both a letter and a postcard. She wrote only occasional postcards to her other seven servicemen—Gordon Green; Walter; Alex; Jean Stacy; Jim Bowden; Carolyn's new husband, Ray Nelson;[3] and Bobby Jr., who joined the Marines at age seventeen. Bobby was seriously wounded on Okinawa, in the last battle of the war. The others came home unharmed.

William married Ethelene Huff Booth in 1948 and bought his own farm—about one hundred acres—in Russell, a mile from the homeplace. They moved into an old farmhouse, which he named, in his merry way, Bumblebee Haven.

Fielding received his doctorate in English literature from George Washington University in 1947 and went on teaching in Statesboro.

Dick Jr. never married, and scholarly opinion today is that he was too busy being married to the Senate, where he earned a reputation as one of the hardest-working and most effective senators of all time. Yet he always headed home to Russell for his brief vacations. There was no other place he wanted to be more. Although it is certain that Ina would have loved to see him happily married, she was content to remain his validating female support.

During Ina's last years she had Sarah and Sybil nearby, and she had Modine Thomas as cook and housekeeper. Modine was an indomitable black woman, so fierce that Alex Russell, who sewed her up after more than one fracas, said if he knew he was going to be in the worst barroom brawl in the history of humankind and he could pick one person to be on his side, he wouldn't pick Muhammad Ali, Joe Lewis, or Jack Dempsey. He'd pick Modine Thomas. Modine loved as fiercely as she fought, and she loved Ina Russell. Thanks to her, Ina in her last days did not have to worry about her household being cared for. With such a lieutenant, the serenity and order that Ina had worked for in her home remained intact till the end of her days.

In 1950 Ina Dillard Russell was chosen Georgia's Mother of the Year. Although she cared little for such honors and less for any hoopla, she was too gracious to refuse, and Winder carried out a gala parade and celebration. The parade started when a big black limousine convertible pulled up to the front door at the homeplace and collected Ina. The floats in the parade represented the professions of her children. Governor Herman Talmadge, Gene Talmadge's son, delivered the main address in the Winder football stadium. All Ina's children were there except Walter, who, having remained in the Army after the war, was stationed in Japan. After it was all over, Ina insisted on writing to him. Billie was amanuensis. Ina said how much they missed him and that they called his name several times. A reporter from *Colliers* magazine spent two days at the Russell homeplace that summer, and the resulting article, "Cheaper by the Baker's Dozen," proves he fell in love with Ina.

In 1952 Richard Russell Jr. campaigned for the Democratic nomination for president, his first unsuccessful candidacy. Ina was interviewed several times during the campaign. After the convention was over, a reporter asked Ina how she felt about her son's defeat. "I'm glad he tried," she answered.

Ina pushed for family reunions each year, and the family loved the gatherings, usually in June, close to the date of their parents' wedding anniversary. In June 1953 all of Ina's children managed to make the family party. It was the first time in many years that they had all been together. At this time Ina had thirty-six living grandchildren, most of whom were also present. Although Sarah, Carolyn, and Ala Jo had relatively young babies, the newest babies were great-grandchildren in the Walter Russell, Robert Lee Russell, and Jim Bowden families. Ina once more rejoiced to have her kin gather under her roof. The old house was filled to bursting, as were the other Russell houses in the settlement, Rob's, Alex's, and William's. Inlanders could always make room for outlanders. A photographer from the *Atlanta Journal Constitution* took pictures of Ina on the front-porch steps of her home with her teeming family that day, and his photograph of her and the thirteen children shows everyone laughing. There is no telling who cracked the joke, but it's certain there was at least one.

On August 30, 1953, Ina suffered a cerebral hemorrhage and died at home.

On September 1, 1953, three days after her death, Ina's children were gathered again, this time in sadness. Although they knew that their mother's favorite hymn was "O Happy Day," a hymn in which the day of death is celebrated as the day of reentry into the heavenly kingdom, they grieved their loss. Nevertheless, they sang "O Happy Day" with gusto at the simple funeral service held in her living room, for she had long decreed that all rites be held from her home. Only the family and a few close friends could be seated in the house, but under the oaks, sycamores, and pecan trees she and Richard planted, chairs were set up for the hundreds who came from all walks of life to honor the life and work of Ina Dillard Russell. When her body was taken to the family cemetery on a knoll behind the house, the great throng, led by her senator son, walked behind the hearse along the dirt road to her burial place beside Richard among the pines. Writing of the funeral, Ralph McGill, editor of the *Atlanta Constitution,* said: "[When] the flower-covered casket was lowered into the earth, we all turned back to our respective ways—humbled by the presence of death, but exalted by the great dignity of this passage from earthly home to the eternal one." To the last she adhered to her ideal of simplicity and achieved her quiet eloquence.

Ina's children continued to succeed according to her definition of success: they led useful lives and were probably as happy as human beings can hope to be. Although heir to all human ills, having no immunity against marital difficulties, debilitating illnesses, job losses, or loss of faith, when one of their number fell or was knocked down, others more able to help at the time lifted him or her up. A functional family is not one without problems. It is one that can handle the trials and vicissitudes that are bound to come.

Richard Russell and Ina Dillard began their lives together with a determined desire to found a strong family. Both had in early youth pledged to try to leave a lasting influence for good on their world through their work. The newspaper accounts of their deaths illustrate in black and white that they achieved their mutual and individual ambitions. In 1938 Richard Russell's blazing front-page headlines accompanied by eloquent articles describing his fifty years of service to his beloved Georgia took precedence over a one-column report about the Nazis systematically going through German towns in the night, destroying Jewish places of business and forcing Jews into ghettos. An even smaller column mentioned a Mussolini speech. Georgia was still a separate country in those days, and her native sons more important than remote European troubles. To the last Richard Russell had longed for honor in his own country: In 1937 he paid for a four-page entry under his name in a book about distinguished Georgians. Yet to the last he worked on as chief justice, going to his office almost every day, never stinting or excusing himself because of the inevitable infirmities of age. That his name, through that of his son, is today emblazoned on schools, parks, lakes, highways, and federal buildings, must be counted a sweet irony.

When Ina died, her story did not make huge headlines. Such would never have occurred in a patriarchy under any conditions. In addition, because World War II had given the entire United States a sense of the global community that Americans had never had before, the top story of August 31, 1953, was of American GIs being released from prisoner-of-war camps in Korea. Nevertheless, Ina's death and her picture, a frail Ina in her rocking chair, made the front page, and a further story about her successful children filled an entire page inside. Notice of her funeral and description of it were front-page material for the next two days. On her burial day flags in Georgia drooped at half-mast in her honor. Clearly if you are counting success in these ways, Ina's work as wife and mother was recognized and acclaimed in an extraordinary way.

Ina did not count success by newspaper stories or names on public monuments. For her, success was defined in the reliable characters of those children she reared. She had lived long enough to know that they were strong in brain and training to serve their society in worthwhile positions and that they were serving. She knew, too, they were heart-strong, that they knew how to obey love's command, that not one was a stranger to the stern ideal of integrity or the daily use of the balm of human kindness. She knew, also, that having done her best in word and action to teach them how to live a life, she would have "to leave the subject with them."

When she had left it with them for the last time, they chose a traditional epitaph from the Book of Proverbs: "Her children arise up and call her blessed, her husband also and he praiseth her." She asked for no other praise.

Ina Dillard Russell lived her life accepting "woman's place" in a male-dominated world. Nevertheless, she believed that she—and everyone else—counted to a Higher Power with a worth going far beyond flesh, bone, or any other peculiar construction of earthly life, while she also celebrated earthly life completely. Her devout faith cannot be discounted in considering the enormous success of her life and her legacy. It fostered both her enviable equilibrium and her vision.

Endowed with rich talents for love and work, she developed the capacity to spend these generously. Of her age, but in any age, her life stands as an outstanding example of the power of the human spirit to remain faithful to the highest ideals to which our species may aspire.

Notes

1. Annie Dillard Launius's husband died soon after the birth of their first child, a daughter, who also died tragically at the age of nineteen. Annie never went out of mourning, always wearing black in winter and white in summer.

2. Fite, *Richard B. Russell, Jr.,* 143, 144.

3. When Carolyn married a Presbyterian minister, Ina saw another of her dreams come true. All those years of having ministers at her Sunday dinner table, she had hoped for a preacher for Carolyn. Carolyn found Ray Nelson on her own, however, with a little help from her brother Jeb. They were married on February 18, 1942.

INDEX

Russell, Sybil Millsaps (*continued*)
318; marriage of, 214–15n; and politics,
310; pregnancies of, 277, 291; travels with
Ina, 274

Russell, Virginia Wilson (daughter-in-law),
273, 274, 276, 285, 296; birth of first child
of, 312; and politics, 310; teaches, 299, 304

Russell, Walter Brown (son): advised on
work and school, 216–17; birth of, 43,
45; home chores of, 91, 92; in Japan, 339;
as Ina Jr.'s special boy, 46, 225, 231; at
Monroe Agricultural and Mechanical
School, 189, 193; at Oglethorpe University,
193–94; picks cotton, 75, 120, 121, 182;
shoots dog, 173; at University of Georgia,
202, 203, 213–14; wedding of, 231–32;
works at the A&P, 214, 217, 225n

Russell, William John (brother-in-law), 7,
13, 31, 131, 134, 216, 225, 269

Russell, William John (father-in-law), 4, 11,
12, 13, 26, 38

Russell, William John (son): advised,
298–99, 301–2, 312; birth of, 46; buys
farm, 339; early growth and development
of, 54–55, 84, 87, 108, 165; as fair prize
winner, 192; farms, 322, 332; in Florida,
225–26, 227; and generosity to twin
brother, 276, 295; in grade school,
127, 163, 186; home chores of, 187;
homesickness of, 299, 301; at Monroe
Agricultural and Mechanical School, 201,
210; and politics, 238; at Winder High
School, 217, 218; works at the A&P, 235,
276, 321–22, 324. *See also* Georgia
gubernatorial campaigns: 1930, 1932

Sanger, Margaret, 289, 290n, 292
school: books for, 54, 97, 102, 116, 241, 242,
243, 249; importance of, 100–101, 103, 119;
Latin in, 87, 97, 106, 115, 118, 119n, 122, 133,
139; report cards from, 6, 87, 90, 103–4,
114, 115, 122, 125, 138–39, 242, 271–72;

subjects in, 102, 113, 118, 139, 185; summer,
271–72; teacher-student relationships in,
53, 101, 153; uniforms for, 97, 102. *See also*
education; Russell, Georgia: schools at
scuppernongs, 36, 37, 234, 268, 272, 275
servants: in Atlanta, 316, 317, 323; attitudes
toward, 75, 78, 101, 137, 143, 160, 187; at
Christmas, 276; in Governor's Mansion,
289, 291, 294, 297, 302, 317, 319; housing
for, 140, 245; payment or gifts to, 66, 68,
255, 317; traveling with, 275; as yard help,
199, 204–5, 215, 238, 244, 275. *See also*
Annie Lou; Bell; Doscia; Gus; Laura;
Millie; Thomas, Modine; Waters, Shirley
Sharpton, Ralph (son-in-law), 71, 72n, 136,
147, 177, 204, 234–35; automobile accident
of, 326; employment history of, 303, 304,
312, 318; moves to West Coast, 287n, 292n
Sharpton, Mrs. Ralph. *See* Russell, Harriette
Brumby
Sigma Alpha Epsilon (S.A.E.) fraternity, 150,
202, 241
slavery, 4, 9–10; Dillards as slave-owners, 10
Smith, Hoke, 45, 73n, 248
Stacy, Jean Killough (son-in-law), 335, 338
Stacy, Mrs. Jean Killough. *See* Russell, Ina
Dillard (Ina Jr.)
Stephens, Alex (Court of Appeals judge), 111
Stephens, Alexander H., 302, 303n, 327
Supreme Court of North Carolina, 256, 258
Sweetwater factory. *See* textiles

Talmadge, Eugene, 263n, 332, 333, 334, 339
Talmadge, Mrs. Eugene, 315, 317, 320
Talmadge, Herman, 339
teeth, 239; care of, 165, 327; loss of, 308,
309n; and toothache, 30, 137; work on,
50, 98, 139–40, 167, 265
telephones, 86, 129, 135, 216, 244
tenant farming, 45, 63, 91, 92, 132, 133; Bone
family, 121–22, 123; Polk Manders, 120,
121n; and trouble with black laborers, 140

SOUTHERN VOICES FROM THE PAST
Women's Letters, Diaries, and Writings

Chained to the Rock of Adversity:
To Be Free, Black, and Female in the Old South,
edited by Virginia Meacham Gould

The Diary of Dolly Lunt Burge, 1848–1879,
edited by Christine Jacobson Carter

A Heritage of Woe: The Civil War Diary of
Grace Brown Elmore, 1861–1868,
edited by Marli F. Weiner

Roots and Ever Green:
The Selected Letters of Ina Dillard Russell,
edited by Sally Russell

Shadows on My Heart: The Civil War Diary of
Lucy Rebecca Buck of Virginia,
edited by Elizabeth R. Baer

Tokens of Affection: The Letters of
a Planter's Daughter in the Old South,
edited by Carol Bleser